"*Cultural Representation and Cultural Studies* is an innovative and insightful account of the all-important 'cultural turn' in contemporary scholarship. In lucid prose, Zhou Xian's study perspicuously reconstructs the way that the methodologies of Cultural Studies and Visual Culture have revolutionized our understanding of the modalities of legitimation in post-industrial society. Zhou Xian's book is especially original and compelling in the way that it applies the techniques of 'cultural analysis' to the convulsive socio-historical transformations that have impacted post-revolutionary China. In sum, *Cultural Representation and Cultural Studies* is a pathbreaking contribution to the field of Cultural Studies scholarship."

Richard Wolin, *Distinguished Professor of History and Comparative Literature, CUNY Graduate Center*

"Zhou Xian has for decades now been one of China's and East Asia's leading thinkers in cultural theory and aesthetics. In this book he brings his considerable learning to the investigation of visual culture in contemporary China. Zhou is one of the few who have successfully crossed over from comparative literature to thinking about art. This book is also a major contribution to our understanding of the visual landscape of the contemporary city."

Scott Lash, *Professor of Sociology, School of Anthropology, Oxford University*

"The immense culture of Zhou Xian, his continual dialogue with Western theoreticians, his great power of analysis and synthesis make the translation of his texts a reference work. Focusing particularly on the effects of differentiation in an artistic field that reflects the evolution of Chinese culture and society as a whole, this book is also an important contribution to contemporary aesthetics."

Carole Talon-Hugon, *Professor, Philosophy Department, Sorbonne University, France*

CULTURAL REPRESENTATION AND CULTURAL STUDIES

From the perspective of critical cultural sociology, this book delves into the intertwining relations of cultural transformation and social evolution, illuminating contemporary Chinese culture's landscape and underlying logic since the 1980s.

With a special focus on the tensions among politics, economy, and culture itself, this book examines the transitions of Chinese culture from tradition to the modern age. It expounds the cultural differentiation and its effect in contemporary China. Within this framework, the author addresses some key issues and phenomena that figure in the cultural scene of modern China, ranging from the crisis of Chinese cultural identity in the context of globalization, the media culture, and its impacts on everyday life, to the visual culture and social transformation.

Offering a panoramic view of Chinese contemporary culture, literature, arts, and society, this title will serve as an essential read for scholars of China studies, Cultural studies, and visual culture, as well as anyone interested in what's going on in Chinese contemporary culture.

Zhou Xian is a distinguished professor at Nanjing University, China. His research interests include cultural studies, aesthetics, and literary theory. His books cover a wide range of topics and he has been published in Chinese, English, and French.

China Perspectives

The *China Perspectives* series focuses on translating and publishing works by leading Chinese scholars, writing about both global topics and China-related themes. It covers Humanities & Social Sciences, Education, Media and Psychology, as well as many interdisciplinary themes.

This is the first time any of these books have been published in English for international readers. The series aims to put forward a Chinese perspective, give insights into cutting-edge academic thinking in China, and inspire researchers globally.

To submit proposals, please contact the Taylor & Francis Publisher for the China Publishing Programme, Lian Sun (Lian.Sun@informa.com)

Titles in media communication currently include:

Environmental Risk Communication in China
Actors, Issues, and Governance
Jia Dai, Fanxu Zeng

Documentaries and China's National Image
Chen Yi

Rural-Urban Migration in China
The Impact of New Media
Zheng Xin

Social Mentality and Public Opinion in China
Fanbin Zeng

The Global Film Market Transformation in the Post-Pandemic Era
Production, Distribution and Consumption
Edited by Qiao Li, David Wilson, Yanqiu Guan

Cultural Representation and Cultural Studies
Zhou Xian

For more information, please visit https://www.routledge.com/China-Perspectives/book-series/CPH

Cultural Representation
and Cultural Studies

Zhou Xian

Taylor & Francis Group

LONDON AND NEW YORK

This book is published with financial support from Chinese Fund for the Humanities and Social Sciences.

First published in English 2023
by Routledge
4 Park Square, Milton Park, Abingdon, Oxon OX14 4RN

and by Routledge
605 Third Avenue, New York, NY 10158

Routledge is an imprint of the Taylor & Francis Group, an informa business

© 2023 Zhou Xian

Translated by Dan Hansong

The right of Zhou Xian to be identified as author of this work has been asserted in accordance with sections 77 and 78 of the Copyright, Designs and Patents Act 1988.

All rights reserved. No part of this book may be reprinted or reproduced or utilised in any form or by any electronic, mechanical, or other means, now known or hereafter invented, including photocopying and recording, or in any information storage or retrieval system, without permission in writing from the publishers.

Trademark notice: Product or corporate names may be trademarks or registered trademarks, and are used only for identification and explanation without intent to infringe.

English Version by permission of Nanjing University Press.

British Library Cataloguing-in-Publication Data
A catalogue record for this book is available from the British Library

ISBN: 978-1-032-52536-5 (hbk)
ISBN: 978-1-032-52537-2 (pbk)
ISBN: 978-1-003-40708-9 (ebk)

DOI: 10.4324/9781003407089

Typeset in Times New Roman
by codeMantra

Contents

Preface   ix

Introduction   1

PART I
From Tradition to the Modern Age   21

1. From primitive culture to classical culture: integration and differentiation   23
2. From classical culture to modern culture: harmony vs. conflict   32

PART II
Chinese Culture in the Context of Globalization   45

3. "Legitimation" and identity anxiety   47
4. Sinologism as a problematic   61
5. Literature and identity   73
6. Cross-cultural understanding and interpretation   86
7. Globalization and cultural identity   97

PART III
Media Culture and Everyday Life   109

8. The changing landscape of contemporary Chinese media culture   111

9	The emergence of Micro Culture and its discontents	123
10	From "immersive reading" to "fast reading"	137
11	The construction of critical rationality in a technology-oriented society	161
12	The aestheticization of everyday life in the "post-revolutionary time"	173

PART IV
Visual Culture and Social Transformation — 183

13	Contemporary Chinese society and visual culture	185
14	From text reading to picture reading	204
15	Spectacle cinema and visual culture	217
16	Wang Guangyi's *The Great Criticism* and pop iconography	230
17	Spatial practices in the space of haze city	246

Index — *263*

Preface

Over the past 40 years, there have been profound changes in Chinese society and culture, which have brought about a series of convoluted problems that need to be addressed. While there is no doubt that economic reform and marketization of the 1980s were important causes of these transformations, the sea changes of Chinese culture cannot be simply reduced to economic determinism. Therefore, it is necessary to establish a cross-disciplinary perspective on contemporary Chinese culture, a perspective that entails an integrated analysis of economy, politics, society, and culture in a broader locus of critical inquiry, in order to explain why and how contemporary Chinese culture has transformed.

China has a long history, featuring a living and continuing 5,000-year civilization. Due to its inherent "ultra-stable system", the evolution of Chinese society and culture used to be a matter of *inheritance*, rather than *transformation*, stability taking precedence over innovation. However, with the outbreak of the Opium War in the 1840s, the internal and external problems in China had reached a tipping point, ending up with the fast disintegration of the ultra-stable system of Imperial China. Hereafter, modern China witnessed an avalanche of drastic societal changes and entered an epoch of great transformation—the 1911 Revolution, the establishment of the Republic of China, the war between the warlords, the alliance between the ruling Kuomintang (KMT) and the Chinese Communist Party (CCP), the Anti-Japanese War, the founding of the People's Republic of China, the Cultural Revolution, and eventually, the reform and opening-up. These drastic changes have had a widespread and profound impact on Chinese economy, politics, and culture, with an array of forces competing with one another and creating a unique tension structure in Chinese society and culture. In terms of traditional culture, there is a historical transition from *subversion* to *restoration*, from the May Fourth & New Culture Movement appealing for "down with the Confucian shop" to the recent official slogan that "vintage traditional Chinese culture is the root and soul of China". The reorientation of ideology has its historical context, and caters to some current practical needs. This clearly shows that whenever there is a major social change, a nation would readjust, either officially or unofficially, its relationship with tradition, and, as Hobsbawm put it, engage in "the invention of tradition". This invention is not so much arbitrary as logical—or, more precisely, conditioned by the holistic interaction of various external and internal agents, which result in a tension structure as compromise. These are the main issues discussed in the first part of my book.

My analysis and interpretation of tension structure are not only focused on the multifarious relationship between the modern and tradition, but also manifest in the tension between globalization and localization, which further evolves into the crisis of contemporary cultural identity and identity reconfiguration. On the one hand, China is trying to integrate into the process of globalization, learning from and racing against the West; on the other hand, the so-called Westernization and its cultural "invasion" have raised intractable anxiety about one's local culture. How to maintain the necessary tension between the two is a puzzle we have to solve in Chinese culture today. Historically speaking, during the last two decades of the 20th century, we were more inclined to emulate the West—Chinese literature, plastic arts, and films are the best cases in point. Since the 21st century, as China rose to become the second largest economy in the world, an all-around progress boosts national self-confidence in its culture, the project of cultural identity tilting more and more to autonomy. This is actually the two sides of modernity: the advocacy of learning from the West has led to the reforms in China, which in turn stokes vigilant anxiety about Western cultures. Such a situation is like a gigantic pendulum that keeps moving back and forth before reaching a balance. As an old Chinese saying puts it, "Fortune was in the east of bank thirty years ago, but turns to west when thirty years has passed". This is the gist of the second part of the book.

The third type of tension structure, unique to Chinese culture, is the dichotomy of political discourse and entertainment discourse. From the historical perspective of aesthetics, it is a modern version of traditional pedagogy featuring "education through entertainment". Judging from modernity, it is a game between the political system and the market, which is unique to contemporary Chinese society. The reasons for this tension are various. For one thing, it has something to do with the tightening of political propaganda inherent in China, and the other is the brand-new media culture brought about by technological innovation, which has fundamentally changed the original cultural landscape—mass entertainment and market-oriented needs become more prominent, the traditional revolutionary culture being replaced by a new consumer culture. As a result, blatant political propaganda is covertly integrated into mass entertainment. The iterative development of media technology in China is a "double-edged sword", providing space for mass entertainment and democratic expression, on the one hand, and technical means for harsher cultural control, on the other. Such a tendency is best captured in the rapid development of "micro cultures" and the concomitant "micro phenomena". In China, however, we still fall short of a critical rationality when it comes to technology, and the critical theory of technology, a conspicuous "short plank" in the contemporary humanities in China, is quite marginalized. An examination of these issues forms the third part of this book.

The last kind of tension structure is from *within*—that is to say, from the "image vs. word" contradiction as seen in contemporary Chinese cultures. Due to the galloping expansion of media culture, the dominance of visuality has become the quintessential spectacle in contemporary Chinese culture. The once word-centered culture constructed by print civilization has gradually given way to a new image-centered culture. Our obsession with images has been seen in every aspect of daily lives, from work to entertainment, from art to science. The acculturation of visuality and the visualization of culture are the two sides of the same coin of contemporary Chinese culture. Everyone is immersed in a visual culture, which in turn participates in the construction of human subjectivity. This book's fourth part therefore revolves around a panoramic inspection of Chinese visual culture, reading, film, and painting, and finally takes issue with haze in urban China through the lens of visual culture.

Parts of several chapters of this book have been previously published in international academic journals—*Philosophy and Literature, Space and Culture, Neohelicon, Contemporary Chinese Thought*. I am grateful to He Chengzhou, He Ning, Xu Lei, and others for their kind help and assistance in drafting and revising these English-speaking journal articles. An earlier version of "The Aestheticization of Everyday Life in 'the Post-Revolutionary Time'" in Part III appeared in *The Bloomsbury Research Handbook of Chinese Aesthetics and Philosophy of Art* (Bloomsbury, 2021) edited by Marcello Ghilardi and Hans-Georg Moeller, and "Wang Guangyi's *The Great Criticism* and Pop Iconography" in Part IV appeared in *The Philosophy and Art of Wang Guangyi* (Bloomsbury, 2019) edited by Tiziana Andina and Erica Onnis. I like to thank the original copyright holders for permission to reprint these chapters.

Introduction

The evolution of Chinese culture is filled with inexplicable conundrums. In the long history of ancient China, cultural shifts occurred at an extremely slow pace—through micro changes, in sociological terms. Since the mid-19th century, however, Chinese society and culture have undergone drastic changes at an unprecedented speed. Tumultuous, seismic shifts have instead taken place, which sociology would term macro changes. The Opium Wars, the May Fourth Movement, the founding of the People's Republic of China, and the most recent reform and opening-up have brought about sea changes in Chinese culture. At the same time, the inhabitants of this culture have continually felt the impact of "cultural shock". Strictly speaking, societal cultural changes not only refer to objective, physical, factual ones—such as urban expansion or improved living standards—that have occurred or are going to take place, but also include one's newly acquired feelings and mentality in response to these physical changes. In other words, change is also a matter of subjectivity. To some extent, our shifting ideas trigger changes, and these ideas are also part of the reality we perceive in our mind. When we gear up to interpret the physical and spiritual realities undergoing changes, new changes might come into being. Thus, given the variability of Chinese society and culture, we face three tasks: first, to describe the objective changes that have taken place; second, to survey how we reflect on and further change these changes; and third, to analyze how the first two tasks *impinge* on each other, in particular how conceptual changes in our society bring about behavioral changes, or vice versa.

Since the early 1990s, the remaking of Chinese society and culture has attracted tremendous scholarly attention. Many scholars were attracted to these issues and attempted to offer a sweeping explanation, tracing out the genealogy and driving home the causes of the transformation. That most of their theoretical endeavors, however, did not pay off reveals not only the limit of current theories but also the urgency of alternative analysis. The top issue is the crisis of theory. When it comes to new social and cultural phenomena, preexisting theoretical framework and vocabulary always fall short of explanatory power. We must upgrade our "weaponry/toolkit of critique", which also means the need to "critique our weaponry/toolkit". The second issue is our impulse to interpret and anxiety about interpretation. Those eager to account for new social-cultural phenomena are usually charlatan theoreticians or poorly trained researchers. They simply have no idea how to *do* theory properly. A bulk of cultural studies either succumb to the pitfalls of overgeneralization or focus too much on odds and ends. The third issue is the absence of critical insights into the connection between society and culture in our current cultural discourse. An integrated research is yet to come—an interdisciplinary approach, combining and integrating knowledge from different subjects; a collaboration between social sciences (including economics, law, sociology) and the humanities (literature, history, philosophy, art). The three issues serve as a reminder of how necessary it is to embrace an integrated theoretical scheme and fuse horizons of various disciplines, when studying the cultural transformation in China today.

The concept of culture and cultural sociology

The concept of culture is so expansive and all-encompassing that all human activities and artifacts, it seems, are associated with the umbrella term "culture". The more familiar a thing appears, as Bertolt Brecht remarks, the less thought of. The same is true of "culture", a word that seems to cover such a wide range in everyday life that we are supposed to automatically understand what it means. But what *does* culture actually mean? Academics have come up with many answers over the years. American anthropologist Alfred L. Kroeber, for example, lists over 170 definitions of "culture".

Broadly speaking, there are two ways of defining culture: one is the macro, holistic approach; the other, the micro, specific approach. Philosophers tend to adopt the former, while experts prefer the latter. In archeology, culture is the tangible, material aspects of archeological records; in anthropology, culture is a specific way of living and what one personally identifies with; in sociology, culture is the blueprint for a social group that lives in the same region and shares the same language. None of those definitions are wrong, but looking at culture through the lens of a specific subject has its obvious limitations. In comparison, a general, eclectic approach may be more productive:

> Culture is the "social inheritance" of a community, which includes all material artifacts (i.e. tools, weapons, houses, jobs, rituals, administrative and reproductive venues, works of art, etc.), all spiritual products (i.e. symbols, thoughts, beliefs, aesthetic sentiments, values, et.), and special behavioral patterns (such as institutions, groups, rites, and social organizational modules) formulated by a nation under certain living conditions in history and through constant accumulation of all kinds of activities passed down from generation to generation.[1]

I find the definition above reasonably satisfying because it takes into equal consideration the material, spiritual, and behavioral aspects of culture. Hence, it will serve as a frame of reference, and a point of departure, for my cultural analysis in this book. For sure, there are many other similarly valid definitions, a widely accepted one in sociological studies running as follows: "Culture is often defined as a living blueprint for a community, the members of which share a common territory and language, feeling obliged to each other, and calling the community by the same name".[2] In general, sociology culture is defined in a way that emphasizes practicality and boundaries—which, while useful in many ways, still presents problems for critical sociology.

Some recent trends in cultural studies are vastly promising, and provide my project with inspiring critical resources. First, cultural studies of late years have weighed in on the debate about cultural behavior—paying attention to the individual subject's understanding and awareness of its own behavior, and to the ethos of a particular demographic group while studying its cultural behavior. "Culture", as American sociologist Robert Redfield points out, "is the conventional understanding manifest in behavior and artifacts".[3] Redfield's emphasis on the subject and on understanding reflects an interest in the explanation of the meaning of culture. Second, recent cultural studies emphasize how culture participates in the production and explanation of meaning, thereby positioning language and signs at the center of culture. A representative voice is American anthropologist Clifford Geertz, who has influenced cultural studies profoundly since the late 1970s. Inspired by Max Weber's definition of men, Geertz views culture as an interpretation of signs. In *The Interpretation of Cultures*, a book celebrated widely throughout Western academia, Geertz writes,

> The concept of culture I espouse...is essentially a semiotic one. Believing, with Max Webber, that man is an animal suspended in webs of significance he himself has spun, I take culture to be those webs, and the analysis of it to be therefore not an experimental science in search of law but an interpretive one in search of meaning.[4]

Geertz's oft-quoted view has been treated as a sign of the turn from applied anthropology toward interpretive anthropology. It illustrates how semantics has become the vital part of cultural studies. Scholars are increasingly aware that the relationship between signs (or languages) and human behavior resembles that between grammar and speech.[5] Third, Walter Benjamin calls our attention to the mode of cultural production, and a new paradigm of cultural analysis comes into being. Recently, many Western scholars treat culture as a process of "production and consumption", especially with the rise of postmodernism and post-industrialism. New cultural phenomena—such as the society of production, the consumer society, or the culture of reproduction—have occupied the center of cultural studies. The rise of various subcultures and the change they bring about to the fabric of social structure are all contributing to new forms of cultural production and consumption. The unique spectacle of culture is therefore shaped by the real, complex processes of interaction and exchange in culture. Finally, culture, as a system, is not affected by a single source of influence; rather, the formation of culture is a result of negotiation and transaction. That is to say, culture is not a passive, static fact, but a developing, changing process, during which we create and remake culture itself, rather than unthinkingly accepting the heritage of a given tradition or history. Meanwhile, culture itself eventually evolves into something different, deviating from its original aims and concerns, because, as I argued early on, culture is the synergetic outcome of negotiation and transaction among numerous coactors.

What if we have a critical cultural sociology that does justice to these trends in cultural studies? The implications, from my point of view, are enormous. First, we shall pay close attention in cultural studies to not only how reality changes, but more importantly to how those who have brought about these changes interpret or understand them. In this sense, as Geertz says, cultural studies is fundamentally "the interpretation of interpretation" and "the text of a text", wherein the first "text" refers to history itself, and the second is an interpretation of the first. Second, regarding signs as what represent culture is to tease out the root causes of changes in the meaning of culture, by digging into the volatile forms, structures, and rules of signs. This approach could be highly productive for aesthetic culture studies. Aesthetic culture is essentially a semantic and symbolic system, a barometer that measures in detail all changes in society. If we recall the first point, cultural studies then becomes a *re*-understanding and *re*-interpretation of the way we understand and interpret logograms, which in turn leads to semantic analysis, the cornerstone of critical cultural sociology. Here, the interpretation of meaning is different from traditional positivism, because it no longer sees culture as an assemblage of physical facts, but as a meaning-making process, as a kind of relationship between the subject in culture and cultural interpretation. We may have recourse to cultural sociology, the scope and methodology of which is aptly summarized by Scott Lash as follows:

> More specifically, postmodernism and other cultural paradigms are what I want to call *"regimes of signification"*. The idea for this comes from the political economists of the "Regulation School" and their notion of "regime of accumulation" … In "regimes of *signification*", however, only *cultural* objects are produced. All regimes of signification comprise two main components. The first is a specific "cultural economy". A given cultural economy will include (1) specific relations of production of cultural objects, (2) specific conditions of reception, (3) a particular institutional framework that mediates between production and reception, and (4) a particular way in which cultural objects circulate. The second component of any regime of signification is its specific *mode* of signification, by which I mean that its cultural objects depend on a particular relationship between signifier, signified, and referent.[6]

To me, what Lash lays out here is a framework for cultural sociology. What I want to stress is the interconnectedness between cultural economy and mode of signification. Mode of signification is the process reflected in the cultural economy—not Saussure's abstract, theoretical model of language. Therefore, when inquiring into contemporary Chinese aesthetic culture, we must translate the mode of signification into the interrelationship between meaning-making and meaning-receiving. This interrelationship and countless changes it brings into view are the core issues of cultural sociology I am engaging with. The way we tackle these issues brings us to the third concern of critical cultural sociology: we must be especially wary of two inclinations. The first tendency is "cultural elitism", or "cultural conservatism"—a narrow-minded way of thinking that repudiates all changes in culture, sticking to its elitist standpoint, and opposing the democratization, expansion of the public sphere, and bemoaning the increasing marginalization of the elite as a result of rising mass culture. Another alarming tendency is a populist view of culture that eschews all principles. By "the populist", I mean the unconditional, undifferentiated, and uncritical endorsement of all cultural changes. Such a cultural position, at its most extreme, would do away with critical thinking altogether, and compromise the standard of theoretical inquiry by acquiescing to consumerism and hedonism. Finally, we need to better understand the synergism of cultural development, analyzing the different agents involved in the synergy, and envisioning a larger picture about the formation of cultures in the future. In an analysis like this, we usually have recourse to "ideal types"—looking into, albeit reasonably, a complex web of socio-cultural phenomena, and yet dwelling upon a few strains of culture, which are placed at the top of our agenda because of their salient features. The cultural study of ideal types, however, is but a first step in our analysis of the complex synergism of Chinese aesthetic culture. More importantly, we must fully take into account the complexity and volatility of cultural facts. While using ideal types of culture as a basis and a point of reference, therefore, we must embark on an in-depth investigation of the negotiations, transactions, and achievements among various mediators intertwined in Chinese aesthetic culture.

After mapping out the tenets of cultural sociology, it becomes necessary to propose a methodology, which is not only possible but indeed necessary, in the light of the current research on contemporary Chinese culture. I define critical cultural sociology as a body of scholarly accounts that revolves around culture as its primary target of investigation, and views changes in culture as a key index of societal transformation. Society, culture, and aesthetic culture, respectively, form what Pierre Bourdieu calls a "field": society constitutes the contextual field of culture, which in turn represents society; aesthetic culture is studied as an individual field, while culture, as a whole, serves as the backdrop of aesthetic culture. What we refer to as synergy is the complex interaction between the "field" of aesthetic culture and the other "fields", such as society and culture. A sociologist often starts from a specific phenomenon. Similarly, our approach to cultural sociology will start with a specific field, that is, aesthetic culture, so as to avoid the pitfalls of empty generalizations. Furthermore, bearing in mind a total and inseparable picture of culture and society, my study of aesthetic culture takes into equal consideration the complex relationship between the two domains.

For sure, critical cultural sociology is an open system. In other words, its approach is neither one of positivist, empirical sociology, nor purely abstract and metaphysical. I propose a third path of its own. More importantly, critical cultural sociology is at its core interdisciplinary, receptive to diverse theories and methodologies. Here, there are four tenets I hope to highlight. First, its basic framework is indebted to sociology, and keeping the socio-cultural elements in mind is fundamental to critical cultural sociology. We must champion, as C. Wright Mills aptly puts it, a "sociological imagination". Second, a cultural sociologist must have an acute sense of history, the key to deciphering socio-cultural changes. The sense of history not only refers to an awareness of changing reality, but entails an incisive observation of the evolution of theory. Third, a global and anthropological vision is pivotal. On the one hand, such a vision will enable us to gauge the development of Chinese culture in the global context. On the other hand, anthropological thinking is essential to maintaining our cultural integrity and keeping at bay Eurocentrism and cultural imperialism. Fourth, what the word "critical" adds to cultural sociology, I believe, is more than a particular attitude or mood of thinking—critical of the current status of our culture, this kind of sociology also attends to social relationships and the fate of culture, committed to laying bare suppression, objectification, and injustice in culture under consideration. It analyzes, from historical and social perspectives, relationships and powers as found in social culture; explains the complex conflicts between those relationships; and predicts the culture yet to come, with the help of "sociological imagination". Our intellectual life is imbued with neologisms with a prefix "post-" or a suffix "-ism", and the talk of diversity, tolerance, and micro politics is an academic fad. However, we should continue to pore over meta-theory and pay due attention to social culture and its internal relationships, while retaining our theoretical vision characterized by diversity and tolerance. We must not privilege a certain type of discourse at the expense of other discourses. Instead, we should keep all doors open.

If we combine these arguments about critical cultural sociology with the concept of culture, as discussed earlier, we will arrive at a schema of critical cultural sociology. In a word, critical cultural sociology is a discipline that critically explicates the signification of society and culture, treating Marxism as the cornerstone.

Social evolution and cultural transformation

As previously mentioned, the historical development of Chinese society is the dynamics behind all cultural changes in China. If we want to get to the bottom of the historical changes in culture, in particular aesthetic culture, reflecting on social changes becomes an imperative.

Different visions and methods can be employed to analyze Chinese society. Here, I suggest using critical cultural sociology as a lens. That is, we make an overarching description of social structures in China, invoking the term "ideal types" associated with the works of Marx and Weber, who were pioneers of critical theory. Chinese society has developed unevenly, and social reality and cultural phenomena of different phases of history are intertwined—one can find in China traditional, modern, and even postmodern cultures mixed up. When focusing on ideal types, therefore, we must keep the status of amalgamation in mind. In other words, the method of ideal types is only one way of engaging with the dazzling changes in Chinese society, and should not be grafted in a simplistic manner. Just as any theoretical model can be reductive when facing a complex society, my analysis might err on the side of oversimplification. As Weber points out,

> An ideal type is formed by the one-side accentuation of one or more points of view and by the synthesis of a great many diffuse, discrete, more or less

present and occasionally absent, concrete individual phenomena, which are arranged according to those one-sidedly emphasized viewpoints into a unified *analytical* construct. In its conceptual purity, this mental construct cannot be found empirically anywhere in reality…It has the significance of a purely ideal limiting concept with which the real situation or action is compared and surveyed for the explication of certain of its significant components. Such concepts are constructs in terms of which we formulate relationships by the application of the category of objective possibility. By means of this category, the adequacy of our imagination, oriented and disciplined by the society, is *judged*.[7]

Let's look at China since the reform and opening-up, a period when remarkable changes take place—the shift from a society of homogeneity to one of diversity, from socialist egalitarianism to disparity in wealth, from everything-is-politics to marketization, from an over-politicized society to a civil society, et cetera. One of the most significant and salient changes is the transformation from a society featuring solidarity and low differentiation to one that is increasingly differentiated. I use the word "solidarity" in the sense of Émile Durkheim, referring to the transformation from "mechanical solidarity" to "organic solidarity". The word "differentiation" is used as an inclusive and complex concept in sociology. For starters, it refers to how a society changes from an undifferentiated, hybrid one, to one of increased differentiation—in particular, the differentiation in politics, economy, and culture. Society as a system is composed of different subsystems. That Marx describes the constructions of society as "superstructure" and "economic base" has been an enormously illuminating idea for my analysis of Chinese society. In a similar vein, more binary structures can be added to the map of differentiation. According to structural functionalism, especially the theory of Talcott Parsons, each subsystem must function in harmony if the society, as a whole, hopes to work well. According to Parsons, there are four conditions for the functioning of a society: adaptation, goal attainment, latency or pattern maintenance, and integration. Correspondingly, a society comprises four subsystems: economy, politics, family, and communal cultural groups. Parsons posits that every subsystem comprises a series of institutions, which in turn are based on a set of behavioral roles that are ultimately governed by our core values. The transition from traditional to modern society is marked by how the larger system is no longer homogeneous, and how subsystems continually differentiate when acquiring more autonomy and functions. Of course, this is not to say that subsystems are self-contained, autonomous, and hermetic; rather, they each maintain their own independent rules of operation, and interact with one another on a higher level.

Some sociologists maintain that the development of society is essentially a process of differentiation. If we make comparisons across history, traditional societies, to a large extent, were highly unified and homogeneous. Differentiation in various societal sectors explains how traditional societies morph into modern ones. Social subsystems begin to acquire and develop their own autonomy. Many even think that modernization (or the expansion of modernity) is no more than the result of continuous differentiation. Both Weber and Habermas think that the process of modernization is reflected in the way those previously integrated fields gradually come apart. For Weber, differentiation and the attainment of autonomy are fundamentally a matter of acquiring legitimacy. In a traditional society, all proof of the legitimacy of values or fields relies on "meta-narratives", such as rationality, nature, or deity. An important sign of differentiation is that various fields step by step develop their own rules and criteria for securing their own legitimacy. This in turn means that self-legitimization stands in opposition to the foundationalist legitimization: in the light of the former, the legitimacy of a field or a set of values is up to itself, rather than relying on some "meta-standard"; in the light of the latter, all values are derived from a transcendental meta-category. Habermas also points out that cultural modernity and the modernization of society are the two sides of the same process, accompanied by ongoing differentiation. Since the Renaissance, in particular the time of Enlightenment philosophy and rationalism, the theory, the ethics, and the aesthetics have become three disparate spheres, subject to respective rules. Habermas writes,

> [Max Weber] characterized cultural modernity as the separation of the substantive reason expressed in religion and metaphysics into three autonomous spheres. They are: science, morality, and art. These came to be differentiated because the unified world-views of religion and metaphysics fell apart. Since the 18th century, the problems inherited from these older world-views could be arranged so as to fall under specific aspects of validity: truth, normative rightness, authenticity, and beauty. They could then be handled as questions of knowledge, or of justice and morality, or of taste. Scientific discourse, theories of morality, jurisprudence, and the production and criticism of art could in turn be institutionalized. Each domain of culture could be made to correspond to cultural professions in which problems could be dealt with as the concern of special experts. This professionalized treatment of the cultural tradition brings to the fore the intrinsic structures of each of the three dimensions of culture. There appear the structures of cognitive-instrumental, of moral-practical, and of aesthetic-expressive rationality, each of these under the control of specialists who seem more adept at being logical in these particular ways than other people are.[8]

For Habermas, cultural modernity is synonymous with the modernization of society—the differentiation of cultural modernity is saliently characterized by the establishment of different rational principles for theory, ethics, and aesthetics. Pierre Bourdieu, a disciple of Max Weber, takes on the issue of modernity in a different way. Bourdieu discovers a cardinal sign of the transition from traditional to modern society: the increasing autonomy of what he calls "fields". In traditional society, power relations were of direct transaction free from intermediaries, having shaped social status, cultural value, and ranking. But with the development of society, all "fields" are bound to develop, to various degrees, a kind of autonomy. For Bourdieu, the more autonomous a field is, the more likely it is the case that its production caters for other producers, instead of mere consumers, in social (power) realms. In contrast, science is the field with the greatest autonomy, followed by academia and art (in particular, the high art). The autonomy of academia is manifest in its separation from power, while the autonomy of art is granted by its separation from consumers. In this scale of autonomy, law scores poorly, and the field of politics turns out to be least autonomous, because it is intractably entangled with power relations. According to Bourdieu's analysis, the social field and the power field are two sides of the same coin—the farther other fields are from the two, the more autonomous. A crucial factor is the intermediary. When a field is gradually developed and matured, there will be a set of protocols applicable to this certain field. In such a situation, the relationship between power and social fields shifts from one of traditional, unmediated transaction to the mediated one, hence giving birth to autonomy, or, as Althusser puts it, "semi-autonomy". Claus Offe coins a term, "structural disparity", to describe this shift, pointing out that the process of differentiation in modern society starts from the separation of home and workplace, which used to be one and the same in traditional society. This fundamental separation led to a series of further separations: church and state, laws and ethics, nation and civil society, and the division of labor. For Offe, these differentiations are what have made possible the birth of a modern society of more possibilities and liberty.[9]

Of course, all of the theories discussed above are based on historical accounts of Western culture and society. Fundamentally, they might only apply to the West, but it doesn't mean we can't invoke these theories as useful frames of reference, when it comes to the modern and contemporary Chinese culture. If we crudely divide the development of Chinese society into two phases—traditional society and modern society—the process of differentiation in the changing China is eye-catching. Going a step further, the phenomenon of differentiation is even more salient, if we divide Chinese culture since the Opium War into three phases: the May Fourth Movement, the post-1949 socialist culture, and the post-reform and opening-up. The last one is a perfect case for my argument here. Before the reform, China was highly centralized, with monism and politicization being its most prominent characteristics. Politics, economics, and culture were all forcibly tied together, and everything was but an aspect of politics. Some scholars remark that China at this stage was characterized by a state monopoly of social and economic resources, which in turn led to the integration of politics, economics, and ideology in a society with a low degree of differentiation.[10] In Bourdieu's terms, autonomous fields have not yet come into being. All values and social activities in China were tangled up with the field of politics, with no mediation whatsoever.

Before the reform and opening-up, the high degree of integration and totality of Chinese society was clearly achieved by means of institutional centralization, monopolization of resources, modeling of social life, and self-enclosure. At this point, there was no such thing as a subsystem or an autonomous "field", since the political agenda was of paramount importance. China, first and foremost, had a direct control over all subsystems, including economy and culture. In this kind of society, subsystems enjoy no autonomy. That is to say, no subsystems in China were functional at the moment, a larger system reigning above all other systems. In short, it might be more accurate to say that no subsystems could operate independently in China. The political system, functioning as an overall system and seeping into every corner of life, penetrated every aspect of Chinese economy and culture. In a certain way, all economic and cultural activities before the reform and opening-up were visibly and forcefully controlled by the political branch, that is, the power discourse manifest in institutional means. All non-political, economic, or cultural activities became politicized, economy and culture being the direct extensions of politics. Not only did the state, as a power apparatus, plan and directly control all economic sectors, and monopolize all economic resources, but also economy itself was tinted with politics. The result was that the running of economy didn't abide by economic laws, but was hinged on politics. There is no better example of this than the negative impact of various political movements (caused by domestic and international conflicts) on economic performance.

If this is true for the economy, what about culture? From science and technology to literature and art, even to marriage, food, clothing, and housing, all are obviously under the direct control of the political field. To use Bourdieu's term, all fields belonged to the "super-field" of politics. Be it the natural sciences, or other fields of scholarship, or literature and arts, or the judicial system, nothing was free from the grip of political system; nor was it possible for each sector to claim autonomy of any kind. Clearly, the rules of operation for all other fields were a direct application and extension of the rules of the political system. Any branch of science, or any discipline, could be branded "legal" or "illegal", depending on specific external demands. Psychology and sociology, for example, could be denounced as "pseudo-science", based on some "legalized" evidence. Literature and art became tools for political propaganda and mouthpieces for the discourse of power, and thus became unmistakably sterile, a fact that was aptly illustrated by the eight so-called "Model Plays", the only staple of theater allowed for a nation of 800 million. Of course, there were, once in a while, some little rebellions, as a backlash against such a state of social control. But whether these rebellions were the result of opposing forces or of the field of politics attempting to reinforce its own dominance, they could only strengthen the process of social integration and unification. This lack of differentiation reached its peak during the Cultural Revolution, and drove China to the brink of social collapse.

In a structure where politics, economy, and culture were so tightly integrated, the political system alone functioned above all else, while the economic and cultural systems were deprived of their own tracks, unable to invigorate themselves. The unworking of all subsystems was what happened next. In the cultural sphere, political discourse, wielded as a tool, was the only legitimate form of discourse, and all other voices were denied the right to exist. The cultural system gradually stopped communicating with the outside world, becoming more and more sealed-off. The sole legitimacy of political discourse made discourse structures highly exclusive. And culture, especially aesthetic culture, speaks the language of political discourse. In this closed, monolithic, centralized social structure, only the official culture had the legitimate status. With its political backing, it made culture entirely subservient to politics. In the late 1970s and early 1980s, the reform and opening-up opened a new chapter for China. Systemic reforms led to the coexistence of multiple forms of ownership and therefore inevitably to the separation of the Party and politics, and of politics and enterprises. The centralized administrative system gradually crumbled. Economic reforms helped the China get rid of the planned economy and gear up to the market one. The unified, planned system gave way to a new market system, allowing for the binding relationship of supply and demand, and encouraging competition. The state no longer controlled economic activities directly. Instead, it exerted macro-control over the market, through a series of intermediaries. The changes that have taken place here were extremely dramatic, most obviously in that economy was no longer directly conditioned by politicized regulation, and that it has acquired a certain degree of autonomy. The relative separateness of politics and culture changed national and social relations, and at the same time propelled Chinese economy forward. The boom of economy affected all aspects of Chinese society beyond estimation. Without reducing everything to economic determinism, it is beyond denying that a series of further differentiation in China had much to do with the relative separation of politics and economy. In other words, many other differentiations were no more than a part of the chain reaction following this first one.

The results of differentiation in China varied, and differences made possible the creation of autonomy. As the Chinese economy sought to find and establish its own rules, it differentiated itself from politic on the one hand, and made changes on politics and culture on the other. With the differentiation of politics and the economy, more fields began straying away from the field of power relations. The natural sciences, unsurprisingly, gained the greatest autonomy, followed by other fields of knowledge. Aesthetic culture, represented by literature and art, also became an autonomous domain in a certain way, over the course of differentiation. Bourdieu, when analyzing the transformation from traditional society to modern society, notes an interesting phenomenon. In traditional society, power operated as a defender of the orthodox. The true-or-false logic, therefore, would be replaced in traditional power relations by the friend-foe logic. This phenomenon was witnessed in the Cultural Revolution, when academia and art were similarly judged in accordance with a friend-foe dichotomy, transforming a question of cognition to a matter of ethics. Historically, as differentiation emerges, the more a field gains autonomy, Bourdieu finds, the more it will use the language of science, replacing the friend-foe logic with that of true-or-false. This argument is best illustrated in the debate on whether "practice is the sole criterion for testing truth", a proposition that is enormously significant in that it diverts us from the friend-foe opposition to the autonomous scientific axiom featuring true-false logic.

In literature and the arts, there has been a similar shift. Before the reform and opening-up, literature and art, taking class struggle as the top agenda, emphasize the instrumentality of artworks. At that time, it was a must to apply the friend-foe evaluation to "flower or grass", for the arts have been totally subject to the control of politics. After "the Gang of Four" were ousted, Chinese art started to develop into a new phase, "writing about the real" becoming the earliest, and the most cogent weaponry for human mind. Here, our concern about the "real" was not only a matter of aesthetics, but also of epistemology. This new trend reflects the fact that art had steered away from the "friend-foe" logic and began to embrace the "true-false" logic. Such an intellectual and conceptual change in part justifies the newly acquired autonomy of literature and art in China. It can be regarded as the effort of aesthetic culture, whose producers were striving to establish their own game rules, and as a process of securing new paradigms of aesthetic culture—a paradigm different from instrumentalist thinking. Hence, contemporary Chinese culture, after differentiation, still had a close tie with politics, but this tie was either mediated or embodied in direct administrative regulation and governmental intervention. On the other hand, culture in contemporary China was under the pressure of economy. The main manifestation is found in the fact that when culture was no longer directly manipulated by government, some cultural sectors began to woo an unfledged market. As a result, the game rules of economy, or market/business values, began to permeate the realm of culture. A more lucid statement may be as follows: contemporary Chinese culture, especially its aesthetic culture, has to some degree or in some way been freed from the role of political instrument, but it has not turned aesthetic culture into a completely autonomous domain. At the same time, it is swayed by economy in an unprecedented way, which inevitably allows cultural industry or mass culture to gain a secure foothold in contemporary Chinese culture. In this sense, differentiation is no more than a further development of the complicated interaction across different sectors in China, rather than leading to an absolute autonomy. Acknowledging this point will be very methodologically useful for our further discussion of the transformation of Chinese culture.

Differentiation is a basic scale or index for our understanding of Chinese society and culture in transformation. In sociology, from Marx to Weber, from Parsons to Habermas and Bourdieu, a leitmotif running throughout their works is the differentiation of modern societies. With further analysis, we can discover that differentiation takes place in many societal fields. For example, the differentiation of social formation makes it possible that a society made of egalitarian politicized men is replaced by that comprising consumption-oriented men of unmistakable social gaps. Another example is the opposition between the modern masses and the elite minorities. Of course, what interests me here most is cultural differentiation *per se*. Put in another way, when we notice the relative disengagement of culture from politics, we must also pay attention to the differentiation happening in culture itself. Prior to the reform and opening-up, Chinese culture, on the one hand, was controlled by the branch of politics; on the other hand, it was invariably one-dimensional. Culture at that time was synonymous with ideology and politics. In this sense, there was no such thing as difference or distinctive ingredients in this culture. Even if there had been some sort of difference, its existence would have been transient, and the dominant culture endorsed by the state was the only choice, no alternatives allowed. Why? The reason is simple. The rationale centering on "friend or foe" could deter any alternatives. Nevertheless, as the reform gave rise to the uncoupling of economy, politics, and culture, culture had witnessed some differentiation within itself. The differentiation of culture has multiple meanings. First, it can refer to horizontal differentiation, that is, differentiation happening in aesthetics, science, law, morality, and other cultural domains. Another type is vertical. That is to say, a certain culture develops into different subcategories from within. What concerns this book most is the latter. Through the lens of vertical differentiation, we can find that inside contemporary Chinese aesthetic culture is a tripartite structure—dominant culture (or, mainstream culture, official culture, and orthodox culture), elite culture (or high culture, minorities culture, clique culture), and mass culture (or cultural industry, popular culture, folk culture). The emergence of such differentiation is the necessary condition of pluralist culture. In my opinion, to look into and reflect upon the differentiation in contemporary China's aesthetic culture is essential to fully understanding the evolution of Chinese society and culture. If one gives no sight of the evolution of such differentiation, he or she would interpret Chinese culture in a simplistic, or even conservative, way. If one pays no attention to the complex, dialectical interaction of such differentiation, he or she would mistake the plural for the monistic, cancel cultural dialogism and polyphony, and retreat to cultural monologism. Besides, it is equally dangerous to overstate the role of differentiation, or to privilege one cultural mode, because it will bring about some sort of radicalism or conservatism—beware, the conservative here is often disguised as the radical, the two being the two sides of a coin, and even interchangeable). Historically speaking, aesthetic culture in contemporary China is of a plural, differentiated status, which signals a remarkable progress. Of course, the reason for such a situation is rather complex.

As yet, we have mapped out the social differentiation (and the collateral cultural differentiation) in contemporary China. Our analysis of social differentiation is horizontal and sociological, while cultural differentiation begets a vertical and morphological discussion. The former serves as the very backdrop against which the latter emerges. Cultural differentiation always points to a case study of some "field" or "realm" related to social differentiation. With the cultural sociological approach I chose to endorse earlier on, we can make elaborate analysis of the historical process of differentiation. As I said, society and culture are made up of different forces that play a functional role in them, and are therefore ultimately nothing more than a process of "compromise, transaction and achievement". The unique landscape of contemporary Chinese politics, economy and culture, and their complex relationships constitute the totality of contemporary Chinese society (a totality that is characterized by organic integration and thus differs from the mechanical integration of the pre-reform and opening-up period). In a further sense, the complex interaction among politics, economy, and culture leads to the differentiation of culture, giving rise to the tripartite structure of dominant culture, elite culture, and mass culture. The three cultures are interrelated but distinctive, subject to all kinds of constraints of ref. These constraints include the institutional regulation, the market pressure, the conflict and interplay between state and market, and the differentiation and compromise of cultural producers. Therefore, the enormous, game-changing transformation in contemporary China's aesthetic culture is actually the product of the three cultures' interaction and reconciliation, a product that sooner or later must be constrained by the totality of politics, economy, and cultural milieu. Cultural sociological analysis must always focus on the complex relations and changes of this kind.

However, the trend of differentiation in contemporary Chinese culture has stagnated in recent years, for the binary structure of administration and market is more and more subject to the control of the administrative branch of political authority. A culture that was once governed by a true-false logic seems to be giving way to a friend-versus-foe logic. In other words, the cultural differentiation that had been underway since the reform and opening-up is being compromised by a recentralized cultural hegemony. To complicate matters further, while at times cultural differentiation and the construction of autonomy may appear to be underway, the control over these differentiations is increasing, with the decline of autonomy in various cultural spheres. The apparently autonomous functioning of market is increasingly at the mercy of administrative intervention and regulation. Aesthetic culture, which once boasted of the notion of artistic autonomy and even aesthetic autonomy, has now suffered such a setback that a new wave of centralization is fundamentally altering the current structure of contemporary Chinese culture. This situation is similar to that discussed by Habermas in the preface to the 1989 new edition of *The Structural Transformation of the Public Sphere*. When the first edition of the book appeared in 1962, the author was still optimistic, believing that the public sphere can provide the institutional guarantee of democracy, especially the autonomy of various civic institutions, organizations, and groups, and that the public sphere can ensure social democracy and freedom of expression. But less than 30 years later, when he added a new preface to the book, Habermas had to admit that many of his earlier judgments had been naïve. He argues that with the rise of electronic media, advertising has obtained new meanings; that with the increasing intermingling of entertainment and information, there is a tendency toward centralization in all spheres; that the disintegration of liberal associations and local public sphere would bring about another transformation to the fabric of public sphere.[11] Of course, what I mean here by "recentralization" is not the same as what Habermas means by "centralization", the former underscoring the recolonization of culture by an authoritarian regime.

Cultural production-reception mode

Having pointed out the status of cultural differentiation in China, my next concern is how to analyze the effect of such differentiation on aesthetic culture. Or, given differentiation of this kind, how can we explain the significance of aesthetic culture in contemporary China? If critical cultural sociology is concerned with the interaction among all kinds of social forces under the condition of differentiation, how can this concern, in a further sense, be explained in a dynamic process in which culture is deemed as the production and reception (i.e., consumption) of symbols? In other words, I will employ an analytical logic characteristic of critical cultural sociology. Above all, I regard culture (including aesthetic culture) as productive and consumptive phenomena. That is to say, my premise is the Marxist theory on productive society and consumer society, while those sociological theories on production and consumption are an integral part of our "fused horizon". Second, to study culture against the background of production-consumption relationship, I go further to define culture as a process of producing and consuming signs. Aesthetic culture, as a peculiar as much as representative assemblage of cultural signs, not only reflects a set of field-specific game rules about production and consumption, but represents, to a considerable degree, the overall conditions of Chinese culture. Thus, the rules of symbolic production and consumption in aesthetic culture are an epitome of culture as a whole. As mentioned earlier, modern cultural sociology offers several definitions of culture, which in turn point to different research approaches. The three definitions below are most commonplace: culture as language and apparatus, culture as tradition and value orientation, and culture as production and consumption.[12] In fat, the three are not unrelated, which is why I prefer to take them as the three dimensions of a greater process. Hence, critical cultural sociology ought to take culture as a processive relationship of symbolic production and consumption inside a certain apparatus. Finally, in light of these basic definitions, we have actually established a research model—using critical cultural sociology to study aesthetic culture within a cultural production-reception framework. This model has four features. First, it overcomes the limitations of static, isolated cultural studies, and interprets culture in terms of the dynamic configuration of production and consumption. Therefore, it is a dynamic, dialectical study of interactions. Second, as pointed out by Marx in a dialectical way, production not only creates the object for the subject, but the subject for the object. Marx's take on production-consumption process is dynamic, both on the synchronic level and on the diachronic one. That said, his dynamic inquiry is in fact a historical investigation. When it comes to contemporary Chinese aesthetic culture, it is necessary for us to extend our research to history, historically interpreting the transformation of contemporary Chinese aesthetic culture and its implications. Third, this research model offers a cogent perspective on the differentiation of society and culture. As we know, differentiation manifests itself in disparity, which in turn inevitably leads to contradiction and interaction. Be it production or consumption, it involves a sophisticated study of difference and interaction incurred by differentiation. Not only can the production-consumption model help us explore the interactive relationship of the two, but it also enables us to analyze how the structure of aesthetic culture's production and consumption bears resemblance to social structure. Four, there is a more important reason that the developments of contemporary Chinese aesthetic culture have far exceeded the scope of classical art. The development and impact of technology, the ubiquity of mass media, the emergence of the masses with literacy, the transformation of artistic production from artisanship to mechanical reproduction, the changes of how art is disseminated, the influence of fashion and taste, and the relationship between communities and subcultures are among the issues that cannot be adequately addressed in light of the traditional paradigm, which centers around individual creativity and case studies. What we need now is a research model that is not only holistic, but concerned with new dimensions. The sociological paradigm of "production vs. consumption" just caters to the needs listed above.

Historically speaking, regarding the theory of cultural production, there are several major theoretical models in cultural sociology. First of all, Marxist political economics. For Marx, production and consumption are dialectical categories.

Classical Marxist theorists give many in-depth analyses of inequality and alienated labor, by making historical inquiry into the mode of production in capitalism, and by debunking the myth of surplus value. Marx has never established a theory of cultural sociology, but for his apostles, the theories of labor as the reification of men and of aesthetic capability and the socialization of human beings have enabled the followers to extend Marxism to cultural sociology. It is a great leap from classical Marxism's political economics to Frankfurt School's critical theory. Those theoreticians in Frankfurt School reflect on the Enlightenment historically and explicate mass culture (as cultural industry) on the basis of economic analysis of post-liberal capitalist societies. They put forward some critical paradigms when analyzing cultural production and consumption in capitalist societies, revealing in particular the ideological control of cultural industry upon the masse, and advocating the redemptive power of the avant-garde art and its utopian ideal. Their work is rather radical insofar as their critique of society and culture is concerned. The later Critical Theory is more concerned with the relationship between the dominant culture and the dominated under the condition of globalization, interested in how to dismantle and critique the cultural hegemony and repression of capitalism.[13]

Second, besides the mode of cultural production as explicated in Marx's political economics, Weber's sociology also offers an influential model. Weber puts forward a cultural sociology in his treatise on the Protestant ethics and the rise of capitalism. This theoretical model can be used elsewhere. For example, Weber's religious sociology construes an intricate system for structural analysis. He divides into two types the leaders: the bureaucratic and the charismatic. Accordingly, in the case of religion, these two leader types specifically refer to priests and prophets. Both produce signs and compete with each other for consumers. In the scheme of religious sociology, there are three elements of symbolic production, as is the case of Marxist political economics: cultural purveyor or cultural producer, cultural product, and those who demand or consume cultural product. In Weber's system, a priest is supposed to maintain the existing religious system, while a prophet represents the force of religious reformation. The conflict between the two not only unfolds the hidden contradiction of religion, but reveals the complicated relationship between production and consumption. Marx's model was later renovated by Bourdieu, who changes it into a highly influential analytical mode in today's cultural sociology. By looking into the relationship between "limited field of production" (i.e., "high art" or the avant-garde art) and "massive field of production (i.e., mass culture or folk art), Bourdieu points out that the two modes of cultural production involve disparate subjects and have different characteristics. For the former, production is for the producers themselves (i.e., fellow artists, critics, gallery owners, art agents). In other words, for this kind of symbolic production, the provider is at the same time its demander. Those avant-garde artists, acting as the subject of production, are the *de facto* "prophet" in the name of "pagan" or "heretic", standing up against the existing system and tradition. The latter is for the sake of consumers, belonging to the vast social field. Bourdieu notices that the avant-garde artist as "prophet", in his limited filed of production, often begets violent resistance from the "priest"— painters and critics in academia. Thus, Bourdieu introduces cultural system to the study of symbolic production. A telling example regarding such institutionalization is the French Academy (*L'Académie française*), whose function, according to Weber's religious sociology, is similar to the church (a bureaucratic apparatus). Such institutionalization also includes museums, critics, agents, gallery owners, and art institutes. Orthodox painters and heretic avant-garde painters compete with each other to woo the establishment. An interesting phenomenon came to Bourdieu's notice: critics, galleries, and the catalogues published by museums of fine arts can consecrate some sort of art, by virtue of their special "power of appellation". A case in point is their designation of the Impressionist paintings or the Cubist paintings. The "power of appellation" is in fact a means of "symbolic violence" imposed on the ordinary consumers in "massive field of production". "Limited filed of production" is composed of some activists and institutions, which pertain to three forms of resistance: the struggle among different art producers (those consecrated artists, avant-garde artists, heretic artists, bourgeois artists, etc.), all of whom pine for recognition and consecration from the establishment; the struggle between producers and market owners (in essence, another name for the established system); the struggle among different market owners.[14]

Be it Marx's political economics or Weber's cultural sociology, a core issue is the interactive relationship of different cultural or subcultural forces in both production and consumption. The two thinkers' work can help us analyze production and consumption in contemporary Chinese society/culture. Judging from the latest trend of cultural sociology, the theory on production and consumption is of great critical prowess and feasibility. No wonder it has become a crucial mode of cultural interpretation. As pointed out by some scholars,

> In recent years, however, a more specialised notion of production has developed which emphasises the role of ideology and politics. The relation of art to ideology has been radically recast in terms of a materialist aesthetic produced from within ideology itself...Production theory thus focused on the transition from nineteenth-century capitalist individualism to twentieth-century collectivist modes of political life and culture demanding art-forms that engaged with the active masses of the 'scientific age'.[15]

Studying Chinese aesthetic culture, I think, entails the following basic issues, which constitute the mainstay of our "production-reception" mode. First, cultural production (a.k.a., symbolic production, textual production, or semantic production) is a field in Bourdieu's sense, a "combined force" in Fredrick Engels' sense, and in Clifford Geertz's sense, "compromise and transaction" (which means the conflict, interaction, and coordination of all kinds of forces). Therefore, one's analysis of cultural production would necessitate an anatomy of various cultural contradictions. Second, based on such an anatomy of "contradictions", one's study must pay special attention to the subject of production (i.e., artists, critics and consumers), whose cultural behavior and taste are linked, and whose mode of production is evolving; to the changing channel of dissemination; to the interpretation of how cultural object (product) produces meanings. Third, cultural production here is regarded as semantic production, so a central issue is about the generation and interpretation of symbolic and textual meaning—this issue can be aptly rephrased as one related to discourse, dialogue, and communication. Thus, the production of aesthetic culture is a specialized production of discourse, and the primary task of cultural sociology is to examine such discourse. In cultural sociology, I want to alert you to two inappropriate tendencies. The first one is an obsession with the subject in cultural production, taking production as the basic or, even the only, link of the whole culture, and giving no sight of the subject of consumption and consumer behavior. In fact, it is at this point that Bourdieu's theory is flawed. The second one is attaching much importance to semantic interpretation, but downplaying production. The myth is that what matters is how to interpret the texts at hand, so the subject of reception deserves more scrutiny. We can find such an inclination in Anthony Giddens's theory. Giddens maintains that "Cultural analysis focuses on the relation between discourse and what I shall henceforth call 'cultural objects'... As a consequence of this, the 'consumer' or receiver becomes more important than the producer in the interpretative process".[16] I think, we should establish a more balanced, symmetrical cultural production-reception model. Here, semantic production and interpretation are paralleled, as all interpretative processes entail what Habermas calls "symmetrical intersubjectivity". According to his communication theory, all speech acts consist an addresser and, in a symmetrical sense, an addressee. This symmetrical relation is the premise of all speech acts or communicative actions. After all, both semantic production and semantic consumption reflect such a symmetrical intersubjective relation; otherwise, all communicative action would be in peril. Habermas points out,

> Pure intersubjectivity is determined by a symmetrical relation between I and You (We and You), I and He (We and They). An unlimited interchangeability of dialogue roles demands that no side be privileged in the performance of these roles; pure intersubjectivity exists only when there is complete symmetry in the distribution of assertion and dispute, revelation and concealment, prescription and conformity, among the partners of communication.[17]

What Habermas discusses here is communicative relation, but such a relation in fact exists between cultural production and consumption, because it is a process of transmission and transformation of cultural meanings. Thus, in this process, both the producer and the consumer are indispensable. Dialectically speaking, the two roles are symmetrical and interchangeable.

Notes

1. Alan Bullock and Oliver Stallybrass, eds. *The Fontana Dictionary of Modern Thought*. London: Fontana, 1982. p.150.
2. Beth B. Hess, Elizabeth W. Markson and Peter J. Stein. *Sociology*. New York: Macmillan, 1988. p.56.
3. Joel M. Charon, ed. *Meaning of Sociology*. Englwood Cliffs: Prentice Hall, 1990. p.204.
4. Clifford Geertz. *Interpretation of Cultures*. New York: Basic Books, 1973. p.5.

5 See Clifford Geertz. *Nagara: The Theatre-State in the Nineteenth-Century Bali*. Princeton: Princeton University Press, 1980. Also see Marshall Sahlins. *Culture and Practical Reason*. Chicago: University of Chicago Press, 1971.
6 Scott Lash. *Sociology of Postmodernism*. London: Routledge, 1990. pp.4–5.
7 Zhou Qi. *Social Structure in the Contemporary West*. Beijing: Chinese Social Sciences Press, 1996. pp.9–10.
8 Jürgen Habermas. "On Modernity", in *Postmodernist Culture and Aesthetics*. Ed. Wang Yuechuan and Shang Shui. Beijing: Peking University Press, 1992. p.6.
9 Pierre Bourdieu. "The Specificity of the Scientific Field and the Social Conditions of the Reason", *Social Science Information* 14.6 (1975), pp.19–47. Also see Claus Offe. *Contradictions of Welfare State*. London: Hutchinson, 1984.
10 See Deng Zhenglai and Jing Yuejin. "Constructing Civic Society in China". *Proceedings on Chinese Social Sciences*, No. 4, 1992; Sun Liping, "On a Society of Totality". *Proceedings on Chinese Social Sciences*, No. 1, 1993.
11 Jürgen Habermas. *The Structural Transformation of the Public Sphere: An Inquiry into a Category of Bourgeois Society*. Trans. Cao Weidong, et al. Beijing: Xuelin Press, 1999. p.15.
12 Hans Haferkemp, ed. *Social Structure and Culture*. Berlin: Walter de Gruyter, 1989. pp.68–73.
13 See Theodor W. Adorno. "Culture Industry Reconsidered", in *Culture and Society*. Eds. Jeffrey C. Alexander and Steven Seidman. Cambridge: Cambridge University Press, 1990; also see Theodor W. Adorno, *Aesthetic Theory*. London: Routledge & Kegan Paul, 1984.
14 Pierre Bourdieu. "The Production of Belief: Contribution to an Economy of Symbolic Goods", in *Culture & Society* 2.3 (1980), pp.261–294.
15 Alan Swingewood. *Sociological Poetics and Aesthetic Theory*. London: Macmillan, 1986. p.80.
16 Anthony Giddens. "Structuralism, Post-structuralism and the Production of Culture", in *Social Theory Today*. Eds. Anthony Giddens and Bryan S. Turner. Stanford: Stanford University Press, 1987. pp.215–216.
17 Jurgen Habermas. "Social Analysis and Communication Competence", in *Social Theory*. Ed. Charles C. Lemert. Boulder: Westview, 1993. p.416.

PART I
From Tradition to the Modern Age

1 From primitive culture to classical culture

Integration and differentiation

With a 5,000-year history of advanced civilization, Chinese culture boasts countless glory and treasure. Nevertheless, since the 1840s, Chinese culture began to transform itself, yet in an excruciating way. The transformation from a traditional society to a modern one hinges on cultural changes. As a matter of fact, the modernization of society and its cultural modernity are two correlated matters. Cultural modernity is always the prerequisite for social modernization.

The historical trajectory of traditional Chinese culture, one may say, is rather clear, whereas this culture's transformation in modern era seems quite inexplicable. It is worth noting that given the vast expanse of China's territory and the enormous cultural and economic differences across various areas, whilst some regions have crossed the threshold of modern society, the others might still remain in a somewhat primitive state. Cultural disparities are even more striking, when comparing China's urban culture and country culture, cultures in coastal areas and in inland, youth culture and alternative culture, to name but a few. Hence, some scholars conclude that modern China is actually a bizarre hybridity that consists of the pre-modern, the modern, and even the postmodern cultural elements. When some seemingly "avant-garde" pundits indulge in empty talks about Chinese postmodernity, or all kinds of "post-" theories, "post-" eras, "post-" phenomena, some significant issues are usually overlooked by them. It is safe to say that our pre-modern traditions are entwined with China's modern problems, the two making a real vista of contemporary Chinese culture. Generally speaking, the trend of social and cultural developments in China is a metamorphosis from the traditional to the modern. If we fail to grasp this basic fact and trend, and indulge in various "postmodern" talks, it is like, as Lu Xun mocks, pulling one's hair in the hope of escaping the grip of Earth's gravity. As a result, we might have turned a deaf ear to some more pressing issues regarding Chinese culture.

In modern times, culture has received much scrutiny from academia. The recurring cataclysmic changes that happen to human cultures and societies have led to a series of inscrutable cultural riddles. When the scholarly interest in Chinese culture, especially the changes in aesthetic culture, is on the increase, any discussion on the contemporary transformation of Chinese culture shall offer a historical slant, fully aware of the essential context in which the passage from traditional to modern took place.

DOI: 10.4324/9781003407089-3

Culture is an all-encompassing meta-category. We never reach a consensus as to the exact meanings of this concept. In "Introduction", I've given a preliminary delineation of the conception of culture, and attempt to address the complex relationship between culture as an idea of totality and culture as a subsystem. In this section, I am to make a diachronic investigation into culture, analyzing the different historical modes of culture and their internal makeup, paving the way for further understanding of the contemporary transformation of Chinese culture.

In the field of sociology, Max Weber, in his study of the legitimacy of political order, uses the method of "ideal types" and divides legitimate power into three categories—the traditional, the charismatic, and the rational—which are used to account for the legitimation of power in different societies, cultures, and times. However, the so-called "ideal types" have been used by many great thinkers prior to Weber, though in different registers. A convenient case in Germany is Schiller, who found his time undergoing a sea change. He rightly concluded that such a cultural shift means a transition from "naïve poetry" to "sentimental poetry". Starting from his philosophy of idealism, Hegel also made an insightful inquiry into the evolution of culture, and famously divided human arts into three consecutive, but totally distinct, phases and basic genres, namely, "Symbolic Art", "Classical Art", and "Romantic Art". Karl Marx, by comparing the different modes of production in history, classified human society into four basic types: slave society, feudal society, capitalist society, and communist society to come. Thus, an efficient way to make a historical investigation into culture is morphology plus typology (i.e., the method of ideal types).[1]

From the vantage point of a more mature version of historical morphology, we can roughly divide the long history of human civilization, or a nation's culture, into several historical modes. The same morphological rules apply to aesthetic culture, a subsystem within culture, and a larger system of totality. Generally speaking, we can make a tripartite classification of the cultural modes in history: primitive culture, classical culture, and modern culture (maybe postmodern culture?[2]). Every type has its internal logic and configuration, with a set of characteristics in its own right.[3] If we look into the interior of the three cultural forms, it is evident that many a change taking place in contemporary Chinese culture indeed originates from a distant past. Primitive culture, the primordial cultural mode, is characterized by high-level integrity and utilitarianism. The so-called "high-level integrity" refers to the fact that inside primitive culture, there was no specific stratification yet, with all cultural activities or realms (fields) entangled and bound up in one. What we today call art or aesthetic culture was in primitive culture closely connected with prehistoric religion and witchcraft, the dividing line between both being barely noticeable. The naturalistic art in the Paleolithic age was tied up with witchcraft, and in Neolithic times, pantheism, totemism, and art were always inseparable from one another. We can safely deduce that aesthetic culture in such a form was not autonomous and that there were no specialized producers and consumers of aesthetic culture. High-level integrity was embodied in those undifferentiated group activities in clan tribes, and as a result, aesthetic activities were integrated into the collective practice of pristine religions and witchcraft, production and consumption being two sides of the same coin. The high degree of unity and undifferentiation in primitive culture was found in many aspects—the low-level differentiation of social classes, the absence of professionalization and labor division, the lack of differentiation among economic, cultural, and other activities, and the mixture of individuals and communities. According to the art historian Arnold Hauser, it takes tens of thousands of years for a "professional" artist to emerge, as a result of differentiation. When hunting and animal husbandry were replaced by agriculture, seasonal labor for the first time made leisure time available. The earliest cave paintings were for the purpose of witchcraft and economy. It was not until the role of artists was separated from that of magicians that "professional" artists were born into the world.[4]

Utilitarianism is another feature of primitive art, because the arts in undifferentiated primitive culture did not have *raison d'être*. Art at that time, as I pointed out earlier, was no more than the means of primitive religion and economic activities. The utilitarian feature, to some degree, cancelled the process of stratification and differentiation within primitive culture. In my point of view, stratification and differentiation are the source of cultural development and its internal conflicts. In this sense, there were no significant contradictions and conflicts in primitive culture, which was essentially homogeneous. The undifferentiated status of primitive culture and society merits a lengthy quote from Scott Lash:

> In broadest outline here, in primitive societies, culture and the social are as yet undifferentiated. Indeed religion and its rituals are part and parcel of the social. The sacred is immanent in the profane. Further, nature and the spiritual remain undifferentiated in animism and totemism. The magician's role underscores the ambiguity of distinction between this-worldly and other-worldly, and the priests' functions have not yet become separate and specialized.[5]

The passage from primitive culture to classical culture is a great leap forward for human civilizations. The time of each civilization's entry into the classical age is inconsistent; however, judging from the history of some major civilizations, 500 B.C. seems to be a significant historical watershed. That said, it is during this period that China, India, Greece, Egypt, and Persia turned into mature civilizations and entered the classical age. As Karl Jaspers points out,

> The axis of history is to be found in the period around 500 B.C.—between 800 and 200 B.C.—when the spiritual foundation of humankind simultaneously or independently came into being in China, India, Persia, Palestine and Greece. Man, as we know him today, is still based on such a foundation.[6]

Jaspers calls this pivotal period the "Axial Period", the time when the classical civilization matured.

As another historical mode, classical culture is different from primitive culture. First of all, classical culture was not as indivisible and undifferentiated as primitive culture; on the contrary, the former became differentiated and stratified. A sociological term, differentiation has plenty of meanings. Speaking of the differences between classical and primitive cultures, differentiation is found in many aspects. Echoing Max Weber's theory, Lash maintains that classical culture actually entailed a process leading to the modern. During this process, differentiation was embodied conspicuously in two aspects: first, the dissociation between the culture and the social; and second, the dissociation between the sacred and the secular. As to the first differentiation, it means that the culture had gradually gained autonomy and become independent of the social. Culture and the social were no longer an undifferentiated "field". Such division is of great significance, because aesthetic culture, as a subcategory of culture, could develop into a "field" merely under the condition of a differentiation somewhat between culture and the social. Given the more and more differentiated classical culture, not only did aesthetic culture emerge as an increasingly independent cultural mode, but it was made up of various subcultures. The first type of differentiation went hand in hand with the second one, that is, the separation between the religious and the secular. As mentioned previously, in the primitive societies, religion, as a basic socially binding force, exerted an enormous restrictive power upon all aspects of the social culture, and under such conditions, the culture was part and parcel of primitive religions. In the classical era, with the separation of the secular and the religious, aesthetic culture was established as human activities different from religion. The dissociation of the culture would mean the dissociation of aesthetic culture, which naturally gave rise to the emergence of the artist specializing in art. Needless to say, it is a great leap forward for our civilizations. Various kinds of art genres and forms, in consequence, began to sprout. Had the above-mentioned two differentiations failed to happen, it would have been totally inconceivable for art to appear and develop. The development of all national arts, as Pitirim Sorokin contends, was subject to a common law—all art styles and categories developed not simultaneously, but in a sequence. The turning point was first witnessed in architecture and sculpture, followed by painting, and then by literature, music, etc.[7] We can regard it as another differentiation within art, without which the so-called real art would not have sprouted and bloomed.

Apart from the above-mentioned differentiations, there are other social differentiations that merit further consideration. Although culture and the social started being differentiated, it does not mean the two were totally irrelevant. Rather, the development of culture and the differentiation of society share weal and woe. In the classical age, the emergence of city-state (*polis*) is quite a contrast to the countryside. Furthermore, the differentiation of social classes brings about social hierarchy. The old saying "Whilst criminal penalties do not apply to the noble, civic rites are not created for the rabble" (刑不上大夫, 礼不下庶人) is just a case in point. The "noble" and the "rabble" are simply designations for social hierarchy in classical times. If primitive culture is an indivisible unity, the culture in the classical era has obviously been more prone to differentiation. With the development of social differentiation, cultural differentiation is not so much the formation of various art genres as the diversification of subcultural forms. Similar to the differences between the "noble" (大夫 *dafu*) and the "rabble"(庶人 *shuren*), classical culture also develops into two corresponding categories. One can be loosely categorized as "elite culture", and the other as "folk culture". The former belongs to the privileged gentry, such as the pre-Qin aristocracy famous for "patronizing the intellectual", and the Italian noble or royal families Velázquez and Michelangelo used to serve. The latter is totally different in that it is pristine and popular, at the service of most people, even including those uncivilized people. To be more specific, the patrician culture, insofar as the classical mode of aesthetic culture is concerned, was normative as much as prerogative. By "normative", I mean it had a strict set of standard tastes and a system of styles historically developed and fostered by generation of artists, genteel scholars, cultivated patrons, or connoisseurs, and was embodied in a whole normative system of cultural conventions. For example, there is a hierarchical idea of "taste"(品 ping) in traditional Chinese aesthetics in classical poems and paintings. By "prerogative", I mean this culture was monopolized by a select class strong in cultivation. In ancient China, the aristocracy usually practiced Six Classical Arts, namely, rites, music, archery, horsemanship, calligraphy, and arithmetic. Folklore culture falls into another category, and is characterized by pristine, natural, and naïve aesthetic proclivity. It has little interest in personalized, stylish, overwrought expression; rather, it emphasizes the vibrant life of common people as a whole, without the taint of patrician pretension and scholarly pedantry. Elite culture conforms to a set of norms, whereas folk art is never short of diversity, with a broad spectrum of regions, communities, and conventions. Comparatively speaking, patrician art belongs to the ruling class, while folk art is of the ruled mass. There is a conspicuous contrast between classical culture and primitive culture, a contrast particularly pointed out by Arnold Hauser in his analysis of the two cultures. He contends that not until the agrarian population in primitive societies was differentiated into classes did folk art come into being. According to Hauser, "for 'folk art' only has a meaning, as has been said, in contrast to the 'art of a ruling class'; the art of a mass of people which has not yet divided into 'ruling and serving classes, high and fastidious and low and modest classes' cannot be described as 'folk art', for one reason because there is no other kind of art at all".[8] That said, in the age of classical culture, culture was differentiated into two disparate fields, that is, the minority's and the majority's. Not only are the two different in terms of cultural production and consumption, but they have totally different configurations of meaning. Disparity means contradiction, the movement of which in turn contributes to the evolution of culture. Therefore, to understand the internal dynamics and trajectory of classical culture, one must pay attention to the binary opposition between aristocratic culture and folk culture.

Generally speaking, in the classical age, the opposition between aristocratic culture and folk culture was not as poignant as that one finds in modern culture. Classical culture is by and large harmonious, though the two subcultures are different. In fact, there is no such thing as a mutually exclusive relationship or rivalry between the two, which have their own target customers and operational realms. Through the lens of politics, aristocratic culture, as the ideology of the ruling class, usually entails "cultural hegemony" for folk culture, and is apt to impose its ideology on other cultures. However, in terms of structural relationship in total, the two cultures would not come into direct conflict or antagonism which yet defines modern culture. Without class disparity and cultural difference, or without targeted customer group and taste difference, it would be impossible for these two subcultures to develop in parallel. Here, it is by no means to say that patrician and folk cultures are unrelated; rather, they have rather complex relations, one of which is the fact that the renewal and reformation of patrician culture usually depend on folk culture, as the latter is a vast, dynamic "field" free from doctrinal rules, and full of lively improvisations. The typically aristocratic norms and conventions of art are not found in folk art. The patrician art depends on a few artists, and is constrained by the aristocracy's gusto and somewhat narrow-minded standards. Consequently, such art could easily drain off its vitality and develop into a rigid and barren culture. It is therefore indispensable for aristocratic art in classical times to absorb raw materials and inspirations from folk art. There are ample examples, ranging from Chinese Music Bureau Poetry to *Book of Poetry*, from monologue storytelling popular with urban masses to traditional chapter novels read by the intellectuals. The Soviet Formalist theoretician Yury Tynyanov pointed out that there was a pattern in literary history—"orthodox literature" (patrician culture) and "marginal literature" (folk literature) always trade with each other. In other words, the less exquisite or mature genre, technique, style, and language in folk culture are processed by the learned and thereby transformed into elegant literature. Viktor Shklovsky calls it "defamiliarization".

Of course, the absence of acute conflict does not mean there is no such thing as friction or rivalry between the two cultures. When aristocratic culture exercises its "cultural hegemony", folk culture in various ways tends to do away with those cultural restrictions imposed by the aristocracy, so as to express its own cultural tastes and lifestyles. Mikhail Bakhtin has an excellent observation in this regard. Bakhtin notes that there was a folk culture of humor derived from the Middle Ages in the West, a culture in many aspects antithetical to the serious, orthodox official culture (i.e., patrician culture). He maintains that the folk culture of humor is "a second world and a second life" outside of the orthodox culture. There are several differences between the two cultures, the first being popularity. While patrician culture is limited to the select few, the folk culture of humor means cultural activities joined by the entirety of people. Bakhtin writes,

> These forms of ritual based on laughter, which existed in all the countries of medieval Europe, offered a completely different, nonofficial, extraecclesiastical and extrapolitical aspect of the world and of human relations. They built a second world and a second life outside officialdom, a world in which all medieval people lived during a given time of the year.[9]

According to Bakhtin, to understand Western culture since the Middle Ages, one must first understand the dualistic relation between the official/ecclesiastical and the folk/culture; otherwise, there is no way to grasp the nature of a culture in this epoch. According to Bakhtin's cultural morphology, the basic structure of classical culture is such a dualistic pattern featuring official culture and folk culture. During a medieval carnival, the stage is boundless, players and audience being the same people. There are no other lives outside of carnival, and no one can dodge it. Thus, in such a cultural ritual, the feudal culture representing the select ruling class is dissolved, replaced by a carnival celebrated by people from all walks of life. On the occasion of carnival, men must follow the carnival's law, which yet stipulates utmost freedom. Hence, carnival has a tint of cosmos, pointing to the rebirth and regeneration of the world, and inviting everyone to be a part of it. The second characteristic of folk culture is that it has the proclivity of interpersonal intimacy. Folk culture (particularly carnival in the town square), so to speak, makes all hierarchy and differences disappear, people being allowed to touch each other willfully.

> It was a consecration of inequality. On the contrary, all were considered equal during carnival. Here, in the town square, a special form of free and familiar contact reigned among people who were usually divided by the barriers of caste, property, profession, and age...People were, so to speak, reborn for new, purely human relations. These truly human relations were not only a fruit of imagination or abstract thought; they were experienced.[10]

The third feature is a logic of inversion. The sublime and the abject in reality, the great and the small, the wise and the stupid, etc., were totally turned upside down. Kings became the object of mockery, while underlings were empowered to laugh at kings. As an important characteristic of folk culture, this inversion renders a self-contained logic absolutely incompatible with official culture. Put in another way, carnival realized a complete reversal of all social norms and values established by official culture. Bakhtin further writes,

> All the symbols of the carnival idiom are filled with this pathos of change and renewal, with the sense of the gay relativity of prevailing truths and authorities. We find here a characteristic logic, the peculiar logic of the 'inside out', of the 'turnabout,' of a continual shifting from top to bottom, from front to rear, of numerous parodies and travesties, humiliations, profanations, comic crownings and uncrownings. We must stress, however, that the carnival is far distant from the negative and formal parody of modern times. Folk humor denies, but it revives and renews at the same time. Bare negation is completely alien to folk culture.[11]

Finally, folk culture turned into art, with a vulgarity of official culture frowned upon. Bakhtinian morphology offers a peculiar frame of reference for our understanding of classical culture. That he views folk culture and official culture as two antithetical categories sheds light on the internal contradiction and its dynamics inside classical culture, and inspires us in many ways.

What we have discussed so far seems to be about Western cultures, but to a considerable extent, the same is true of Chinese culture. In the overall structure of classical Chinese culture, there were also two basic categories: aristocratic culture and folk culture. Although Western carnival-style culture is alien to our culture, folk culture and patrician culture, comparatively speaking, were antipodal in many aspects. Simply put, the two cultures operated with their own logic and principles. As we see the dualistic structure of classical culture, we must be aware of another characteristic of classical culture, a characteristic unfound in primitive and modern cultures—cultural harmony. The term "harmony" actually has a two-fold meaning. First, compared with undifferentiated, holistic primitive culture, classical culture had experienced social and cultural differentiation, which brought about different subcultural forms and concomitant interrelations. If difference and contradiction were nonexistence in primitive culture, the dualistic structure of patrician culture and folk culture had evolved into a complex relationship between difference and contradiction. Nevertheless, difference and contradiction, at this point, were by and large harmonious. Regardless of sporadic conflicts, the two were not purely antagonistic and divided. Culturally speaking, that classical culture was characterized by harmony is a proposition unanimously accepted by academia. Let's take Chinese culture for instance. Insofar as the reality of Chinese culture is concerned, the notion of "modesty and harmony" (中和, *zhonghe*) in Confucianism reflects a typical quest for harmonious relationship in terms of man and nature, individual and society, so on and so forth. From the vantage point of aesthetics, Confucianism advocates that art as a special method should be used to help us "think, observe, live with others, and make good judgment" (兴 *xing*、观 *guan*、群 *qun*、怨 *yuan*), and eventually contribute to the overall harmony of society and culture. In the second volume of *Virtuous Discussions of the White Tiger Hall* (白虎通德论), there is a chapter titled "Ritual and Music", in which a quote from Confucius is recorded. The quote as follows features the idea of "harmony" in Confucianism:

> Confucius said, music being performed in royal temples, the upper and the lower listen to it, and then learn together to be respectful. Music being performed in tribal communities, the elder and the young listen to it, and then learn together to be harmonious. Music being performed in personal households, parents and siblings listen to it, and then learn together to keep filial affection. That is why musicians worship harmony and smoothness, and work on instruments and rhythms. Good music cannot go without harmonious relationship between melody and rhythm. The same is true of the relationship between fathers and sons, the monarch and his subjects, so on and so forth. To make the world harmonious is the purpose of music created by the ancient dynasty. (子曰，乐在宗庙之中，上下同听之，则莫不知敬。族长乡里之中，长幼同听之，则莫不和顺。在闺门之内，父子兄弟同听之，则莫不和亲。故乐者所以崇和顺，比物饰节。节文奏合以成文，所以和合父子君臣，附亲万民也。是先王立乐之意也。)[12]

Second, that classical culture was essentially harmonious is a reasonable proposition as one compares it with modern culture. In contrast to modern culture, classical culture, in spite of the tension, and entanglement between aristocratic culture and folk culture, the differentiation was far from the mutually exclusive antagonism we witness in modern culture. It is in this sense that I say classical culture was a culture of harmony. Hegel, in his analysis of the basic differences among the symbolic (primitive), the classical, and the romantic (modern) art, put forward a reference frame, that is, form vs. content. In his view, primitive culture was highly symbolic in that the predominant concern of this art was to represent object, rather than spirit. Thus, primitive culture cannot be harmonious. Romantic art is opposite, as spiritual content overwhelms material representation. Of course, this mode of culture was not harmonious, either. As to classical culture, material representation and spiritual content are in accordance with each other. Here, Hegel's discussion is derived from his philosophy of idealism that highlights the development of idea; nevertheless, his observation to some degree grasps the essence of classical culture, that is, harmony. Since the modern age, more and more scholars have shown, in different ways or with different terms, their rapport with, or nostalgia for the harmonious culture in classical times. Wilhelm Schubart once classified culture into four types, one of which is "the harmonious culture". He believes that the representatives of the harmonious culture are Homer's ancient Greek culture and the Confucian Chinese culture.[13]

Notes

1 Pitirim A. Sorokin. *Sociological Theories of Today*. New York: Harper & Row, 1966.
2 Western scholars are largely divided as to whether postmodern culture belongs to a distinct historical period. One view is that (i.e., Habermas and Giddens) modernity is far from complete and the so-called postmodern is no more than an illusion. Lyotard and others assert that the postmodern is an early stage of the modern. Another popular opinion is that the postmodern is a new phase after the modernist culture—the postmodern, according to Fredric Jameson, is no longer a matter of *-ism* but of *-isms*.
3 For the different historical forms of culture and their characteristics, see the works of Schiller, Hegel, Spengler, Jaspers, Adorno, and others; also see the cultural anthropological works of Benedict, Boas, Kroeber, and others. In addition, Riesman's theory of sociological categorization and McLuhan's work on the modes of transmission are also noteworthy critical resources.
4 Arnold Hauser. *The Social History of Art, Vol. 1*. New York: Vintage, 1957. pp.21–26.
5 Scott Lash. *Sociology of Postmodernism*. London: Routledge, 1990. p.6.
6 Karl Jaspers. "The History of Man", in *Selected Essays on Modern Western History Studies*. Shanghai: Shanghai People's Publishing House, 1982. p.38.
7 Pitirim A. Sorokin. *Sociological Theories of Today*. New York: Harpper & Row, 1966. p.366.
8 Arnold Hauser. *The Social History of Art, Vol. 1*. New York: Vintage, 1957, p.24.
9 Mikhail Bakhtin. *Selected Essays by Mikhail Bakhtin*. Trans. Tong Jinghan. Beijing: China Social Science Press, 1996. p.100.
10 Mikhail Bakhtin. *Selected Essays by Mikhail Bakhtin*. Trans. Tong Jinghan. Beijing: China Social Science Press, 1996, p.176.
11 Ibid. pp.106–107.
12 See Ban Gu, eds. *Virtuous Discussions of the White Tiger Hall*. Beijing: China Literature and History Press, 1999.
13 Pitirim A. Sorokin. *Sociological Theories of Today*. New York: Harper & Row, 1966. p.325.

2 From classical culture to modern culture
Harmony vs. conflict

When culture changed from its classical mode to modern mode, there are two basic signals worth our attention. First, further differentiation led to the disintegration of classical culture, and the primary momentum of modern culture was more violent and in-depth differentiation. As pointed out by some cultural sociologists, differentiation is the major characteristic of cultural modernity. Second, based on further differentiation, there were more conspicuous conflicts and contradictions. If classical culture is mainly defined by harmony, the distinguishing features of modern culture are contradiction and conflict. In classical culture, spirit and object, individual and society, and sense and sensibility were still in a harmonious state; nevertheless, the emergence of modern culture brought the harmony to an end, and gave rise to sharp conflicts and contradictions.

In light of the history of Western culture, Schiller and Hegel were among the earliest ones who realized the advent of modern culture. Schiller touched upon the issue of the end of classical culture by drawing a line between "naïve poems" and "sentimental poems", while Hegel, in a different manner, described the transition in terms of "the age of prose" which replaced "the age of poetry". Marx, in his analysis of capitalism, particularly alienated labor, pointed out the vast difference between feudal societies and capitalist ones. Oswald Spengler once announced that since the Romantic period, Western civilization had tolled the bell of its decline; Georg Simmel proclaimed at the turn of 20th century that Western civilization had entered into the age of "cultural tragedy"; Heidegger asserted that as technical reason transcends spirit, it is no longer possible for men to "dwell poetically"… All these great German thinkers stated a self-evident truth; that is, a modern culture totally different from classical culture was looming large in front of them.

Obviously, the modern originated in the West. The debate over cultural modernity began in the West, too. If we're concerned about China's turning to social and cultural modernization, there are two problems that merit further study. First, the transformation of Western culture can be taken as a reference frame for our understanding of Chinese culture's turning to modernity. By virtue of this reference frame, we can better grasp the characteristics of Chinese culture's modern transformation. Second, taking Western culture as a frame of reference is a research approach of great value, but we must err on the side of caution. On the one hand, one can't deduce a universal pattern from the trajectory of Western culture and then apply it to studies on Chinese cultures. In China's cultural studies, we must be alert to such a fallacy. On the other hand, one must pay attention to the singularity of Chinese culture, to the fact that the transformation from classical culture to modern culture in the case of China was a rather long and complex process. Not only does it concern manifestations of some universal principles regarding the culture of the whole human race, but it has to do with the representation of Chinese culture, which has its unique forms and developmental route. Given these recognitions, we first delineate the trajectory of Western culture's modern development and then investigate the case of China.

Modern culture was the inevitable product of industrialization, urbanization, free market economy, and technical advances. Industrialization made agricultural societies obsolete in the West. The influx of agrarian laborers to towns created cities of unprecedented size and drastic increase in civic population. Free market economy extended supply-demand relationship and the rationale of commercial transaction to every corner of one's societal life. The gallop of technology fundamentally changed behavioral pattern of production and consumption of material and spiritual products. Thus, what underlies modern culture makes it different from classical culture in terms of internal logic and features.

According to a consensus in Western academia, modern culture originated in the Renaissance; nevertheless, modernist culture (i.e., avant-garde culture) in the strict historical sense did not exist until the second half of 19th century. Web in his famous treatise on religious sociology observes that the modern transformation of Western culture took place at the time when theoretical, ethical, and aesthetic knowledge and practice became independent of the unity of religion and metaphysics. In other words, the historical process of differentiation gradually led to a modern culture unlike traditional culture defined by religion-metaphysics. Habermas, following Weber's argument, points out that cultural modernity stemmed from such differentiation, which further gave rise to specialization of occupations, to the tripartite opposition among the cognitive/implemental, the moral/practical, and the aesthetic/representational. What are the implications of such differentiation for art? An obvious tendency is that art is more and more assigned to a self-contained, autonomous realm, that the justification of art is not found in religion or other realms, and that art ought to and is necessarily being-in-self and being-for-self. These are the inherent characteristics of modernist art. According to Daniel Bell,

> The modern movement disrupts that unity. It does so in three ways: by insisting on the autonomy of the aesthetic from moral norms; by valuing more highly the new and experimental; and by taking the self (in its quest for originality and uniqueness) as the touchstone of cultural judgment.

The three features, so to speak, summarize the gist of modernism. As to the autonomy of modern art, the most representative case is found in the quest for so-called "the pure".[1] The artistic notion of "the pure" seems to suggest that it dawned upon modern artists that in the past art was actually adulterated. Here, "impurity" has multiple meanings, the first being that art is not for art's sake (instead, for the purpose of morality and politics) and the second being all art genres were not so developed as to claim its normativity and singularity. For example, the ideas of painting and sculpture were caught in a mesh, and fiction, poetry, and drama are somewhat interchangeable. However, a primary objective of modern artists was to identify the uniqueness of a particular art genre. It was commonplace to see some terms such as "pure poetry", "pure form" in modern art. Some aestheticians boil modernist art down to "stylish alienation" or "aesthetic isolationism". As to the characteristics of modern art, Jose Ortega y Gasset in the 1930s was among the earliest theoreticians who gave a brilliant summary:

> When analyzing art styles in this century, we came to find some closely related tendencies. The "new style" tends to: 1) dehumanize art 2) avoid living forms (note: it refers to the old-fashioned verisimilitude); 3) see the work of art as nothing but a work of art; 4) consider art as play and nothing else; 5) be essentially ironic; 6) beware of sham and hence to aspire to scrupulous realization; 7) regard art as a thing of no transcending consequence.[2]

In Jose Ortega y Gasset's view, modern art divided people into two categories. The first is the upscale, genteel minorities who are connoisseurs of modern art; the second is the masses who neither understand nor appreciate it. Overall, modern art took the line of elitism and distanced itself from the mass, gradually developing into, as Marcuse puts it, a clique art.

When modern art was in full swing, an art closely related to the masses came into being. As mentioned earlier, with the change in modern societies (in particular, industrialization and urbanization), more and more people were drawn to cities. Hence, Ortega found that, in contrast to the last century, Western societies in the 20th century had witnessed a spectacular change, that is, the emergence of modern multitude. He discovered that after the WWI, in all European major cities, one could see a throng of strangers in restaurants, theaters, beaches, parks, trains, and steamers, which in the past belonged to a few and were never open to everyone. The masses become a new social class in modern society, and were the product of modern society itself. Jose Ortega y Gasset in *The Revolt of the Masses* writes,

> Society is always a dynamic unity of two component factors: minorities and masses. The minorities are individuals or groups of individuals which are specially qualified. The mass is the assemblage of persons not specially qualified. By masses, then, is not to be understood, solely or mainly, 'the working masses.' The mass is the average man. In this way what was mere quantity—the multitude—is converted into a qualitative determination: it becomes the common social quality, man as undifferentiated from other men, but as repeating in himself a generic type. What have we gained by this conversion of quantity into quality? Simply this: by means of the latter we understand the genesis of the former.

³That said, modern societies consist of the masses strikingly different from the folk in traditional societies, because the masses have little difference among each other, similarity or conformity having become the chief characteristic of them. That is why the masses become "the average men". Ortega's argument delicately resonates with American sociologist David Riesman's theory, which states that traditional societies were "tradition-directed", while early modern capitalist societies were "inner-directed", and contemporary capitalist societies are "other-directed". The birth of the masses also gave rise to the so-called capitalist "super-democracy", which means that those norms and rules that used to differentiate people and their behaviors in traditional societies have lost their potency in modern societies. Culture exclusively prepared for the few is now consumed by the multitude. Ortega contends that the masses would come to dominate not only culture but also politics. If modern art is in accordance with, as Ortega puts it, the "select few", the masses then are in alliance with another kind of culture, that is, mass culture. As opposed to modernism or avant-garde art, mass culture came into being as a result of Western modernization (in particular, cultural modernity). If modern art remains "elegant culture", mass culture is none other than "vulgar culture". The differentiation of culture just corresponds to social differentiation in the modern age.

At the turn of the 19th century, Georg Simmel sadly pointed out the rising modern culture signals the advent of "cultural tragedy", which features the material objectivity ruling over the spiritual, and the death of individual freedom incurred by the collective life in a society. Oswald Spengler bemoaned the corruption of art as a result of commodification, and the demise of art's autonomous value, which was increasingly replaced by external merchandise. In the 1920s and 1930s, with the processes of massive urbanization and the burgeoning of urban masses, mass culture with a tint of cultural industry came into being, accompanying the appearance of mass media. The rapid development of mass culture became the game-changing ingredient of modern culture and stipulated the "rules of game". Mass culture resembles folk culture in the sense that both claim a large number of addressees; otherwise, this culture is essentially different from folk culture, which I will return to later on. As the sociologist Leo Löwenthal states,

> The decline of the individual in the mechanized working processes of modern civilization brings about the emergence of mass culture, which replaces folk art and 'high' art. A product of popular culture has none of the features of genuine art, but in all its media popular culture prove to have its own genuine characteristics: standardization, stereotype, conservatism, mendacity, manipulated consumer goods.⁴

There is a particular issue worth our attention, that is to say, our morphological conception of modern Western art must heed the binary opposition between modern culture and mass culture. In other words, that these two cultures are mutually exclusive and antagonistic is a key to understanding why modern culture was drifted to a road of "Against Communication" and "Against Interpretation". Some Western aestheticians in particular stress that modern culture, besieged by mass culture, must adopt a radical strategy, if it hopes to exert itself as a subversive counterforce, that is to say, a force of "counter-culture" or "anti-culture", and to keep its identity. Around the 1900s, Simmel poignantly argued,

> Every day and from all sides, the wealth of objective culture increases, but the individual mind can enrich the forms and contents of its own development only by distancing itself still further from that culture and developing its own at a much slower pace.[5]

That said, under the enormous pressure of material culture, there is only one way out, that is to say, distancing itself from it. From the ensuing Frankfurt School to the critical theories and leftist theories in the 1970s, most academics adopt this line of thought to clarify the historical contour of modern culture. Viewed by modern aestheticians, the notion of "artistic autonomy" is not only the property of art but also what underlies modern culture, because the autonomy of art justifies modern culture itself. Adorno bluntly says,

> The fetish character of art works is a condition of their truth, including their social truth. The principles of being-for-other only seems to be antagonistic to fetishism; in reality it is the principle of exchange, and therein lies concealed real domination. Freedom from repression can be represented only by what does not succumb to repression use value, only by what is useless. Works of art are plenipotentiaries of things beyond the mutilating sway exchange, profit and false human needs. Against the background of an illusory, social totality, art's illusory being-in-itself is like a mask of truth.

Hence, "Modernism's refusal to communicate is a necessary but not a sufficient condition of ideology-free art. Such art also requires vitality of expression—a kind of expression that is tensed so as to articulate the tacit posture of art works".[6] Herbert Marcuse, totally concurring with Adorno, writes:

> Artistic activities (including, to a large extent, its receptive capability) have become the privilege of the 'select few' who are exempt from production... Art cannot do away with the social division that cultivates the clique character; nor can it compromise its liberating effect by 'vulgarizing' itself.[7]

From this perspective, it is easy for us to understand why modern art is so obsessed with innovation and self, which to a large degree can be taken as radical resistance against the status quo of capitalism and mass culture. Fredric Jameson rightly argues,

> "a primary question of modernist literature is expression. First of all, in a society with growing masses, language is more and more standardized by journalism, and daily language in industrialized cities become devalued. The country folks used to have colorful languages, and so did the patricians.

However, as people swarmed into cities, language is no longer organic, vibrant, or lively. Instead, language has been manufactured as machines and turned into industrial language. Those poets famous for writing obscure poems are actually attempting to change the depreciation of human language, and to restore the long lost vitality of it.[8]

In a nutshell, modern culture and mass culture are antithetical, with totally antipodal property and function. Of course, as a natural law, there is a vast "gray" area between the two poles, and between the two subcultures, there are many transitional modes of culture. Nevertheless, it is quite clear that the two cultures are the two extremes of the broad cultural spectrum.

First, modern culture is autonomous, while mass culture is heteronomous. The term "autonomy" means modern culture is being-in-itself and being-for-itself, justified by its self-contained aesthetic nature. The term "heteronomy" means mass culture is being-in-others and being-for-others, which further reflects its commercial nature of cultural "mimesis". The principle of autonomy reveals that modern culture is concerned with its own aesthetics, assuming the role as a subversive rebel in the present society and as a guardian of aesthetic values. In contrast, heteronomy is indicative of the fact that mass culture pursues commercial value rather than aesthetic one, acting as a potential accomplice of today's capitalism. When the classical Western culture swerved to modern culture, Kant was among the earliest ones to propose the idea of "aesthetic disinterestedness". Since then, the principle of autonomy in aesthetic culture has received more and more scholarly attention. Historically speaking, the notion of aesthetic autonomy manifests itself in bourgeois aesthetics that arose in modern times, and is the historical product of continuous differentiation of society and culture. The endorsement of aesthetic autonomy never means the cancellation of art's social and ethical functions; rather, it suggests a more dialectical approach to understanding art. Hegel points out that if the end of art is deemed as irrelevant to art itself, it amounts to saying that art has no essence and end *sui generis*, but is used as a means in service of other things, which are responsible for art's definition. Adorno has made a more incisive assertion:

> Rather, [art] is social primarily because it stands opposed to society. Now this opposition art can mount only when it has become autonomous. By congealing into an entity unto itself – rather than obeying existing social norms and thus proving itself to be 'social useful'—at criticizes society just by being there. Pure and immanently elaborated art is a tacit critique of the debasement of man by a condition that is moving towards a total exchange society where everything is a for-other.[9]

The passage above seems a little baffling. Why does art have to "stand opposed to society" if art means to criticize society? What is "a total exchange society where everything is a for-other"? Western thinkers have found out that, since the end of 19th century, there have been some disturbing tendencies in the development of aesthetic culture. Simmel acutely notes that men's creative mind is being corroded by fetishism, and spiritual culture of the subject is giving way to objective culture of the material. In the 1950s, such a trend showed no sign of abating. Adorno holds that this cultural turning to thing-like essence is a self-evident fact. During this process, the autonomy of aesthetics is under severe threat. Accompanying the establishment of a total exchange commercial society, culture is more and more tinted with "commodity fetishism". As Adorno writes, "The aspect of cultural commodities that is subject to human consumption is their abstract being-for-other. Yet, by being forced to cater to the consumer's interest they necessarily defraud him".[10] This culture's internal logic is not different from the exchange logic of commodity, which never points to the internal aesthetic value of art itself, but aims at the exterior commercial value. Hence, this culture is not autonomous. Adorno names it "desubstantialization of art". Since mass culture is in accordance with a total exchange commercial society in modern times, the former naturally assumes the "hegemony" of a dominant culture and poses a threat to modern culture. Under such cultural circumstance, modern culture would have to turn to autonomy to sustain its survival. Using autonomy or even narcissism to battle mass culture is exactly what happened to modern Western art.

Second, the opposition between modern culture and mass culture is also manifest in the two's different tastes. Taste is an aesthetic category of extremely complicated meanings. When it comes to aesthetic subjectivity, taste is embodied in aesthetic norms and connoisseurship; speaking of aesthetic objectivity, it manifests itself in a style, form, characteristic of reified object created by the subject. From literature's vantage point, taste is the concrete manifestation of some internal property of culture, reflecting not only the individual judgment and selection but also the commonality of a group or subculture. Through the lens of taste, one can have a glance at the multiple discrepancies between modern culture and mass culture.

Generally speaking, modern culture aims at establishing and maintaining a sort of distinctive norms and standards and is concerned with the internal value of aesthetics. Mass culture, on the contrary, hopes to create transient vogues, which are necessitated by its quest for endless commercial value. To put it in another way, the two cultures have virtually different discourses, the former being called "elegant taste" and the latter being called "distorted taste" (the German word *kitsch* originally means mass culture). In contrast, modern culture entails a complex set of aesthetic discourse, for it pursues from within subversion, creativity, individual style, and historical awareness. In consequence, there is a relentless internal drive in modern culture to transcend itself. As pointed out by American literary critic Irving Howe, modernism, based on the insurgence against vogues, is unflagging furious attacks on orthodox orders. Unlike modernism, mass culture is reproducible discourse, and, owing to its inherent marketing rules, is characterized by standardization, impersonality, formulation, and kitsch. If modern culture still makes new norms as it smashes many a norm in classical culture, mass culture never gets tired of imitating the former, and attempts to formularize, stereotype, and standardize those mature norms in modern culture. Therefore, on the one hand, modern culture is constantly in pursuit of innovation and "defamiliarization" and seeks for new subject matters and technical styles, but it seldom learns from mass culture.

At this point, it differs from classical culture, in which aristocratic culture sucked out nutrition from folk culture; in modern culture, the two subcultures have reciprocal antagonism. On the other hand, mass/consumer culture is always shoplifting valuable gems from modern culture, only to reduce them to some formulaic clichés. Modernism always ventures to creatively transform what is familiar into something "strange", while mass culture takes the opposite way, that is to say, a safe and cheap approach, simply in hope of translating all "unfamiliar" innovations into something familiar, and acceptable.

As to the issue of taste, some Western scholars of cultural studies discover that in the field of mass culture, there is "Gresham's Law" at work, which states that "bad money drives out good". Dwight MacDonald suggests that "Gresham's Law" manifests itself in the 1950s Western culture:

> Good art competes with *kitsch*, serious ideas compete with commercialized formulae—and the advantage lies all on one side. There seems to be a Gresham's Law in cultural as well as monetary circulation: bad stuff drives out the good, since it is more easily understood and enjoyed. It is the facility of access which at once sells *kitsch* on a wide market and also prevents it from achieving quality. Clement Greenberg writes that the special aesthetic quality of *kitsch* is that it "predigests art for the spectator and spares him effort, provides him with a shortcut to the pleasure of art that detours what is necessarily difficult in genuine art" because it includes the spectator's reactions in the work of art itself instead of forcing him to make his own responses. Thus "Eddie Guest and the Indian Love Lyrics are more 'poetic' than T.S. Eliot and Shakespeare."[11]

Given the accessibility of mass cultural products, MacDonald points out the mechanism of "Gresham's Law", because these products are the most commonplace and convenient objects of consumption, ready-made for the spectator. In my opinion, "Gresham's Law" has more implications here. In the 1980s, another American art sociologist Robert N. Wilson had a different view. He observes:

> [...] a mass business society inevitably imposes a sort of aesthetic Gresham's Law, in which bad art drives out good. The good, at any rate, is taken to be the enemy of the best; a combination of business values and the proficiency of the mass media lends to this enemy an overwhelming advantage. Thus the great variety and bulk of popular culture are assumed to drown out the lonely but elegant voice of high culture.[12]

Wilson stresses the combination of business values and the mass media, which is a crucial point. Mass culture is always wooing business values, because the mass media are capable of disseminating mass culture's standardization, formulae, and reproducibility, and hereby bestows overwhelming advantages upon it. In contrast, avant-garde culture is obsessed with creativity and individual styles, which cannot fit in with the needs of standardization and reproducibility in the mass media.

Wilson's theory tilts to media technique, but I think it is not convincing enough to explicate "Gresham's Law". In a broad sense of social culture, the reason why "Gresham's Law" frequents the domain of mass culture is related to many factors in modern societies. We can easily pay attention to how mass culture seeks for business values so as to give no sight of ethical norms and aesthetic conventions. However, this line of thought only points out the surface, without revealing the hidden reasons. In my opinion, this phenomenon has a lot to do with the masses forged by the modern urban societies. To be more specific, "Gresham's Law" is decided by the lifestyle of the modern multitude and their cultural characteristics. Industrialization significantly increases the density of urban population, and the democratization of education brings about the so-called *culturati*, those equipped with literacy and intensely interested in cultural affairs. Furthermore, the technical progress and the increase in work efficiency enable them to have more and more spare time. As a result, leisure becomes a part of life. On the other hand, the civilized masses created by urbanization differ from the country folks in agricultural civilization, as the former no longer hinge on family, but are connected more and more by social organizations—businesses, public institutions, social services, etc. Hence, individual personality, or even a small group's identity, has been gradually leveled; what comes next is, using a term in sociology, "social masses". Under such conditions, cultural masses breed a strong tendency to conformity. As remarked by David Riesman, the "other-directed" modern men are strikingly different from the "tradition-direction" ones in traditional societies or the "inner-directed" ones in early modern societies. The American psychologist Carl Ransom Rogers suggests that the modern men have a kind of invisible collective pressure, because individual differences always evoke anxiety and disquiet. Conformity is the safest policy. The dullness of spare time and the tendency to conformity, plus the impact of consumer hedonism prevalent in business societies, give rise to a vulgar taste which prefers immediate sensational stimulations. The homogeneous masses of modern culture are in need of similarly homogeneous entertainment to kill their abundant spare time. It is at this point that pornography, violence, and gossips about one's privacy inside stories circulating in mass consumer culture cater to the masses. Daniel Bell, in his *The Cultural Contradictions of Capitalism*, particularly emphasizes the connection between the distorted taste and the *culturati*. He writes,

> In this double contradiction of capitalism, what has been established in the last thirty years has been the tawdry rule of fad and fashion: of "multiples" for the *culturati*, hedonism for the middle classes, and pornotopia for the masses. And in the very nature of fashion, it has trivialized the culture.[13]

Different cultures have different functionality. The functional opposition between modern culture and mass culture points to another fundamental differentiation between the two cultures. Comparatively speaking, modern culture, by and large, is a serious culture, with moral concerns and aesthetic pursuit which usually underlie the reflection, critique, and reconstruction of extant cultures. As mentioned in my previous discussion on autonomy, such a culture insists on autonomy because it goes against the grain of society so as to launch a critique of it. Since the total exchange relationship in mass business society has taken shape, the hegemony of commercial culture is omniscient, with inflated consumer hedonism constituting phony ideology and covering up authentic relationship of dominance. Therefore, it is very pressing for art to reflect on and critique society. On the contrary, modern mass culture, generally speaking, is a business culture inclined to being other-directed, and aims to maintain the status quo of dominant culture, boost the fake ideology of consumer hedonism, and strengthen the cultural hegemony of mass business society. The Frankfurt School has elaborated on this point. Leo Löwenthal points out that mass culture "offer nothing but entertainment and distraction—that, ultimately, they expedite flight from an unbearable reality. Wherever revolutionary tendencies show a timid head, they are mitigated and cut short by a false fulfilment of wish dreams, like wealth, adventure, passionate love, power, and sensationalism in general".[14]

Hauser is even more blunt:

High, serious, uncompromising art has a disturbing effect, often distressing and torturing; popular art, on the other hand, wants to soothe, distract us from the painful problems of existence, and instead of inspiring us to activity and exertion, criticism and self-examination, moves us on the contrary to passivity and self-satisfaction.[15]

Thus, we can see the tremendous changes that happened when classical culture turned into modern one. While classical culture is characterized by the relative harmony of aristocratic culture and folk culture, such harmony had been smashed by modern culture. Modern culture replaced it with an antagonistic binary opposition between avant-garde art and popular culture (or high culture vs. mass culture). In other words, modern culture is composed of two subcultures, which are sheerly differently the binary in classical culture. Modern culture, of course, is not a legitimate heir to classical aristocratic culture. Sometimes, the revolt against tradition takes the form of negating traditional patrician culture. In many ways, modern culture radically diverges from and negates classical culture, even bringing a fatal blow to the very foundation of culture itself. Literature turns into anti-literature; painting, non-painting; and theater, anti-theater. Ortega boils this culture down to "dehumanization", which accounts for its unpopularity and lack of audience. Later on, Adorno even asserts that this culture is an art of narcissism, an art that refuses exchange relationship and distances itself from the mass. But modern culture merits further consideration in two aspects. First, it is a denial of classical art in tradition. Some Futurists even threaten to burn off all traditional artworks. Second, compared with classical aristocratic art, it seems to be even more "privileged", never feeling concerned by its lack of market and audience. Rather, modern art takes pride in its isolation, championing the principle of autonomy to such a degree that it borders on stubborn narcissism. If the first point still reflects its acute impulse to create and innovate, the second one would envision modern culture's innate crisis.

After pointing out the binary opposition in modern Western culture, I think there are still a couple of things worth mentioning here. First, the opposition between modern culture and mass culture is no more than the overall condition of Western culture. As mentioned earlier, when invoking such "ideal types", one must pay attention to the vast "gray area" between the two poles. Binary opposition, eventually, is a reference frame that helps us understand modern Western culture. Second, my typological study of modern culture and mass culture is just a reductive analysis of the global pattern, allowing for plenty of counter-evidence and more complicated phenomena. There are two kinds of phenomena we must be alert to. First, the gap between modern culture and mass culture is sometimes closing. According to Clement Greenberg, a renowned American art theorist, avant-garde art (modernism) and vulgar art are twins, fathered by specific social, economic, and political conditions in capitalism. The two categories are only opposed on the surface, but they have internal consistency deep down. Greenberg writes,

> And in the case of the avant-garde, this was provided by an elite among the ruling class of that society from which it assumed itself to be cut off, but to which it has always remained attached by an umbilical cord of gold... Kitsch's enormous profits are a source of temptation to the avant-garde itself, and its members have not always resisted this temptation. Ambitious writers and artists will modify their work under the pressure of kitsch, if they do not succumb to it entirely.[16]

In the 1960s, Renato Poggioli, an Italian scholar on the avant-garde, explicitly pointed out that there was no essential demarcation between avant-gardism and those fads and clichés in mass culture, the two even walking in the same shoes. In his opinion, the characteristic impulse to make anew in the avant-garde is actually a revision of the notion of "eternal beauty" in classical art. Here, the concept of "beauty" is reduced to some passing fashions or clichés. Poggioli writes,

> The connection between the avant-garde and fashion is therefore evident: fashion too is a Penelope's web; fashion too passes through the phase of novelty and strangeness, surprise and scandal, before abandoning the new forms when they become clichés, kitsch, stereotype. Hence the profound truth of Baudelaire's paradox, which gives to genius the task of creating stereotypes. And from that follows, by the principle of contradiction inherent in the obsessive cult of genius in modern culture, that the avant-garde is condemned to conquer, through the influence of fashion, that very popularity it once disdained—and this is the beginning of its end.[17]

His observation provides us with a new perspective on the relationship between modern culture and mass culture. That said, by penetrating the apparent opposition of the two, we can find the deep interaction and bond of the two. The innovation in the name of avant-gardism is at the same time a conversion to stereotypes. In Ezra Pound's words, the artistic beauty pursued by the avant-garde is no more than "a brief gasp between one cliché and another."

Second, as to the *culturati*, most critics, be it the 1930s Frankfurt School, or the postmodern theories in the 1970s, regard mass culture as negative cultural phenomena. Yet, mass culture is not monolithic, and has complicated makeup. Since the 1980s, the critical theory and cultural studies developed in the West have been interested in the subversiveness of mass culture and its inner contradiction and produced a series of new insights. Take, Adorno, for instance. Since the birth of his 1940s *Dialectics of Enlightenment*, Adorno always advocated a critique of cultural industry, taking modern culture and mass culture as two antithetical categories. However, in the late 1960s, shortly before his death, Adorno came to realize that mass culture could also be used to subvert the existing capitalism. We should be aware that some scholars of later critical theory had a different opinion of this issue.[18] This new trend will help us understand mass culture in contemporary Chinese culture.

Notes

[1] Daniel Bell. *The Cultural Contradictions of Capitalism*. Trans. Zhao Yifan, et al. Beijing: Sanlian Bookstore, 1989. p.30.
[2] Jose Ortega y Gasset. "The Dehumanization of Art", in *Criticism: The Major Texts*. Ed. Walter Jackson Bate. New York: Harcourt Brace Jovanovich, 1970. p.661.
[3] Jose Ortega y Gasset. "The Coming of the Masses", in *Mass Culture*. Eds. Bernard Rosenberg and David M. White. New York: The Free Press of Glencoe, 1957. p.42.
[4] Bernard Rosenberg and David M. White, eds. *Mass Culture*. New York: The Free Press of Glencoe, 1957. p.55.
[5] Georg Simmel. *The Philosophy of Money*. London: Routledge & Kegan Paul, 1978. p.446.
[6] Theodor W. Adorno. *Aesthetic Theory*. London: Routledge & Kegan Paul, 1984. p.323–337.
[7] Herbert Marcuse. *Modern Aesthetics in Question*. Trans. Lv Yuan. Beijing: Culture and Art Press, 1987. pp.15–16.
[8] Fredric Jameson. *Postmodernism and Cultural Theory*. Trans. Tang Xiaobing. Xi'an: Shaanxi Normal University Press, 1987, p.160.
[9] Theodor W. Adorno. *Aesthetic Theory*. p.321.
[10] Theodor W. Adorno. *Aesthetic Theory*. p.25.
[11] Bernard Rosenberg and David M. White, eds. *Mass Culture*. New York: The Free Press of Glencoe, 1957. p.61.
[12] Robert N. Wilson. *Experiencing Creativity*. New Brunswick: Transaction, 1986. p.97.
[13] Daniel Bell. *The Cultural Contradictions of Capitalism*. p.37.
[14] Bernard Rosenberg and David M. White, eds. *Mass Culture*. p.55
[15] Arnold Hauser. *The Sociology of Art*. p.582.
[16] Clement Greenberg. "Avant-Garde and Kitsch", in *Modern Culture and the Arts*. Eds. James B. Hall and Barry Ulanov. New York: MaGraw-Hill, 1967. p.180, pp.182–183.
[17] Renato Poggioli. *The Theory of the Avant-Garde*. Cambridge: Harvard University Press, 1968. p.82.
[18] See Douglas Kellner. *Critical Theory, Marxism, and Modernity*. Baltimore: JHUP, 1989; Also see Raymond A. Morrow and David D. Brown. *Critical Theory and Methodology*. Thousand Oaks: Sage, 1994.

PART II
Chinese Culture in the Context of Globalization

3 "Legitimation" and identity anxiety

"Legitimation" and "legislators"

"Legitimation" is a concept of political governance in Weber's sociology. Simply put, it is the ground on which power is endowed and enforced. According to Weber, there are three types of legitimate rule: legal authority, traditional authority, and charismatic authority.[1] I suggest we transplant Weber's concept of legitimation to the domain of culture. I am of the opinion that in any culture, there is a process of legitimation similar to that in politics. A culture, or a type of literature, regardless of its content, form, or style, will be either accepted and endorsed or simply rejected and criticized within the social or cultural community it belongs to. This process is what I call a "lawsuit" that determines its legitimacy or illegitimacy. In spite of Hegel's axiom that "whatever is true is reasonable", the legitimacy of something's *raison d'etre* needs to be justified time and again.

After the First Opium War of 1840, Chinese culture has undergone profound changes—controversies over the ancient vs. the present, the Chinese vs. the foreign arose time and again. In 1995, some new scholarly debates resurfaced in China and some influential theories were put forward. Not only were these theories conceived for theoretical polemics, but also they reflected some anxiety in contemporary Chinese culture and therefore deserved more scrutiny.

In my opinion, cultural legitimacy is substantiated in various ways, political and legal discourse on legitimacy being one form, and theoretical polemic being another. Now, I venture to take a few liberties with Weber's idea of legitimation. Our conception of cultural and literary history is far from static, permanently open to revision and debate when a new culture or cultural form emerges. On the surface, such debates simply usher in different ideas and stances, but in fact they are wars for paradigm inside a cultural community. I am inclined to regard the debate on legitimation as an outcome of paradigmatic differences in a cultural community. According to Thomas Kuhn, scientific research hinges on a scientific community, that is, an apparatus composed of professional researchers working in a specific discipline. The workings of such a community depend on some shared disciplinary norms, which Kuhn calls "paradigm" or "disciplinary matrix". Kuhn writes, "A scientific community consists, on this view, of the practitioners of a scientific specialty…Within such groups communication is relatively full and professional judgment relatively unanimous".[2] As to the definition of paradigm, it is "what the members of a scientific community share, and, conversely, a scientific community consists of men who share a paradigm".[3] More specifically, there are four dimensions of a paradigm or disciplinary matrix: first, "symbolic generalizations", which are symbols and expressions cast in a logical form; second, "the metaphysical parts of paradigms", which are "shared commitment to such beliefs"; third, "values", which are "more widely shared among different communities than either symbolic generalizations or models", such as "quantitative predictions are preferable to qualitative predictions"; and fourth, "paradigms as share examples", which are some examples about how to conduct research as told by one's laboratory, textbook, or research protocols.[4] All in all, "it stands for the entire constellation of beliefs, values, techniques, and so on shared by the members of a given community".[5] By adopting Kuhn's theory on paradigm, we can make a preliminary attempt to define one form of cultural legitimacy as the consensus reached in a cultural community. When a culture or cultural phenomenon is in face of tremendous controversies and disagreements, or being critiqued and censured by a certain theory, we can conclude that it is subject to "a crisis of legitimation".

Furthermore, I suggest that Kuhn's theory be grafted on Zygmunt Bauman's notion of "legislator". Bauman holds that modern intellectual elite (who constitute the so-called cultural community) in the domain of aesthetics has played the role of "legislators" for a long time. He writes,

> [F]or several centuries [intellectuals] seemed to remain uncontestably their own monopolistic domain of authority—the area of culture in general, 'high culture' in particular...Throughout the modern era, including the modernist period, aestheticians remained firmly in control of the area of taste and artistic judgement...Being in control meant operating, without much challenge, the mechanisms transforming uncertainty into certainty; making decisions, pronouncing authoritative statements, segregating and classifying, imposing binding definitions upon reality. In other words—it meant exercising power over the field of art.[6]

Obviously, "legislators" here refers to the professional elite in a cultural community, in particular those working on theoretical studies, ranging from critics, art historians, to theoreticians and aestheticians. They specialize on critical inquiry, always putting forward their opinions and value judgments regarding different cultural phenomena. The way they advance arguments, debate, or quarrel is in fact the "legislatorial process" of cultural "legitimation", which functions as an apparatus controlling culture and its valuation. Although today Bauman's "legislators" are morphing into "interpreter", it is always their callings to repudiate or defend cultural legitimacy.

That said, the latest disputes over theory are quite interesting and meaningful.

The "legitimation" debate

The last 150 years has been the most turbulent period for Chinese society and culture. Chinese culture, in particular its literature, is always prone to complicated tension, often alternating between endorsement and denial, acclaim and repudiation, and radicalism and conservatism. This phenomenon illustrates, as an English proverb vividly says, "every dog will have its day". Since the late 1980s, some debates over cultural and literary legitimacy have achieved particular prominence, which to some degree demonstrates the profound anxiety about cultural identity in Chinese cultural communities. I'll focus on two cases in point, which are perhaps not directly related, though both took place in the middle and late 1990s and had considerable impact on Chinese literature and its scholarship.

The first paradigmatic controversy is concerned with the "aphasia" of Chinese literary theory. This issue was broached in 1995, and according to its major initiator, Cao Shunqing, the contemporary Chinese literary theory is "aphasiac" in that:

> What is the most urgent problem of today's literary theory studies? My answer: the "aphasia" of Chinese literary theory! For many years, the modern and contemporary Chinese literary theory has been almost exclusively using a whole set of terminologies and discourses originating in the West, which results in the "aphasiac" state of our literary theory in terms of publication, communication and interpretation.
>
> Why can't we speak with our own voice and employ our own theory? An essential reason is that we failed to create our own theoretical system, a set of discourse that belongs to ourselves, and a set of scholarly norms that features our characteristic speech, communication and interpretation. Without the Western literary theory, we, like a "dumb" scholar, could barely speak. Let's think about it! How can a "dumb" person give an eloquent talk on the podium of academia? How can we count on a group of "aphasiac" scholars to speak up for our own opinions in face of those foreign colleagues, to voice our own message? How can a nation, without its own scholarly language, stand out in the international forum of literary theory studies? How can such a nation create its own system of literary thought and never shy away from competing with all kinds of "-isms" in the world?[7]

The above remark is full of melancholy, disappointment, and *ressentiment*. Brought to the fore is a harrowing fact that Western theory has gained a dominant foothold in China, and that Chinese theoreticians are unable to sound "their own voice". More importantly, it implies a value judgment that on the one hand there is a synchronic disparity between "us" and "them", and on the other there is a diachronic affective difference between the past and the present. Cao and his followers assert that "this aphasia is a severe cultural disease".[8] This indictment immediately set off a tsunami of debates, yet with no consensus having been reached. Some said it hit the bull's eye, while others dismissed it as a "fake question".

Not long after the polemic of the "aphasia of Chinese theory", another theory on the failure of modern Chinese poetry (a.k.a. New Poetry) over the last century had attracted much attention in our cultural community in 1998. This theory is predicated on the indictment that modern Chinese poetry went astray in the direction of

"Westernization", at the expense of losing the signifying and aesthetic characteristics of traditional Chinese poetry:

> To understand the emergence of "post-new poetic trend" and its features, we must begin with the nearly 100-year history of new poetry. Starting from Hu Shih's (胡适) "Old Duck" and Guo Moruo's (郭沫若) "Goddess," our New Poetry has been evolving for nearly a century. The New Poetry, developing from the scratch, has now accumulated a large volume of poetic works, but as a form of Chinese poetry, it is still in search of its identity, questing for its poetic personality, poetic imagery as well as its Chinese characteristics. Today, the New Poetry has departed from its classical precedents, displaced from the family of classical Chinese, and always on the road of wandering. Neither has it any intention of connecting with its family lineage of thousands of years, nor does it desire any family resemblance with its forefathers. Hu Shih once compared such a genetic association to "the blood smell of the Foot-Binding Age". The New Poetry has broken up with the tradition, totally freeing itself from any constraints of the poetic language and spirit that define the traditional Chinese poems. It defected to the West, embracing the criterion of Western poetry.[9]

Of course, while the first polemic is focused on literary theory, the second has a different target, that is, poetic writings. However, it is worth noting that the two share a strikingly similar line of thought, which can be explicated as follows.

First, both believe that modern Chinese poetry and contemporary Chinese literary theory have been *over*-Westernized or *over*-otherized. The "symptom" is that we can do nothing but parroting others, cut off from our own cultural "root". For all the necessity of learning from the West, we are too obsessed with others to remember who we are. I think the "aphasia" of literary theory is a vital judgment, which underscores the fact that our Chinese theoreticians can't speak our thoughts without the Western lexicon, or we can't speak on our own terms, as the ancient sages did. For instance, the idea of "*feng gu*"(风骨)in Chinese poetics is now respectively interpreted, paralleling to the form/content dichotomy in Western theory, as form and content. Another example is James J. Y. Liu's *Chinese Theories of Literature*, which according to some critics has been reduced to "a pile of materials within the discourse of Western theory, or an annotative text for M. H. Abrams's theoretical model".[10] Those who criticize the "Westernization" of New Poetry assert that the achievement of modern Chinese poetry has obviously been "exaggerated", while scant attention is paid to its problems or negative impact.

> "Today, some practitioners of New Poetry largely ignore the characteristics of both Chinese poetry and Chinese culture, producing an array of *quasi*-Chinese and *quasi*-Western poems, which are embarrassing to both the Chinese poetic tradition and the Western one".[11]

If the above remark is merely confined to the surface, these critics go further to lay bare the deep problem here. The "aphasia" that inflicts Chinese theory is, most crucially, caused by our abandonment of the traditional Chinese "academic norms", which determines the making of categories in a deep sense. The ancient prepositions, such as Laozi's "the way that can be named is not the way" (道可道，非常道), "being and non-being beget each other" (虚实相生), "less is more" (以少总多), and "the debate of word and meaning" (言意之辩), are subject to these "academic norms".[12] The in-depth reason why modern Chinese poetry has been "Westernized" is that the "spiritual realm" (境界) of classical poetry is bygone.

> "The spiritual realm had been vigorously pursued by ancient Chinese intellectuals in the fields of literature, history and philosophy for thousands of years. Such a realm, the compound of ethics, aesthetics and knowledge, is concerned with life experience and evaluation, a realm between religion and philosophy. It is like the breath of Chinese soul, tangible and intangible, the absence of which will result in the lusterlessness of a poem, as if a stack of words. In Western poetry one can find ethics, religion and knowledge, but not this mixed breathing of soul".[13]

Thus, these arguments seem to add up to the dubious "legitimacy" of modern and contemporary Chinese literary theory and modern Chinese poetry. Literary critics are simply parrots, and the New Poetry is not "Chinese" anymore. That said, it is amount to judging "illegitimate" both the current Chinese literary theory and the New Poetry.

Second, the two indictments make similar cause-analyses or reach similar conclusions, which is say that the targeted problem is resulted from our contempt for or "discontent" about the traditional culture. The clinic diagnosis of the "aphasia" points to the unbalanced national mentality, the deluge of radical sentiment, cultural nihilism, and distorted cultural values. Cao Shunqing, for instance, writes,

> "Over the last hundred years, there is an insurmountable cultural complex, that is, hating one's traditional culture, and blaming the tradition for China's backwardness. Indoctrinated with this self-critical, self-debasing and self-disparaging mentality, some mid-aged and young scholars and students have begun to harbor such an viewpoint: traditional Chinese culture is at odds with modernization and will block the historical progress of China. Therefore, if one dares to advocate traditional culture in China, it is tantamount to taking the side of backwardness, regression and anti-modernization. This is the mentality we're having today".[14]

The detractors of the "Westernized" New Poetry have expressed the same idea, though in different words:

> "It never occurs to them (the school of New Poetry) to include 'classical Chinese poetry' into the dictionary of New Poetry, let alone to inherit it. The home-leaving of New Poetry at the turn of the twentieth-century was stimulated by a rebellious spirit, and the vagrant has no reason to turn back, to say

nothing of inheriting the ancestral legacy. The thousands-years-old poem collections of our forebears on the book shelf have now given way to the translated Western poems. Books in classical Chinese characters and with vertical layout are anything but pleasing. Driven by the self-hating mentality, the slogans such as "Right to rebel", "Poisonous is patrimony" have influenced us for decades. The last resort is to take refuge in the Western culture".[15]

Moreover, "(the New Poetry) always takes pride in their 'revolution', which in turn eclipses their artistic sluggishness and contributes to the maldevelopment of New Poetry".[16]

The biting criticism I quote above intends to underscore a historic rupture in culture. On the one hand, it takes the form of cultural radicalism in our cultural community; on the other, it calls attention to a historical fact about the cultural turn. It is the aforementioned attitude or idea that results in such an approach to cultural praxis. As Foucault would put it, this attitude leads to a binary opposition between the old and the new. By negating the old, the new is confirmed in such a way as to realize the new complicity between power and knowledge. Thus, both of the two debates emphasize the reversal of the originally reversed relationship. In other words, as per the two polemics, the cultural praxis of abandoning the old and wooing the new is essentially illegal, because it would mean the uprooting of one's culture. Put in a blunt way, those who ignore their cultural ancestry are "illegitimate" heirs.

Third, both of the two critiques want to alert people to the critical moment of facing our cultural disease and seeking for therapy. The only cure for the "aphasia", according to these apologists of traditional culture, is to return to the tradition.

> We shall take root in the 5,000-years-old cultural China, striving to revive our national spirit, standing on the solid foundation of national culture, absorbing cultural nutrition from China and abroad, from the past and the present, and synthesizing the East and the West so as to create our independent discourse. The aim is to establish a well-functioning discourse system of literary theory that can give voice to, and exert influence on, the living condition of contemporary China and the concomitant literary and artistic phenomena. To realize this project, it is a vital step, during the process of restoration, to re-examine the traditional discourse and to prepare it for modern transformation. Specifically, our method and means: first, we collect and edit the archive of traditional discourse, clarifying what is a traditionally Chinese way of communication and what is our cultural spirit; then, use the traditional discourse to have a dialogue with its contemporary counterpart, and endeavor to transform it into a modern version; finally, in an eclectic manner, reconstruct the traditional discourse.[17]

The critics who lash the "Westernization" of New Poetry say:

> The survival of modern Chinese poetry in the 21st-century depends on whether we can understand the valence of the revival of our tradition when

we are entering into the modern age and learning from the West. How is innovation possible when tradition is abandoned? Without standing on the ground of tradition, innovation can merely take the form of slavish westernization. Are we merely struggling to join the club of Western culture? Obviously, it is most unfit for a nation proud for her long-history of language and culture to be so humble. On the eve of a new century, the top issue (which is also a matter of life-and-death) of modern Chinese poetry is to seek for its poetic traditional, to resuscitate its heart, and to dig out the spring hole buried under the earth.[18]

In my view, these arguments not only cast doubt on the legitimacy of literary theory and modern Chinese poetry, but reaffirm that tradition is the premise of re-legitimation, because only those that are local, national, and traditional are entitled to authentic legitimacy. With a second thought, one can detect in the two debates a visceral concern about Chinese culture, as well as a strong indignation about the status quo of literary theory and Chinese poetry. It is a manifestation of our anxiety about cultural identity, an anxiety like a ghost haunting our cultural community since the 1840s. This anxiety, in essence, is rooted in an acute awareness of Chinese culture being "otherized". In the 1970s, Yu-sheng Lin (林毓生) proposed a theory on "the crisis of Chinese consciousness" and expressed such an anxiety:

> There is a lack of real authorities in the cultural world of China; China is experiencing an authority crisis. Why? The main reason is that authorities in various fields either fall apart or become very weak after the May Fourth Movement which is mainly a kind of anti-traditional movement... Some people are emotionally unstable when their inherent authorities are thrown into profound crisis; their irritation is because of the collapse of their own tradition, so people in this circumstance often try to protect their tradition in irrational ways.[19]

In light of Lin's theory, since the May Fourth Movement, the authority of traditional Chinese culture has been almost worn out. Without an authority, what's the point of talking about cultural legitimation? It is quite similar to Nietzsche's aphorism that "God is dead", or more appropriately, to Dostoevsky's words in *The Brothers Karamazov*: "If God is gone, we can do whatever we want!" For Lin, the loss of traditional authority means the crisis of legitimation (i.e., "the crisis of Chinese consciousness"). Although some "new authorities" managed to replace the old ones, the former's legitimacy is dubious. Lin concludes:

> The iconoclasts in the May Fourth Era believed that the traditional culture and regime were sources of a particular national way of life. However, they found themselves greatly estranged from the traditional culture and regime. What is more, they vehemently rejected and criticized the traditional culture and regime, so as to seek national survival and development. They were also nationalists, yet their nationalism was iconoclastic. On the ideological

level, the all-encompassing anti-traditionalism did not allow for any positive estimation or understanding of traditional components. Nevertheless, the intellectual compound of radical anti-traditionalism and nationalism gave rise to great tension, which later caused many thorny problems in the intellectual history and the history of politics in China.[20]

Lin's analysis could be seen as a footnote to the "aphasia" discourse in Chinese literary theory and the discourse of the "Westernization" of modern Chinese poetry. It reveals the internal causes of the violent iconoclastic nature of Chinese culture since the early modern age, and also provides a kind of historical analysis of the rupture in tradition. The three theories above show profound suspicion of Chinese culture during China's transformation into modernization. This kind of suspicion reflects some kind of value orientation and cultural choice inside our cultural community and also, to some degree, mirrors our anxiety about cultural identity.

Re-legitimation and identity construction

These theoretical suspicions of cultural legitimacy posit a critique of the "aphasia" of literary theory and the "defection" or "Westernization" of modern Chinese poetry. Thus, re-legitimation becomes an issue one must grapple today. But, how? The discontent voices I quote above unanimously suggest retraditionalization.

In my view, having been through sea change in history, our society and culture are in face of a profound and grim identity crisis. Given the rupture in history and chasm in culture, the enormous transformation of society entails a deluge of uncertainties and possibilities. Such is case of China since the early modern age. Thus, the cultural community takes it on itself to play the role of cultural "legislator", interrogating the legitimacy of the present culture, and, at the same time, seeking for evidence of re-legitimation. The transformation from the traditional to the modern can be interpreted as a two-way process: one the one hand, it is a process of "de-traditionalization", and on the other, "retraditionalization". In other words, the two-way process is dialectic, like the sides of the same coin. It is the very process of "de-traditionalization" that incurs its antithesis, that is, "retraditionalization", because the latter is an acute stress reaction to the former.

Admittedly, "retraditionalization" is not to relive the past; rather, it is to reformulate the current culture by referring to the good old tradition, with the purpose of "creative transformation of tradition". At this point, I have no value judgment to pass. My main concern is, instead, how is "retraditionalization" related to identity construction in the present culture. Or, I can rephrase the question: Why is "retraditionalization" an antidote to our anxiety about cultural identity? I think, the aforementioned three theories, without doubt, are part of the endeavor to "retraditionalize" modern Chinese culture. To illustrate their connection with identity construction in culture, I would use Giddens's concept of "ontological security", which according to him is the basic feature of human life. Giddens writes, "all individuals develop a framework of ontological security of some sort, based on routines of various forms".[21] Therefore, routines and ontological security are interdependent. When a child leaves his primal guardian (mother), his sense of security is compromised and is replaced by anxiety about insecurity. This highly symbolic principle also applies to cultural "ontological security". When a certain culture severs its bond with "maternal tradition", the culture's "ontological security" is under threat and identity anxiety then arises. Identity anxiety here means restless worries caused by one's uncertain identity. I would like to extend Giddens's theory a little bit. The interaction between ontological security and routines, as far as a human individual is concerned, refers to the routinization of individual life and behavior; when it comes to a group and its culture, the process of routinization is far more complicated and extensive, and can't be equal to tradition itself. That said, this process to a large extent includes tradition or its functions. Thus, the relationship of ontological security with routines is the same as the one with tradition. The interdependence between ontological security and tradition discloses the inseparable bond of the two. Tradition often provides firm ground for ontological security, which in turn reinforces or confirms the legitimacy of tradition. Because the moral and emotional factors in the tradition can be transformed into some kind of binding-power and control, "[traditional] morality offers a measure of ontological security to those who adhere to it".[22]

Specifically, I think "retraditionalization" can buttress ontological security and alleviate our anxiety about cultural identity in three aspects. First, on the psychological level, "retraditionalization" can produce a sense of belonging to our "great tradition", and renew people's pride in such a tradition. The "great tradition", in its primary sense, points to the past, which stands for a complex framework of reference for the present; second, its "greatness" distinguishes it from the "minor traditions" or local ones. The "great tradition" was glorious not merely for what it created within a culture, but for its profound impact on the outside world. Obviously, the traditional Chinese civilization exemplifies such an idea of "great tradition". No wonder those who repudiate the "aphasia" of literary theory and the "Westernization" of New Poetry are deeply nostalgic for and proud of such a "great tradition". Furthermore, in the legitimation debate, "great tradition" is not a bunch of empty figures of speech, nor is it an abstract category. On the contrary, it is an effective container of emotion, which can be transformed into specific symbolic codes, such as classical literary theory and classical poems. "Great tradition" means "glorious past". For a cultural community, "retraditionalization" can not only reconfirm the past but also fulfill, in an imaginary way, the "Centrality Complex" related to the old glorious, but irretrievable, days.[23] The sense of belonging and happiness helps to revitalize the long-desired cultural identity under construction in reality, binding the past with the present, and extending the ancient "great tradition" to today's cultural praxis, and emotionally undergirding our cultural community. In this context, classical poetry and classical literary theory turn out to be such congenial symbols that they can appeal to readers and at the same time enact as cultural resources to impact the current culture. This accounts for the past-oriented "ontological security" newly acquired by the cultural community.

Second, "retraditionalization", historically speaking, offers some pure, authentic, and reliable cultural origin or source. "Ontological security" hinges on conventions, which in turn are fostered through tradition. Any cultural identity has or would "invent" its foundation myth, explain its cultural origin or roots. With modernization and globalization intensifying the cultural exchanges and interactions, the pervasive infiltration of the alien, "other", or heterogeneous memes results in cultural hybridity of the present. The intensification of hybridity will inevitably stimulate some acute stress reaction to the local culture, bringing about a crisis of cultural ontological security.

Hence, it is common practice to confirm, explicate, or reconstitute, and to insist on the legitimacy of, one's peculiar locality and distinctive tradition. Naturally, to return to local cultural tradition is in fact a return to a distinctive or even singular culture. Although the social soil that used to cultivate such a culture—say, the traditional agrarian society has already given way to the industrial one—is bygone or is disappearing, this culture is still appealing and desirable. The reason is that the old tradition, in contrast to the hybridity of the present culture, seems to retain some cultural purity. The "aphasia" indictment and the charge against "Westernized" New Poetry share one argument in common: modern and contemporary literary theory and modern Chinese poetry have been "otherized" or "Westernized". Put in another way, the two are no longer pure, mixed with too many "heterogeneous" elements. The two camps sing a hymn to the lost tradition, which implies a statement that the old tradition is pure and trustworthy, because it belongs to us and makes "who" we "are". A synonym for "purity" is authenticity. The anxiety incurred by the hybridity and heterogeneity of contemporary culture is an anxiety about authenticity, about one's loss of self, and about one's "stopping being oneself". Anthony D. Smith finds that the most important way to maintain authenticity is through language because language is a medium of differentiation, distinguishing "us" from "others".[24] Critics against the "Westernization" of New Poetry are in favor of the classical poetic language (including the vertical writing layout) and disparage colloquialism in modern poetry. Those critical of "aphasia" reject the Western terminology and advocate the traditional vocabulary of ancient literary theory. Both approaches can be regarded as a theoretical defense of cultural authenticity, a strategy of preserving the authentic cultural identity via language. Purity and authenticity provide a source of trust and certainty, laying solid foundation for identity construction. But it is worth noting that such a form of purity and authenticity is always illusive and utopian.

Third, "retraditionalization" constructs a unique and congenial "discourse of homesickness", which in turn gives rise to a cultural "sense of homeland". Under the conditions of relentlessly changing modernity, nostalgia is often created as a peculiar type of discourse, giving spiritual consolation to those sentimental men of letters. So the discourse of nostalgia plays an important role in confirming the cultural legitimacy of modern cultural community and in constructing cultural identities. Fred Davis holds that "nostalgia thrives on transition, on the subjective discontinuities that engender our yearning for continuity".[25] That is to say, when a society and a culture undergo gargantuan changes, nostalgia arises. Bryan S. Turner argues that nostalgia as a discourse has four basic meanings: first, nostalgia breeds a sense of historical decline and loss, because one is far away from the "golden age" of homeland; second, the discourse of nostalgia entails a lack of human wholeness and ethical certainty, and a sense of scarcity. The universal values that used to bestow upon us social relation, knowledge, and personal experience are in wane. Third, with the loss of authentic social relations, in the discourse of nostalgia there develops a feeling of losing one's freedom and subjectivity. Finally, the discourse of nostalgia bemoans the loss of innocence, personal authenticity, and emotional spontaneity.[26] In this regard, I believe that "retraditionalization" is a nostalgic reaction to such a kind of condition, showing affectionate reminiscence of the good old days. As a result, nostalgia is always intertwined with the past, always discoursing on the lives or things bygone. Speaking of its temporality, nostalgia usually means to maintain the continuity with the past. But it is notable that nostalgia frequently occurs at present, especially during a period of great social and cultural transformation. Thus, nostalgia posits a complex dialectic between the past and the present: on the one hand, it always points to the past, remembering and recollecting the past; on the other, nostalgia always takes place at present, as a product of the specific social and culture changes of the present. Davis highlights two features of nostalgia. First of all, nostalgia is affirmative of the past glory, and its overall relation with the past is always positive, affirmative, and active. "The good old days" is such an idiomatic expression. When it comes to specific poetic technique,

> modern Chinese poetry is absolutely comparable to, if not better than, classical poetry in terms of shifty imagery-making, but not in such aspects as the expressiveness of words. The dominance of colloquialism and the archaic status of some Chinese characters, owing to the codifying of simplified Chinese, have made New Poetry a lesser art. And today nothing can be done to fix its flaws".[27]

Another feature of nostalgia is its relation with the present. "Nostalgic feeling", Davies writes, "is infused with imputation of past beauty, pleasure, job, satisfaction, goodness, happiness, love and the life, in sum, any or several of the positive affects of being".[28] The "Westernization" of New Poetry also illustrates such an affirmative/negative dichotomy.

> The classical tradition of Chinese poetry was dismantled in the beginning of the 20th century. During the May Fourth Movement, new normativity of poetry, known as the new tradition, came into being and has since been practiced and experimented for over eighty years. However, a complete set of rules regarding the writing and criticism of modern poetry is nowhere around the corner till today".[29]

Robert Nisbet rightly says, "nostalgia tells us more about present moods than about past realities, explains the current wave of nostalgia".[30] This explains the controversies over cultural legitimacy and our anxiety about cultural identity.

In a nutshell, "retraditionalization" is essential for ontological security, which then plays a significant role in the construction of cultural identity.

Some critical reflections

Undoubtedly, tradition is an indispensable resource for contemporary Chinese culture in the midst of great transformation. If we go beyond the either-or mindset, beyond the binary oppositions such as radical vs. conservative, revolutionary vs. reactionary, modern vs. traditional, progressive vs. regressive, how can we reflect, in a broader context, on the latest trend of retraditionalization? Both the appeal for "retraditionalization" and "re-legitimation", I think, are a natural development, with considerable reasonability and necessity. However, for all its reasonability and necessity, we must call attention to some neglected aspects, to its problems and limits.

First of all, when advocating for "retraditionalization", one should heed the narrow-minded "politicization of culture", which imposes the segregation of "us" and "them", or even rejects "cultural politics" as a whole, by manipulating the partiality of cultural identity and exaggerating cultural differences. Differences are natural as much as necessary, which accounts for the justification of cultural multiculturalism. The danger, however, is that if differences are inappropriately magnified to the point of ideology, differences are likely to be translated into the criteria of *either-or* value judgment. Thus, we must guard against the concomitant cultural violence, a violence that is inclined to reduce the question of cultural judgment or cultural identity to the trial of political loyalty or national allegiance. Of course, there is no escape from "identity politics", but we should caution against parochial, simplistic "politicization of culture". Under the circumstances of equality, multiplicity, and democracy, one's adherence to local differences shouldn't contradict one's respect for other's differences.

Here arises another question: when returning to local and indigenous traditions, how can we avoid "otherizing" (the other is always the West) and "demonization". It is evident that the imagery of "Orientalism" abounds in Western culture, an imagery that is in accordance with a distorted Oriental "other" the Western mind gets used to. In Edward Said's words, people from European cultures usually deal with, or even invent, the Orient in various ideological ways, displaying between the West and the East a relationship between power, dominance, and hegemony. Orientalism, he says, is

> a collective notion identifying "us" Europeans as against all "those" non-Europeans, and indeed it can be argued that the major component in European culture is precisely what made that culture hegemonic both in and outside Europe: the idea of European identity as a superior one in comparison with all the non-European peoples and cultures. Furthermore, there is hegemony in the eastern concept of the Europeans which continuously reaffirms European's superiority to the east, thus repelling more independent consciousness and questioning spirit of thinkers.[31]

Obviously, from the standpoint of Chinese culture, such "Orientalism" is pernicious. However, in the framework of Oriental culture, the propagation of and adherence to traditional are always operated with "the other" as the reference frame. Is it possible that we might unwittingly distort the Western "other", when regarding it as the peer or even antithesis of our local, indigenous tradition? Let's rephrase the question: during the process of "retraditionalization", what if we produce an "Occidentalism", which is not essentially different from the "Orientalism" we lash? What if we persecute some dissidents of independent spirit and healthy skepticism, in the name reviving and championing local cultural tradition? These questions beget more scrutiny.

Third, we must be vigilant against cultural fundamentalism of all sorts. In my opinion, the so-called purity and authenticity of national culture are no more than illusory and utopian dreams. Tradition is not immutable and frozen, and the development of traditional Chinese culture in history was and is always indebted to the foreign resources. The presumption of an absolute origin, an authentic root is often than not a cultural fantasy. We need to inspect our tradition in a dynamic and open way. Anthony Giddens rightly interprets fundamentalism as "tradition in its traditional sense".[32] In the time of great transformation, what we need at this moment is certainly not "tradition in its traditional sense", but "tradition in the modern sense".

Finally, let me be clear: multiculturalism is right. Strictly speaking, traditional culture itself is not so much monolithic as complex and diverse. It is absolutely untenable to conceptualize an absolute cultural source and to instigate us to return to such a starting point. The confirmation and legitimation of differences are not meant to privilege a single culture or value, but to endorse the co-existence of difference cultures and values. Hence, multiculturalism can do the best to our cultural development at present.

As a concluding remark, I want to bring up the issue of cultural legitimacy again. I am convinced that legitimacy must be renewed time and again, and can be proved in different ways. The proof of a certain culture's legitimacy entails an appeal for some kind of cultural identity, and the process of legitimacy approval is a process of ascertaining or seeking for the roots of cultural identity. If we hold to the commitment to multiculturalism, and deal with cultural identity in a more open and diverse way, rather than taking identity as some closed, ossified, essentialist category, it is more likely to grasp the rich meaning and to understand the dynamic possibilities of cultural identity in today's world. That said, to insist on "tradition in the modern sense" requires us to take the present as the baseline of all cultural activities and theories. If the contemporary project of cultural identity can meet the requirements of the social and cultural developments in China today, our traditional culture should be used as a resource of modernity, rather than restraints on it. It is my firm belief that the cultural development and the building of cultural identity can join hands and negotiate with each other, and can be adaptive and self-adjustable. It is natural to witness some tension as a result of different forces or elements entangled, and the structure of culture can evolve to soften the tension. In this sense, "retraditionalization" might be considered as the effort to ease the tension. In fact, the project of cultural development cannot "totally Westernized" as feared by some people, nor is it possible to "return to the ancient way". Rather, a more constructive scenario is "the middle ground", that is, the negotiation and compromise of all of the different forces involved. Only under this circumstance is cultural identity viable.

Notes

1. See Max Weber. *Economy and Society.* New York: Bedminster Press, 1968.
2. Thomas S Kuhn. *The Structure of Scientific Revolutionaries.* 3rd Edition. Chicago: The University of Chicago Press, 1996. p.177.
3. Thomas S. Kuhn. *The Structure of Scientific Revolutionaries.* p.176,
4. See Thomas S. Kuhn. *The Structure of Scientific Revolutionaries.* pp.182–188.
5. Thomas S. Kuhn. *The Structure of Scientific Revolutionaries.* p.176.
6. Zygmunt Bauman. *Legislators and Interpreters: On Modernity, Post-Modernity and Intellectuals.* Cambridge: Polity Press. pp.124–134
7. Cao Shunqing. "Aphasia in Modern Chinese Literary Theories and Cultural Morbidity", in *Debates on Literature and Art* 2 (1996). pp.50–51.
8. Ibid. p.51.
9. Zheng Min. "One Hundred-Year Exploration of New Chinese Poetry and Trends of Post-New Poetry", in *Literary Review* 4 (1998). p.77.
10. Cao Shunqing. "New Thoughts on Aphasia in Modern Chinese Literary Theories", in *Journal of Zhejiang University* 1 (2006). pp.12–13.
11. Zheng Min. "On the Characteristics of Traditional Chinese Poetry", in *Literature and Art Studies* 4 (1998). p.84.
12. Cao Shunqing. "New Thoughts on Aphasia in Modern Chinese Literary Theories", 13.
13. Zheng Min. "The Classicality and Modernity of Chinese Poetry", in *Literary Review* 6 (1995). pp.88–89.
14. Cao Shunqing. "New Thoughts on Aphasia in Modern Chinese Literary Theories". p.14.
15. Zheng Min. "One Hundred-Year Exploration of New Chinese Poetry and Trends of Post-New Poetry." p.79.
16. Zheng Min, "Composing New Poetry in Tradition", in *Hebei Academic Journal* 1 (2005). p.130.
17. Cao Shunqing and Li Siqu. "The Basic Path and Methods of Rebuilding the Chinese Literary Theories", in *Literature and Art Studies* 2 (1996). p.12.
18. Zheng Min. "One Hundred-Year Exploration of New Chinese Poetry and Trends of Post-New Poetry". p.81.
19. Lin Yusheng. *The Creative Transformation of Chinese Tradition.* Beijing: Sanlian Press, 1988. pp.7–8.
20. Ibid, p.152.
21. Anthony Giddens. *Modernity and Self-Identity.* Cambridge: Polity, 1991. p.44.
22. Ulrich Beck, Anthony Giddens and Scott Lash. *Reflexive Modernization.* Cambridge: Polity, 1994. p.65.
23. For more discussion on "Chineseness", see Zhang Fa, Zhang Yiwu, and Wang Yichuan. "From 'Modernity' to 'Chineseness': Towards a New Episteme, in *Debates on Literature and Art* 2 (1994). pp.10–20.
24. See Anthony D. Smith. *Nations and Nationalism in a Global Era.* Cambridge: Polity, 1996.
25. Fred Davis. *Yearning for Yesterday: Sociology of Nostalgia.* New York: Free Press, 1979. p.49.
26. Bryan S. Turner. "A Note on Nostalgia", in *Theory, Culture, Society* 4 (1987). pp.150–151.
27. Zheng Min. "The Classicality and Modernity of Chinese Poetry". p.84.
28. Fred Davis. *Yearning for Yesterday: Sociology of Nostalgia.* pp.14–15.
29. Zheng Min. "On the Tradition of Poetry", in *Debates on Literature and Art* 3 (2004). p.16.
30. See Fred Davis. *Yearning for Yesterday: Sociology of Nostalgia.* p.10.
31. Edward Said. *Orientalism.* New York: Vintage, 1979. p.7.
32. Ulrich Beck, Anthony Giddens and Scott Lash. *Reflexive Modernization.* p.100.

4 Sinologism as a problematic

Sinologism as a problematic

Sinologism has been a heated topic both in China and abroad over the last few years. Since the issue was first broached in the 1990s, it has attracted more and more critical attention, discussions, and even polemics. It is endorsed as much as it is repudiated, and more people choose the middle ground. Sinologism is not so much an academic topic as an issue of cultural politics related to the cultural awareness of China as a rising world power in the global age. This concept was at first put forward as a problem against the academic backdrop of postmodernism, postcolonialism in the West, and against the domestic backdrop of the rise of China and the growth of Chinese cultural awareness. In my view, the reason why Sinologism is rife with controversies is two-fold: one the one hand, it reflects the thirst of Chinese scholars to pursue cultural leadership in the world; on the other, it is caused by the impulse to redress the imbalance between Chinese scholarship and the Western counterpart since the late Qing dynasty.

On a global scale, modernization is always accompanied by a modern consciousness of indigenous culture. With the ascendancy of globalization, the rise of modern nation-states is not merely an empowerment of national politics, economy, and society, but also a zeal for national culture. Therefore, in the realm of academic studies, those taken-for-granted or allegedly natural ideas and methods are subject to reconsideration so as to reevaluate the relation between self and the other in knowledge production and transmission. This tendency seems to be unavoidable for a nation-state's engagement with the world in terms of culture and scholarship. From the perspective of sociology, it is the re-legitimation of a nation-state's cultural identity; from the perspective of political science, it manifests the political awareness of a nation-state's cultural ethnicity. Many a country in the West had undergone such a transformation. The ascendant of the United States since the second half of the 19th century, as the old European powers were in wane, is a case in point. The self-consciousness of "Americanness", for example, in the 19th-century philosophy, literature, and arts, was centered on the singularity and autonomy of American culture, and many American intellectual elites strived to break away from the grip of European cultural precedents, to seek for the Americanness of its own culture.[1] Thus, American art historians are inclined to downplay the effect of

European tradition, starting their historical narrative with the cultural legacy of North American Indians, rather than with Greco-Roman classicalism or the modern tradition of Renaissance. By doing so, American art was from the very roots differentiated from European art. For example, more and more studies on "Hudson River School" and the American landscape paintings to follow deliberately avoid referring to landscape painting in European art, emphasizing the geographical features of the Wild West, in particular its vast, primitive, and sublime landscape, which make American landscape painting intrinsically different from its Western counterparts (such as those by the French School or Dutch School). The bulk of European art since Giorgio Vasari consists of traditional architecture, sculpture, and painting, photography having no place in art history. But the United States is a different case. Given the complex entanglement of 20th-century American art and photography, American art historians usually single out photography as a distinguishing characteristic of American art in contrast to European one. Therefore, cultural locality inevitably breeds the quest for a culture's indigenous discourse, and the situation in China is the same case.

The new century has witnessed China's rise to the world's second largest economy, together with China's rapid development in economy, politics, science, and technology. It is in this broad context that Sinologism gained its prominence and became a heated topic. Furthermore, the surge of the Civil Rights movements in the second half of the 20th century gave rise to ethnic studies and postcolonial critique in Western academia. Edward Said's critique of Orientalism paved the way for the critique of Sinologism. It is almost certain that the emergence of Sinologism was inconceivable had it not been for Said's books on Orientalism. Yet, it is worth noting that in many aspects the critique of Sinologism surpasses that of Orientalism.

We therefore have every reason to assert that the debate over Sinologism is closely linked to the increasingly acute cultural self-consciousness in the course of China's rise. It not only reflects the new rivalry between China and the West in terms of knowledge production in Chinese academia and academic exchange with the world but also reflects China's urge to address such a rivalry. The Sinologism debate mirrors China's impulse to increase its cultural leverage when the global impact of Chinese politics and economy is on the ascendant, and posits a critical reflection on the Western Sinologists' misreading of and prejudice against China studies. Undoubtedly, it is more than timing to raise the issue of Sinologism at the moment, as it may yield more constructive reconsideration of Chinese cultural subjectivity and autonomy in the course of globalization.

What we are talking about when talking about Sinologism?

What is "Sinologism"? Since the birth of the concept, it has been rife with controversies, scholars radically divided on what it means. The absence of consensus indicates that Sinologism ushers us into a shifty domain of knowledge in growth, a domain that consists of too many cultural and political issues of historical complexity. According to Ming Dong Gu, the term "Sinologism" can be defined in at least eight ways:

1) A knowledge system of external investigation into China and Chinese civilization; 2) A knowledge-processing system governed by a China-oriented ideology, 3) The total of problematics concerning China studies; 4) A critical theory on the problems of Sinology; 5) An intellectual product co-created by scholars from multiple countries and regions; 6) The alienated knowledge and scholarship in the field of China-and-the-West studies; 7) The product of intellectual ideology transformed from epistemology and methodology in the field of China-and-the-West studies; 8) A critical theory based on self-conscious reflection, calling for the production of knowledge on China in as objective and impartial ways as possible.[2]

The eight definitions of Sinologism showcase the diversity and variances of scholarly interest. Before we proceed to a detailed analysis, it is necessary to straighten out the methods used to define Sinologism.

First, there is a gap between descriptive definition and prescriptive definition, either of which corresponds to a different critical stance. The descriptive one usually stresses what Sinologism is, presupposed as a factual statement about Sinologism as an intact object. However, the prescriptive one is completely different in that it entails a value judgment, and intends to illustrate the conditions of Sinologism and explain why it is so. The two approaches indicate not only the fundamental disagreement on what is Sinologism, but also the complicated social and political relations between a Sinologist and Sinology one engages with. While the descriptive approach aims to make an empirical study, explicating what is Sinologism, seeing it as an autonomous field of scholarship, the prescriptive approach from the outset presupposes that Sinologism is shaped by a kind of cultural politics, which means that Sinologism was and is unable to develop into an objective knowledge system.

Second, from the normative vantage point of Chinese culture, we can categorize these definitions into three groups. The first group consists of those that define Sinologism as a negative concept, that is to say, underscoring the hidden ideology of partiality or hostility against Chinese culture. In other words, these definitions (i.e., No. 2, No. 6, and No. 7) misinterpret the knowledge forms or research strategies regarding China studies. The second group, on the contrary, takes Sinologism as an affirmative concept, or, in other words, a kind of knowledge production and research strategy serving the purpose of critically engaging with China studies (i.e., No. 4 and No. 8). The last group is more neutral, such as No. 1, No. 3, and No. 5, which are supposed to be descriptive methods. The three groups of definitions—negative, affirmative, and neutral—actually correspond to the three basic positions in Sinologism or even Sinology. To discuss Sinologism, we must see the faultlines in the first place.

For all the different definitions, if we take a closer look at the debate over Sinologism, it is easy to find that the focal point is not so much how to define Sinologism as whether Sinologism is equal to Sinology or not. Put another way, there is at least one consensus; that is, Sinology is largely tinted with a streak of Sinologism, which accounts for the prejudiced interpretation of Chinese issues. There are three bodies of opinion to corroborate this claim.

The first typical observation is held by Zhou Ning. In his 2004 article "Sinology, or 'Sinologism'", Zhou offers a clear definition of Sinologism:

> Is sinology knowledge, or imagination? Is it "truth," or "myth"? Is it a discipline, or an ideology?... Sinology is more like a "narrative", a kind of discourse, with the agency to select, represent, construct and generate meanings. Its arbitrariness does not refer to any objective reality; rather, the meaning is created in a specific context of cultural ideology.
>
> ...Sinology has entered into the phase of post-sinology, which on the one hand is about reflexive critique of sinology, and on the other becomes ideological discourse to a great degree. China studies, derived from the ideology of the Cold War, is involved in the containment of China, and helps with the construction of the myth of "China's threat". Sinologism runs throughout the development of sinology.[3]

If Zhou Ning has touched upon the problem of Western Sinology, Wen Rumin takes issues with the supposed "Sinologist mood" prevalent in Chinese academia. He writes,

> The reason I suggest we outgrow the "sinologist mood" is for the purpose of scholarly self-criticism. Such a mood is unhealthy because it abets blind "parroting". Recently, some Chinese scholars and critics specializing in modern and contemporary literature, including some famous ones, seem to idolize sinology, in particular sinology in the United States. They take great pains to keep tabs on sinology. For some of them, sinology is not merely a source of reference, but an exemplar one must look up to. Sinology has become a fad we never get tired of.[4]

According to Zhou and Wen, Sinologism is found among Western Sinologists as much as Chinese local scholars. Bearing different names, "Sinologist mood" and "Sinologism" point to the same form or strategy of knowledge, though the two might vary in terms of manifestation. Therefore, Sinologism is a universal problem, plaguing both the West and China. Ming Dong Gu makes a more in-depth examination of the complex relation between Sinology and Sinologism. He says,

> Sinologism is primarily an implicit system of ideas, notions, theories, approaches, and paradigms, first conceived and employed by the West in the encounter with China to deal with all things Chinese and to make sense of the bewildering complexity of Chinese civilization. As the political and intellectual spectrum has been dominated by the West, and the world has to observe China and consume knowledge about China through the Western lens, Sinologism has been complicated and enriched by the non-Western peoples'

perceptions, conceptions, and evaluations of Chinese civilization. Because the ways of observing China and producing knowledge and scholarship on China are controlled by an inner logic that operates frequently beyond our conscious awareness, Sinologism is basically a cultural unconscious in China-West studies and cross-cultural studies.[5]

Gu astutely observes that this "cultural unconscious" hinges on a structure of tension between external and internal forces. On the one hand, it is the implicit "colonization of the other" in Western Sinology, and on the other, it has something to do with the mood of "self-colonization" haunting the local Sinologists. The two forces work together, contributing to the dominance of Sinologism in the West and in China. Therefore, Gu believes that central to the problem is the mindset of Chinese scholars whose interpretation of China has been firmly fostered by Western conception, Western notion, and Western value judgment, who have developed the habit of valuing and judging their own culture by the Western standard. The same is even true of the whole world, where the tendency is such that Western ideas, conception, and evaluation have become the universal yardstick.[6]

Maybe Gu's definition of Sinologism is not accepted by everyone, but I trust it is generally acknowledged that the inclination of Sinologism is explicitly observable in Sinology. Thus, what really matters is not what *is* Sinologism, but to what extent such a Sinologism takes a foothold in Sinology—we may ask, for example, "Is Sinologism dominant or subordinate in Sinology? And how is it related to other inclinations in Sinology?" In fact, the focal point is whether Sinology is equal to Sinologism or not. There are two completely different positions here. The radical one is to assume that Western Sinology is nothing but Sinologism, while the moderate one argues that the two are not the same thing, because both encapsulate very different sets of theories and ideas. This debate touches upon many issues on cultural politics in the process of knowledge production, and involves some critical theoretical questions in the field of cross-cultural studies.

Back to the concept of Sinologism. I think we must take into consideration the nature of definition when it comes to Sinologism. Is Sinologism a global concept, or a local one? In the case of the former, Sinologism is the equivalent of Sinology. Put another way, every wrinkle of Sinology has the streak of Sinologism. In the case of the latter, Sinology and Sinologism are not concepts on the same level—Sinologism is found in Sinology, but only limited to some parts.

In my opinion, there are three points we must take notice of. First, Sinologism is an orientation of knowledge production closely related to Sinology, and we must lavish our attention on it. Second, Sinologism is not synonymous with Sinology, because Sinology is a field of complexity and heterogeneity. Whether in terms of the various historical stages of Sinology's evolution, or speaking of the miscellaneousness of ideas, approaches, and topics, Sinologism is not an omnipresent and constant phenomenon in Sinology. Third, if one takes such a reflexive stance, it is then necessary to distinguish and contrast Sinologistic Sinology and non-Sinologistic one, so as to reveal the ideological implications of Sinologism and its dangers, and to find a strategy that can forestall the baleful effect of Sinologism.

Sinologism as misinterpreted knowledge

It is true to say that, when it comes to Chinese culture, there are certain biases, misinterpretations, or even explicit hostility in Western Sinology. The distorted misinterpretation is rooted in different reasons and takes different forms. However, the present discussion of Sinologism has not touched upon the very texture of Sinology, failing to acknowledge its complexity and variance. If there were different kinds of Sinologism, it would be very arbitrary and reductive to use one label to identify them, and hereby overlook the multiple facets of Sinologism.

Maybe we can regard Sinologism as a structural system of knowledge production, in which there are actually different strains of Sinologism. To be more specific, the system consists of a series of polarized units—one end is black and another white, with vast gray area in between. If the salient characteristic of Sinologism is prejudiced misinterpretation, there must be two poles: intentional misinterpretation and unintentional misinterpretation. The intentional misinterpretation is usually based on deliberately distorted facts, or hostile presumptions that lead to negative judgment by default, or Euro-centric reference framework in which Chinese history and culture are violently situated, or presupposed ideology applied to some certain questions. All in all, the conclusion is ready-made because the interpretation is conditioned by some Western ideology. Here is an example. In her analysis of *Great Criticism* series by contemporary Chinese pop artist Wang Guangyi, American scholar Mary Binttner Wiseman comments on the significance of his works:

> Political themes from the Cultural Revolution joined Pop Art in a series of oil painting by Wang Guangyi, one of which, Great Castigation: Coca-Cola [1993], combines the image of three workers lined up side by side with the soft drink logo. Only the heads and raised left arms of the second and third workers can be seen. The first clutches a red book and all the three hold one large fountain pen whose nib lies just above the second C in the white letter "Coca-Cola" and whose length appears to be the pole of a red flag. If the first C is communism, then the second, the one threatened by the pen's nib, is "capitalism", [...] The conjunction of the two reduces the revolutionary workers and the log of China's most popular company to kitsch, trivializing the ideologies of Maoism and Western economies. To reduce Maoism to kitsch is to subvert its authority over the people's beliefs and values. Great Castigation: Coca-Cola is nothing more than an exemplification of materialism, historical and consumer, where "nothing can escape being material".[7]

In fact, in Chinese cultural context, in particular in the case of Wang Guangyi, there is no such thing as explicit political intentionality. In the local context, the two letters "C" have nothing to do with "communism" and "capitalism" as suggested by this American scholar. Evidently, such an allegorical analysis is typical of many Western scholars with the presupposition of Western ideology, and her findings are no more than what she hopes we see from Wang Guangyi's works.[8]

In contrast, unintentional misinterpretation probably stems from the lack of critical resources, or the misunderstanding of basic facts, or the misuse of materials, which leads to a conclusion not well-informed, or untenable. Given the forbidding difficulty of learning Chinese (in particular Classical Chinese) as a foreign language, it is inevitable for a non-Chinese scholar to conduct an inadequate study or make an erroneous interpretation. Therefore, we must draw a line between the two kinds of misinterpretation, especially guarding against the intentional one. The intentional misinterpretation bespeaks, as Foucault would put it, the complicity of discourse between knowledge and power, the result of which is that materials on China are tailored or customized to fit in with the presupposed framework of Western ideas on authenticity and inauthenticity, virtue and vice, and beauty and ugliness. Such an arbitrary tailoring and anatomy of Chinese knowledge would ultimately serve the purpose of Westernized ideology or cultural hegemony. As is summarized by Stuart Hall, in Foucault's discourse theory,

> Discourses are ways of referring to or constructing knowledge about a particular topic of practice: a cluster (or formation) of ideas, images and practices, which provide ways of talking about, forms of knowledge and conduct associated with, a particular topic, social activity or institutional site in society. These discursive formations, as they are known, define what is and is not appropriate in our formulation of, and our practices in relation to, a particular subject or site of social activity; what knowledge is considered useful, relevant and "true" in that context; and what sorts of persons or "subjects" embody its characteristics.[9]

An extreme form of intentional misinterpretation is antagonistic interpretation, which is fraught with prejudices and biases produced by Western ideology, and is carefully schemed to reduce China issues to the ready-made proof of West-supremacism, to disparage or negate Chinese civilization, and, ultimately, to serve Western imperialism and hegemony. The latest discussion on Sinologism centers on intentional misinterpretation in Sinology, largely overlooking unintentional misinterpretation, though the two poles coexist in the field of Sinology. Of course, between the two kinds of misinterpretation is a vast stretch of gray zone, which is even more complicated and deserves meticulous differentiation and analysis.

The categorization of unintentional and intentional misinterpretations further elicits two questions. The first is the Western Sinologists' attitudes to China. Generally speaking, three kinds of attitudes can be found, which are pro-China, neutral, and anti-China. A part of the humanities and social sciences, Sinology is unlike natural sciences and technoscience in that it usually takes an explicitly ideological and political stand. Scholars usually start with a presupposed political or ideological position, on the basis of which they proceed to probe into China studies. Therefore, such a presupposed position plays a vital role in the orientation of their Sinologist studies. Speaking of the highly selectiveness of an artist's choice of his or her painting's subject matter, Ernst H. Gombrich points out that "the artist will therefore tend to see what he paints rather than to paint what he sees".[10] The same is true of Sinology. A Sinologist's attitude to China decides what a Sinologist research he makes. The preexisting political stance is like what Gombrich calls schemata, which provides a precondition for what a Sinologist wants to see and can see. Gombrich, to elucidate the mechanism and workings of schemata, compares and contrasts an anonymous English painter and the Chinese-British painter Chiang Yee (蒋彝), both of whom faced the same Derwentwater but created totally different scenery paintings. He writes,

> It is a view of Derwentwater. Here we have crossed the line that separates documentation from art. Mr. Chiang Yee certainly enjoys the adaptation of the Chinese idiom to a new purpose; he wants us to see the English scenery for once "through Chinese eye". But it is precisely for this reason that it is so instructive to compare his view with a typical "picturesque" rendering from the Romantic period. We see how the relatively rigid vocabulary of the Chinese tradition acts as a selective screen which admits only the features for which schemata exist. The artist will be attracted by motifs which can be rendered in his idiom. As he scans the landscape, the sight which can be matched successfully with the schemata he has learned to handle will leap forward as centers of attention.[11]

Actually, one's political position decides what he or she sees and how. As for those Sinologists with entrenched biases against China, their research shows a rather explicit inclination. That said, there are some anti-China Sinologists in the West, whose political stance and attitude toward China from the outset predetermine their research and would automatically drive at a conclusion in favor of Western-centrism or the West's supremacy. It is especially true of some scholars engaging in topical or think-tank studies on the West's strategies for China. Such studies are less the politicization of Sinology than the *Sinologization* of politics. In contrast, the pro-China scholars often have a congenial approach to Chinese civilization and are more prone to reach a relatively objective and fair conclusion. Of course, those who stand in between account for the majority of Sinologists, who have no specific presupposed position and will develop their own attitude toward China as their research moves on and their first-hand knowledge about Chinese culture deepens. If one takes Sinologism as a local concept, I think it is necessary to apply this term merely to those anti-China Sinologists, whose studies are rife with biases, misinterpretation, and the West-oriented ideologies.

The second question is the difference between indigenous culture's supremacism and Western-centrism. It is a self-evident truth in intercultural studies that all researchers are accustomed to examining other cultures through the lens of their mother culture. As a proverb goes, "home is home though it is never so homely". When it comes to the relationship between self and the others in intercultural studies, it is inevitable for us to unwittingly display, though to different degrees, the sense of superiority about one's native culture or civilization. I think there are two kinds of cultural supremacism: "weak supremacism of native culture" and "strong supremacism of native culture". The two kinds of supremacism comprise the two poles of indigenous scholars' attitudes toward alien civilization or culture. It is characteristic of the former to curb one's sense of cultural superiority and feel free to study and even endorse the cream of foreign cultures. Therefore, in terms of Sinology, "weak supremacism of native culture" is not necessarily a bad thing, while "weak supremacism of native culture" is nothing but bloated, hyperbolic, and parochial, which blinds the researchers to objective and balanced observation and makes them wear tainted glasses to view the other's culture. For those influenced by "strong supremacism of native culture", the conclusion is ready-made even before their research kicks off. Their research is no more than a routine to corroborate the presumed conclusion. Frank Lentricchia once made a poignant remark on some unthinking literary criticism based on unreflecting routines, which I think is also true of Sinology: "I believe that what is now called literary criticism is a form of Xeroxing. Tell me your theory and I'll tell you in advance what you'll say about any work of literature, especially those you haven't read".[12] The anti-China Sinologists have a similar approach to China, though they for sure won't admit it.

Thus, if we agree to differentiate Sinologism and inspect it on a local level, this term should only refer to "strong supremacism of native culture" and nothing else. The salient feature of such studies is to impose a presumed conclusion on the materials, to butcher or tamper with facts, only to secure the conclusion that the Other's culture or civilization is inferior to the Western one. When allied with imperialism and colonialism, this Western-centrism would be more risky, because the conclusion on the inferiority of the Other's culture helps to justify the dominance and exploitation of the Empire and the colonists.

Intercultural studies: Is it possible to understand the Other?

Let's turn to a more forbidding conundrum: in intercultural studies, when we view, from our standpoint, the Other's civilization or culture, how can we avoid preexisting prejudices and try to achieve maximal objectivity and fairness? This is perhaps the most thorny, and unsolvable puzzle in the Sinologism debate. Zhou Ning and Ming Dong Gu, in their critique of Sinologism, have raised the question as to how to make a fair and sound study on Chinese civilization, but some other scholars are quite dubious about it. To illustrate this problem, it is necessary that we turn to other disciplinaries to better understand this conundrum. I notice that in the latest cross-cultural psychology studies, there are some new theories and ideas worth our attention. For example, it is proposed that there are four basic principles in cross-cultural psychology:

1 People view and evaluate other cultures from the perspective of their own.
2 Some psychological principles are universal, and some are culture-specific.
3 Several key cultural dimensions aid our understanding and study of cross-cultural phenomena.
4 Despite the many cultural differences identified by cross-cultural researchers, people in various cultures share some commonalities than differences.[13]

The content and sequence of the four principles are very interesting, relevant to the intercultural conundrum under discussion here. First, these principles touch upon four aspects of intercultural understanding and interpretation: a) the focus of intercultural studies is the differences and commonalities of various cultures; b) cross-cultural commonalities are more than differences; c) the study on commonalities and differences can begin with some key cultural dimensions; and d) people view other cultures from the perspective of one's own. The sequence of the four principles is noticeable. The leading principle is the unavoidability of viewing other cultures from self-perspective. But how can we, through the lens of our own culture, view other cultures' differences and commonalities? Put another way, is such a self-perspective deceptive and limited? The answer would decide whether *objective* and *fair* cross-cultural studies are possible or not.

In my opinion, since it is inevitable to mix our point of view with prejudices and even biases, some adjustment of strategy and methodology will be necessary. Generally speaking, seeking for commonalities is an effective approach to reaching agreement in cross-cultural dialogue and communication. When we view other cultures with our own eyes, what strikes us are usually differences, which are yet not absolute. The safe logic of understanding and interpreting other cultures is to discover commonalities among differences. The key issue here is not *whether* there are differences, but *how* to deal with them. To solve this issue, we must seek help from other theories and methods.

First, let's take a look at Habermas's communicative rationality, which is enabled by intersubjectivity. In Habermas's view, that intersubjective communication and understanding are possible is premised on the interchangeability and equality of both parties involved in communication. It is the transformability of one's role that lays the foundation of the so-called "intersubjectivity". He writes,

> Pure intersubjectivity is determined by a symmetrical relation between I and You (We and You), I and He (We and They). An unlimited interchangeability of dialogue roles demands that no side be privileged in the performance of these roles: pure intersubjectivity exists only when there is complex symmetry in the distribution of assertion and disputation, revelation and hiding, prescription and following among the partners of communication.[14]

Such an intersubjectivity, I believe, is pivotal to interpretation and understanding in intercultural studies. Its significance is not only manifest in the principles of rationality in intercultural communication, but also stipulated by the "political correctness" of academic inquiry. Only as equal rejoinders of dialogue can we transpose ourselves and enter into other cultures, appreciating the idiosyncrasies and properties of the Other's culture, and avoiding narrow-minded conclusions, without being swayed by stereotypes.

A further question arises: How to escape from the limits of self-perspective? Gadamer's hermeneutics offers an inspiring method. In dealing with the historical distance between present interpreters and ancient texts, Gadamer puts forward a strategy called "fusion of horizons", which means to combine the interpreter's horizon of expectation at present and ancient texts' horizon of expectation in the past. Because either one has some sort of limitedness, the combination of two horizons would produce a larger, better horizon. The fusion of horizons, Gadamer says,

> [...] involves rising to a higher universality that overcomes not only our own particularity but also that of the other. The concept of "horizon" suggests itself because it expresses the superior breath of vision that the person who is trying to understand must have. To acquire a horizon means that one learns to look beyond what is close at hand—not in order to look away from it but see it better, within a larger whole and in truer proportion.[15]

As far as intercultural studies are concerned, the fusion of horizons refers to the fusion of one's self-horizon and the other's horizon. Although everyone views the other from the perspective of one's own, the fusion of horizons is possible in intercultural studies. To realize such a fusion, scholars must learn to shift their own vantage points, enter into the other's culture, observe and experience the other's culture in an empathetic manner, and hereby combine the two horizons. By doing so, we can continue to understand other cultures from self-perspective, and at the same time add the perspective of other cultures so as to correct some limits or blind-spots characteristic of self-perspective and arrive at a more objective and fair interpretation of the other's culture.

Back to the topic of this section. To reflect on Sinologism as a local concept, we should take into consideration the methodology of intercultural studies, not only pointing out the flaws of Sinologism but also suggesting a method by means of which we can avoid falling into the trap of Sinologism. If we can apply Habermas's notion of intersubjectivity to the research on other cultures, it is then possible to realize the fusion of two horizons and transcend the regional vision of Sinologism, acquiring a horizon of totality, which would enable a better observation of other cultures. Therefore, in the field of Sinology, we must advocate more reflection on methodology itself, curbing the Sinologism in service of Western imperialism and colonialism, and striving for a "paradigmatic revolution" of Sinology.

The discussion above is meant to illustrate two points. First, featuring the tension between various elements of various cultures, intercultural studies is a miscellaneous field of knowledge, which is different from the unicity of the cultural studies by and for the Chinese. Considering the asymmetry in global academe and the fact that cultural exchange is largely dominated by the hegemonic Westerners, how intercultural studies stave off Western-centrism and Western culture supremacism is a pressing question worth more reflection. There is stark disparity between perfectly scientific knowledge and cultural politics in reality, especially in the case of the humanities, where absolutely autonomous and free values of neutrality are nowhere to be found. When China is on the rise to be a world power, more debates over the cultural politics in knowledge production will emerge. Second, in spite of the friction of cultural politics, it should remain as the most desirable vision to have a more objective and fair interpretation of our own or the Other's culture. The scholarly world is not insulated from politics, but it doesn't mean all learning must be politicized. It is possible, and even necessary, to sustain a kind of tension between the two. Compared with other disciplines, intercultural studies necessitate more humanist wisdom and ethical tolerance.

Notes

1 See Stewart Buettner. *American Art Theory, 1945–1970*. Ann Arbor: UMI, 1981. pp.15–36.
2 Ming Dong Gu and Zhou Xian, eds. *Current Debates on Sinologism*. Beijing: China Social Science Press, 2017. p.1.
3 Zhou Ning. "Sinology and Sinologism," in *Current Debates on Sinologism*. p.27–31.
4 Wen Rumin. "The Sinological Mindset in Literary Studies," in *Current Debates on Sinologism*. p.36.
5 Ming Dong Gu. *Sinologism: An Alternative to Orientalism and Postcolonialism*. London: Routledge, 2015. p.7.
6 Ming Dong Gu. *Sinologism: An Alternative to Orientalism and Postcolonialism*. p.106.
7 Mary Bittner Wiseman. "Subversive Strategies in Chinese Avant-Garde Art," in *Journal of Aesthetics and Art Criticism* 65.1 (Winter 2007). pp.112–113.
8 See Zhou Xian. "On Wang Guangyi's Chinese Pop Art Iconography," in *Academic Monthly* 1 (2018). pp.14–150.
9 Stuart Hall, ed. *Representation: Cultural Representations and Signifying Practices*. London: Sage, 1997. p.6.
10 Ernst H. Gombrich. *Art and Illusion: A Study in the Psychology of Pictorial Representation*. London: Phaidon Press, 1969. p.69.
11 Ibid.
12 Frank Lentricchia. "Last Will and Testament of an Ex-Literary Critic: A Theorist Rejects His Calling," in *Quick Studies*. Ed. Alexander Star. New York: Farrar, Straus and Giroux, 2002. p.31.
13 See Kenneth Keith. *Cross Cultural Psychology: Contemporary Themes and Perspectives*. Oxford: Blackwell, 2010. p.12.
14 Jürgen Habermas. "Social Analysis and Communicative Competence," in *Social Theory*. Ed. Charles Lemert. Boulder: Westview, 1993. p.416.
15 Hans-Georg Gadamer. *Truth and Method*. Trans. Joel Weinsheimer and Donald G. Marshall. London: Bloomsbury, 2013. p.316.

5 Literature and identity

Identity as a phenomenon/problem

We all live in a specific sociocultural context. As a "social animal" and a subject capable of self-reflection, we are confronted with the following questions: "Who am I? And who are we?" In one's social communication with various other people or groups, in our imaginary connection with others, in a variety of literary and artistic works, we can't help noticing many a difference between "me" and "him", "us" and "them", and "my" and "our" cultural rootedness. Furthermore, against the backdrop of globalization on the rise and increasingly frequent cultural exchange and travels, in a time when time-space has been more and more condensed, China witnesses, on the one hand, the influx of various Western festivals, Western fast food, Hollywood blockbusters, and *Harry Porter* series, and on the other, the fad of Chinese Knots, Tang suits, traditional festivities, collection of classical calligraphy and painting, folk villages, and cultural heritage preservation. As different cultures meet and clash, some entangled questions, such as difference and conformity, heterogeneity and homogeneity, the sense of homeland, and the sense of alienation, have further complicated the issue of identity.

The problem of identity is manifest not only in the general realm of socio-culture but also in the domain of literature, where a number of identity issues emerge. Temporally speaking, the transformation of tradition to the modern brings about the faultline between the new tradition and the old one; spatially speaking, the progress of globalization leads to the conflict between the foreign cultures and the local ones, a situation that begets a series of questions concerning our identity. At the same time, urban literature is on the rise, while rural literature is at a low ebb; popular literature is expanding, whereas serious literature is shrinking; women's writings pose a challenge to traditional patriarchal hegemony; Chinese diasporic literature is booming, and the petty bourgeoisie taste is fashionable. All of these phenomena have posited some cultural riddles, beckoning literary critics to solve them. Strictly speaking, identity as an issue abounds in all sectors of our sociocultural apparatus. It entails complicated "politics of difference" and power relations, ranging from ethnic and racial differences, through class and social differences, to gender, subcultural, and even regional differences. The question of identity, as some scholars put it, is brought up because of its association with a series of polemics, such as feminism, ethnicity, sexual orientation, Eurocentrism, diaspora, postcolonialism, and postnational issues.[1] Paula M. L. Moya says,

> "'Identity' remains one of the most urgent—as well as hotly disputed—topics in literary and cultural studies. For nearly two decades, it has been a central focus of debate for psychoanalytic, poststructuralist, and cultural materialist criticism in areas ranging from postcolonial and ethnic studies to feminism and queer theory".[2]

Since China's reform and opening-up, we have witnessed a sea change in Chinese culture and literature, where a host of movements, trends, debates, and theories—whether it is "Chinese cultural fever", "high culture *versus* low culture", "aphasia of Chinese theory", "classical Chinese poetry *versus* modern Chinese poetry", or "the modern transformation of ancient Chinese theory"—are more or less related to identity, and can be innovatively examined and elucidated from the perspective of identity.

Identity studies: from psychoanalysis to cultural studies

Identity is one of the most frequently used critical idioms in today's academe. Semantically speaking, it can signify a lot of things. In personality studies, identity, a concept about one's innate self and subjectivity, refers to the essential and continuous self. In this case, one can have gender identity, racial identity, or communal identity. Logically speaking, it signifies the relation between two or among more elements which can replace one another without changing its value in syllogism. A broader usage: it can describe a "deep" relation between seemingly different factors, such as functional identity.[3] In philosophy, identity means the correspondence between psychological activities and physical activities, such as the identification between the feeling of pain and physiological source of pain.[4]

In our time, the earliest study of identity was found in Sigmund Freud's psychoanalysis of identification. For Freud, identification is an important and complicated psychological mechanism, and "identification is known to psychoanalysis as the earliest expression of an emotional tie with another person".[5] There are several noticeable points with regard to identification. First, identification is an emotional tie with the others and is realized by means of "introjection". Second, identification from the outset is ambivalent, with intimacy and repulsion at the same time. Third, self is produced by identification. Super-ego is usually the first special force exerted by identification; with the development of ego, ego's resistance against identification will be increasingly accentuated.[6] As far as the genealogy of identity studies is concerned, Freud's view on the ambivalent nature of identity has a far-reaching influence on other identity theories, which similarly stress identity's ambivalence and refute the myth of essentialism in identity.[7] After Freud, the psychologist Erik Erikson puts forward a famous theory named "identity crisis". Here, identity is "a feeling of knowing oneself, a feeling of 'knowing one's future goal', an inner confidence that one would get the desired recognition from his trustworthy people".[8] Erikson observes that identification takes place in the childhood stages, while the formal integration of identity in adolescence far outnumbers identification. Identity is "the process of the natural growth of self which integrates all the changes caused by identification and libido into the natural aptitude shaped by heritage and the opportunities provided by various social roles".[9] Erikson's theory contains an important argument that individual identity is not inborn, but acquired in the adolescent stages by integrating different factors and impacts. In other words, individual identity is a process of constant volatility and multiple possibilities. Besides Erikson, the most influential theory on identity is Lacan's psychoanalysis. The subject, Lacan believes, learns to tell the distinction between self and the other at the mirror stage, and establishes the relationship between the internal world and the external world through the prism of mirror image:

> The child at the *infans* stage, still sunk in his motor incapacity and nursling dependence, would seem to exhibit in an exemplary situation the symbolic matrix in which the *I* is precipitated in a primordial form, before it is objectified in the dialectic of identification with the other, and before language restores to it, in the universal, its function as subject.[10]

Lacan's identity theory is notoriously complicated, but there are several points worth our attention. First, he finds that identity is decentralized, a fact that casts doubt on Descartes's notion of "cogito" by the subject. Second, during the process of *I*'s formation, it starts with mirror image, followed by language, and both are pivotal to the formation of identity. Lacan also says, "The form in which language expresses itself in and of itself defines subjectivity...I identify myself in language".[11] These ideas help the other scholars to formulate new theories premised on the analogous structure between identity and language. Third, Lacan calls our attention to imaginary identity, which means one's symbolic identification with an ideal "*I*". This identity is concerned with a specific cultural group's vocabulary, norms, and orientation. That is to say, it is the subject's identification with the constructional way of intersubjective social space in which one's imaginary identity is sustained. Fourth, Lacan stresses the same structure of language and unconscious.

From the classic Freudian psychoanalysis to Lacanian poststructural psychoanalysis, identity studies have evolved greatly, in spite of the fact that these theories are limited to personal identity and individual subjectivity. The significance of identity studies lies in its innovative, changeable, and decentralized idea of subjectivity, which posits a powerful challenge to the traditional, static, and Cartesian notion of subjectivity. Besides, that identity studies combine identity with language, paying special attention to symbolic identity, has a far-reaching impact on the development of identity theories in the future.

Since the 1980s, with the rising prominence of globalization and cross-cultural communication, identity becomes a central issue in cultural studies, the new vogue in academe. If the most topical issue prior to the 90s was ideology and hegemony, the post-90s scholarly buzzword is *identity*. Not only has the question of identity been widely discussed in literary studies and cultural studies, but it also extends to social theories, philosophy, education studies, politics, and media studies. Stuart Hall, the leading exponent of cultural studies in England, inherits the Marxist tradition and absorbs intellectual cream from psychoanalysis and poststructuralism, having built an influential brand of identity theory. According to Hall, central to the question of identity is subjectivity. He notes that the recent attention to identity issues is against the backdrop of "post-Cartesian metaphysics", which makes an influential critique of the autonomous subject. Hence, identity studies can't adhere to the traditional approaches; rather, it must open itself up to new critical thinking. In his view, the traditional concept of identity is characterized by the combination of totality and intrinsicity, its core tinted with essentialism. To critique this tendency is actually to cast doubt on the Cartesian subjectivity of "cogito". But Hall insists that his theory should not negate the subject; rather, it aims to reconstruct a decentralized subject, which is not abstract, static, but mediated. This explains his preference for the idea of agency of the subject. Here, we can see Hall's indebtedness to Foucault's theory, in which the study of subjectivity is not so much to produce the knowing subject, but to produce a theory of discursive practice. The reason why Hall emphasizes the agency of the subject is that he wants to sketch out the actual conditions—the domain of discursive practice—under which the subject emerges. Put another way, the question of subjectification can only be formulated in discursive practice, on the basis of which the question of identification arises.[12] To introduce discursive practice to identity studies is actually a method used in psychoanalysis, in particular the deconstructive one. He writes,

> In common sense language, identification is constructed on the back of a recognition of some common origin or shared characteristics with another person or group, or with an ideal, and with the natural closure of solidarity and allegiance established on this foundation. In contrast with the "naturalism" of this definition, the discursive approach sees identification as a construction, a process never completed—always "in process". It is not determined in the sense that it can always be "won" or "lost", sustained or abandoned. Though not without its determinate conditions of existence, including the material and symbolic resources required to sustain it, identification is in the end conditional, lodged in contingency. Once secured, it does not obliterate difference. The total merging it suggests is, in fact, a fantasy of incorporation.[13]

Evidently, Hall abandons the essentialist notion of the subject and identification, which is static and centralized. On the other hand, under the impact of ideology and hegemony studies, Hall is against the "naturalistic" definition of identity, which holds that identity is inborn and predetermined, beyond any change. He points out the *unfinalizability* and the *becoming* of identity, revealing the openness and plasticity of this process. By using the category of discourse, he stresses the fact that identity emerges in discursive practice, and is produced by discursive practice (or, to be more specific, by signifying practices). Hall, nevertheless, pays a lot of attention to identity studies in the past (or historicization and contextualization). He understands that the late modernity we are living in has totally changed identity as was known in the past. Identity is now getting more and more fragmented, so the discursive practice of identity is in no way singular or unified. Rather, it is often the case that identity straddles many different, complicated, or even conflicting discursive practices, which makes identification in the present world extremely complicated. Above all, Stuart Hall, by introducing discursive practice and signifying practice to his theory, has transformed the focal issue of identity studies from "who we are" to "what we might become". He writes:

> Though they seem to invoke an origin in a historical past with which they continue to correspond, actually identities are about questions of using the resources of history, language and culture in the process of becoming rather than being: not "who we are" or "where we came from", so much as what we might become, how we have been represented and how that bears on how we might represent ourselves. Identities are therefore constituted within, not outside representation. They relate to the invention of tradition as much as to tradition itself, which they oblige us to read not as an endless reiteration but as "the changing same": not the so-called return to roots but a coming-to-terms-with our "routes". They arise from the narrativization of the self, but the necessarily fictional nature of this process in no way undermines its discursive, material or political effectivity, even if the belongingness, the "suturing into the story" through which identities arise is, partly, in the imaginary (as well as the symbolic) and therefore, always, partly constructed in fantasy, or at least within a fantasmatic field.[14]

The latest "turns" of identity theories

Identity studies, by shifting from psychoanalysis to cultural studies, by changing its focal point from the individual subjectivity to the collective subjectivity, can now boil down to Hall's questioning formula: instead of asking "who we are" and "where we were from", now the master questions are "what we may become", "how we are represented", and "what affect the way we are represented". In my view, this "turn" has profound implications.

First of all, this "turn" is embedded in the particular context of late modernity. Without doubt, the prominence of identity issues is closely related to the transformation of the socio-historical conditions in our time. Late modernity has a series of salient characteristics which was unseen before, such as the demise of totality and grand narrative (Lyotard), liquidity and ambivalence (Bauman), multiplicity (Welsh), and time-space compression (Harvey). Post-Fordist production mode is manifest not only in economy but also in culture. The bipolarity of globalization and localization accounts for the urgency of the question of identity, while the tension between dominant cultures and marginal cultures abets the surge of nationalism. Therefore, it is inevitable for identity studies to change from a static inquiry into the past to a dynamic examination of the present and the future. Changing the fixed question of "who we are" to the question about contingency, that is, "what we may become", Hall reveals that identity is always unfinalized and in the process of becoming. With the decline in totality and the growth of multiplicity, and with the enhanced fluidity and fragmentation, identity is correspondingly in face of dissolved totality and increased uncertainties. Negatively speaking, identity in late modernity is contingent, facing more complexity and dilemma. Positively speaking, it subverts the old-fashioned idea of identity that is static, fixed, and undivided, allowing for more possibilities for the shaping and development of identity. At the same time, the emphasis on uncertainty and volatility also justifies the reforms made to change the status quo of global and regional cultures. Late modernity enables us to recalibrate the definition of identity. As Hall puts it, his concept of identity is not that of naturalism and essentialism, but a strategic and descriptive one. Recently, some scholars also argue that "identity categories provide modes of articulating and examining significant correlations between lived experience and social location".[15] This approach can inspire us to reflect on ethnical or collective identity in contemporary Chinese culture. We were accustomed to centering on historical traditions, which by and large is a retrospective methodology. We'd better change the old habit of *looking back on* the past cultures and seeking for resources in tradition. If we learn to *look forward*, as suggested by Hall, the most urgent question then is not how to restore the great tradition in the past, but how to deal with the future. The contemporary Chinese scholars are simply too apt to ask, as Hall cautions against, "Who we are? Where we are from?", rather than asking "Who we may become?" a question that invites us to formulate the national identity of Chinese culture, with present or future orientation, but without cutting the tie with history. In Hobsbawm's words, it aims at the "invention of tradition".[16] The May Fourth Movement, in spite of its future orientation, adopted a radical approach to severing the historical tie and rejecting the great tradition, whereas the recent trend in Chinese culture is the return to tradition, which yet makes people forget about the present or future. In light of Hall's theory, identity in the past doesn't make much difference, and the primary concern is what we may become. In our culture and literature today, the unreconstructed force is ingrained, and we must be alert to it.

Second, this "turn" highlights the change in the significance of subjectivity. That is to say, the subject centering on Cartesian "cogito" is now replaced by the subject decentralized. As mentioned earlier, the question of identity is actually concerned with the subject. To be more specific, identity is how the subject locates and ascertains oneself in some specific socio-cultural relations, with regard to the construction of and inquiry about one's subjectivity. The Cartesian subjectivity is autonomous and rational, with generally effective and constant qualities, sometimes taking the form of Kantian transcendental subject. Judging from Hall's theory of identity, such a notion of subjectivity is problematic. The Marxist approach to subjectivity stresses the production of the subject based on specific production mode and economic basis, dismissing the idea of the abstract subject that transcends social restraints. The school of psychoanalysis, by looking into human unconscious, the structure of personality and its internal conflict, posits a powerful challenge to Cartesian and Kantian notions of subjectivity. This school is inclined to take the subject as dynamic, contingent, or even questionable agency.[17] The poststructuralists make a more radical critique of the subject. Foucault reveals the interrelatedness of discourse and the subject in his famous examination of the symbiosis of power and knowledge, which completely subverts the Cartesian subject as autonomous entity.[18] Suppose the question of identity is merely concerned with subjectivity, the transformation of the idea on subjectivity will inevitably lead to the change of identity theories, a salient manifestation being the shift from the fixed, abstract (or transcendental), and universal subject, to the local, changeable subject contingent upon some certain contexts. In other words, the centralized and unified subject is turned into the decentralized, or even fragmented, subject. Therefore, the previous line of identity thinking is now redirected to a heterogeneous, dynamic and multiple one. More importantly, today's analysis of identity is, methodologically, focused on "exteriority" or "alterity". Unlike the traditionally self-referential theory on subjectivity, identity studies center on association. Because any identification, be it individual or collective, is a reflection on the relation between *I* and the other, a meditation on relationality. A methodological principle proposed by the postmodernists is such a contemplation of exteriority or relationality. Hence, it is necessary for us to employ the idea of "constitutive otherness" to anatomize socio-cultural phenomena.[19] Any form of socio-cultural phenomena operates within a certain hierarchical system, confirming something and negating other things simultaneously, which is the reason why otherness or difference sometimes is brutally excluded. Hall therefore argues that "Identification is, then, a process of articulation, a suturing, an over-determination not a subsumption".[20] Like all kinds of signifying practice, identification is contingent upon a "game", that is to say, the game of *différance*, which is in turn conditioned by a logic of more than *one*. Since identification is a dynamic process of crossing differences, it results in a discursive function, which is to correlate and mark the symbolic boundaries, and ultimately is production of "boundary effect". It insists on its outsidedness, acting as a constitutive outsider, which in turn reinforces this very process.[21] Bauman illustrates this method from another perspective. He contends that the project of modernity is to reflect upon itself from *within*, while the idea of postmodernism takes a cool and critical outsider's view of modernity.[22] Therefore, the two are totally different in terms of thinking style and have a distinctive vision of the world. It is from such a vantage point that we can see clearly distinction, contradiction, repression, and periphery, see what is veiled by essentialism or dominant ideology, and understand the complex correlations of identities.

Third, the shifting of identity studies gives rise to the so-called, as Hall puts it, "discursive turn", which can be interpreted as what the "linguistic turn" brings about to identity studies. This new turn translates the epistemological and conscious issues into linguistic ones. Wittgenstein famously says, "All philosophy is a critique of language". Human language is not a transparent, neutral, or natural tool for communication, but a means to shape ourselves and the world. Peter L. Berger and Thomas Luckmann rightly argue:

> This reality-generating potency of conversation is already given in the fact of linguistic objectification. We have seen how language objectifies the world, transforming the *panta rhei* of experience into a cohesive order. In

> the establishment of this order language realizes a world, in the double sense of apprehending and producing it. Conversation is the actualizing of this realizing efficacy of language in the face-to-face situations of individual existence. In conversation the objectifications of language become objects of individual consciousness. Thus the fundamental reality-maintaining fact is the continuing use of the same language to objectify unfolding biographical experience.[23]

When Foucault subverts the Cartesian notion of subjectivity, he calls our attention to the discourse's disciplinary power on the subject, a power caused by the symbiosis of power and knowledge. To be more precise, subjectivity is in fact shaped by discourse, which in turn is produced by power. Hall specifies that identity arises and develops in discursive practice, without which identity is groundless. Identity is, by nature, formulated linguistically.[24] The latest identity theories can help one understand that identity stems from difference, the notion of which is obviously exposed to the influence of the post-structuralist theories on language and its semantic aspects. Linguistic studies have shown that meaning is generated within the linguistic system of difference, a fact that explains the contingency of meaning. Only in the changeable and volatile relationship with a signifying network can meaning exist, so there is no such thing as an "absolutely true" meaning. Moreover, the fixed corresponding relation between symbol and its referent in reality doesn't exist; nor is it possible to have an innate meaning independent of human thought, behavior, and knowledge.[25] The same is true of the formation or production of identity. It is impossible to claim an originary or authentic identity outside discourse, for identity is the produce of difference.

Finally, as indicated by what Hall calls "discursive turn", identity is closely entwined with symbols or signs, one of which, of course, is language. The recent scholarly discussion about cultural identity and national identity lavishes attention on symbolic identity, which Freud and Lacan have elaborated on in their own studies. The "fictionality" of cultural and national identity is an interesting topic in the latest development of identity theories. In this regard, Eric Hobsbawm's "invented tradition" and Benedict R. Anderson's "imagined communities" are the most noteworthy ideas. Hobsbawm discovers that the quest for ancient tradition is something new in the modern age and that sometimes tradition is "invented" during a certain movement or a short period.

> "Invented tradition" is taken to mean a set of practices, normally governed by overtly or tacitly accepted rules and of a ritual or symbolic nature, which seek to inculcate certain values and norms of behaviour by repetition, which automatically implies continuity with the past. In fact, where possible, they normally attempt establish continuity with a suitable historic past... However, insofar as there is such reference to a historic past, the peculiarity of "invented" traditions is that the continuity with it is largely factitious. In short, they are responses to novel situations which take the form of reference to old situations, or which establish their own past by quasi-obligatory repetition.[26]

Hobsbawm's term is reminiscent of Benedetto Croce's axiom, "All history is contemporary history". In the above-quoted paragraph, Hobsbawm underscores some crucial issues. First, tradition is "factitious" because it is "invented" consciously. Second, the "invented tradition" is a necessary response to the novel situations of the present, for the purpose of building continuity with the past, catering to the needs of the changed socio-cultural context. Third, the continuity with the past is selective, for people aims to look for "a suitable historic past". Four, "invented tradition" is realized through automatic reference to the past and quasi-obligatory repetition. Anderson's "imagined communities" resonates with "invented tradition" in many ways. In Anderson's view, nation-state, the product of modernity, was born into the world as the result of the rise of modern national languages and print culture, while at the same time, religious communities, monarchies, and traditional views of time declined. He takes nation-ness and nationalism as cultural artifacts of a particular kind, arguing that "once created, they became 'modular', capable of being transplanted, with varying degrees of self-consciousness, to a great variety of social terrains, to merge and be merged with a correspondingly wide variety of political and ideological constellations".[27] Anderson emphasizes the imaginedness of national community, but he doesn't mean the nonexistence of it. Nor does he want to say nation-ness is something fabricated. Rather, what he points out is that nation-ness is a social recognition, or a psychological product of social facts. A point worth noting is that Anderson attaches great importance to print media, in particular literature and newspaper, which can help shape the imagination about national communities. All in all, these theories tend to underscore the symbolic and creative (i.e., to say, fictional, imagined, or representational) dimensions of cultural (or national) identity, largely in accordance with the aforementioned poststructuralist identity theories in which identity is regarded as a constitutive process, dynamic and unfinished. At the same time, Anderson's theory highlights the effect of symbolic representations, ranging language to literature, from journalism to media, from festivities to everyday life, on the formation of identity.

Identity as signifying practice in literature

Two preliminary conclusions can be reached so far: one the one hand, identity is a dynamic, developing, and unfinished process, a process that is open-ended and constitutive; on the other hand, identity is formulated in discursive practice, with language and literature playing key roles in the formation of symbolic identities. Based on the first conclusion, we can infer that identity is a future-oriented process, starting with the present. The second one proves that literature is indispensable for identity, because literature itself is a constitutive practice of identity discourse.

Now, let's come back to the relationship between literature and identity. In my view, the relationship is manifest in two aspects: first, how literature represents "us", or in Hall's words, "how we are represented"; second, how literature impacts or formulates identity, or as Hall puts it, "how literature influences our way of representing ourselves". Combined together, the two questions boil down to one question, "what we may become". The first question is a matter of literary criticism and literary history, which I'd prefer to leave out here. The second one, however, is exactly what literary theory and cultural studies should focus on.

Those who specialize on the question of identity would discover that there are a lot of ways of identification in our real life. Anderson, for example, has discussed the important functions of festive rituals, monuments, and museums, which in Chinese tradition have undoubtedly been reinforcing the cultural identity of Chinese nationals. However, in contrast with these cultural forms, literature, along with many "para-literary" forms (such as drama, film, TV, and radio), represents discursive practice of identity in more regular, continuous, and immediate ways. These sorts of discourse, obviously, are capable of impacting identity more comprehensively, lastingly, and deeply than other discourse. From elementary and secondary school Chinese textbooks to all kinds of works of literature, reading is a significant epistemological form of identification, for language functions as a vital portal to the development of the conception of "us". It is in this sense that we speak of "the engineer of human souls", "a study of humanity", "casting national personality", and "national epic" in literary studies. What I'm going to talk about is not whether it is possible for literature to exert impact on identification, but *how* literature contributes to the formation of identity.

To be more specific, there are several points worth our further attention: first of all, the founding myth of a nation. In identity studies, it is believed that each nation has its own founding myth, which plays a vital role in constructing the source or fountainhead of a nation and its culture. Such a myth usually tells us about the time, space, ancestors, and tales of a nation's origination, which are of vital significance for the shaping of a set of commonly shared symbols. In Chinese literary history, there are a great deal of "myths" of this kind, ranging from the legend of Nuwa who patches the Sky to the tales of Three Sovereigns and Five Emperors. Speaking of Mongolian and Tibetan ethnic groups, both claim their own national epics. Second, literary works canonized in history. Each nation has its own literary history, though varying in terms of content and form. A specific set of literary canons, sooner or later, emerges or will be produced from national literature. The classic works of literature are usually texts most frequently read and cited within a long time span. If we can trust Hobsbawm's assertion that repetition is the means of sustaining a continuity with the past, classic works of literature, after being read and interpreted time and again, are likely to cement generations of people together as "imagined communities", producing lots of shared experiences and conceptions. Third, from literary classics one can distill some exemplary figures, which, from the perspective of cognitive psychology, can function as "personality templates". In other words, these figures could serve as examples of personality, on which the future generations are modeled. In Chinese literary history, there are many apotheoses of human character, ranging from men of letters such as Qu Yuan, Tao Yuanming, Li Bai, and Tu Fu, to fictional characters in The Romance of Three Kingdoms, to the patriotic General Wen Tian-xiang and the righteous Bao Zheng. If these heroic examples are instrumental in shaping "positive" identification, there are many negative figures in literature which take part in identification in more complicated ways, such as Lu Xun's Ah Q, whose "spiritual victory" is important in exposing our national defects. Finally, the space of homeland and its lifestyle as represented in literature, in particular some symbolic sceneries in nature and of humanities, such as the Yellow River and the Loess Plateau. Homeland is one's destination in space, and the sense of homeland is an experience of familiarity, intimacy, and involution, an experience that repeatedly reinforces people's affection, homesickness, and longing toward homeland, which reminds us of our cultural identity, particularly the haunting memory about childhood.

Obviously, that literature can play a part in identification illustrates the connection between the current society/culture and the past. Since identity is something dynamic, developing, and unfinished, its connection with tradition becomes a key issue in our discussion of identification. In my opinion, there are two tendencies we must caution against. One can be broadly defined as "cultural fundamentalism", while another as "cultural nihilism". The former usually takes a position of essentialism, insisting that one should go back to a unified, originary, and essential fountainhead, without which it is impossible to build cultural or national identity. Such a line of thinking is "past-oriented" and "retrospective". The once famous debate over the "aphasia" of Chinese literary theory, to some extent, is a case in point. Given its obsession with identity as an originary, and constant entity, the "cultural fundamentalist" tendency stresses that only the return to classical literary theory and its thinking mode can ensure the stability of our identity. I think this approach is neither viable theoretically nor feasible in reality. The latter is exactly the opposite, generally denying the present's influence on the past, and regarding identity as something empty. That said, identity has no historicity, nor does it have any sense of reality. When it comes to the relationship between history and the present, we'd better take a "future-oriented" position based on the present. Hall aptly says, identities

> relate to the invention of tradition as much as to tradition itself, which they oblige us to read not as an endless reiteration but as 'the changing same': not the so-called return to the roots but coming-to-terms with our 'routes'.[28]

Hobsbawm also argues that the invention of tradition is to establish continuity with "a suitable historic past". By "suitable", Hobsbawm doesn't mean suitable for the past, but for the present, which undergoes changes and finds the historic past suitable. Invented traditions, for Hobsbawm, are therefore a certain response to the updated conditions of the present, which means our relationship with history is not fixed, but contingent on the current context. Such a relationship illuminates the subject's agency and changeability in the process of identification, which is neither to encapsulate the past influences in a passive way, nor to simply return to the traditions. If we combine this theory with Hayden White's theory of history, some interesting findings might emerge. For White, history is not merely about a bunch of events, but about the network of relations that historical events are embedded in. It is up to the historian, rather than the events *per se*, to unveil the significance of the relational network. Hayden White writes,

> So too for historical narratives. They succeed in endowing sets of past events with meanings, over and above whatever comprehension they provide by appeal to putative causal laws, by exploiting the metaphorical similarities

between sets of real events and the conventional structures of our fictions. By the very constitution of a set of events in such a way as to make a comprehensible story out of them, the historian charges those events with the symbolic significance of a comprehensible plot structure.[29]

Hayden White maintains that historians should unravel historical meaning from the current context, which is an inspiring argument for our understanding of identification. I think Hobsbawm's "invented traditions" exactly means the same thing. Or, in Hall's words, we are in face of a "changing same". Thus, when dealing with our continuous relations with the historic past, we are continuously interpreting and "inventing" tradition, rather than absorbing the past passively. Literary discourse, as an agent of identification, is therefore always evolving. A literary historian's view on literary canons, and a literary critic's innovative interpretation of typical characters, and a writer's fresh representation of homeland, are open-ended and unfinished. In a similar vein, the way literature engages with identification is also open-ended and unfinished. If we look into literature from this perspective, literature is certainly more than entertainment and moral education. Considering the complicated tension between globalization and localization, literature will repeatedly spell out conundrums of identity, asking "who we might become of", as China is in the midst of its modern transformation, with contemporary cultural identity in the process of reconfiguration.

Notes

1. Marjorie Ferguson and Peter Golding. "Cultural Studies and Changing Times: An Introduction", in *Cultural Studies in Question*. Eds. Mariorie Ferguson and Peter Golding. London: Sage, 1997. p.xxvi.
2. Paula M. L. Moya and Michael R. Hames-Garcia, eds. *Reclaiming Identity: Realist Theory and the Predicament of Postmodernism*. Berkeley: University of California Press, 2000. p.1.
3. See Arthur S. Reber. *The Penguin Dictionary of Psychology*. Harmondsworth: Penguin, 1995.
4. Kenneth McLeish. *Bloomsbury Guide to Human Thought*. London: Bloomsbury, 1993.
5. Sigmund Freud. *Selected Later Writings of Sigmund Freud*. Translated by Lin Chen et al. Shanghai: Shanghai Translation Press, 1986, pp.112–115.
6. Sigmund Freud. *Selected Later Writings of Sigmund Freud*. p.112–198.
7. Stuart Hall and Paul de Gey, eds. *Questions of Cultural Identity*. London: Sage, 1996. p.3.
8. Quoted in Baldwin R. Hergenhahn, *An Introduction to Theories of Personality*. Trans. He Jing and Feng Zengjun. Haikou: Hainan People's Publishing House, 1988. p.162.
9. Ibid.
10. Jacques Lacan. "The Mirror Stage as Formative of the Function of the I as Revealed in Psychoanalytic Experience", in *Selected Works of Jacques Lacan*. Trans. Chu Xiaoquan. Shanghai: Sanlian Bookstore, 2001. p.90.
11. Jacques Lacan. "The Function and Field of Speech and Language in Psychoanalysis", in *Selected Works of Jacques Lacan*. pp.311–312.
12. Stuart Hall and Paul de Gey, eds. *Questions of Cultural Identity*. pp.1–2.
13. Stuart Hall and Paul de Gey, eds. *Questions of Cultural Identity*. pp.2–3.
14. Stuart Hall and Paul de Gey, eds. *Questions of Cultural Identity*. p.4.

15 Paula M. L. Moya and Michael R. Hames-Garcia, eds. *Reclaiming Identity: Realist Theory and the Predicament of Postmodernism.* p.4.
16 See Eric Hobsbawm and Terence Ranger, eds. *The Invention of Tradition.* Cambridge: Cambridge University Press, 1983. pp.1–14.
17 Robert C. Davis and Ronald Schleifer. *Criticism and Culture.* Essex: Longman, 1991. p.84.
18 See Michel Foucault, "The Discourse on Language", in *Critical Theory Since 1965.* Eds. Hazard Adams and Leroy Searle. Tallahassee: Florida State University Press, 1986. pp.148–163.
19 Lawrence Cahoone, ed. *From Modernism to Postmodernism: Anthology.* Oxford: Blackwell, 1996. pp.15–16.
20 Stuart Hall and Paul de Gey, eds. *Questions of Cultural Identity.* p.3.
21 Stuart Hall and Paul de Gey, eds. *Questions of Cultural Identity.* p.4.
22 Zygmunt Bauman. *Modernity and Ambivalence.* Cambridge: Polity, 1991. p.272.
23 Peter L. Berger and Thomas Luckmann. *The Social Construction of Reality: A Treatise in the Sociology of Knowledge.* London: Penguin, 1967. p.173.
24 Hall's emphasis on the discursive or ideational practices of identity has also attracted some criticism. Some critics have pointed out that his theory gives too much prominence to the immaterial praxis of identification, while considerably ignoring the profound influence of material circumstances and praxis on identification.。
25 Paula M. L. Moya and Michael R. Hames-Garcia, eds. *Reclaiming Identity: Realist Theory and the Predicament of Postmodernism.* p.5.
26 Eric Hobsbawm and Terence Ranger, eds. *The Invention of Tradition.* pp.1–2.
27 Benedict Anderson. *Imagined Communities: Reflections on the Origin and Spread of Nationalism.* London: Verso, 1991. p.4.
28 Stuart Hall and Paul de Gey, eds. *Questions of Cultural Identity.* p.4.
29 Hayden White. *Tropics of Discourse: Essays in Cultural Criticism.* Baltimore: John Hopkins University Press, 1985. pp.91–92.

6 Cross-cultural understanding and interpretation

Cross-cultural studies of the humanities

In different domains of cultural production, cross-cultural studies have disparate features, which deserve special scrutiny and discussion. The cross-cultural research of the humanities is unique in many ways, with comparative literature and cross-cultural literary studies as salient examples. First, the humanities are characterized by overtly ideological properties and cultural differences in terms of interpretation. Let's compare natural sciences and the humanities. The cross-cultural communication in natural sciences usually seldom leads to severe disagreement and disparity. A piece of medical literature in the field of cancer science, though written in English, won't bring about much different interpretations for non-English-speaking readers. However, in the field of the humanities, there are a legion of different, cultural-specific interpretations. It is no exaggeration to say that the cross-cultural research in the humanities is rife with interpretive disparities, ambiguities, and conflicts. Science and art (i.e., the liberal arts) represent two totally different knowledge paradigms, because the scientists pursue a singular and up-to-date answer, whereas in art different interpretations are tolerated.[1] To borrow two terms from Wolfgang Iser's hermeneutics, science is "hard-core theory", which can deduce many laws to make predictions, but literature (the humanities) is "soft theory", which cannot make predictions.[2] Obviously, the distinctive knowledge paradigm of the humanities decides the complexity and diversity of cross-cultural studies and communication. Thus, it is inevitable to have, as a hermeneutician would put it, "interpretive conflicts".

Second, the research method of the humanities also decides the complexity of cross-cultural understanding and interpretation. A typical cross-cultural research of the humanities usually takes the form of local scholars interpreting the other culture's texts and trying to make some analyses. Textual studies are very different from the face-to-face cross-cultural communication, as the former lacks the chance of intersubjective dialogue which might correct interpretive mistakes on spot. It is often the case that a humanities scholar takes up a text from the other's culture and makes his own interpretation, an interpretation located in a specific context and an interpretive community. This scenario is much like touring or theater-going. A researcher enters into an alien land by means of his imagined interpretation of the

DOI: 10.4324/9781003407089-9

other's text, like a tourist setting one's foot in a foreign country for sightseeing, whose own culture background must be different from the target culture and then may bring about a number of disparities, ambiguities, or even conflicts. A classic example is a Chinese director trying to stage a foreign play (say, Beckett's *Waiting for Godot*). The way a Chinese director interprets a foreign play, including its characters, conflicts, plots, or themes, is unanimously related to the intercultural relation between *I* (or *We*) and the other.

Third, the cross-cultural studies in the humanities have more complicated and volatile interactive relations than other disciplines do. Ranging from the researcher (the subject) and the text (the target), to languages (media) and interpretive methods and cultural contexts, there are various forms of interactive relationship. From this angle, we can describe the cross-cultural studies in the humanities as some humanities scholars interpreting the other's text through the mediation of languages. According to this simple definition, we can detect several layers of interactive relationship: *intersubjectivity*, *intertextuality*, and the *inter-lingual*, *inter-contextual*, and *intercultural* relations. It is in this dynamic interactive relation that cross-cultural studies take place, so we can further define the *intercultural* studies in the humanities as a group of local researchers in an *inter-contextual* and *inter-lingual* position engaging in *intersubjective* cross-cultural dialogues with the other's text and its *intertextuality*.

The three points decide the traits of cross-cultural studies in the humanities, which can be further translated into other puzzles: How do the cultural differences or even ideological conflicts between self and the other impact intercultural understanding and interpretation? How can one transform those intercultural obstacles, such as biases, misunderstandings, prejudices, into positive resources? How can these interactive relations do good to cross-cultural understanding and interpretation in the field of the humanities?

Coding and decoding in interactivity

If we regard cross-cultural studies as a sort of information communication, informatics and semiotics can provide different analytical frames. In terms of informatics, cross-cultural studies are a process of information production, transmission, and reception between senders and receivers, which entails the trio of sender-media-receiver. For the sender, his work is the coding of information; for the receiver, the decoding of information. Given the distinctions between the coding and decoding languages and cultures, the other's text is likely to be distorted on the side of local receivers. This outcome is what we all "conflicts of interpretation".

In his study on TV texts, Stuart Hall puts forward a semiotic coding-decoding mode. He believes that multiple differences exist between coding and decoding, which is caused by the semiotic variance, locational asymmetry between senders and receivers, and other reasons. During the coding-decoding process, the structural difference on the part of information receivers will lead to information distortion and misinterpretation. As information is sent out and received, dominant cultural order, on the one hand, exerts significant impact; on the other, there are various private or individual forms of decoding process, pointing to all kinds of "selective perception". Generally speaking, Hall's decoding process can boil down to three types. The first one is decoding in "dominant or hegemonic position", featuring a decoding process within the range of dominant signs, a process of ideally lucid transmission. In brief, decoding of this kind is in accordance with coding. That is to say, the decoder interprets information largely according to the coder's intention. The second one is decoding of the "negotiated code or position", which means the decoder partially agrees with the dominant meaning of coding, and at the same time partially resists or deviates from the original meaning. It is thus a state of compromise and negotiation. The third one is decoding of "oppositional code", which totally defies the coding rules, understanding codes in a different or even contrapuntal way, radically departing from the coding.[3] We can, as a form of shorthand, name the three TV decoding approaches, submissive decoding, compromised decoding, and oppositional decoding, which can apply to cross-cultural studies of the humanities and reveal a law; that is, there are at least three kinds of interpretations for local researchers specializing in decoding the other's text.

Of course, the reality is way more complex than the tripartite playbook of cross-cultural understanding and interpretation. The reason is rather simple: different cultures differ greatly, and the asymmetry between senders and receivers, as described by Hall, is commonplace. Hence, the more the participants interpreting the other's text, the more the possible interpretations. Insofar as China receives Western literature and art, some highly influential works from the Western cultures didn't make a splash in China, while some less important ones have made tremendous impact when introduced to China. Take drama for instance. Ibsen's *A Doll's House* became a phenomenal play during the May Fourth and New Culture Movement, whereas his other plays failed to have a similar reach in China. The expressionist paintings of Edvard Munch, another Norwegian artist, were barely known in China for quite a long time.[4] Another example is German playwright Brecht, whose idea on theater had far-reaching influence on a number of young Chinese playwrights in the early years of reform and opening-up, greatly stimulating the conceptual innovation and formal experimentation of contemporary Chinese theater. However, some equally important Western playwrights, such as Vsevolod Meyerhold, Antonin Artaud, Samuel Beckett, and Harold Pinter, enjoyed much less popularity in the 1980s China.[5] All of these make clear two points: first, cross-cultural communication is culturally selective, as a local culture is always accustomed to receiving the other's culture selectively, according to specific cultural and historical contexts; and second, one's understanding and interpretation of the other's culture is always exposed to the influence of local cultural tradition and historical reality.

"Cultural correctness" and intersubjectivity

Cross-cultural studies include a series of cultural interrelations. However, over the course of the long history of cross-cultural studies, there are always a myriad of ingrained biases, misinterpretations, and distortions. Orientalism prevalent in the Western academe is a salient case in point. According to Edward Said, the

Westerners' studies of the East are rife with deliberate distortion and misinterpretation. In the Western intellectual world, the idea of "Orient" is anything but natural; rather, it is the target of intentional construction by the ideologies of imperialism and colonialism in the apparatus of Western power/knowledge. Orientalism, as a set of Western knowledge discourse about the East, obviously contains numerous conceptual stereotypes or prejudices, which are manifest in a series of binary oppositions between the West and the East. In brief, the Western civilization is advanced, rational, scientific, industrious, and superior, while the Eastern one is backward, irrational, mysterious, sluggish, and gross. By examining the knowledge lineage of Orientalist scholarship in the West, Said reveals the complicated and implicit Western supremacism and ideology. The key argument Said wants to make is that the West's interest in the "Orient" is not cultural, but political. To be more specific, the Westerners' cultural interest in the Orient is entwined with some political, economic, and military considerations. He writes,

> Orientalism, therefore, is not any airy European fantasy about the Orient, but a created body of theory and practice in which, for many generations, there has been a considerable material investment. Continued investment made Orientalism, as a system of knowledge about the Orient, an accepted grid for filtering through the Orient into Western consciousness, just as that same investment multiplied—indeed, made truly productive—the statements proliferating out from Orientalism into the general culture....Orientalism is never far from what Denys Hay has called the idea of Europe, a collective notion identifying "us" Europeans as against all "those" non-Europeans, and indeed it can be argued that the major component in European culture is precisely what made that culture hegemonic both in and outside Europe: the idea of European identity as a superior one in comparison with all the non-European peoples and cultures. There is in addition the hegemony of European ideas about the Orient, themselves reiterating European superiority over Oriental backwardness, usually overriding the possibility that a more independent, or more skeptical, thinker might have had different views on the matter.[6]

Within the knowledge system of Orientalism lies an invisible "filter framework", the function of which is to filter those thinkers of more independence and skepticism, who might say something heretical. What is left, finally, is no more than a body of knowledge or so-called "truth" endorsing Western supremacy. The implicit ideology of Orientalism, in fact, is an implicit version of Western supremacism. Starting with such a motivation, the West's understanding of the other's culture is bound to be full of distortion, misconception, and prejudice. Interpreting the other's culture then morphs into a construction of some specific ideology. Actually, it is very likely for a cross-cultural scholar to champion the idea of "China-centered culture supremacy" in one's interpretation of the other's culture. What's more, there are other non-cultural objectives in politics, economy, and military, which add up to making cross-cultural studies a cultural "battle field", where many researches have but dubious academic value, because they have almost completely departed from the tenets of cultural equality and reciprocity. Therefore, when laying bare the ideology of cultural imperialism in Orientalism, we must advocate an egalitarian idea of cross-cultural studies and cultivate a congenial attitude toward the other's culture. To use a philosophical term, the aim is to cherish and hold to "intersubjectivity" in cross-cultural communication. Habermas has an accurate statement about this position:

> Pure intersubjectivity is determined by a symmetrical relation between I and You (We and You), I and He (We and They). An unlimited interchangeability of dialogue roles demands that no side be privileged in the performance of these roles; pure intersubjectivity exists only when there is complete symmetry in the distribution of assertion and disputation, revelation and hiding, prescription and following among the partners of communication.[7]

Pure intersubjectivity means an equal interchangeability of social roles, aiming to enact a dialogue. Dialogicity, in Habermas's opinion, is tantamount to the reversibility of *I* as the addresser and the other as the addressee. In the cross-cultural studies modeled on Orientalism as described by Said, the researcher has no intention of listening to the other, and would rather distort the other's text according to one's own ideology. Put another way, the reciprocity of dialogue is what Habermas calls "pure intersubjectivity", which differs greatly from all kinds of cultural supremacism. It has been a trend in the recent cross-cultural communication theories to pay more and more attention to intersubjectivity, which is now taken as the pivotal approach to cross-cultural understanding and Interpretation.[8] Furthermore, as per Heidegger's philosophy on the dialogical dichotomy of listening and speaking, listening takes precedence over speaking, and speaking hinges on listening. Therefore, logically speaking, listening happens before speaking, and speaking is for the sake of listening, without which speaking is meaningless. That said, the primary condition of dialogicity in cross-cultural studies is listening to the other's voice. Orientalism is no so much dialogue as monologue, because the Western scholars studying the Orient have little interest in listening to the other's speaking. This explains why Orientalism is conditioned by the cultural hegemony practiced in Western cultural supremacism. Considering the trendy term "political correctness", I think it is necessary to advance the idea of "cultural correctness", an analogous "political correctness" in cross-cultural studies. "Cultural correctness" stipulates that different cultures should be equal to each other, and it is the prerequisite for cross-cultural studies to avoid the trap of cultural imperialism in favor of one's own cultural supremacy.

Fusion of horizons in interactive context

It has been a consensus in cross-cultural studies that everyone observes the other's culture through one's own cultural lens.[9] A conundrum arises: How to construct pure intersubjectivity? How to make the self-centered observation more effective, reasonable, and productive? In a nutshell, how to hold to "cultural correctness" in cross-cultural studies?

A local scholar's reading of the other's text produced in an alien culture is inevitably coded by his or her own horizon and experience. Husserl in his phenomenology postulates two propositions, namely, "phenomenological reduction" and "eidetic intuition". He maintains that we can exclude precedent knowledge in our probe into the world, for the purpose of reaching an intuition about the essence of phenomena. However, the later hermeneutic scholars make an opposite case, arguing that the precondition that makes interpretation possible is an interpreter's "fore-understanding". That said, it is actually impossible to suppose that any interpreter may abdicate his or her fore-understanding before entering into a concrete context. Gadamer points out that the primary condition of any interpretation is fore-understanding, which "determines what can be realized as unified meaning".[10] However, what might be included in the "fore-"? There are both "productive prejudice that enables understanding" and "prejudices that hinder it and lead to misunderstanding".[11] Generally speaking, it is unlikely for us neither to manipulate the two types of prejudices nor to separate them. Only by one's grasp of "the prejudice of completeness" can the complete truth in text be obtained.[12] The key issue, then, is how to construct "the prejudice of completeness"? Gadamer never gives us an explicit answer. He only posits the "fusion of horizons", which means the fusion of the present horizon and the past one. In his opinion, fusion of horizons would promise a wider horizon that transcends the limits of the present and the past, enabling us to discover more enriching meanings. On the basis of "fusion of horizons", he puts forward another conclusion: "the discovery of the true meaning of a text or a work of art is never finished; it is in fact an infinite process", in which "fresh sources of error constantly excluded", and "new sources of understanding are continually emerging that reveal unsuspected elements of meaning".[13] All of these depend on "the temporal distance that performs the filtering process".[14] Gadamer's findings help justify different kinds of reasonable interpretations. Here, let's clarify the question Gadamer discusses. What he attempts to explicate is how an interpreter located in the present context can set out to understand and interpret historical texts, which have a long temporal distance from we are now. If we transform this question from historical context to cross-cultural context, from a local researcher's hermeneutic work on historical texts to a local researcher's hermeneutic work on the other's text, from the temporal distance in history to the spatial and temporal distance between different cultures, I think Gadamer's conclusion also holds true.

Now, I'll try to combine Gadamer's "fusion of horizons" with other theories, exploring how cultural studies can turn a local scholar's fore-understanding into productive resources. First, there is indeed historical distance, as noted by Gadamer, between the present and the past in cross-cultural studies. Fusion of horizons is not to cancel the distance, but rather render the distance productive and provide fresh resources for textual interpretation. Second, apart from the historical distance, a more important distance in cross-cultural studies is the (spatial) distinction between local cultures and the other's cultures. Fusion of horizons therefore begets the question of how to translate the local cultural context into positive resources. I suggest two possible approaches. First, as far as cross-cultural studies are concerned, fusion of horizons can take the form of contextual fusion, which means a process from local contextualization to re-contextualization (of the other) to fusion of different contexts. Second, cross-cultural studies are usually accompanied by a cyclic process from assimilation to accommodation in the sense of genetic epistemology of the subject, a process that expands a local researcher's horizon in cross-cultural studies.

Let's start with the first approach. Introducing the other's text to a local culture's context is the first step of cross-cultural studies. At the beginning, the local hermeneutic scholars in their reading of the other's text usually depend on their fore-understanding. However, this is far from the end. Cross-cultural studies need to realize the transfer of contexts, that is to say, to construct a cultural context for the other's text through imagination. There is an old Chinese saying to the effect that "put oneself in others' position", which means we must enter into the other's context to understand them. This is "de-contextualization", the second step of cross-cultural studies, which means one's entry into the other's culture in an imagined way, putting aside the restraint of local contexts for the time being. Of course, such an imagined transfer would depend on the researcher's knowledge about the other's culture and other relevant expertise. The third step is to arrive at the in-betweenness of contexts, a state much like Gadamer's "fusion of horizons". To be more specific, it means the hermeneutic scholar can shuttle between local context and the other's context, developing an inter-contextual relation or tension.[15] At this point, two kinds of context affect the other's text being interpreted. Gadamer rightly remarks, "To acquire a horizon means that one learns to look beyond what is close at hand—not in order to look away from it but to see it better, within a larger whole and in truer proportion".[16] However, I want to emphasize that a wider horizon is neither fixed nor constant; rather, it will develop and change over the course of interaction between two different contexts that respectively belong to self and the other. A wider horizon is usually used to influence and discover each other. It means neither slavish adherence to local context nor plunging oneself into the other's culture by rejecting selfhood. In Wang Guowei's apt words, it is the alternation and interaction between the state of "I am present" and that of "I am absent".[17] In this sense, the productive dynamics behind one's interpretation of the other's text in cross-cultural studies is the cultural interaction between self and the other, the incessant dialogue between self and the other. Here, the interpreter's fore-understanding and cultural elements in the other's text are mixed to such a degree that they are neither the pure product of self's fore-understanding nor the facile impact of the context of the other's text. It is at this point where what Said describes as "a more independent, or more skeptical, thinker" who "might have had different views" can show up; similarly, it is in this sense that Gadamer's "new sources of understanding" might emerge. All those Orientalist cross-cultural interpretations are evidently no more than self-serving and parochial understanding.

Now, let's turn to another issue, which is that local interpreters in cross-cultural studies are also confronted with continuous construction of subjective episteme. According to Jean Piaget's genetic epistemology, hermeneutic activities are carried out within specific cognitive schemes, a key concept central to Kant's epistemology. After Kant, this concept attracts much critical attention from scholars studying the philosophy about subjective cognition. Art psychologist Ernst Gombrich also draws on this concept, analyzing how painters from different cultures represent the same scene in different ways. His explanation is that every cultural scheme, like a filtering mechanism, exerts a potent control over a painter's artistic work. These schemes determine an artist's representation as vocabulary does in a certain language. He proceeds to arrive at an important conclusion: "Painting is an activity, and the artist will therefore tend to see what he paints rather than to paint what he sees".[18] However, for an artist, scheme is not fixed and constant, but rather subject to ongoing assimilation and accommodation, the two of which alternate and evolve together. This is the gist of Jean Piaget's genetic epistemology. In Piaget's opinion, assimilation is the adaptation to familiar stimuli on the part of an interpreter's cognitive scheme, employing the present schemes to understand and interpret stimuli; accommodation, on the contrary, means that some fresh sources of stimuli bring about adjustment and adaptation of scheme.[19] According to this theory, when facing new texts of the other, cross-cultural interpreters will employ his old schemes and at the same time adjust or reconstruct his preexisting schemes so as to accommodate new situations and develop new schemes of understanding and interpretation. By using this principle to explain fusion of contexts or horizons, we may regard an interpreter's role as the continuous construction of cognitive scheme by balancing assimilation and accommodation. If one interpreter blindly adheres to preexisting schemes and assimilation, it would inevitably lead to biases, misunderstanding, and distortion. Orientalism can be seen as a polarized form of this inclination.

Interpretive strategy about cross-cultural text

Cross-cultural studies bring about productive interpretation of the other's text. By "productive", I mean new meanings arise in cross-cultural interpretation of the other's text. Gadamer rightly says "the discovery of the true meaning of a text or a work of art is never finished; it is in fact an infinite process", in which "fresh sources of error constantly excluded" and "new sources of understanding are continually emerging that reveal unsuspected elements of meaning".[20] Poststructuralism insists on the deconstruction of the centrality of textual meaning, such as Barthes' "the death of the author", Foucault's "author function", Kristeva's "textual productivity and intertextuality", and Fish's "interpretive communities". This intellectual trend has made cross-cultural studies pay close attention to the productivity of textual meaning. Hall's theory on the diversity of decoding suggests that textual interpretation serves the important function of meaning-finding or construction. Such constructiveness refers not only to the discovery of meaning in the other's text, but also to the construction of an interpreter's identity. Unlike the previous identity theories centered on originary or authentic identity, Hall's theory argues that the subject's identification is less about "who we are" than about "what we may become". He asserts that identification is a process of articulation, a game of *différance*, the inner logic of which is not "derived from one", but "more than one".[21] If we combine Hall's theory on multiple decoding and his theory of identification, we can then find a new approach to intercultural studies, that is to say, taking an interpreter's identification and the production of meaning in the other's text as the two sides of a coin. Since there is no such thing as singular, constant textual meaning, since cross-cultural understanding and interpretation is an event between different cultures and between different historical times, every interpreter thus wanders between what Eric D. Hirsch's hermeneutics calls meaning and significance. According to Hirsh, the text has two sides, changeable and unchangeable. The changeable side refers to different understandings made by readers in different times and cultures, whereas the unchangeable side refers to the author's original intention when writing the text. The former means a dynamic relation between the text and its endlessly different readers, who absorb significance from the text; the latter points to the implicit meaning, which is relatively stable, in the text established by the author's explicit purpose.[22] Applying Hirsch's hermeneutics to fusion of horizons or inter-contextuality, it becomes clear that the purpose of cross-cultural studies lies between meaning and significance, and to explain the meaning of the other's text means to shuttle between the two. The so-called fixed and constant textual meaning is no more than an ideal target for hermeneutics. All hermeneutic work is actually a necessarily unfinished endeavor to approach this target.

Now, I think it is necessary to put forward a new term, "inter-interpretations". In the humanities, the most interesting, and the most difficult, part of cross-cultural understanding and interpretation is inter-interpretations, an exceedingly complicated issue. To be more specific, inter-interpretation in cross-cultural studies means a certain text being understood and interpreted differently in various cultures and the interaction of these interpretations. During a text's travel from its local culture to an alien culture, its indigenous interpretations are different from its newly acquired meanings in the target culture. The transformation of interpretations leads to complicated, differing, and conflicting interpretation, pervasion, integration, and resistance, among other relations. From exporting a text through its reception to returning to the mother culture, the interpretations of this certain text are exposed mutual influences from different cultures. As Hirsch would put it, the textual meaning is repeatedly being enriched and complicated by new discoveries of "significance". Although the humanities studies are usually individualistic, all studies are subject to the restraints of the interpretive codes in interpretive communities. Only in such interpretive communities can an interpretation be historical, communicable, and intelligible. The significance of pure intersubjectivity is again brought to the fore.

Finally, I'll dwell upon the complicated relations between negotiation and constructivism in cross-cultural understanding and interpretation. As mentioned before, cross-cultural studies are not a travel of theories, with a self-denied interpreter. However, I don't concur with the Foucauldian proposition that all discourses are merely deliberate construct, there being no such thing as a real entity or truth. In my opinion, construction in cross-cultural studies, more precisely speaking, is a kind of "negotiable construct", rather than willful distortion or misinterpretation as in Orientalism. Therefore, interpreting the other's text, as far as cross-cultural studies is concerned, is a process of negotiation in "interpretive communities", a process rigorously regulated by multiple contexts, historicity, intercultural communication, and interpretive communities. I think negotiation here is a descriptive, rather than prescriptive, notion, which illustrates the interrelatedness and reciprocity between different interpretations in cross-cultural studies.

So far, I have made use of a series of concepts with regard to "inter-" to prescribe interpretive principles and strategies in cross-cultural interpretation of the other's text. These concepts shed light on the nature of relationality in my theorization. To borrow a vivid term from Engels behind the cross-cultural interpretation of the other's text is an axiom of "parallelogram".[23] This axiom tells us that history consists of various conflicting wills, which work together to form "parallelograms" comprised of countless parameters of force, "parallelograms", which in turn form a totality of interaction. Cross-cultural studies are none other than the overall "parallelogram" made of innumerable smaller ""parallelograms", that is to say, the individual interpreters' interpretations. The interplay of negotiation and construction is unstoppable, because without negotiation, construction is impossible and vice versa. Such is the dialectics of cross-cultural interpretation of the other's text.

Notes

1 Thomas Kuhn. *The Essential Tension*. Chicago: University of Chicago Press, 1977. pp.340–351.
2 Wolfgang Iser. *How to Do Theory*. Oxford: Blackwell, 2006. pp.5–10.
3 Stuart Hall. "The Television Discourse – Encoding and Decoding", in *Studying Culture: An Introductory Reader*. Eds. Ann Gray and Jim McGuigan. London: Arnold, 1997. pp.32–34.
4 See Zhou Xian, "Ibsen's and Munch's Mirror-Image of China", in *Comparative Chinese Literature* 1 (2012). pp.59–69.
5 See Zhou Xian, "Brecht's Seduction and Our 'Misreading'", in *Theatre Arts* 4 (1998). pp.42–56.
6 Edward Said. *Orientalism*. New York: Penguin, 1978. pp.6–7.
7 Jürgen Habermas. "Social Analysis and Communicative Competence", in *Social Theory: The Multicultural & Classic Readings*. Ed. Charles Lemert. Boulder: Westview, 1993. p.416.
8 See Jordan Zlatev, et al, eds., *The Shared Mind: Perspectives on Intersubjectivity*. Amsterdam: John Benjamins, 2008.
9 See Keith, Kenneth, *Cross Cultural Psychology: Contemporary Themes and Perspectives*. Oxford: Blackwell, 2010.
10 Hans-Georg Gadamer. *Truth and Method*. London: Continuum, 2004. p.294.
11 Hans-Georg Gadamer. *Truth and Method*. p.295.
12 Ibid.
13 Hans-Georg Gadamer. *Truth and Method*. p.298.
14 Ibid.
15 Recent research on cross-cultural interactions of immigrants into the culture of the other has found that such interactions are characterized by three stages: the first stage is confusion; the second, delayed understanding; and the third, anticipation. The three-stage model also applies to the interpretation of the other's text by the native interpreter specializing in cross-cultural studies. See Anna Mindess, *Reading Between the Signs: Intercultural Communication for Sign Language Interpreters*. Boston: Intercultural Press, 2006. p.157.
16 Hans-Georg Gadamer. *Truth and Method*. p.304.

17 Wang Guowei names two different realms in Words on Earth: "The realm of me, with me to see things, so things are tinted with my color. The realm without me, with things to see things; I cannot distinguish me from things". *Wang Guowei's Essays on Scholarship*. Ed. Fu Jie. Beijing: China Social Science Press, 1997. pp.319–320.
18 Richard Woodfield, ed. *The Essential Gombrich*. London: Phaidon, 1996. p.107.
19 Piaget writes, "Taking the term in its broadest sense, 'assimilation' may be used to describe the action of the organism on surrounding objects, in so far as this action depends on previous behaviour involving the same or similar objects…Conversely, the environment acts on the organism and, following the practice of biologists, we can describe this converse action by the term 'accommodation', it being understood that the individual never suffers the impact of surrounding stimuli as such, but they simply modify the assimilatory cycle by accommodating him to themselves". See Jean Piaget, *The Psychology of Intelligence*. London: Routledge, 2003. p.8–9.
20 Hans-Georg Gadamer. *Truth and Method*. p.298.
21 Stuart Hall and Paul de Gey, eds. *Questions of Cultural Identity*. p.4.
22 Hirsch writes: "In 1960 I first proposed the analytical distinction between two aspects of textual interpretation. One of them, meaning, was fixed and immutable; the other, significance, was open to change…*Meaning*, then, may be conceived as a self-identical schema whose boundaries are determined by an originating speech event, while *significance* may be conceived as a relationship drawn between that self-identical meaning and something, anything, else". See E. D. Hirsch, Jr., "Meaning and Significance Reinterpreted", in *Critical Inquiry* 2 (1984). p.202–204.
23 Engels writes: "[H]istory is made in such a way that the final result always arises from conflicts between many individual wills, of which each in turn has been made what it is by a host of particular conditions of life. Thus there are innumerable intersecting forces, an infinite series of parallelograms of forces which give rise to one resultant — the historical event. This may again itself be viewed as the product of a power which works as a whole unconsciously and without volition". See "Engels to J. Bloch", in *Selected Works of Marx and Engels*. Beijing: People's Publishing House, 1972. p.478.

7 Globalization and cultural identity

There is an interesting story about the earl of the Ho in "The Floods of Autumn", a chapter of *Zhuang Zi*.

The time of the autumnal floods was come, and the hundred streams were all discharging themselves into the Ho. Its current was greatly swollen so that across its channel from bank to bank, one could not distinguish an ox from a horse. On this the (Spirit-)earl of the Ho laughed with delight, thinking that all the beauty of the world was to be found in his charge. Along the course of the river, he walked east till he came to the North Sea, over which he looked, with his face to the east, without being able to see where its waters began. Then, he began to turn his face round, looked across the expanse, (as if he were) confronting Zo, and said with a sigh, "What the vulgar saying expresses about him who has learned a hundred points (of the Tao), and thinks that there is no one equal to himself, was surely spoken of me". (秋水时至，百涘渚崖之间，不辨牛马。于是焉河伯欣然自喜，以为天下之美，为尽在已，顺流而东行，至于北海，东面而视，不见水端，于是焉河伯始旋其面目，望洋向若而叹曰：'野语有之曰：闻道百，以为莫几若者，'我之谓也！")[1]

To interpret it in another way, we can liken the earl's travel to the North Sea to the Chinese people's response to globalization. Before seeing the North Sea, the earl is rather complacent, having no idea about the outside world. Upon setting foot on the North Sea, he began to realize how parochial he used to be, because the beauty of the world more often than not lies beyond one's horizon. In other words, when limited by a narrow and fixed horizon, we are usually immune to identity crisis. Only when one outgrows his own horizon can he realize the differences between his familiar society and culture and the new ones he encounters, acquiring new opinions about himself. This is the representation of identity crisis.

Today, the globalized world is like the "North Sea", which dismantles the old worldviews of countless "earls of Ho" during their encounters with the others. The tension and dialogue created by cultural diversity and differences help them understand the distinction between "me" and "him", and "us" and "them". It is the practice of difference carried out in cultural exchange that brings to the fore the question of cultural identity, either individual or collective, as a burning issue.

Globalization and "identity crisis"

Identity usually refers to one's cognition about oneself. Many studies have shown that self-knowledge is not so much the outcome of isolated "*cogito*" as the "product" of comparing and contrasting *I* and the other. I call it the "Effect of the Earl of Ho". The cultural impact caused by globalization is rather complicated and far-reaching, involving many different nations and cultures that are forced to encounter and collide with one another, bringing about complex consequences. Jorge Larrain points out,

> Whenever there is a conflictive and asymmetric encounter between different cultures, be it by means of invasion, colonization or extensive forms of communication, the issue of cultural identity arises. The question of cultural identity does not usually arise in situations of relative isolation, prosperity and stability. For identity to become an issue, a period of instability and crisis, a threat to the old-established ways, seems to be required, especially if this happens in the presence of, or in relation to, other cultural formations. As Kobena Mercer has put it, "identity only becomes an issue when it is in crisis, when something assumed to be fixed, coherent and stable is displaced by the experience of doubt and uncertainty". This provides us with a clue as to what is normally meant by identity. The main ideas associated with it seem to be those of permanence, cohesion and recognition. When we talk of identity, we usually imply a certain continuity, an overall unity and self-awareness. Most of the time these characteristics are taken for granted, unless there is a perceived threat to an established way of life.[2]

Why is it so that "in a relatively isolated, prosperous, and stable environment cultural identity is seldom an issue"? It is because identity, all in all, is a problem of differences, which are imperceptible unless compared with dissimilar things or environments. As in psychology, self-knowledge is usually acquired through the lens of the others. Thus, we can regard globalization as a process that elicits our awareness of differences, and a process that brings about our reflection upon identification, and a process that would inevitably lead to identity crisis.

The reason why globalization results in identity crisis is rather complex. To answer this question, we must start with the dichotomy of globalization and localization. The true meaning of globalization is always contentious, its different aspects being stressed in different definitions. John Tomlinson's observation is inspiring. He contends that globalization means complex connectivity of the modern world, referring to "the rapidly developing and ever-densening network of interconnections and interdependences that characterize modern social life".[3] If so, what does the complex connectivity look like? Some argue that it is a kind of "homogenization", which means every corner of the world is turning more and more similar and local heterogeneity is facing unprecedented risk of extinction. Some argue that it is no more than "Westernization", which means the economic, political, and cultural domination of the West over non-Western ones. The others argue that globalization is a process of generalization that overcomes the limitation of particularization. All of these sayings share one thing in common: globalization acts as a sort of universal or homogeneous external force, which unites different places into one. Mike Featherstone writes,

> The process of globalization suggests simultaneously two images of culture. The first image entails the extension of outwards of a particular culture to its limit, the global. Heterogeneous cultures become incorporated and integrated into a dominant culture which eventually covers the whole world. The second image points to the compression of cultures. Things formerly held apart are now brought into contact and juxtaposition... The first image suggests a process of conquest and unification of the global space. The world becomes a singular domesticated space, a place where everyone becomes assimilated into a common culture.[4]

In fact, the consequences of globalization are rather complex, as homogenization and universalization are merely a part of the whole picture, the other part being that this process at the same time stimulates strong impulse of localization. Bauman rightly points out that "globalization divides as much as it unites—the causes of division being identical with those which promote the uniformity of the globe".[5] We may take its unifying effect as a process of the world being integrated into a whole, and regard the dividing effect as a process that pushes each local culture to stick to its indigenous particularities. Many globalization scholars have noticed such a contradictory trend. For example, Jonathan Friedman in *Cultural Identity and Global Process* argues that globalizing and localizing are two tendencies that appear at the same time and work on each other; Roland Robertson in *Globalization: Social Theory and Global Culture* stresses that universalism and particularism are the indivisible movements pertinent to globalization. In my opinion, the reason why globalization and localization, two seemingly antipodal tendencies, are actually concurrent is that both revolve around two axes: a spatial axis, which is an index for how the local and the outside world are related; a temporal axis, on which the relevance between the present (the modern) and the past (the tradition) is marked. If the core of identity is difference, difference must have manifested itself in the two interconnected axes. Integration results in differentiation; globalization gives rise to localization; universalism elicits particularism. On the spatial axis, our differences from the outside world cause our self-identification; on the temporal axis, the current changes give birth to our identification with and nostalgia for the past, to our concern about and reflection on the demise of tradition. Obviously, modernization and globalization go hand in hand—industrialization, urbanization, commercialization, rationalization, differentiation, bureaucracy, social division of labor force, the growth of individualism, and the rise of nation-state bring about the expansion of globalization, but at the same time beget acute vigilance against or even boycott of such a trend. The backlash against globalizing usually takes the form of reaffirmation of indigenous culture and nostalgia for a secure, authentic "homeland" in the past. Such a contradictory tendency manifests itself in a neologism, "glocalization", which originally refers to a marketing strategy of adapting alien goods to a local market. This term is now applied to broadly explain a cultural phenomenon, that is to say, the concurrence of globalization and localization.

In the light of the symbiosis of globalization and localization, there is another dimension of globalization and identity crisis, that is to say, the global condensing of time-space and disappearance of placeness. With the acceleration of modernization, in particular the rapid growth of transportation and communication technologies, the globe is shrinking drastically. Our traveling speed spectacularly increases, with the invention of vehicles from carriage to train, and, finally, to jet planes. As a result, the Earth is getting smaller and smaller, giving rise to some terms such as "global village". David Harvey says that in the 1960s, the earth is approximately 1/15 of its size in the sixteenth century. By "time-space compression", he mean to signal "processes that so revolutionize the objective qualities of space and time that we are forced to alter, sometimes in quite radical ways, how we represent the world to ourselves".[6] Harvey holds that in a relatively isolated traditional society, a certain venue has its own autonomy and authority; when time-space is compressed, time is condensed into space, or space into time, simultaneity and ephemerality being commonplace in everyday life. Harvey writes,

> Mass television ownership coupled with satellite communication makes it possible to experience a rush of images from different spaces almost simultaneously, collapsing the world's spaces into a series of images on a television screen. The whole world can watch the Olympic Games, the World Cup, the fall of a dictator, a political summit, a deadly tragedy... while mass tourism, films made in spectacular locations, make a wide range of simulated or vicarious experiences of what the world contains available to many people. The image of places and spaces becomes as open to production and ephemeral use as any other.[7]

Obviously, globalization induces cultural diversity and the influx of heterogeneous elements, which to different degrees alter the original form of indigenous life. Owing to the unprecedented convenience of telecommunication and transportation, Marx's famous prophesy has now come true: "All fixed, fast-frozen relations, with their train of ancient and venerable prejudices and opinions, are swept away, all new-formed ones become antiquated before they can ossify. All that is solid melts into air".[8] In my view, the ephemerality and simultaneity produced by the compression of time-space are actually the two sides of the same coin, both being symbiotic and indivisible. It is the reason why Giddens believes that the era of modernity sets into motion" "the sheer pace of change", which explains why "traditional civilisations may have been more dynamic than other pre-modern systems, but the rapidity of change in conditions of modernity is extreme".[9]

This tendency is most manifest in the separation of time and space and its "emptiness". The "presence" of traditional life is now replaced by the "absence" of globalized life now, which then gives rise to the so-called "disembedding". By "disembedding", Giddens means "the 'lifting out' of social relations from local contexts of interaction and their reconstructing across indefinite spans of time-space".[10] The "present" system of high stability and slow change in the traditional society has been destroyed, replaced by the profound impact of distant events on the local "life world". While Giddens calls it "distanciation", Bauman describes this condition as "liquidity". Bauman discovers that modernity is after all time's victory over space, because time is positive and active, and space is awkward and passive. Therefore, more means of high-speed transport appears. "'Solid' modernity was an era of mutual engagement. 'Fluid' modernity is the epoch of disengagement, elusiveness, facile escape and hopeless chase. In 'liquid' modernity, it is the most elusive, those free to move without notice, who rule".[11] When the obstacle of space is now overcome by the compression of time-space, what Bauman describes as "liquid" state inevitably dissolves the authenticity and presence (*Anwesenheit*) of an otherwise stable traditional society. Today, we have already been deeply influenced by the "liquidation" effect. It is worth noting that when the ephemerality and simultaneity brought about by time-space compression add up to more volatility and uncertainty in local life, identity crisis is inevitable. Our response to such a crisis in turn leads to some complicated or even contradictory impulse. As Harvey says, "The greater the ephemerality, the more pressing the need to discover or manufacture some kind of eternal truth that might lie therein".[12] The loss of tradition results in the impulse to cherish and sustain the tradition; similarly, in the context of compressed time-space, cultural identity, be it individual, collective, or even national, will become a more and more urgent issue.

The correlation between globalization and identity crisis is also manifest in the cultural hybridity induced by globalization. Hybridity is a result of the influx of heterogeneous factors. The term "hybridity" is used to refer to the traits of colonial cultures, frequently investigated within the framework of "us vs. them", a dichotomy that implies the invasion or even conquest of local discourse ("us") by colonial discourse (the Other). Here, I invoke this term in a broader sense, referring to the entangled condition of heterogeneous cultural factors brought about by globalization. Put another way, hybridity is a third state of neither-local-nor-foreign. As Friedman points out,

> Cultures flow into on another and mix. And the more movement of culture in the world, by means of migration, media transmission, etc., the more mixture until finally we have a hybridized world equivalent in cultural terms to the economic globalization process. This can occur because cultures are substances that flow into one another from disparate origins producing mixtures that maintain the properties of those origins.[13]

The more the prominent globalization is, the greater such a hybridity. In traditional societies, those relatively autonomous and indigenous cultures are now under threat, giving way to the influx of foreign cultures in the name of "traveling" in local contexts. A myriad of alien cultural elements, such as translated works, Hollywood blockbusters, online games, cartoons, foreign shows and contests, exotic fashions, become trendy in China. Behind such phenomena lurk some deep and complex values and ideologies. Of course, it is not an either-or issue, for the imported alien cultures, upon its entry into local context, are unlike what they are in their original environment. Rather, the traveling foreign cultures are actually conditioned by their sophisticated interrelation with local cultures and the convergence of two. Hence, local misinterpretation, distortion, and appropriation are not only possible but also necessary. As Stuart Hall's three "decoding" models suggest, local interpretation sometimes can change the original textual and symbolic meaning, breeding new sources of interpretation and understanding. Hybridity demonstrates the "alternative" status of cultures being mixed and converged. As Hall writes,

> "[T]he hybridity of all cultures as something which is a product of the encounter between cultures. Hybridity points to the situation of being neither inside nor outside a culture, but in a third space on the borderline, where one is inside and outside at the same time".[14]

Admittedly, the infiltration of alien cultures is everything but time-specific, but it is certainly the case that the reign of telecommunication technologies, globalized media, and virtual reality has rendered such a hybridity virtually unprecedented either in terms of extent or in range. Some scholars are of the opinion that in this "Third Space", a kind of "cosmopolitan identity" has come into being and that the so-called global culture (as the "Third Culture") is around the corner. However, I think this observation is largely problematic. On the one hand, the hybridity induced by incoming alien cultures in the Third Space is likely to jeopardize the traditional cultural identity; on the other hand, hybridity, as a form of experience, is bound to bring about some complicated and heterogeneous impulses, some of which even result in cultural fundamentalism. Globalization can endanger the existence of differences, on the one hand, and create new differences that reinforce our awareness of disparity, on the other. As Roland Robertson aptly says, "[A]s the entire world becomes more compressed and singular the bases of doing identity are increasingly, but problematically 'shared,' even though they may at the same time collide".[15] One can interpret this sentence in an inverted way: the "shared" bases of doing identity are actually an acknowledgment of differences, or illustrate the "controversiality" of such sharing.

The time-space compression and hybridity in the age of globalization weaken the identity-doing played out in the local space of traditional culture. Generally speaking, the stability and homogeneity of some specific space play a vital role in sustaining identity, whereas the spatial fluidity and hybridity induced by globalization render the traditional space's identity-doing uncertain and diverse. As Harvey notes, we are committed to

> the search for personal or collective identity, the search for secure moorings in a shifting world. Place-identity, in this collage of superimposed spatial images that implode in upon us, becomes an important issue, because everyone occupies a space of individuation (a body, a room, a home, a shaping community, a nation), and how we individuate ourselves shapes identity.[16]

Given the influence and infiltration of external space, and owing to the shrinking importance of local presence, particularly due to the facile invasion of local space by media and network that can penetrate spatial obstacles easily, what Giddens calls "distanciation" is therefore reinforced. Or, as Joshua Meyrowitz argues, what kind of information we receive has nothing to do with the place where we are.[17] The aforementioned simultaneity is manifested in the synchronous reception of information in different locales. The local information field abounds with all kinds of incoming information. The life world originally characterized by indigenous characteristics is now more and more complicated and diverse. It is in such a context that place's identity-doing function becomes problematic, owing to the confusing space created by globalization. When describing his notion of "imagined communities", Anderson stresses that hundreds of millions of people form imagined connection with one another through certain languages and texts, which is actually a sea change that has taken place in the contemporary world. As Tomlinson emphasizes,

> The opposition we are thus pushed towards is one between local direct face-to-face interaction and experience, and a qualitatively different order of mediated experience that we, in the developed world, have increasingly routine access to in our localities.[18]

From the connection between globalization and locality, we can see a series of binary oppositions, such as ephemerality vs. eternality, simultaneity vs. immediacy, distanciation vs. localization, absence vs. presence, complexity vs. unitarity, and decentralization vs. centralization. It is within these binary structures of interaction and tension that we find identity a pressing issue, and that the form and structure of identity undergo significant changes.

Identity building in locality

Globalization, in my view, is a double-edged sword. It results in the impasse of traditional culture and consequently identity crises on the one hand, and provides local cultures with precious opportunities to reconstruct themselves, on the other. In this light, globalization is actually an incentive for cultural identity and its crisis, but the contemporary transformation of cultural identity is of positive consequences. Fredric Jameson eloquently writes,

> Thus, if you insist on the cultural contents of this new communication form, I think you will slowly emerge into a postmodern celebration of difference and differentiation: suddenly all the cultures around the world are placed in tolerant contact with each other in a kind of immense cultural pluralism which it would be very difficult not to welcome. Beyond that, beyond the dawning celebration of cultural difference, and often very closely linked to it, is a celebration of the emergence of a whole immense range of groups, races, genders, ethnicities, into the speech of the public sphere; a falling away of

those structures that condemned whole segments of the population to silence and to subalternity; a worldwide growth of popular democratization—why not?—which seems to have some relationship to the evolution of the media, but which is immediately expressed by a new richness and variety of cultures in the new world space.[19]

Here, Jameson tries to anatomize a complicated consequence of globalization, that is, the endorsement and celebration of difference. If one can say that cultural identity is to identify with and reflect upon difference, globalization then not only brings about identity crisis but also enhances our tolerance of difference and awareness of identity.

The evolution of globalization has an actual effect on difference making and identity issues: by collecting and grouping local symbolic resources, globalization can probe into some ingrained *memes* (cultural "genes") within our specific identity. As we know, language is at the very core of the symbolic for national communities. A language can unite some people and at the same time distinguish them from others speaking different languages. For each one, the mother tongue is a foundational element of identifying with one's homeland and culture. As an everyday practice of signifying, literature plays an indispensable role in the process of creating identity and consciousness of difference. Since China's reform and opening-up, literature, or cultural practice as a whole, has witnessed many a trend and inclination, which to different degrees concerns the building of local cultural identity. Recently, China is trying to reorient itself to Confucian culture and to champion Chinese traditions. The so-called "Root Seeking Literature" and "cultural fever", the debate over Vernacular Poetry and Metrical Poetry, and some influential Chinese novels such as *White Deer Plain* and *Wolf Totem* can all be regarded as a sort of response to the globalization and modernization of Chinese literature and culture. More broadly speaking, language, along with other forms of cultural symbolic systems—ranging from plastic art, film, TV to drama, from folk art to festive rituals—is deeply entwined with local cultural identification. The recent vogue of historical TV drama, the rise of folk crosstalk, the emphasis on the preservation of intangible cultural heritage, the construction fever of historical museum and folk museum, the cultural relic fever, the fad of Tang suit, and other traditional costumes can all be interpreted as a part of identity crisis under the pressure of globalization and our stress responses to such a crisis. A rediscovery and celebration of these traditional symbolic resources are not accidental at all; our exploitation and regrouping of these resources are necessary initiatives taken to address the current identity crisis. As Anthony Smith writes,

> For the nation and its identity is expressed and revealed in the 'authentic' memories, symbols, myths, heritage and vernacular culture of the 'people' who form a community of history and destiny, and whose intellectuals and professionals seek to authenticate, safeguard and embody that heritage and culture through cultural and educational institutions in an autonomous homeland. The need for protection, recognition and belonging encourages

the nation and its members, especially its intellectuals and professionals, to seek to institutionalize their symbols, culture and heritage in and through a national state which will both embody that heritage, symbols and culture and fulfil these needs. So the intellectuals and professionals who guard and run the cultural and educational institutions in the autonomous homeland or national state form the locus of the nationalism of the popular ethnic nation; they do so not just in terms of their material and status interests, but as an expression and embodiment of the identity, unity and autonomy of the people of the nation, who are generally represented by ethnic intellectuals and professionals who direct the nation's cultural policies and authenticate its heritage, culture and symbols on behalf of "the people".[20]

In the light of culture in a broader sense, such a local response to identity reconstruction has manifested itself in many domains, not limited to literature. Over the recent years, as globalization is played out in China, there emerge in local culture a series of noteworthy phenomena, which are closely related to the local construction of cultural identity. Recently, a catchy term is nostalgia, which not only appears in all kinds of literary works but also manifests itself in various cultural representations, ranging from media to arts. Undoubtedly, the process of globalization begets many complicated responses locally, one of which is our anxiety about the loss of homeland and the impulse to reconstruct it. Mike Featherstone discovers that a backlash against globalization is to reaffirm or even strengthen local cultures. Given the loss of a sense of place induced by what Joshua Meyrowitz names "electronic media culture", it is natural for people to pine for a sweet homeland idealized in memory or tradition. In his view, homesickness is a response to "the loss of home in the sense of physical locale", whereas nostalgia points to "a more general loss of a sense of wholeness, moral certainty, genuine social relationship, spontaneity and expressiveness".[21] Authenticity is enticing only because the present life is becoming more and more ephemeral and shallow. The latest fever of reconstructing local cultures is a case in point. For example, traditional customs, festivals, folk customs, old streets, Chinese opera, old workshops, folk houses, native dialects, a peddler's hawking, and traditional food can all be regarded as the representation of our thirst for the sense of home. The reconstruction of cultural symbols of homeland is also widely found in works of literature and media programs. One's attachment to a sense of home is tantamount to a nostalgia for something lost, a demand for something scarce, which Featherstone calls "willful nostalgia". Homesickness or nostalgia, as an enactment of collective memory, is actually our remembrance of the good old days. Over the course of rebuilding the past, it satisfies people's seemingly innocent yearning for the past. Like the elders reminiscing about their golden days in childhood, our nostalgic reconstruction of the past must have entailed idealization and beautification in the light of our present need. What reappears are always what we are in dire need of in reality. Therefore, the past always means the memorable and cherishable in one's nostalgia. At the same time, "willful nostalgia" also glosses over, or even dismantles the bitter and grim part of the old days, a process that renders the past innocent and desirable for people attracted by its particular charm today. As I mentioned earlier, a locale is vital for sustaining identity, but the time-space compression and hybridity brought about by globalization have comprised such an identity-sustaining function served by traditional locales. Therefore, contemporary culture is crucial for the material and spiritual reconstruction of all sorts of "homes". Paul Connerton writes,

> "We conserve our recollections by referring them to the material milieu that surrounds us. It is to our social spaces — those which we occupy, which we frequently retrace with our steps, where we always have access, which at each moment we are capable of mentally reconstructing — that we must turn our attention, if our memories are to reappear".[22]

For this reason, the preservation of traditional cultural relics and the restoration of them have become urgent tasks today.

In fact, reconstructing the sense of home is always associated with festive rituals. As Hobsbawm would put it, these festive rituals in our time can be interpreted as "invented tradition", which serves a constructive function similar to Anderson's "imagined communities". A salient example is the recent debate over the defense of local festivals, which are increasingly "marginalized" by a variety of foreign festivals to such a degree that some advocate "to defend our Spring Festival". The fall and rise of traditional festivals, however, is not an evidentiary story to illustrate the aphorism that "fortune was in the east of bank 30 years ago, but turns to west when 30 years has passed", nor is it a proof of the cyclicity of fashion. Rather, it sheds light on the multiple influences of globalization on local cultures. Some researchers find that under the condition of increasing hybridity of globalized cultures, traditional festivals play a crucial role in identity construction. Featherstone finds that

> A sense of home is sustained by collective memory, which itself depends upon ritual performances, bodily practices and commemorative ceremonies. The important point here is that our sense of the past does not primarily depend upon written sources, but rather on enacted ritual performances and the formalism of ritual language. This may entail commemorative rituals such as weddings, funerals, Christmas, New Year, and participation or involved spectatorship at local, regional and national ritual (e.g. royal weddings, nation days, etc.).[23]

In this regard, Connerton has a more blunt statement: "All rites are repetitive, and repetition automatically implies continuity with the past".[24] In other words, traditional festivals are not only a repetitive rite but some rite through which we are connected with our past, retrieving the cultural tradition we belong to and collapsing the distance between the past and the present and finally escaping from fragmentation and shallowness and returning to authenticity. As Connerton aptly says,

Commemorative ceremonies share two features of all other rituals, formalism and performativity; and in so far as they function effectively as mnemonic devices, they are able to execute that function in large part because they possess such features. But commemorative ceremonies are distinguishable from all other rituals by the fact that they explicitly refer to prototypical persons and events, whether these are understood to have a historical or a mythological existence; and by virtue of that fact rites of this sort possess a further characteristic and one that is distinctively their own. We may describe this feature as that of ritual re-enactment, and it is a quality of cardinal importance in the shaping of communal memory.[25]

It is by means of collective participation that cultural identity—that is to say, identifying "us" with "imagined communities"—is incessantly produced.

In short

In this section, I have discussed the complex situation of cultural identity brought about by globalization: identity crisis on the one hand, and response to this crisis (in the form of strengthened identity) on the other. Given the conflicting relation between the two, identity itself takes a variety of forms. Radical anti-traditionalism and conservative fundamentalism constitute the two poles of this contradiction. Although the renaissance or invention of tradition has an indispensable role to play in the formation of contemporary cultural identity, we must be fully aware of the utopian character of such a position on identity, which pursues nothing but authenticity, purity, and essence, sometimes at the cost of disaster. For the same reason, radical anti-traditionalism is also problematic, because of its contempt for local cultures and traditions. In particular, I want to point out that cultural identity in the context of globalization is first of all a process of opening-up and substantiation, a process of enrichment and diversification. It is neither necessary nor impossible to fantasize about a facile return to the past. Furthermore, globalization being an unstoppable trend, we need to take seriously the impact of globalization on locality. The benchmark against which we think about cultural identity is no so much the irretrievable past as the present socio-cultural context we are living in. Our current need determines the gist of cultural identification. For this reason, we can conclude that globalization and local cultural identity may bring out the best in each other. Those binary relations, such as tradition vs. modernity, the local vs. the foreign, work together to shape the open-ended structure of identity and mold the collective identity of contemporary Chinese people.

Notes

1 Sun Tonghai, trans & eds. *Zhuangzi*. Beijing: China Bookstore, 2007. p.243.
2 Jorge Larrain. *Ideology and Cultural Identity: Modernity and the Third World Presence*. New York: Polity Press, 1994. pp.142–143.
3 John Tomlinson, *Globalization and Culture*. New York: John Wiley & Sons, 2013. p.1.
4 Mike Featherstone. *Undoing Culture: Globalization, Postmodernism, and Identity*. London: Sage, 1995. p.6.
5 Zygmunt Bauman. *Globalization: The Human Consequences*. New York: Columbia UP, 1998. p.2.

6   David Harvey. *The Condition of Postmodernity*. Cambridge, MA: Blackwell Publishers, 1989. p.240.
7   David Harvey. *The Condition of Postmodernity*. p.293.
8   Karl Marx and Friedrich Engels. "The Communist Manifesto", in *Selected Works of Marx and Engels, Vol. 1*. Beijing: People's Publishing House, 1972. p.254.
9   Anthony Giddens. *The Consequences of Modernity*. New York: John Wiley & Sons, 2013. p.4.
10 Anthony Giddens. *The Consequences of Modernity*. p.21.
11 Zygmun Bauman. *Liquid Modernity*. New York: Polity, 2000. p.120.
12 David Harvey. *The Condition of Postmodernity*. p.292.
13 Jonathan Friedman. "The Hybridization of Roots and the Abhorrence of the Bush", in *Space of Culture*. Eds. Mike Featherstone and Scott Lash. London: Sage, 1999. pp.235–236.
14 Mike Featherstone and Scott Lash, eds. *Space of Culture*. p.10.
15 Roland Robertson. *Globalization: Social Theory and Global Culture*. New York: Sage Publications, 1998. p.99.
16 David Harvey. *The Condition of Postmodernity*. p.302.
17 See Joshua Meyrowitz. *No Sense of Place*. New York: Oxford University Press, 1985.
18 John Tomlinson. *Globalization and Culture*. p.156.
19 Fredric Jameson. *Valences of the Dialectic*. New York: Verso, 2010. p.437.
20 Anthony Smith. *Nations and Nationalism in a Global Era*. New York: John Wiley & Sons, 2013. p.17.
21 Mike Featherstone. *Undoing Culture: Globalization, Postmodernism and Identity*. p.93.
22 Paul Connerton. *How Societies Remember*. Cambridge: Cambridge UP, 1989. p.37.
23 Mike Featherstone. *Undoing Culture: Globalization, Postmodernism and Identity*. p.94.
24 Paul Connerton. *How Societies Remember*. p.45.
25 Paul Connerton. *How Societies Remember*. p.61.

PART III
Media Culture and Everyday Life

8 The changing landscape of contemporary Chinese media culture

Since the 1990s, Chinese media culture, along with the stunning growth of Chinese economy, has undergone a series of remarkable changes. Thanks to the reform of cultural institutions, the media industry has become more market-oriented, turning into a dualistic structure of administrative regulation and market-based allocation. Such a dualistic system leads to some inherent tension in media culture, which further brings about the structural separation and functional division of political discourse and entertainment discourse, creating a rather complicated media effect. At the same time, the rise of grassroots media stemmed from folk cultures has changed the topography of Chinese media culture, and exerted significant impacts on contemporary society and culture. An inquiry into these issues shows that when Chinese economy is booming and society is making progress, Chinese media culture will be further diversified and enriched, and tensions within media itself will be heightened.

The soaring development of Chinese economy has propelled the profound transformation of all sectors. In 2008, China's GDP exceeded 3 trillion (CNY), ranking the third in the world. In 2010, China's GDP has surpassed Japan, the second largest economy in the world. Obviously, economic reform as a locomotive propels the transformation of Chinese social culture from traditional to modern. The changes in social base will naturally result in the change of superstructure. Everyone living in China can be acutely aware of the sea change in various socio-cultural sectors. Media as a culture is the cultural reality we are in face of everyday, ranging from TV to radio, from newspapers to books, from the Internet to cell-phone messages. When one says "we are living in the world", it more or less means that "we are living in media". The latest epic transformation of media culture is what we are living through.

These changes also arouse strong interest in contemporary China's media culture, not only among Chinese scholars but also abroad.[1] Over the last few years, studies on this topic abound, attracting vehement debates and diverse opinions. In this chapter, I will analyze several trends in the evolution of Chinese media culture since the 1990s and investigate the complex contradictions lurking behind contemporary Chinese society and culture, as well as their implications.

Tensions in media institutions

Since the reform and opening-up initiated in 1978, China has been shifting from planned economy to a market one, aiming to build a socialist market-oriented economy with Chinese characteristics. As suggested by the slightly oxymoronic term "socialist market economy", socialism in the political sense and market economy in the economic sense coexist in China, a design that seems to defy the tenets of classical economics and political theories. It is against this backdrop that Chinese media culture has undergone similarly complex changes, with its institutions gradually morphing into a particular system analogous to "socialist market economy", a system characterized by dualistic media culture. As we know, media is of peculiar importance to modern China's social cultures. Since the New Democratic Revolution (1919–1949), all forms of literature and art are no more than the propaganda devices of the Communist Party, with the purpose of motivating and educating the masses. "To educate through entertainment" is the guiding principle of Chinese media. Prior to the reform and opening-up, all media are the Party's mouthpiece, and the administrative branch has a direct control on the production and transmission of media. Nevertheless, the huge success of economic reform brings both pressure on and opportunities for media culture. The market reform, or the appeal of industrialization, has been changing the makeup of media culture from the outside. Reforming cultural institutions entails a much-needed transformation of such an external pressure into internal momentum, a transformation that can solve the problems of Chinese media in reality.

Generally speaking, there are three reasons to account for the formation of dualistic system in contemporary Chinese media culture.

First, the success of cultural industrialization in Western countries has served as a useful model for the transformation of China's media culture. From Hollywood in the United States to the animation industry in Japan, the highly developed market-based industrialization of media culture is obviously a recommendable path for other countries to take. With the ascendency of China's national power, it is now a pressing mission to boost its soft power. China is not only supposed to be an economic giant but also a cultural power. Therefore, media culture as the most influential channel of culture has to be industrialized.

Second, when China's economic reform has achieved a great success, a reform of cultural establishment naturally tops the agenda. The economic reform has greatly changed the cultural topography and internal structure of China. Some developments, the rise of consumer culture and the gargantuan demand of popular entertainment in particular, render the old-fashioned media culture centering on the Communist mouthpiece function obsolete. Hence, how to construct a new mode of media culture which can both serve the function of political propaganda and that of popular entertainment and how to strike a balance between the two have become the new issues the decision-makers of Chinese media culture must deal with.

Third, the old mode of administration-oriented cultural institutions overburdens the government, some art and media institutions failing to make ends meet and facing grim crises of survival. How to alleviate the government's burden, how to revitalize these flagging cultural institutions, and how to develop cultural industries capable of innovation and self-regeneration are burning questions to be answered. To reform China's cultural institutions is a choice we have to make.

From 1992 onward, the Central Committee of the CPC has adopted new policies to promote the reform of cultural institutions.[2] In 1996, the CPC announced that such reforms should strengthen the positive role of market.[3] The real turning point emerged in 2000, when the Fifth Plenary Session of the Fifteenth Central Committee of the Party explicitly reiterated the objective, method, and procedure of the institutional reform of culture. It was decided that the Chinese government would offer better policies to improve cultural industry, to optimize its regulation of cultural market, and to propel the development of relevant cultural industries.[4]

The market-based institutional reform of media culture is obviously a complicated and systematic project. The first step was to replace the old budget system with a "budget lumpsum", which naturally saves budget making from the administration's intervention. Once this reform was enacted, the gross revenue of China Central Television Station (CCTV) grew from 120 million yuan in 1990 to 5.75 billion yuan in 2000; the number of channels increased from three in 1991 to nine in 2000, and the average broadcasting time rose from 31 hours a day in 1991 to 156 hours a day in 2000. During this period, CCTV spent approximately 1.2 billion yuan on global broadcasting, and by 2000, CCTV's programs reached 98% of countries and regions in the world.[5]

The second step was to integrate different media institutions into several large media conglomerates in order to better address new challenges after China's entry into the WTO. Since 2001, China has set out to merge journalism, publishing, broadcasting, film, television, and showbiz, aiming to enhance the competence of cultural enterprises. By 2002, China had established 72 media groups, including 38 newspaper groups, 10 publishing groups, 5 distribution groups, 12 broadcasting and television groups, and 5 film groups. By the end of 2008, a total of 13 enterprises in China's cultural industry were listed on the stock market, operating on the principle of financing. The biggest change is that mass media, which used to be the propaganda mouthpiece exclusively controlled by the Party, are now a part of China's top strategic mission to develop national "soft power". As State Councilor Liu Yandong said, it is necessary to develop an advanced culture that matches China's newly acquired economic prowess, making it a source of strength for a modernized power like China, and offering spiritual support that enables us to stand high among all the nations in the world.[6] During the aftershock of global financial crises, the State Council in 2009 advanced the "Cultural Industry Revitalization Plan", which emphasized that social benefits should be the top priority, and called for the unity of social and economic benefits, the specific goal being to transform for-profit cultural public institutions into enterprises and complete the shareholding system reform.[7]

Undoubtedly, the transformation of cultural institutions has to a great extent changed the topography of Chinese media culture. But what kinds of change have been brought out by introducing industrialization and market to media in China? Some scholars assert that the commercialization of Chinese media will totally revolutionize the present media culture and bring new challenges to our reality; other scholars believe that the industrialization of media culture is merely an institutional reform and will not lead to any substantial transformation in Chinese medial culture.[8] In my view, the two seemingly conflicting opinions are actually similarly shallow.

Before the reform of cultural institutions, the establishment of media culture remained largely monotonous; no sooner had the market reform been introduced did institutional tension within media culture arise. On the one hand, media culture still has the function of political propaganda on behalf of extant dominant culture, strictly circumscribed by the administrative establishment. On the other hand, the pressure of market economy and the demand of mass entertainment—the effective model of cultural industry in developed countries in particular—exert impact incessantly on the existing construction of media culture. Hence, there is a tension between the old restraints of administration and the new competitions in market, because the two are not totally congruous in terms of media orientation, content production, claim for objective, and transmission process, and would inevitably lead to contradictions, disparities, and friction. Given such a complicated institutional tension, we naturally appeal for structural reform and adjustment to redress the consequent problems, and arrive at a state of equilibrium after a series of complex games. Viewing from the structural-functional perspective of media culture, a salient consequence of this tension is the structural division and functional differentiation of entertainment discourse and political discourse in media.

Division of media discourse

The double system of administration and market in Chinese media culture gives rise to an internal tension that inevitably pushes people to seek for a method to relieve such a tension. Put it another way, the relationship between the demands of media market and the requirements of dominant political propaganda is necessarily contradictory. The former is purely market-oriented, aiming at media industrialization, whereas the latter is ideology-oriented, freighted with the tasks of political propaganda on behalf of the Party and government. If so, how could we redress this tension?

If we pay some attention to the current topography of Chinese media culture, a simple but effective solution is available, which is to segregate its structure-function according to the disparities of content production and transmission method, to distinguish the space of political propaganda from that of entertainment consumption, and to sustain their relative autonomy. For example, in the mainstream media such as newspaper, broadcasting, TV, and publishing, there are usually some specific programs with a heavy dose of political propaganda. Some salient examples can be found in the news report or topical features broadcast by CCTV, or the front pages of those CCP newspapers at either the top or the provincial levels. The expansion of media market and entertainment industry can't be tolerated if it competes for the autonomous space of political publicity, the uniform function of which is to ensure that in the age of media market reform, the dominant culture is firmly harnessed by the Party. In the other spaces surges a flood of colorful entertainment forms and information, which are solely market-oriented and accommodate the mass's need of recreation. Entertainment discourse here is not only diverse in terms of form but also inclusive in terms of content, ranging from celebrity anecdotes and tabloid gossips to exotic yarns and cultural-sports news. The gap between the two kinds of discourse is not unlike the classification of *wen* (文) and *bi* (笔) in classical Chinese literary theory—entertainment discourse is always seeking for the sensual pleasure of flamboyant rhetoric, while political discourse is more concerned with the functional efficiency of verbal communication. Although political discourse always strives for the combination of "delight and instruction", the structural and functional differentiation in media has actually led to the separation of "instruction" and "delight".

From the perspective of content analysis, the two strikingly distinctive types of discourse are subject to different protocols and point to different realms. Political discourse has its fixed expressions and unique rhetoric, with a rigid set of criteria for content and transmission. Yet, outside of political discourse, entertainment discourse in various media has its own game rules, having occupied tremendous space and time and developed into highly competitive activities of market. In a number of TV stations and newspapers (in particular those local tabloids and evening papers) and radio stations, entertainment programs or columns are the mainstay. In terms of the "quantity" of media information production, political discourse has a relatively smaller percentage, but quite concentrated, while entertainment discourse produces a deluge of information, which accounts for the majority of present media culture. However, in terms of "content", political discourse conveys specific viewpoints, values, and guidelines, while entertainment discourse is generally vague and ambiguous, consisting of a variety of different views, values, and ideologies.

Correspondingly, such a differentiation of structure and discourse function breeds two distinctive sets of game rules. It is obvious that commercialization and industrialization stipulate that the operation of media be in accordance with market rules, one of which is market competition. In a nutshell, competition in media market is a race for market share and audience, a matter of catching the audience's eyeballs by means of gimmicks and innovative forms. Therefore, in a space teeming with entertainment information, there is always a calling for innovation in the domain of content production and formal techniques. Only through innovations, only when audiences are provided with appealing and sensational products, can a high commercial return be guaranteed. Furthermore, the pressure of fierce competition is from bottom to top, and the production of entertainment programs must take into consideration the demand, taste, and reception of audiences as the ultimate target. On the contrary, in the field of political discourse, the flow of information is usually from top to bottom, and the channel of information transmission must be regulated so as to ensure its absolute correctness and lucidity. The different treatment of the two types of discourse leads to a peculiar landscape in contemporary Chinese media culture: discourse production and transmission, obsessed with competition and innovation, usually manifest themselves in entertainment media, and the fierce race for audience and ratings is even close to the point of a life-or-death battle.

The result is a cycle from innovation to imitation, which means every time when a new genre of program emerges, there will be many competing imitators, who mimic the others until the novelty is worn out or some new fashionable shows kick in. Nevertheless, in the field of political (propaganda) discourse production and transmission, there is no such thing as a competition; nor is there a pressure of innovation. Although political discourse sometimes absorbs some effective methods and techniques from entertainment discourse in order to transform itself stealthily, there is nothing like a life-or-death battle for winning audience.

Let's make a comparison between Chinese and Western media cultures in our time. The recent trend of Western media culture is characterized by "infotainment", a neologism obviously derived from the combination of "information" and "entertainment". According to some scholars, the so-called "infotainment" is to convey and transmit information by the means of mass entertainment.[9] To be more specific, it is a combo that mixes up serious journalism and hard information of politics with purely entertaining shows and programs. Here arises a significant and peculiar landscape of media. When information and entertainment are indiscriminately mixed up, the seriousness, authenticity, and credibility of journalism or political information itself, on the one hand, are largely compromised, and, on the other, are confused with fun-seeking, frivolous attributes of entertainment shows. Such bizarre hybridity is meant to attract audience, to promote ratings, and to increase market share. The phenomenon of "infotainment" is especially salient in TV shows, and so is it in all kinds of print media. However, if one may say nowadays political and entertainment discourse in Western media is characterized with miscellaneous "infotainment", there is an opposite trend in contemporary Chinese media culture. That is to say, political discourse and entertainment discourse are increasingly divided, with totally different modes of transmission, and targeting dissimilar audiences. Technically speaking, the separation of political discourse and entertainment discourse is perhaps a necessary choice, for it ensures the legitimacy and seriousness of political propaganda discourse, and at the same time provides the industry of media culture with a relatively independent space.

It's worth noting that propaganda and entertainment, though belonging to disparate realms, have in some way realized reciprocity and collaboration. For one thing, the separateness and coexistence of the two ensure relatively autonomous space for both. Notwithstanding occasional transgression on the part of entertainment discourse, structural distinction, as a whole, is the necessary means to guarantee functionality. The disparity of the two types of discourse, in terms of agenda setting, content production, forms of communication, and target audience, enables them to run independently for the purpose of reciprocity. For another, recreational entertainment discourse knows its own boundary and self-consciously stands outside serious political discourse, which constitutes the very condition of legality of the former's development and expansion. In a nutshell, entertainment discourse justifies its survival by not crossing the red line, and it is the model of cohabiting that makes possible the mutual support. Second, the market-oriented mechanism of entertainment discourse is ultimately subject to the binding power of executive orders issued by the propaganda departments. Hence, the administrative branch specializing in propaganda has a final say about the content of media and thus secures the central government's ultimate control of entertainment discourse by means of outside-the-market executive orders and administrative regulations. This explains why the duality of contemporary Chinese media culture is special. Some ideas and methods used in political propaganda, in turn, are indebted to the information production in entertainment sector, which to some extent helps change the stereotypical modes of traditional political propaganda. Third, with the boom of entertainment media, it not only creates a colossal market for media consumption but a massive media audience and their thirst for consumption. In the "post-revolutionary" age of consumerism, consumptive entertainment discourse is effective in diluting people's concern about and impulse for public politics. The slogan of "amusing ourselves to death" has more and more influenced the younger generation, obscuring their political vision and disabling their social participation. The *laissez-faire* media entertainment will eventually result in the audience's political apathy and entertainment hysteria.

The impact on the media audience

From another perspective, the stark separation of the two discourses also brings about some cultural and political problems, one of which is the polarization of audiences' attitude toward different media. The media is a vast public sphere in contemporary society, and as Habermas points out, a public sphere should be a place that fosters rational debates and participation among citizens.[10] However, when the political discourse and the entertainment discourse in China's media and cultural industry are structurally differentiated and functionally separated, the political discourse still maintains its seriousness and orthodoxy, while the pan-entertainment of the media has opened up the space for the public to seek sensation. In particular, the diversity and richness of the entertainment discourse have to a considerable extent diverted or soothed the masses' political impulses and public concern, providing them with an alternative channel of catharsis and psychological satiation. Since the information transmission of political discourse in the official media is top-down and unidirectional, it is obviously impossible for citizens to take "bottom-up" participation freely, which somehow results in a sense of political alienation and apathy among the public. On the contrary, the highly entertaining media can provide people with alternative space for pleasure-seeking and expression, especially when ratings lie at the heart of the game rules, and some public participation and interaction, superficial as they might be, stimulate the public's enthusiasm. This contrasts sharply with public participation in the realm of political discourse, and it seems that entertainment discourse actually serves a useful function of diversion and mitigation. Therefore, it is inevitable that politics and entertainment, associated with two different discursive domains, meet with antithetical receptions from the same audience.

Here arises the second issue, that is, the alternation of chronic indifference and temporary eruption of passion. The development of contemporary media is increasingly characterized by entertainment. As the demand of sensation-seeking in a consumer society is continuously on rise, it keeps on cultivating audiences accustomed to or addicted to sensational experiences. When contemporary media culture provides sufficient or even excessive consumption of pleasure, will the audience feel less interested in other issues? The consequences of chronic political indifference as normalcy are disconcerting, because it tends to accumulate considerable psychological energy that would explode in the future. This is the phenomenon known as intermittent political impulses in the form of "hysteria". Although the conventional forms of entertainment discourse have largely satisfied the cultural needs of the media's audience to a certain extent, the destructive power of pent-up political impulses still exists. Once a major event suddenly occurs, this impulse will come under the spotlight in the form of an instantaneous outburst. What is particularly noteworthy is that this type of political hysteria is characterized by two features: first, it is highly emotional and often defies calm rational analysis, especially when it comes to issues such as nationalism. Recently, the phenomenon of "cyber-violence" (or trolling) is a case in point. People involved in such explosive Internet events are often highly emotional, and tend to break the ethical bottom line due to their lack of experience in political participation and basic training in rational discussion. What's more, some people simply draw on their experience regarding entertainment discourse when it comes to political discourse, turning serious political or social issues into playful entertainment. This trend is also very problematic. Second, this phenomenon is characterized by acute "hysteria" because it stimulates unprecedented impulses and enthusiasm for political participation but for a short time. No sooner does the time pass than it quickly melts into air and falls back into a long-term state of apathy, waiting for the next unexpected event to come. The lack of rationality, together with the "bipolar" feature of public psychology, is a noteworthy condition of contemporary Chinese cultural politics.

The rise of grassroots media

What we have discussed so far is limited to the official media in China. If we look at the broader vista of contemporary Chinese media culture, we will find a new trend, namely, the rise of grassroots media. The so-called "grassroots media" have a series of new characteristics that are completely distinct from the official media. This new trend accounts for some remarkable changes in the current pattern of Chinese media culture.

Grassroots media, also known as "private media" or "self-media" in academia, are individuals or organizations that voluntarily upload self-made contents to video websites or online forums. Unlike the official media, they have a distinctly folk character. In terms of production, these media are largely scattered in different geographical and spatial areas, with the Internet or smartphones as the main channels of communication. Grassroots media is the Internet-based folk culture in the information age.

According to the "42nd Statistical Report on the Development of the Internet in China", a report released by the China Internet Network Information Center (CNNIC), as of June 30, 2018, the size of Chinese Internet users reached 802 million, with a penetration rate of 57.7%. In particular, the population of cell-phone netizens has reached 788 million, and the proportion of mobile Internet users is as high as 98.3%.[11] In such a large group of cell-phone users, the SMS is both inexpensive and fast, and has become an important channel for interpersonal communication. When some major events happen, witnesses can instantly pass on the news to friends and relatives through the SMS messages, and the news will have a snow-ball effect as it spreads to the whole society. A more convenient communication channel is the network, which has not only changed the way people communicate, but even changed our lifestyle and mindset. CNNIC's report titled "Major Social Events and the Influence of Network Media" clearly points out that the role of network media during social crises is very significant. The news of the May 12, 2008, earthquake in Wenchuan, Sichuan Province, was initially spread online. According to CNNIC's statistics, 87.4% of Internet users chose to watch the updates on the Wenchuan earthquake, and there are more viewers turning to the Internet media than those watching TV news about earthquake. The openness of the Internet makes it an important channel for people to obtain information about crisis events. The report also shows that 52.1% of those who use the Internet to follow major news in 2008 said they currently prefer to use the Internet over other news media. Chinese netizens spend an average of 55.9 minutes browsing online news each day, and their online behavior is becoming increasingly diversified.

Grassroots media is different from official media in that it reflects more of the will and opinions of the masses. To some extent, grassroots media has inverted the top-down indoctrinatory approach of official propaganda, and created a negotiable model of discussion and dialogue among the public. From online discussions and blogs to podcasts, SMS messages, and emails, grassroots media takes on a variety of forms, and the number of participants, usually highly interactive, is extremely large. There are many popular grassroots websites, such as "Tianya", "Youku", "Tudou", "Blog China", and "Anti-Waves". The 2009 CNNIC report, "Research on China Internet Users' Social Network Application", shows that the population of social media users is close to one-third of the total number of all Chinese netizens, the majority being the post-secondary diploma-holders. The report states that social media websites have become an aggregated platform for various Web applications, including blogs and emails. The data show that the message board is the most popular feature, accounting for 51.2% of online clicks, while the use percentage of pictures/albums is 48.6%, and blog/journal, 41.5%. More and more information interactions are carried out on social media. People like reposting and commenting on news stories, and sharing audio/video clips. It is evident that such grassroots media is actually a public sphere without boundaries, which serves multiple functions such as information sharing, entertainment, and social networking.

Obviously, the rise of grassroots media and the development of communication technology have a lot to do with each other. Some observers have noted that the advance of communication technology has played a rather important role in the emergence of grassroots media in China. In particular, the widespread use of "Web 2.0" technically makes possible the development of various grassroots media. Just as new technologies such as digital cameras and cell-phone photography have completely cancelled out the elitism and high cost of traditional photography. The popularization of "Web 2.0" technologies has changed the old pattern of media production, communication, and reception, allowing most Internet users to freely enter the domain of media and interact with one another. Of course, technology is a double-edged sword, which means it can not only diversify and breathe new life to communication, but also be used to strengthen information control in a more effective way. From the perspective of grassroots media production, advances in communication technology have indeed opened up more possibilities for public participation. Grassroots media have made possible the ideals of "one person, one medium" and of "all communicating to all". In China, there are a large number of young people who are savvy about online media technologies, who are well-educated and have high-level income, and who are eager to use grassroots media to exchange information, launch discussions, and play for entertainment. It gives rise to a boundless media community, a virtual space made of personal information and its distribution, circulation, and reception. It is an "imagined community" in Benedict Anderson's sense. Grassroots media help to gradually develop a prototype of public sphere, where a civil society—no matter how unfledged it might be—can come into being and its protocols of communication be drafted. Take "Tianya" for instance, which was established in March 1999. This virtual community attracted a lot of attention and soon had a large user base. In the next year, this website joined hands with the namesake magazine, and began to promote the humanistic spirit. "Tianya" was hailed as an iconic public website in China, where a host of major issues were vehemently discussed, forging a virtual public sphere of rational debate. In "Tianya", there was a community management committee, and the website's daily operation, the appointment of board moderators, the censorship of posts, the agenda and negotiation of online discussions, etc., all have a streak of public sphere. To a certain extent, this reflects Chinese netizens' social concern and political engagement, which would have a positive effect on the cultivation of rational debates, promote the sense of due process among Chinese citizens, and provide some useful experiences for the trial of political democratization in China.

As Bakhtin points out in his analysis of the differences between folk and official cultures, the two can be contrasted in a variety of ways. Unlike the official media, grassroots media are more diverse in terms of content, which is a fact worthy of more detailed analysis. Through content analysis, we can reveal the indispensability and uniqueness of grassroots media located within China's media and culture system today.

Let's summarize the types of grassroots media in terms of content, and figure out why such communication is important by taking a look at the agenda setting of grassroots media. All-encompassing as grassroots media are, we can categorize them into four major groups: first, media focusing on public emergency, including earthquakes, fires, and some public affairs about the underprivileged, such as "nail households" or the "black brick kilns" incident in Shanxi. In the process of producing, disseminating, and receiving information about these incidents, grassroots media played an extremely important role, ultimately standing up for the interests of the disadvantaged. Second, media to promote corruption crackdown.

By tracking, reporting, and discussing the scandals of some corrupted officials, such media expose their illegality. In particular, some netizens volunteer to take on the so-called "doxxing", an action to some extent bordering on social mobilization. With the joint effort of a multitude of Internet users, corrupt officials were eventually brought to justice. In this regard, the downfall of Zhou Jiugeng, a local official in Nanjing, who sported "overpriced cigarettes", is a famous case in point. Third, media dedicated to discussing social and cultural issues, such as environmental crises and international affairs. Fourth, media joining in the debates on some sensitive policies introduced by the central and local governments, ranging from economy, finance, education, and medical reform, to Internet censorship, real estate, high-speed railroads, and those "vanity projects" run by local officials. In this regard, some online discussions organized on grassroots media did showcase public opinions and collective emotions. Such grassroots media drew the government's attention and have an impact on the administration's decision-making.

The agenda setting of political communication on the part of grassroots media is mostly different from the agenda of official media. Therefore, grassroots media serve the function of voicing out public opinions, a function that can be described as the production and communication of alternative information outside official propaganda. This kind of information in turn has some influence on the government and its decision-making, as well as on the public, and also has an impact on the official media, pushing them to change their information strategy and adopt a more populist line.

Regarding the communication mode and effect of grassroots media, some scholars believe that it has acquired certain leverage to stand for mass opinions and can be used for social organizing and mobilization. Others argue that grassroots media has formed a public sphere of media with Chinese characteristics. And some overseas scholars are more concerned about whether such media has morphed into citizen media or citizen journalism. In any case, the emergence of grassroots media in the current Chinese media culture has undoubtedly positive implications. It has enriched the resources and patterns of media and formed a pluralistic media culture structure with different sources. In addition, grassroots media provides the public with a channel to express their will. Through such expressions, governments at all levels would pay more attention to people's well-being and their voices, and introduce or modify relevant policies. Finally, the tension between grassroots media and official media has given rise to a more interesting trend—official media constantly learn from folk grassroots media and then improve their own strategies and methods. In short, grassroots media are indispensable in contemporary China, and their positive impact is self-evident. Of course, the problems of grassroots media cannot be ignored. A crucial issue is how to cultivate a tradition of rational debate among netizens, how to develop the principle of rational criticism in public sphere discussions, and how to prevent free discussions in the public sphere from turning into immoral trolling.

Over the past decade or so, the landscape of Chinese communication culture has continued to change. From the above analysis, several preliminary conclusions can be drawn as follows: First, the dualistic system of media culture has created an inherent tension, which has been temporarily alleviated through the binary separation of political and entertainment discourses. However, in the long run, the tension still exists and determines the future direction of Chinese media culture. Second, the binary opposition between political discourse and entertainment discourse helps to sustain the respective features of the two, but the concurrent problems should not be underestimated, especially the entertainment-seeking public's political apathy. Therefore, it is important to find a channel that connects the two discourses so as to maintain a balance between the masses' political concerns and their desire for entertainment, and, more importantly, to build an open platform for public participation. Third, the rise of grassroots media has changed the landscape of media culture, its positive effects simply beyond denial. However, how to develop the rules of rational debate and how to avoid irrational cyber-violence will be the key issues to determine the future of grassroots media. In short, contemporary Chinese media culture has broken away from the traditional pattern and entered a brand-new stage of development, which constantly poses new questions and challenges to cultural studies.

Notes

1 Chengju Huang. "From Control to Negotiation: Chinese Media in the 2000s", in *The International Communication Gazette* 69.5 (2007): 402–412.
2 Jiang Zemin. "Report on the Fourteenth National Congress of the Communist Party of China". <http://cpc.people.com.cn/GB/64162/64168/64567/65446/4526308.htm>
3 See "Communiqué of the Sixth Plenary Session of the Fourteenth Central Committee of the Communist Party of China". <http://cpc.people.com.cn/GB/64162/64168/64567/65398/4441784.html>
4 See "Proposal of the Central Committee of the Communist Party of China on the Formulation of the Tenth Five-Year Plan for National Economic and Social Development". <www.gov.cn/gongbao/content/2000/ content_60538.htm>
5 Han Yongjin. "The Reform and Progress of China's Cultural System", in *Publishing Reference* 10 (2005).
6 See Liu Yandong. "To Cultivate a Strong Cultural Soft Power, To Help Build a Modern, Strong, Democratic, Civilized and Harmonious Country". <http://www. mcprc.gov.cn/xxfb/xwzx/whxw/200911/t20091125_75064.html>
7 See "Cultural Industry Revitalization Plan". <http://news.xinhuanet.com/politics/2009-09/26/content_12114302.htm>
8 Huang Chengju. "From Control to Negotiation: Chinese Media in the 2000s", in *The International Communication Gazette* 69.5 (2007), pp.402–412.
9 For more interesting discussion on Infotainment, see Bonnie Anderson. *News Flash, Journalism, Infotainment, and the Button-line Business of Broadcast News*. San Francisco: Jossey-Bass, 2004; also see Bala A. Musa and Cindy J. Price. *Emerging Issues in Contemporary Journalism: Infotainment, Internet, Libel, Censorship*. Lewiston: Edwin Mellen, 2006; Daya Kishan Thussu. *News as Entertainment: The Rise of Global Infotainment*. London: Sage, 2007.
10 See Jürgen Habermas. *The Structural Transformation of the Public Sphere*. Trans. Cao Weidong et al. Beijing: Xue Lin Press, 1999.
11 See "2018 China Internet Report". <https://baijiahao.baidu.com/s?id=160930550-4349531874>

9 The emergence of Micro Culture and its discontents

One day in 2015, I had the opportunity to visit the Tencent headquarters located in Shenzhen. On the second floor of the skyscraper-like headquarters, there were two huge LED screens, showing to visitors how Tencent was changing the world. One display indicated that 380 million WeChat users were online at that moment, with numerous dots flashing across the world map, while the other showed 120 million QQ users online at the time, scattered around every corner of the world. This astounding technological spectacle would have been unimaginable half a century ago, or even 20 years ago. In his 1990 book, *The Condition of Postmodernity: An Enquiry into the Origins of Cultural Change*, David Harvey describes how the world had shrank between the 1850s and 1960s, by the ultimate "annihilation of space through time".[1] Today, with the rapid advance of communication technologies, I think Harvey would cast the world as a tiny dot. McLuhan's notion of "global village" turns out to be an accurate prophecy for this era! However, the world we are experiencing now is completely different from that of McLuhan half a century ago. Today, we can call it the "Micro Era" characterized by the "Micro Culture". Be it WeChat or QQ, many new technologies and innovations are signaling a growing trend: our society and culture are more and more "micronized". If the "Micro Era" is a temporal category, then the "Micro Culture" is a notion of more logical significance, which connotes a new cultural form and its internal development logic. A more specific question can be raised here: What does the "micronization" of society and culture in our time mean? How is "micronization" related to the construction of subjectivity? Does the new Micro Culture give rise to a new type of cultural politics?

The cultural symptoms of "Micro Culture"

When we use the term "Micro Culture" to describe the current cultural transformation, there are actually many issues that need to be carefully considered. There is a term, "microculture", in English, but it refers to the subculture of a minority group of people, who live in a society with their unique languages and ideology.[2] This concept is not the same as the "Micro Culture", which is fervently popular in China today. Here, "Micro Culture" is a loosely defined cultural form, which in particular refers to a new form of culture that is increasingly fragmentized, because of the

DOI: 10.4324/9781003407089-13

ascendance of new technologies and media. It is a culture in which totality is on the wane and people are increasingly obsessed with "smaller" things. The emergence of Micro Culture reminds us of a popular old saying, that is, "Small is beautiful". But in the face of Micro Culture, one must also add, "Small is disturbing!" The rise of Micro Culture does present us with a number of extremely challenging dilemmas. Today, people are simply eager to embrace "micronization" of everything, including texts, behaviors, and ideas. What follows are therefore changed societies, changed cultures, changed technologies, and changed subjectivity.

This tendency is palpably manifested in fragmentation. Fragmentation, which many thinkers have characterized as modernity, has greatly intensified in the postmodern world. Ferdinand Tönnies pointed out in the late 19th century that the so-called "modern" actually implies a shift from the traditional "community" to the present "society". Community here refers to a group of people glued by biological similarities and intimate relationships, and as a result, they essentially share intentionality. Unlike "community", "society" is rationally based on laws and statutes. One of his conclusions is that the modern society stripped of organic communal ties would inevitably result in fragmentation.[3] At the beginning of the 20th century, Max Weber maintained that the emergence of modernity had shattered the religious-metaphysical monolithic worldview characteristic of traditional societies, resulting in the segregation of different value spheres, each of which has its own basis of legitimacy. According to Weber's observation, modern society is constituted by the many self-contained autonomous value systems.[4] Later, Walter Benjamin proposed a very vivid concept, namely, "constellations", subverting the mindset of identity brought about by the Enlightenment modernity. Benjamin's "constellations" is an idea that profoundly touches upon the complex and fragmented state of modern society.[5] Since the rise of postmodernism in the 1960s, while the tendency toward fragmentation has intensified, more sophisticated scholarly discourses on fragmentation were produced. For example, Thomas Kuhn notes that the explosion of scientific knowledge means the loss of universal commensurability; Jean-François Lyotard exclaims that the construction of postmodern knowledge has rendered the demise of grand narrative, which is replaced by small narratives; and Zygmunt Bauman finds that modernity is shifting from weighty to light forms, from solid to liquid.[6] All these propositions reveal an internal logic of social and cultural development, which is the further dissolution of totality and the tendency toward fragmentation.

Here, I would like to emphasize that the Micro Culture, while further intensifying fragmentation, has made fragmentation evolve to a new stage. I suggest that a neologism can be used to more accurately describe this transformation—the "fragmicronization" of society and culture. To borrow Bauman's terminology, if fragmentation is like "water flow", then *fragmicronization* takes the form of "water droplets", which is much smaller, more micronized, and fragmented than the former. Historically and logically speaking, "fragmicronization" is a new phase in the evolution of fragmented modernity, which is mainly characterized by the "fragmicronization" of information production, communication, and reception. The Micro Culture brings about many new micro-phenomena to be interpreted: micro life, micro object, micro consumption, micro narrative, micro thinking, micro psychology, micro emotion, micro subject, micro democracy, micro politics, and so on and so forth.

There are different perspectives on the interpretation of Micro Culture. In my opinion, it is a valid path to examine Micro Culture from the vantage point of modes of information. Marx's analysis of capitalist society as per classical political economics was conducted through the lens of "modes of production", an analysis that cogently unveiled the nature of capitalism. Today, under the social conditions where production and consumption are highly integrated, and where interpersonal communication and information are becoming increasingly important, it is highly apt to examine and interpret Micro Culture from the perspective of "mode of information".[7] Micro Culture is, after all, a symptom of the transformation of the "information mode" in history. It has several features that merit scrutiny, one of which is the fragmicronized composition of information. To put it more graphically, the basic unit of Micro Culture is fragmented, miniature information. As a result, such information is usually less in terms of size, formality, and length. Take WeChat as an example. The Internet is now inundated with WeChat messages, which are usually terse and trifle, but voluminous and extremely swift. The complete, systematic, complex, and relevant information is no longer the mainstream type for interpersonal communication. The second feature is the speed of information transmission in real time. Walter Benjamin once predicted in the 1930s that mechanical reproduction technology could disseminate artworks over a wider spatial and temporal scale, but today, the emergence of Micro Culture has far exceeded Benjamin's prediction. Let's take the example of WeChat again, which is the most typical mode of information communication in the age of Micro Culture. With the technology of wireless networks, information can be transmitted peer to peer in real time, overcoming the barrier of spatial and temporal distances in a swift and extensive manner. The great advantage of Micro Culture lies in the fact that the rate and scope of information transmission is far greater than any other communication media in history, such as print, newspaper, radio, telephone, and television. In the pre–Micro Culture era, the transmission of information had fixed procedures and norms—the collecting, reviewing, fact-checking, editing, copy-editing, and delivering of information are not only complicated but time-consuming. The advance of contemporary information technology has greatly changed the way information is disseminated, giving rise to a variety of grassroots media outside the traditional media system, and thereby unprecedentedly simplifying the standardized procedures in traditional media industry into real-time direct information transmission from peer to peer. Today, the coverage of newsworthy incidents, no matter where they occur, can be effectively disseminated in Micro Culture in real time. Third, the massive transmission and reception of information is an extremely important feature that distinguishes Micro Culture from other cultures we had before. A deluge of unchecked and miscellaneous information in Micro Culture is flowing at tremendous speed between different terminals in the Internet. The heterogeneity, fragmentation, and fracture of such information have completely dismantled the totality and contextualization of information, making a shocking impact on people's grasp and understanding of the information system. This situation has posed many new cognitive challenges to us. In addition to the above three characteristics, the fourth typical symptom of Micro Culture is its tendency toward entertainment. Our contemporary Micro Culture is very different from traditional folk culture and modern orthodox political culture, and has been obviously tinted with the features of consumer culture. As the term "infotainment" suggests, information and entertainment are now completely integrated—news reports, political affairs, and knowledge transmission are all turned into entertainment in the context of consumer culture. When we are reading newspapers / books, watching television, following news, or even reading textbooks, everything tends to be entertaining, and one index of entertainment is the pleasure-seeking during the process of one's information reception. All the supposedly dense, esoteric, and complicated information is reduced to something simplified and fun, with eye-catching visual pleasure being the cornerstone of Micro Information and Micro Narrative characteristic of Micro Culture.

To summarize, the first characteristic is about the scale of the Micro Cultural information's mode, which explicates the sense of "Micro". In Micro Culture, everything tends to be miniaturized, such as information, products, activities, and interactions. The second characteristic points to the communication characteristics of Micro Culture's information mode, highlighting the real-time and efficient nature of miniaturized information communication, which also reveals the high speed of contemporary society and culture. Speed and convenience are the most attractive features of Micro Culture. The third characteristic involves the quantity of information in Micro Culture. A deluge of raw information surges everywhere, without discrimination and discretion, a fact that leads to the reversal of the relationship between men and information. It is not that men are seeking for information, but the other way around. The latest technological devices are constantly forcing people to pay attention to and accept all kinds of information. The last feature is concerned with the qualitative description of Micro Culture, whose tendency toward entertainment and pleasure-seeking has completely changed the game rules of culture. As a result, such a culture inevitably stipulates that all information, things, and even knowledge—ranging from production through dissemination to reception—should follow the principles as per entertainment and pleasure. The above four characteristics are intertwined with each other and constitute the structure of Micro Culture in reality.

The emergence of micro subject

It is very hard to make a precise judgment about Micro Culture, because the fragmicronization of culture is also a double-edged sword, with multiple functions. On the one hand, fragmicronization has led to the dissolution of totality, opening up new space for the free flow of information and the masses' free expression. Therefore, it is much easy for people to notice the new opportunities that Micro Culture brings to the democratization of Chinese society and its public participation. The strictly monolithic information flow in China has been subverted by the peer-to-peer real-time dissemination of fragmicronized information. Micro rights, micro democracy, and micro politics have risen in Micro Culture. On the other hand, while Micro Culture offers more opportunities for the public to express themselves more freely, we must also pay attention to the negative implications of Micro Culture. Some important issues deserve more investigation, such as the complex relationship between the fragmicronization of Micro Culture and the construction of rational subjectivity of modern citizens; the relationship between the free expression of citizens and the spread of immoral and anti-social information; how to construct an overall understanding of society and culture in the midst of fragmicronized and chaotic information; and how to avoid the "spiral of silence" in social media.

A growing number of studies point out that the invention of new technologies such as the Internet, computers, and WeChat has made much latent impact on human beings. Some studies conducted in the United States and Germany in the 1990s found that most webpages won't hold people's attention for more than 10 seconds and that less than 10% of website readers will browse a webpage for over 2 minutes. Nielsen, a senior webpage designer, came to the stunning conclusion that "Web users don't read on the Web!" A decade later, an Israeli study (2008) analyzed data from millions of websites around the world and came to a more precise conclusion: the average time people spend browsing each webpage is between 19 and 27 seconds, including the time of webpage loading. In particular, German and Canadian users spend an average of 20 seconds per page; American and British users, 21 seconds; Indian and Australian users, 24 seconds; and French users, 25 seconds. If this finding was only targeted at the general public, a study by some researches from the University of London in the same year looked specifically into professional users: by investigating the official websites of the British Library and the British Educational Association, one can see how professional website users read academic journal papers. The results were equally surprising—they usually only read the first two or three pages of a paper, skimming no more than the titles and abstracts. The study concluded that a new type of reading had emerged, that is, "power browsing".[8] Also in 2008, N. Katherine Hayles studied the cognitive mode of students at the University of California, and found that the development of information technology had given rise to a "media generation" that was significantly different from the previous generations. She concluded that there was a generational shift or gap in students' cognitive styles and that a new cognitive style and culture had emerged. A new way of perception and culture has emerged. What are the characteristics of the "media generation"? According to Hayles, it is the "hyper attention" that characterizes this generation: "Hyper attention is characterized by switching focus rapidly among different tasks, preferring multiple information streams, seeking a high level of stimulation, and having a low tolerance of boredom".[9] In her view, the opposite of hyper attention, in terms of cognitive style, is another type of attention, which she calls "deep attention", characterized by "concentrating on a single object for long periods (say, a novel by Dickens), ignoring outside stimuli while so engaged, preferring a single information stream, and having a high tolerance for long focus time".[10] Hales found that contemporary social, cultural, and technological developments have led young people to increasingly drift away from the "deep-attention" cognitive mode, who instead more and more embrace "hyper attention" as a cognitive mode. In other words, hyper attention has become the most popular cognitive mode among young people today.

If we transplant the idea of hyper attention to the study of Micro Culture, we can undoubtedly put a new slant on this subculture. Some years ago, I once suggested that the "age of picture reading" was replacing the age of text reading and that the rise of visual culture had changed our reading habits. Now it seems that the new trend not only means the domination of picture reading over text reading, but also means a profound change that happens within text reading itself. The traditional way of reading, marked by "deep attention", is being replaced by the various "micro reading" modes discussed above. The core of "micro reading" is indeed manifested in "hyper attention" as a style of cognition, as is discussed by Hayles. Its four characteristics reveal the striking tendency of Micro Culture's information mode toward fragmicronization, and the extent to which Micro Culture reconfigures subjectivity and its cognitive mode. The rapid shift of focus is actually the symptom of our entire culture. From professional academic research, to hot news browsing, to all kinds of juicy gossips and anecdotes, people are now accustomed to switching their focus quickly, rather than focusing on one object continuously and for a long time. "To spend 10 years making a sword" is a very outdated practice, and as people are more and more prone to utilitarianism, aiming at a short-term end has become everyone's top choice. Another two features—fixation on diversity and addiction to sensational information—also help to explain the shortening of our attention span. The former is about quantity, implying that a man of hyper attention usually prefers the diversity of information, while the latter is about quality of information. Besides leading to a fragmentation of cognitive styles, the diversity of massive information may also make information reception less effective. The agent of Micro Culture prefers sensational information, since bland and ordinary information no longer attracts attention. As a consequence, people are hooked to expect more entertaining information. Today, the so-called "KOL" (key opinion leader) and "clickbait" are very popular, which is precisely the result of such a fervent expectation of stimulating information. This is the product of such stimulating information expectations. Anything that falls short of sensation is unable to hold the public's attention, nor could it attract a large audience. This phenomenon gives rise to a Micro Culture full of nonsensical, falsehood-ridden, redundant but usually sensational information noises. Engaging with such information has now consumed a bulk of our daily time and energy. Finally, the inability to tolerate boredom reveals the psychological motivation inherent in hyper attention. The other three characteristics are all contingent upon this psychological motivation. Long-time attention to a single object can be boring and unbearable, so one constantly changes his focus and seeks a variety of information streams, especially those that are highly stimulating.

In my opinion, if Micro Culture is of the objective cultural reality, hyper attention then is an explication of the cognitive temperament of the subject belonging to this culture, the two being the two sides of the same coin. As we know, the concept of culture itself connotes "nurturing", as culture means a process of forging or influencing men. Therefore, the objective consequence of Micro Culture is always shaping the subject in accordance with such a culture. In turn, this new subject boosts and strengthens the new culture. In this sense, the cognitive mode characterized by hyper attention is both a product of Micro Culture and an agent that enhances and buttresses Micro Culture. It is at this point that we touch upon the subjectivity of Micro Culture, which is different from the previous cultures in that it is shaped by a new kind of "micro subject", especially in the case of the "media generation". From this perspective, when Micro Culture is changing our cultures, it is also changing the subject and its cognitive style. And the change of cognitive style further leads to the change of the subject's way of thinking, feeling, and behavior. I would like to emphasize that Micro Culture brings about not only a reconfiguration of attention patterns in the psychological sense, but also a reconfiguration of practical subjects and their practical behaviors in the sociological and political sense. That is to say, the widespread popularity of hyper attention not only signals the cognitive mode of Micro Culture, but also forecasts the emergence of a certain kind of micro subjects.

Micro narrative and micro politics

The term "micro subject" is coined to contrast the subjectivity typical of the times prior to the age of Micro Culture, and its subjectivity is characterized by the word "micro".

If there was the "age of giants" in the Renaissance and the age of the Cartesian "reflective subject" in the Enlightenment, then, given the highly developed communication technology and media culture today, the conditions that used to make "giants" and "reflective subject" possible are bygone. What newly emerges, instead, is the low-browed "micro subjects". If the "giants" and "reflective subjects" used to live in the three-dimensional space of rationality, today's micro subjects live on the two-dimensional plane of randomness and contingency, a plane signaling the decline of reason, and a plane more fragmicronized and emotional in terms of thoughts and behaviors. I believe that the micro subject accomplishes its socialization and subjectivity through micro cognition, and the basic discourse of micro cognition is "micro narrative". In the light of the current development of Chinese society and culture, it can be said that "micro narratives" are more fragmicronized than the so-called "little narratives", a term coined by Lyotard nearly half a century ago. Micro cognition and its micro narratives constitute the micro subjects who practice micro politics unique to contemporary society. Micro subjects depend on micro cognition, and micro cognition depends on micro narratives. It is necessary to further examine the characteristics of micro cognition and micro narratives.

The first problem to tackle is the habituation of micro cognition under the circumstance of Micro Culture. As mentioned earlier, a salient feature of Micro Culture is the fragmicronization of information. All kinds of media are now rife with a vast amount of raw, unscreened, and unprocessed information, ranging from major news stories or hearsay to anecdotal trivia and myths. Such fragmicronized information constitutes a unique micro narrative. To borrow a term used by Lyotard in his analysis of postmodern knowledge, the shift from modernity to postmodernity means the replacement of "grand narratives" by "little narratives". "Micro narrative" is different from other narratives in that it has its own unique syntactic, grammatical, and semantic rules, its typical form usually being a couple of sentences, no more than a dangling paragraph without a beginning or an ending. The syntax of micro narratives is much more of deconstruction than of construction; its grammar is more often than not transgressive as a result of the compression of information; and its meaning-making is sometimes of partial and inflammatory nature—because of over-compression—at the expense of totality. It is not difficult to find that the basic discursive strategy of micro narratives is to extract some information from a specific context, dismantling the connectivity and configuration between different information. The result is some unconnected and isolated information flowing freely in an entangled social Web. Such information may, on the one hand, distort or one-sidedly reflect the real status of affairs in society and culture, and, on the other hand, reinforce the simplistic and biased interpretation on the part of the audience and stimulate instantaneous emotional reactions among the audience. Perhaps we can put it in this way: micro narratives fragmicronize information in such a way as to facilitate its instant and wide dissemination in real time, but at the cost of compromising the integrity and contextualization of the information. Consequently, one might be misled or misguided when receiving such information, and his interpretation and cognition blocked. Moreover, it would even lead to parochial understanding and judgments on the part of information receivers. As the Chinese saying goes, "a leaf tells us everything about the autumn", which means some seemingly trivial details or clues are associated with and conducive to overall information or omens. Therefore, it is always possible to figure out totality from locality. Yet, since micro cognition is stripped off larger contexts because of the fragmicronization of information, it is merely possible for one to be cognizant of the small through the lens of the miniature, or, even worse, of the miniature through the super-miniature. If the micro narrative is only concerned with the cognitive form, a further problem arises: once men are accustomed to such a cognitive style, micro cognition will be a part of one's knee jerk reaction. Here we may use Piaget's theory of "genetic epistemology" as an explanatory paradigm. According to Piaget, the development of human cognition alternates between assimilation and accommodation. Assimilation is the use of existing cognitive patterns or paradigms to understand the present stimuli or phenomena. Conversely, accommodation is derived from the conflict between the present stimuli or information and the existing cognitive patterns or paradigms, from the subject's cognitive inability to understand or grasp the present, which in turn triggers the change and adjustment of the existing patterns or paradigms.[11] One possibility, I would like to suggest, is that given the chronic exposure to micro narratives and micro information, the concomitant cognitive patterns or paradigms tend to be reinforced, and over time, people are accustomed to, and ultimately addicted to, the dominant presence of such patterns or paradigms, which bring about the mindset in line with micro narratives. To use Piaget's terminology, the characteristics of micro narratives lead to a shift in the existing cognitive pattern and thus to what is known as "accommodation". The consequence of accommodation is the construction of a new micro cognitive pattern compatible with micro narratives. With the establishment of such a pattern, the subject then enters into "assimilation", that is to say, the cognitive subject becomes more and more frequently involved in micro narratives, and increasingly assimilated into such a cognitive pattern. The result is the continuous reinforcement of one's cognitive pattern. This principle also applies to the formation of what Hayles calls the "hyper attention pattern" of the "media generation", and the resulting social and cultural "cognitive generation gap". An increasing number of empirical studies have found that some adolescents in contemporary society have little interest in reading full-length novels and do not have the patience to concentrate on a boring topic of science, which indicates that they have become accustomed to the domination of hyper attention, and have developed micro cognitive habits by spending a lot of time and energy on browsing micro narratives and indulging in them.

Second, the emergence of micro subjects. A great epoch usually creates some vanguards who make grand narrative about the world. Today, the Micro Era and its Micro Culture have jointly shaped through micro narratives micro subjects, a group of men and women who are parochial in terms of their thinking, emotion, and behavior pattern, and are indulged in and accustomed to such fragmicronized cognitive pattern characteristic of Micro Culture, and lack broad vision and global thinking. In general, micro subjects have two distinctive characteristics: first, their cognitive patterns are fragmicronized. They prefer to consume all kinds of micro information, addicted to various micro narratives, and constantly dominated by hyper attention. As a result, they slowly lose the grasp of and interest in grand narratives and big questions. Second, because of the segmentation of fragmicronized information in Micro Culture, Micro Culture creates a variety of micro objects. And on the basis of different types of micro objects, Micro Culture can further categorize subjects into many virtual subgroups, which are generally inclined to be exclusive and hermetic, and share similar interests, congenially and complacently immersed in the same websites or virtual communities. Their nonchalance about the world other than these small groups has resulted in a split of cultural persona: on the one hand, there is a high-level burst of enthusiasm and unstoppable devotion to one's own group of Micro Culture, and on the other hand, an indifference to what is going on in the outside world. These two aspects create a new subjectivity in accordance with the fragmicronization typical of the age of Micro Culture, a subjectivity featuring micro cognition, micro thinking, and micro emotion. Many concepts of cultural subjectivity that have become popular recently are more or less related to this type of subjectivity, ranging from "literary hipsters" to "petite bourgeoisie", "artsy-fartsy", and "loser". All of them, though to different degrees, have the same characteristics of micro subjects. Just like those young people as represented in the movie "Little Times", micro subjects are already the most conspicuous social subjects in this society. Although it is unnecessary to make a simplistic value judgment on micro subjects, there is a serious issue under consideration: the complex relationship between the subjectivity of micro subjects and the modernization of China, as well as its association with the construction of modern citizenship.

China is now in the midst of a radical societal transformation, and the construction of modern citizenship is an urgent task. Yet, the influx of micro subjects poses a serious challenge to such a task. The characteristics of micro subjectivity are much different from the subjectivity as defined by rational self-consciousness and critical traditions. Micro subjects seem to be counterproductive to the construction of such citizenship, nor are they helpful to the cultivation of rational subjects capable of holistic interpretation and judgment. Instead, they may bring about some obstacles to the development of modern citizens' holistic cognition, and invite simplistic judgment and emotional overreaction.

Third, the reliance on micro devices. The emergence of Micro Culture is also the result of innovations in information technology of both hardware and software. In other words, the fragmicronization of culture rests on new technologies and related devices, ranging from cell phones, computers, e-readers to DV camera kit, and various information technologies featuring novel and dazzling interfaces and functions. All of these new devices tend to be increasingly portable, mobile, and miniaturized. Micro Culture, technically speaking, is no more than the product of newly innovated communication technology devices with mobility, which are not only instrumental, but also function as "device paradigms" in the philosophical sense, when they are introduced and widely socialized.[12] These technological devices are not only some devices with functionality, but also a paradigm shaper of people's thoughts, feelings, and behaviors. Accustomed to a certain device, users subconsciously feel a sort of affinity to the device, as well as the culture and ideology opaquely associated with it, and develop a certain sense of "handiness". Users, ultimately, become more and more "addicted to" and "dependent on" a technical device. This "addiction" and "dependence" is manifested in both the hardware and the software. In terms of the hardware, it means one's fascination of or obsession with various technological devices. The so-called "gadget-lover" is a case in point. Those who are engrossed in Micro Culture must be more and more interested in micro devices. One generation of devices will nurture one generation of consumers, who become accustomed to a certain device, and thereby more and more attached to it. The emergence of new devices will reinforce users' addiction to them, even by claiming some minor upgrades or new features. More interestingly, in spite of the evolution of these fancy devices, which are likely to be more and more powerful and convenient, with upgraded functionality, their product life cycle yet becomes shorter and shorter. With generations after generations of products beckoning to consumers, users will have increasingly higher expectations of and stronger "addiction" to up-to-date micro devices. The software "addiction" is an obsession with various operating systems and interfaces. Micro Cultures rely on all kinds of devices to connect people with information, and interfaces become a portal for individuals to access such connected networks. Interfaces help people choose, think, and perceive through operating systems, and they become, in McLuhan's words, "extensions of the person". The various interfaces appear to offer a variety of options, but in fact all the options are predetermined, which means they are no more than some "formulae" for certain ways of thinking and feeling. Once a user visits an interface, he or she is required to abide by a certain "formula", and a fragmicronized way of thinking, feeling, and even behavior is imperceptibly formed, solidified, and reinforced. The use of a certain interface is accompanied by an invisible "addiction", and the more skillful one's use of the interface, the deeper one's dependence. As the subject becomes more and more addicted to the hardware and software of micro devices, our thinking and behavior tend to be more and more fragmicronized.

Fourth, the emergence of micro politics, which is the inevitable result of cultural fragmicronization. From micro subjects through micro cognition to micro devices, the end products Micro Culture helps to create lead to a new kind of cultural politics, namely, micro politics. The so-called "micro politics" is in contrast to the traditional political forms, which rely on face-to-face communication to realize a collective social mobilization and the resulting social practice in general. So, it presents more local and technical demands, taking the form of fragmicronized or incomplete disputes and appeals online. The function of micro politics is an interesting and complex issue, as the conditions under which these localized and fragmicronized requests will form an overall social practice are hard to determine. On the one hand, micro politics creates more gaps, spaces, and possibilities for expression in our society and culture, but it is not immediately clear how these gaps, spaces, and possibilities become relevant and structural. On the other hand, the political potential of micro politics is difficult to predict, because of its decentralized and fragmented nature. Therefore, its relationship with overarching social practices seems rather complicated, and the scope and intensity of its social mobilization sometimes exceed those of traditional social mobilization. That said, micro politics has tremendous potentials. Another question is also worth noting—it is possible for micro politics to make people forget or gloss over some socially and ethically significant issues, when they are addicted to the a large amount of information and exotic sensation, and when they are fixated on disseminating, sharing, and experiencing all kinds of micro information, and are segmented into different social subgroups by Micro Culture.

In addition, the relationship between micro politics and the "spiral of silence" is also a question worthy of further scrutiny. According to Elisabeth Noelle-Neumann, once public opinion or an overwhelming consensus is formed on social media, it will continuously squeeze out those dissenting opinions. The reason is that when a certain viewpoint dominates and becomes widely influential, people will follow the dominant opinion rather than diverging from it, considering the risk of one being isolated or scorned. This theory reveals a pattern that people whose opinions are widely disseminated and accepted tend to act in very confident manner when facing the public and keeps on expressing their opinions. This would have an impact on others who are aware of the dominance of an opinion leader, forcing them to adopt a more conservative and conformist approach. The result of this phenomenon is that those who initially have the dominant opinions will continue to articulate in such a way as to reinforce the status of their viewpoints, while those who disagree are forced to remain silent. The silence of the latter consolidates the strength of the former, and the constant articulateness of the former in turn exacerbates the other side's silence. This gives rise to the so-called "spiral of silence". A growing body of researches has found that "the spiral of silence" is prevalent on the Internet today, and that the micro politics created by WeChat cannot help being implicated.

All of these issues raise a more austere question: does the rise of micro politics as the concomitant of microculture enhance or limit our freedom of expression and imagination?

So far, we have preliminarily described the symptoms and implications of Micro Cultures. Of course, Micro Cultures are much more complex than that. As a new cultural form, and a ubiquitous form of information, Micro Culture has considerably changed our cognition, behavior, and subjectivity, and has raised a series of new and urgent questions. I've made, in this section, some critical reflection on some aspects of Micro Culture, but it is still too early to make a definitive judgment on Micro Culture, which is evolving, and its complex consequences need to be further analyzed.

No matter how Micro Culture might develop, and regardless of the consequences of these developments, there is always the important question of how to choose the most effective strategies to engage with Micro Culture. If we take the cultivation of modern citizenship as the quintessential goal of our project of promoting rational subjects in China nowadays, we must carefully steer away from the restraints of hyper attention, avoiding the negative effects of micro cognition and micro narratives, and, if possible, maximizing the beneficial factors of Micro Culture for the purpose of forging rational subjectivity among citizens. Here, I would like to borrow a buzzword to describe our possible strategy, that is, "crossing-over" (穿越). By "crossing-over", I mean marshaling some overall structural force to traverse the disparate Micro Cultural fragments, to travel through micro cognitive paradigms and micro device paradigms of the subject, and finally to penetrate the diasporic micro subjects. The aim is to gather and link various micro energies, to reconstruct new totality in fragmicronization, and, ultimately, to achieve a systemic cognition of society and self. In other words, "crossing-over" means a new subjectivity under the condition of fragmicronization, a subjectivity capable of grasping the totality in a self-conscious and cognitive way. To be specific, it means three types of cognitive power. First, the ability of contextualization, that is, the ability to restore the fragmicronized information to a specific context, so that the information is no longer an ungrounded "hearsay", but rather something reconstructed in a specific context. Second, the ability to making a structure, which means the ability to link different pieces of information so that not only can the fragments of information be reduced to a contextual product, but also disparate information in different contexts can form a structured schema, which in the end facilitates one's understanding of the tenets of information. Third, the ability of totalizing, that is, the subject's ability to transcend the effect of fragmicronization, and to understand social and cultural phenomena as a whole, in an era of pervasive fragmicronization. This ability can also be seen as the further enhancement and improvement of the previous two cognitive powers. The most important issue here is the modern rationality of our citizens, who can ultimately construct an overall understanding of society and culture through rational cognition, such as reasoning, argumentation, self-criticism, and critique. To a certain extent, the fragmicronization of contemporary society has restricted and even obstructed a citizen's acquisition of "crossing-over" skills. Moreover, we are taught to get used to various cognitive behaviors associated with fragmicronization. Therefore, promoting "crossing-over" is not only a tactic, but also a strategic task.

In the face of the rapidly developing Micro Culture, "crossing-over" has its own dilemma: the entertainmentization of politics or the politicization of entertainment? These are two radically different paths. It is reasonable, I believe, to realize political demands through entertainment, but it is dangerous to entertainmentize politics, because a plethora of entertainment will eventually make its political function run out of steam, or will secretively deconstruct politics by virtue of entertainment. Finally, crossing-over is also a matter of reconfiguring the relationship between miniaturization and totality. While miniaturization is an effective subversion of totality, miniaturization also results in decentralization. The purpose of crossing-over is to subvert the traditional identity through cultural miniaturization, to absorb the diverse resources of Micro Culture, and to reconstruct a kind of pluralistic totality laced with cultural diversity in a new framework. To propel the modernization of Chinese society and culture is its ultimate goal.

Notes

1 David Harvey. *The Condition of Postmodernity: An Enquiry into the Origins of Cultural Change.* Trans. Yan Jia. Beijing: The Commercial Press. pp.301–205.
2 See the entry of "microculture" in Wikipedia. <http://en.wikipedia.org/wiki/Microculture>
3 Ferdinand Tönnies. *Community and Society.* Trans. Lin Rongyuan. Beijing: Peking University Press, 2010.
4 Max Weber. *Religion and the World.* Trans. Kang Le and Jian Huimei. Taipei: Taiwan Yuanliu Publishing Company, 1989.
5 Walter Benjamin. *The Origin of German Tragic Drama.* Trans. Li Shuangzhi. Beijing: Beijing Normal University Press, 2013.
6 See Thomas S. Kuhn. *The Structure of Scientific Revolutions.* Trans. Jin Wulun and Hu Xinhe. Beijing: Peking University Press, 2012; Jean-François Lyotard. *The Postmodern Condition: A Report on Knowledge.* Trans. Che Geun-shan. Beijing: Sanlian Bookstore, 1997; Zygmunt Bauman. *Liquid Modernity.* Trans. Ouyang Jingen. Shanghai: Shanghai Sanlian Bookstore, 2002.
7 The concept of "mode of information" was coined by the American scholar Mark Poster. Imitating Marx's term "mode of production", he proposes that contemporary society is an information society and that its "mode of information" is an important dimension of social and cultural formation. For more details, see Mark Poster, *The Mode of Information: Poststructuralism and Social Contexts.* Trans. Fan Jingwen. Beijing: The Commercial Press, 2000.
8 See Nicholas Carr. *Shallows: What the Internet is Doing Our Brains.* New York: Norton, 2010.
9 N. Katherine Hayles. "Hyper and Deep Attention: The Generational Divide in Cognitive Mode", in *Profession* 1 (2007). p.187.
10 Ibid.
11 "Assimilation" and "accommodation" are the core concepts of Piaget's genetic epistemology. In his psychological research, he found that human cognitive abilities develop in a constant balance of assimilation and accommodation. Assimilation is the acceptance of familiar stimuli by the interpreter's existing cognitive schema, which is used to

understand and interpret the stimuli; accommodation, on the contrary, is the adjustment and adaptation of the schema triggered by the new stimuli. See Jean Piaget. *The Psychology of Intelligence*. London: Routledge, 2003. pp.8–9.

12 The term "device paradigm" was coined by Albert Borgmann, who asserts that contemporary society is one of device paradigm, which provides convenience and efficiency, while profoundly changing our perceptions, behaviors, and human relationships. See Albert Borgmann. *Technology and the Character of Contemporary Life: A Philosophical Inquiry*. Chicago: University of Chicago, 1984.

10 From "immersive reading" to "fast reading"

The crisis of today's reading culture

Each era has its own strength and its own problems. In our time, China's economy has grown far beyond expectations, and technological advances have dramatically changed the life world. However, behind the façade of heartening developments, some bleak omens are slowly emerging. In 2013, Guangxi Normal University Press made an online questionnaire entitled "Those Books You Just Can't Finish Reading". And according to more than 3,000 responses from WeChat, the top ten books in the list were as follows: *Dream of the Red Chamber*, *One Hundred Years of Solitude*, *Romance of the Three Kingdoms*, *In Search of Lost Time*, *Walden*, *Water Margin*, *The Unbearable Lightness of Being*, *Journey to the West*, *How the Steel Was Tempered*, and *Ulysses*. If we take this poll seriously, the questions it begets are deeply disturbing for those professionals specializing in education, cultural studies, and literature. One puzzling question: Why do these classics become books "you just can't finish reading"?

Every era has its own cultural trends. Today, with the high-speed development since the reform and opening-up over 30 years ago, China's economy, society, culture, and education have undergone profound changes, and national reading is no exception! Of course, there is also some good news about reading. For example, the "12th National Reading Survey Report" revealed that 58% of the adults read books in 2014, which is an increase by 0.2% compared with the statistic of the previous year. More importantly, digital reading accounted for 58.1%, up 8% from one year ago, although the annual per capita consumption of print book was only 4.56.[1] We may offer an optimistic explanation: the reason why the consumption of print book is so low is that digital readers are replacing paper books as the "new favorite" medium.

However, behind these seemingly encouraging signs, there are some more complex questions. For example, is there a hidden link between the prevalence of digital e-reading and the decline in Chinese and foreign literary classics into "unreadable books"? In recent years, there is a growing concern that China's contemporary reading culture is in a certain predicament. The way people (especially the youngsters) read has quietly changed, especially as digital media have given rise to a variety of forms of electronic reading, which has greatly changed our reading behavior and habits. The reading ecology today is very different from that of 20 or 30 years ago. Most of those interested in the reading culture in China usually have the impression that the popular reading today has become more and more "speedy", "diverse", "short", "shallow", and "fragmented". Behind these seemingly simple adjectives lie some complicated reasons. Many scholars have analyzed the reading dilemma from different perspectives, and come to different conclusions. Some point out that the current dilemma is due to the fact that print culture has been replaced by digital culture; some assert that it is caused by the development of contemporary Omnimedia; some believe that it is due to the profound influence of visual culture; and others focus on the changed orientation of reading and behavior owing to the transformation of readers' taste, or attribute it to the change of zeitgeist, or highlight the evolution of readerly needs and expectations brought about by cultural changes.[2] Undoubtedly, these discussions reveal the complex causes of the current dilemma of reading culture in China from different perspectives, and shed some light on the topic under consideration.

Among the many diagnoses and analyses, one argument is noteworthy: readers' attention span is shortening in the current mode of digital reading.

> The deluge of texts, information overload and uselessly accumulated discourse are what readers have to face in the digital age. The pursuit of speed is the most basic characteristic of this era, and people are prone to have anxiety, simplifying reading and learning, and lacking patience, calm and the rare ability of meditation in the traditional sense.[3]

This is indeed a worrying tendency in our reading culture today. If we look to other fields, we'll see that people seem to be less and less patient in all professions. The traditional virtue of "exquisite workmanship that comes from toil and moil" is now largely obsolete, and an all-encompassing "high-speed culture" is galloping toward us.[4] For this new form of culture, the law is speed and efficiency, and the principle of "the faster, the better" is unbreakable! Furthermore, since instrumental rationality is now widely championed as common sense for everyday behavior, the old virtue, "patience", is becoming increasingly obsolete. Knowledge, information, documents, databases, and publications are proliferating exponentially. The traditional model of scholarly elucubration is long bygone. Therefore, the "speedy", "diverse", "short", "shallow", and "fragmented" reading style has become the inevitable choice of the reading public.

In my opinion, the current shortage of reading patience is obviously caused by more than one factor. In a broad sense, the modern transformation of our society and culture has greatly changed the ways of knowledge production and acquisition. One can find ample evidence from the social and cultural development since the reform and opening-up. It is beyond the scope of this chapter to make a thorough examination of the causes and their interrelationships. Rather, I select a specific perspective to analyze the reading dilemma that we face at present. A basic assumption here is that a given reading medium shapes a specific type of reading behavior, which in turn constructs the reading habits of readers. Different reading cultures have different reading behaviors, and changes in terms of external behaviors are easier to observe on an empirical level. Changes in reading habits are often difficult to detect, but they are crucial factors in determining reading culture and should never be underestimated.

Obviously, there are many different approaches to understanding the current impasse about reading. We may turn to cultural history, sociology, philosophy, psychology, cognitive science, pedagogy, and even linguistics, all of which offer distinctive perspectives on the status quo of reading culture, and arrive at different conclusions. As mentioned earlier, the causes are extremely complex, and they might act as forces interacting with each other in a "field", with a complex structure of relationships. Therefore, it is impossible to stick to any single path and to provide a thorough and definitive causal analysis here. In this part, we adopt an eclectic method, combining cultural history, philosophy of technology, and cognitive science, and have recourse to some empirical findings to diagnose the current reading dilemma in China in a certain light, and then venture to suggest some solutions.

Many studies tend to assume that electronic reading in the digital age is an important cause of such dramatic changes in our reading culture. In other words, the new reading media and technologies have turned traditional reading upside down, and thus brought about many problems. If we simply follow this line of thought, it might be inevitable to fall into the trap of technological determinism. That is why we should have recourse to a more dialectical approach. Recent studies in the fields of technology history, media archeology, or communication history have revealed the causes of social and cultural evolution from the perspective of technology. The invention of printing, for example, considerably changed the path of modernization; the birth of film, for instance, also had a profound impact on both society and culture. From Benjamin through McLuhan to Baudrillard and so on, their critiques of culture largely chose the same approach.[5] But in my opinion, there is a complex relationship—more precisely, a dialectical interplay—between technological advance and human culture. History has repeatedly shown that technological progress constantly leads to the invention of new devices. On the one hand, new devices reconfigure the human subjectivity and our behavior in a way that corresponds to the paradigm of these new devices; on the other hand, the newly formed subjectivity, in turn, presents new demands for technology and its devices. This highly interdependent and interactive relationship is, I think, a crucial way of understanding the relationship between technology and socio-culture. To illustrate this relationship, I will introduce the term "device paradigm" borrowed from the philosophy of technology as theorized by the German-American philosopher Albert Borgmann. Borgmann's examination of contemporary life reveals that it is characterized by an increasing dependence on the devices that technological progress has given rise to, and that these new devices have formulated the paradigms of our social life. What technological progress helps to create, when constituting new paradigms of life, has profoundly changed our traditional ways of living. For example, in the past people used to do some family chores together, such as wood chopping for building fires, activities that involved all family members and unite them in an emotional, communicative way. However, when centralized heating systems were invented, the device transformed these traditional family activities in a way that makes some skills, participation, and involvement obsolete, and the scenario of a family chopping wood and building a fire together, etc. was out of date. Borgmann notes, in particular, that the emergence of new devices dissolves the inherent relevance between objects and human involvement, while the devices themselves are hidden behind so that no one would even notice them. Thus, objects become commodities, and people are not using objects, but devices as commodities. One of the characteristics of the device paradigm is the mutability of the means and the immutability of the purpose; the purpose of heating, for example, is constant, but new heating devices are bursting unto the scenes all the time. Another feature of the device paradigm is the concealment of the means and the prominence of the purpose, which means that when the devices are making our life more and more convenient, their purpose is always on the board, while the device itself is relegated to the backseat and remains invisible there. More interestingly, as the design of devices becomes more "human" or "user-friendly", the gap between the device's functional accessibility and its structural sophistication becomes wider and wider, but the users are not aware of this discrepancy.[6] Borgmann suggests that an effective way to subvert the domination and negative influence of the device paradigm is through music, jogging, and craftsmanship, which he calls "focal things and practice". It is through such concentration-boosting activities that one is freed from the domination of the device paradigm and return to a life that reflects one's authenticity.

It is true that the device paradigm is not unique to our time and that in different times, there are different kinds of device paradigms. In the long history of human reading, our ancestors did invent a variety of devices and the corresponding paradigms, ranging from images or symbols inscribed by the primitive people in caves or on rocks, through scripts on turtle's shells, bamboo, and cloth, to the invention of paper and printing, and finally to all kinds of trendy electronic readers. However, it is important to stress that the rapid development of contemporary technology has completely reconfigured the device paradigm. And today's digital devices are essentially different from any traditional reading devices, and have given rise to a brand-new reading culture completely different from the old-fashioned print culture. The focus of this section is on how contemporary digital electronic devices are reshaping our reading behaviors and dispositions? How are these behaviors and dispositions in turn hooked by and addicted to the devices? Is there any connection between them and the reading dilemma under consideration?

To answer these questions, we need to make reference to some theories, in particular a new theory with the rubric "comparative textual media" (CTM). The priority of this theory is a comparative study of different textual media technologies, systems, and reading styles. Through a series of comparisons and analyses, one may reveal the truth about electronic digitalized reading. The first task of comparative textual media studies is to establish a "media framework", in which the media characteristics of different texts and the chronicle of their evolution in history can be described as a complex family tree.[7] Although CTM studies are usually applied only in a synchronic manner—that is to say, the complex relationship between different textual media in the same period, such as the relationship between visual and auditory media in contemporary reading culture—I argue that this approach can also be used diachronically, which means we can make a diachronic comparison of various phases of reading culture and of their respective textual media conditioned by the evolving textual media, and relate the comparison to the history of reading culture. As far as the purpose of my analysis is concerned, the "cultural history" approach of CTM is the most effective one, as it allows for a diachronic CTM inquiry, calling our attention to the shift from print culture to electronic culture. By doing so, we can probably tease out some sophisticated explanations about today's reading crisis and its consequences.

Print culture and immersive reading

When it comes to a diachronic investigation of comparative textual media, we will first touch upon the issue of periodization of the cultural history of human reading. According to some cultural historians specializing on textual media, human civilization has roughly gone through four stages: oral culture, codex culture, print culture, and electronic culture.[8] As far as reading is concerned, the reading media and devices in the four stages are completely different. Now, let's we briefly examine these four stages, calling special attention to the peculiar reading behavior shaped by print civilization—immersive reading.

As we know, the "textual" medium of oral culture was no more than human speech, and the so-called "reading" was actually executed through the speaker's spoken language, which is actually a kind of "reading via listening". The typical communication scenario of oral culture is face-to-face communication between people, with salient features of *Anwesenheit* and temporal-spatial restrictions. Only when the speaker and the addressee are together in the same time-space could the "reading" of oral texts happen. For example, the traditional "storytellers" were inseparable from a typical situation of "reading" oral texts. The rise of codex culture was attributed to the invention of writing systems and writing instruments, when reading shifted to interpreting texts written on different mediums. According to some studies, during the time of codex culture, human communication retained much of the oral-auditory character of oral culture—a notable example is the overfamiliarity of recitation. However, the textual medium gradually began to shift from the auditory to the visual, that is, from the verbal to the written. Only at the stage of modern print culture was the shift—a shift from "reading via listening" to "reading"—completed. The textual medium then took the form of black letters printed on white paper, and people no longer used their ears to receive information, but used their eyes to skim the words on the page to grasp their meanings. Such a change in terms of textual medium brought about a new kind of reading, the oral-auditory character of oral culture began to disappear. The new textual medium created by the print culture was decisive in that it led not only to a profound change in reading styles but also to the advent of a new visual paradigm characterized by silent reading.[9] During the transitional period, the ascendency of oral-auditory paradigm was replaced by the visual one, a more important change being that print culture greatly expanded the scope of knowledge production, dissemination, and reception. The prerequisites of *Anwesenheit* and shared time-space in oral culture, as well as the uniqueness of handwritten books in codex culture, were undone, and a large number of reproducible books were able to be widely distributed. The emergence of mechanical reproduction and new devices, as Walter Benjamin points out, would inevitably lead to "the warring breakdown", which in turn helped give birth to modern societies, cultures, and arts.[10] But a special point I want to make here is that this change was also paralleled by the birth of "literacy"—simply put, one's ability to read and write—a quality crucial to modern civilization. Along with the dissemination and popularization of printed artifacts, modern education came into being, with "literacy" being one of the basic goals of public education. The spread of this ability in turn gave rise to a brand-new reading culture. Today, many a domain that we usually associate with modern culture are more or less related to the emergence of print culture and the spread of literacy.

In what follows, I'll focus on the unique reading behavior and dispositions constructed by print culture, and proceed to reveal the dramatic changes that have occurred in contemporary reading culture, by comparing it with the previous reading patterns in oral and codex cultures and, more importantly, with the electronic culture since then. From the perspective of CTM technologies, the emergence of print culture depends on two material conditions: the invention of paper and the invention of movable type. The invention of paper was a revolutionary change to the medium of text. The earliest mediums of engraved scripts are some natural objects, from the rugged stone walls in caves, to the sand or trees, all the way to the turtle shells, bamboo, sheepskin, etc. These rough, uneven, and irregular materials posed serious challenges to transcribing and reading. The emergence of paper, one of China's "Four Great Inventions", dramatically changed the way people wrote and read. To transcribe various literature and anecdotal stories on light, flat and white paper became a major advance in the history of human civilization. The art historian Meyer Shapiro, who made an in-depth study of painting mediums, has an important finding—the colorful and expressive style of the fine art was possible only when a flat wall or canvas was available; moreover, the discovery of perspectivism in particular was in fact indebted to this development. He thus concludes that had the ancient painters only worked on rugged rock walls in caves it would not be possible for them to conceive the methods and ideas of deep three-dimensional perspectivism on a two-dimensional plane, and nor is it possible for Western painting techniques and styles to make a great leap forward.[11] Shapiro's analysis and conclusion of the mediality of painting can be used to explain why the invention of paper mattered. Without paper, many of the valuable legacies and innovations of human civilization would be inconceivable today.

More importantly, movable type, the great gift of ancient Chinese ingenuity, freed mankind from the confines of codex culture and brought it into a new era of mechanical reproduction. The history of China has repeatedly shown that the culture of reading was extremely related to the Empire's apparatus, its cultural traditions, and its scholarly class. The legacy of Chinese civilization would have been insignificant had it not been for the canon in printed form. Some scholars have even argued that the reading and writing style fostered by printing not only shaped the peculiarities of China in cultural history, but was also extremely important to the political and social development of China throughout its imperial periods.[12] In the West, Gutenberg's discovery of movable type in the mid-15th century and the technology of large-scale mechanical reproduction revolutionized Christian culture from the Middle Ages onward, and accelerated the development of modern science and the spread of secular knowledge during the Renaissance. The following conclusion has been widely accepted in academia: the invention of printing marked a shift not only in reading, but in European societies themselves; printed texts had a profound impact on every aspect of European life—"indeed, the invention announced one of world history's greatest social and intellectual ruptures".[13]

The issues I am tackling here are these questions: to what extent did the emergence of paper-based printed texts construct new reading behaviors and habits? What kind of new culture of reading has it given rise to? From the perspective of CTM, what is most noteworthy is the arrival of a new way of reading unique to print civilization—silent reading, which features nothing but immersive reading.

As mentioned earlier, the slow transformation from oral to print culture, paralleled by the change of textual media from oral narrative through hand-copied text to printed text, implies a profound shift from listening-reading (reading by ears) to silent reading (reading by eyes), from auditory comprehension to visual comprehension. Although silent reading existed was nothing new in the pre-printing codex culture, the spread of printing culture definitely reinforced and popularized silent reading, a reading behavior typical of the print-culture era. Steven Fisher writes,

> Whereupon silent reading, wherever it was practised, introduced a new dimension to the performance, one that endures to this day. Reading went from a public to a private act. A reader no longer shared the text with others (who would interrupt with questions or comments), or even tied sounds to letters. She or he could read confidentially, unheard, accessing concepts directly, letting thoughts proceed at a higher level of consciousness, cross-referencing and comparing, considering and evaluating. This changed Western reading habits profoundly, influencing not only reading's external circumstances and matter, but also its psychological effect on the practitioner. The accomplishment became part of one's internalized existence. Reading transcended its social function as a tool, to become a human faculty.[14]

Specifically, what exactly is the act of silent reading? How does it differ from the previous reading acts in oral and codex cultures? In my opinion, there are four features of silent reading.

First of all, silent reading is silent, private, and quiet reading, which is different from recitation or listening-reading (epic, lyric, or *huaben*) characteristic of oral culture. In the age of silent reading, reading no longer takes place in a situation where multiple voices communicate with one another, but a solitary situation in which one communicates with the text. Benjamin in his famous essay "The Storyteller" points out in particular that the storyteller must be in the company of the audience, while the reader of a printed novel is isolated. "In this solitude of his, the reader of a novel seizes upon his material more jealously than anyone else. He is ready to make it completely his own, to devour it, as it were".[15] In *How to Read and Why*, Harold Bloom also makes the case for silent reading as "a habit of solitude".[16] Silent reading is associated with a man's solitary condition, and the individual reader makes some meaningful connection with the world via a particular text. This echoes what Fischer says about the development of silent reading as a move from a public act to a private one.

Although solitude is one's external condition of aloneness, it generates a certain internal cognition and psychological state that helps trigger imagination and thinking. This brings us to the second characteristic of silent reading—the cultivation of rationality. Let's return to the comparison of textual media: unlike the spatial juxtaposition of images or pictures, printed texts are composed of linearly arranged words in a regular manner. The lucidity of language, the logicalness of expression, the normativity of grammar, and the linearity of word sequence all necessarily require the reader to read according to a certain formula. Moreover, any script as a sign is always abstract (even, in some cases, hieroglyphic). Therefore, to understand script means an effort to make sense of the signified via abstract signifiers, and then to grasp the complex meaning of a text. Studies of silent reading show that the eyes scan in an orderly way between the black types on the page, constantly converting them into some specific meaning in the mind, a decoding process that is not only the process of receiving information but also the process of understanding and interpreting it. Therefore, reading is always inseparable from thinking. More interestingly, if compared with the act of "reading" films and TV programs, book-reading is relaxed, bilateral, and repeatable, while film- and TV-watching is one-way, irreversible, and unstoppable. It is commonplace during one's reading that she from time to time pauses, taking her time to peruse the words, thinking about what she is reading, before she resumes reading. Such a state of reading provides the reader with more possibilities to invoke rational thinking. Moreover, the so-called "literacy" I mentioned earlier is also a rational faculty of the subject. Because for those equipped with literary, reading becomes a kind of highly internalized cognitive method, which unwittingly cultivates one's rational thinking as a result of reading. That also accounts for the Chinese proverb, "the more books you read, the more reasonable you are". Many studies have linked the act of reading printed texts to the cultivation of rational subjectivity. In comparing the morphological differences between oral, printed, and electronic cultures, Mark Poster notes, in particular, that

> speech constitutes subjects as members of a community by solidifying the ties between individuals. Print constitutes subjects as rational, autonomous egos, as stable interpreters of culture who, in isolation, make logical connections from linear symbols. Media language replaces the community of speakers and undermines the referentiality of discourse necessary for the rational ego.[17]

This seemingly simple observation delves into the complexities of subjectivity construction from a CTM approach, highlighting the construction of rational subjectivity, a function that characterizes reading in print culture. In other words, while oral culture's speech was related to the constitution of communal subjectivity, electronic media (especially film and TV) imply the potential hazards of disintegrating the rational ego. In contrast, solitude and rational thinking associated with silent reading in print culture are conducive to the construction of "rational, autonomous egos".

The third characteristic of silent reading is the monotony entailed in the austerity of print. Although visual or illustrated books are also a common genre of paper-based text, the major elements of a printed text are texts, and all images are merely an accessory. The monotony of a printed text necessitates concentration and gaze on the one hand, and inevitably results in the monotony of text reading on the other. In aesthetic studies, when making comparative analysis of different symbolic media, scholars usually have to adopt a different set of criteria with regard to linguistic artifact (such as literature). For example, painting, sculpture, and architecture are defined as visual arts, while music is categorized into auditory art, and drama and film into visual-auditory or performing arts. According to this classification, literature would be uncategorizable, so it is often loosely classified into a special category—"imaginative art".[18] In comparison, literature, essentially composed of abstract signs, has neither the immediacy of the plastic arts, nor the directness of some expressive arts such as music, nor the compelling liveness of drama and film. This is why reading literature is different from experiencing other forms of art media, and often seems boring and monotonous. After all, meaning must be understood by decoding abstract scripts. The oneness of printed text inevitably leads to the purity and monotony of silent reading, which both account for the charm of silent reading and bring about its limits owing to its lack of immediacy as felt in audio-visual media. Compared with the multimedia and multi-linkage characteristic of contemporary electronic culture, the dullness, tedium and monotony of reading paper-based texts are obvious. And this is the reason why contemporary electronic reading is so appealing.

From the solitude of silent reading, through its rational thinking to its monotony, we eventually arrive at the fourth, and the most important, characteristic of silent reading: the contemplative nature of immersive reading, which adds to the rationality of reading. In Western languages, the word "contemplation" refers to a state of concentration, which is similar to Zhuangzi's claim that "Where the will is not diverted from its object, the spirit is concentrated" (用志不分，乃凝于神). According to the Oxford English Dictionary, contemplation is "the act of looking at something in a calm and careful way". It has the following connotations: first, a profound state of reflective thinking; second, a state of thinking and planning; and third, meditation in the religious sense. In my opinion, a typical state of mood incurred by silent reading in the face of a paper text is readerly immersiveness. The contemplative meditation produced from time to time or even continuously during the reading process leads to the reader's sense of "self-loss"—completely absorbed in the world created by the text. From the perspective of cognitive psychology, contemplation produced by silent reading is also a unique reading paradigm, that is, immersive reading. Some experts describe such reading as "deep reading": it is "the array of sophisticated processes that propel comprehension and that include inferential and deductive reasoning, analogical skills, critical analysis, reflection, and insight".[19] Therefore, we have every reason to define the characteristics of reading in print culture as immersive reading. In contrast, the symptoms of the current reading crisis in the digital age are, to a considerable extent, the very decline in immersive reading and habitus.

"Hypertext" and "hyper attention" in the digital age

Different cultural forms have their own textual media and unique paradigms of device, which are bound to foster reading behaviors and habitus in their right; in turn, these behaviors and habitus reinforce the subject's dependence on certain media and devices and lead to "addiction". In my view, reading behaviors are the external acts of readers, while habitus are their internalized psychological tendencies. It is easier to observe one's behavior, while habitus is hidden somewhere deep in the subject's psyche, unseen, and intangible. For reading studies, the line of thought should be from the outside to the inside, from the surface to the inside, and from the behavioral analysis to the meditation on habitus. One of my basic arguments is that many of the symptoms of the current reading crisis are more or less related to the changes in the collective reading habitus.

What is habitus? The French sociologist Bourdieu has made a brilliant study on this topic. According to him, habitus is the behavioral disposition of a person's social practice in a particular field. The habitus, thus, is a mental construct that has been or is being structured, which guides the subject's behavior to act in accordance with a certain structure. Habitus, field, and practice, he argues, are three dialectical categories that interact with each other:

> On one side, it is a relation of *conditioning*: the field structures the habitus, which is the product of the embodiment of the immanent necessity of a field...On the other side, it is a relation of knowledge or *cognitive construction*. Habitus contributes to constituting the field as a meaningful world, a world endowed with sense and value, in which it is worth investing one's energy.[20]

According to this theory, people always live in a particular social and cultural field, and their practice must be driven and guided by specific habitus. For example, young people who grow up in different cultural or social classes are always deeply influenced by the class they belong to. As some studies have found, children of the middle class always show rapport with the bourgeois cultural taste and choose to read books peculiar to this class, while the working-class descendants tend to read popular. This contrast is the result of differing cultural habitus. I use the concept of habitus to expose—in light of the dialectical relationship between habitus, field, and practice—how readers change their reading habitus as the textual media changes, and how the changed reading habitus in turn have an impact on our reading behavior and reading ecology.

So far, I have briefly analyzed the immersive reading that characterizes the print culture, which nurtures complex reading habitus. With the decline in print culture and the rise of digital culture, e-reading has replaced paper-based reading, and human reading style has also changed profoundly. The same is true of our reading habitus. By e-reading, I mean reading in the form of mobile or fixed electronic devices (e-readers, cell phones, computers, iPads, etc.). Here is my crucial point: on the one hand, e-reading has greatly changed reading behavior and habitus, due to the emergence of various mobile data terminals or e-readers; on the other hand, it must be fully noted that e-reading is formed against the backdrop of the rapid development of computer hardware and software technology and Internet. Therefore, the rise of e-reading is by no means an isolated phenomenon. Let's return to Bourdieu's theory—the practice resulting from habitus takes place in a specific field. In the case of reading, such a field is the digital electronic culture, which consists of an array of components, ranging from advanced technology to innovative device paradigms, from the formation of consumer ideology to the domination of visual culture, from the ruling tendency of instrumental rationality to the complicated orientation of high-speed culture, and so on and so forth. It is the multiple factors and their interactions that constitute this field, in which the current reading crisis takes place. However, given the scope of my book, it is not possible to make a thorough analysis of all the parameters and their relationships; rather, I will dwell on the impact of e-reading. Still, it is necessary to emphasize that digital e-reading is found in the context of social, cultural, and technological changes in our age. Therefore, an inquiry into e-reading must take full consideration of the changing context, which is also true of a contextualized study of the current reading problems in China.

In the early 1990s, with the popularity of computers and the advancement of digitalization, a large number of old-fashioned paper texts were converted into electronic ones, with computer screen as the basic interface for many readers (especially the teenagers). Although it might be too early to say that the electronic text has completely replaced the paper text, the explosive growth of electronic data resources, together with the incredible convenience and economy of electronic reading, made electronic reading fashionable in no time. The development of the Internet and the new forms of digitalized hypertext endows e-reading with new momentum. There are two issues that deserve our extra attention: one is the emergence of "hypertext", and another, the formation of "hyper attention".

As we know, in the 1980s, when poststructuralism was in its prime years, there emerged many mind-boggling theories, especially Roland Barthes' theory on "the death of the author" and "textuality". "The death of the author", like Nietzsche's pronouncement that "God is dead", deprives the author of the right to interpret the meaning of his or her own text. His idea of "textuality" declares that the meaning of a text is produced through the activities of human speech, rather than being fixed behind the pages. Barthes' textual theory, first of all, emphasizes the etymological meaning in Latin, assuming the text as something "woven". Second, Barthes vividly depicts the text as a web-like system, with thousands of entrances and exits, through which readers can freely come and go and make their own understandings and interpretations. Third, Barthes reiterates that the author is a singular concept, while the readers are "plural". The death of the author is replaced by the birth of the readers, which means a profound transformation from the singular meaning to the plural one.[21] Looking back at Barth's theory of text from the standpoint of 21st-century digital electronic culture, his words may be regarded as a prophecy—about the advent of the electronic reading in the digital age. Now, "hypertext" has proved Barth's theoretical imagination. The hypertext has completely overturned the "God-Author" view of textual meaning and realized the rich "productivity" of text in human linguistic activities. The further result is a radical transformation of our daily reading behavior and habitus.

"Hypertext" has different versions of definition, among which I will use the classic one made by Theodore H. Nelson, one who coined the term in his 1960 book *Literary Machines, 0/2*.

> By "hypertext", I mean non-sequential writing — text that branches and allows choices to the reader, best read at an interactive screen. As popularly conceived, this is a series of text chunks connected by links which offer the reader different pathways.[22]

Simply put, hypertext is realized with the help of today's computer networks and IT technology, taking the forms of e-books, online texts, CD-ROMs, databases, websites, etc. Nelson's definition of "hypertext" highlights three salient features: linking, branching, and non-sequential. "Linking" refers to the fact that hypertext is composed of a web-like structure in which the original text is linked to many subtexts, thus creating a highly productive intertextual relation. With the help of computer networks, an original text is linked to an infinite number of subtexts, thus forming a boundless network, which is akin to Barthes' notion of textual "weaving". "Branching" highlights the diversity of readerly choices and opens up a new space for the production of textual polysemy, which may be regarded as a proof of Barthes' claim that there are countless "entrances and exits" in a text, and as an affirmation of meaning production on the side of the reader. If the two features, linking and branching, are combined, what Barthes calls "the joy of the text" surfaces. The reading of hypertext not only creates numerous links with and choices about subtexts, but also ushers us to a variety of multimedia subtexts—both audio and video—and leads to uncertainties in reading procedures, orientation, attention, understanding, and interpretation. In Nelson's words, linking provides the reader with different paths to the text. Finally, "non-sequential" fundamentally breaks the linear logic of composing and reading paper-based texts, forming a non-linear, non-sequential reading paradigm unique to hypertext. Ultimately, hypertext creates a "non-linear textuality" that is very different from paper text.[23] This creates a "nonlinear textuality" (nonlinear textuality) that is very different from that of paper. At this point, a preliminary conclusion can be drawn that the emergence of hypertext in the digital age has completely overthrown the paper-based reading paradigm of print culture, and has rendered reading increasingly nonlinear, random, and uncertain. It is characterized by the fact that readers can enter and exit from countless possible routeways—title, keyword, index, quote, character name, the event, time, space, etc.—which make reading no longer a definite linear process, but an intertextual process consisting of many pauses, switches, and infinite possibilities.

The emergence of hypertext contributes to a completely new reading behavior, namely, the so-called "reading on the prowl", which is composed of an array of searching, scanning, skimming, and skipping. This mode of reading in turn has given rise to a new type of attention—"hyper attention". In a 2008 study targeting US college students, N. Katherine Hayles found that it is difficult for today's college students to peruse Dickens' novels, noting that this "M generation" (media generation) has newly developed "hyper (or excessive) attention". This is an unprecedented pattern of attention inadvertently formed during the youth's experience in anime, the Internet, films & TV programs, and video games. More importantly, according to Hayles, the hyper-attention model is very different from the traditional deep-attention model. She writes,

> The shift in cognitive styles can be seen in the contrast between deep attention and hyper attention. Deep attention, the cognitive style traditionally associated with the humanities, is characterized by concentrating on a single object for long periods (say, a novel by Dickens), ignoring outside stimuli while so engaged, preferring a single information stream, and having a high tolerance for long focus times. Hyper attention is characterized by switching focus rapidly among different tasks, preferring multiple information streams, seeking a high level of stimulation, and having a low tolerance for boredom. The contrast in the two cognitive modes may be captured in an image: picture a college sophomore, deep in *Pride and Prejudice*, with her legs draped over an easy chair, oblivious to her ten-year-old brother sitting in front of a console, jamming on a joystick while he plays *Grand Theft Auto*. Each cognitive mode has advantages and limitations. Deep attention is superb for solving complex problems represented in a single medium, but it comes at the price of environmental alertness and flexibility of response. Hyper attention excels at negotiating rapidly changing environments in which multiple foci compete for attention; its disadvantage is impatience with focusing for periods on a non-interactive object such as a Victorian novel or complicated math problem.[24]

Those who are concerned about the current reading ecology in China would share the feeling that "hyper attention" has become very commonplace in our reading life today. Hayles summarizes four characteristics of this mode of attention: focus switching, preference for multiple information stream, addiction to stimuli, and impatience with boredom. In my opinion, these characteristics just vividly illustrate the behavior and habitus associated with digital reading today. With further scrutiny, I think the most crucial feature is the fourth one—we are now having an extremely tolerance for monotony or boredom in reading, which accounts for the constant switching of focus and disproportionate preference for information stream and strong stimuli. As we know, reading is very different from watching movies or playing video games, for reading is simple and monotonous, as discussed above. Too many electronic devices today offer too many dazzling tricks and gimmicks, raising the reader's expectations about information in terms of interpretation and experience to an exceedingly high level so that readers will seek more diverse, entertaining, and multimedia-based information.

It is worth our further consideration that deep attention is antithetical to hyper attention precisely in the aforementioned four aspects. Deep attention enables us to focus for a long period of time on a single object and a single information stream, without paying attention to external stimuli—this mode of reading perfectly corresponds to immersive reading in print culture, during the age of which readers were able to be stay attuned to one object, staving off distractions and persisting in the pursuit of a single target in spite of boredom and monotony. The old Chinese saying "a good sword takes ten years to make" or "a bench is not afraid of being cold for ten years" is generally about the same wisdom. In an era when everyone can become famous overnight, in a time when "fast food" culture is knotted into the fabric of daily life, in an era of information explosion and "seckilling", ten years is too long to be bearable. In this light, it is understandable that literary canon would top the list "Those Books You Just Can't Finish Reading".

e-Reading culture and its new habitus

With the invention of various new reading interfaces and devices, and with the change in the textual medium of reading, a new kind of reading culture is gradually taking shape. That is, a digital e-reading culture.

How has e-reading changed our reading ecology? What kind of new reading styles and habitus has it ushered in? Here I will make references to some empirical studies abroad. First, let's take a look at a recent research on reading conducted by Naomi Baron. Based on an extensive survey of college students from more than 30 countries in Europe and North America, Baron clearly outlines the main characteristics of electronic reading:

- Loss of concentration due to distraction (especially by other functions available through digital devices). The exception here may be e-readers that do not have general Internet connection.
- Exchanging linear reading for searching or skimming… [O]nline reading has created a new culture of what elsewhere I have called "snippet literacy".
- Shrinking expectations about reasonable text length. The proliferation of short textual formats (instant messages, text messages, Twitter, mobile apps for news outlets, and even mobile-phone novels) correlates with perceptions that we lack the leisure time for longer reading… and with university faculty members' growing tendency to assign short online readings (chapters, articles) in lieu of entire books.
- Assumption that reading should include instant access to other resources. Platforms with Internet access enable users, in the act of reading, to draw relevant information from other sources. As a subject in the second study reported, what she liked most about reading on a mobile device was being able to "toggle between my book and my foreign language dictionaries easily.[25]

In fact, these four characteristics can be boiled down to an overall trend, that is, the unfeasibility of immersive reading being focused on a single text, although it used to be the dominant way of reading. In the age of electronic media, however, it has been replaced by skimming. While immersive reading, which is often presented as continuous, in-depth reading, corresponds to printed text, skimming, aligned with electronic hypertext, often takes the form of transitory, superficial, and focus-shifting mode of reading. The repeated practice of the latter type of reading in the digital field inevitably cultivates new reading habitus, which is the root of today's reading problems. Some data from Baron's empirical study also strongly support this point. 91% of those students who love electronic reading complain that they are easily distracted when reading on screen and have difficulty concentrating on the text; 78% of those who prefer reading printed texts report that they can easily concentrate on and immerse themselves in the reading.[26] In terms of the functionality of reading, immersive reading tilts to understanding and interpretation, often accompanied by deep thinking or cognitive activities, while skimming functions when one mainly attempts to capture mosaic information, to collect materials, and to browse a large quantity of documents. So, a reader who practices skimming usually has little investment in in-depth interpretation and understanding. The characteristics of these two reading styles respectively correspond to the two modes of attention identified by Hayles—immersive reading relies on deep attention, while skimming hinges on hyper attention.

A number of empirical studies abroad have demonstrated the changes in reading behavior and habitus caused by e-reading. For example, a research team in Norway had two groups of readers read the same short story—one group was assigned to read the paper text, while the other was assigned to read the electronic text. A comparative analysis of the reading effects finds that there was a salient difference between two groups: those who read the paper text had a better memory about the content than those who read electronically.[27] Another study based in the United States also showed that 51% of the students surveyed said that they remembered paper texts better than electronic texts, and only 2% said the other way around.[28] There are many different explanations. A frequently quoted account is that the printed text is a tangible object, which allows the reader to thumb through the pages, and to take notes with a pen. Furthermore, a hardcopy book's binding, the quality of paper, the smell of ink, and the bodily movements accompanied by reading are combined in such a way as to reinforce the memory of the text. In contrast, in electronic reading, whether it is on computer screen or an e-reader/cell phone/tablet, the text is presented in a way that lacks the tangibility as experienced in a print book. In addition to the materiality and tangibility of paper texts, the key difference, I argue, is actually that it is difficult for electronic reading to produce the immersive experience as seen in paper-text reading. Instead, electronic reading is apt to bring about distractions associated with focus switching and the pursuit of information stimuli. Through the contemplative meditation of immersive reading, the reader is in a better position to focus on the pages and delve into deep reading. Compared to the easily distracted interface browsing, the immersive paper-text reading will certainly leave a deeper imprint on the cerebral cortex, making it easier to remember.

In the digital age, what has happened to human reading behavior and habitus, thanks to changes in textual media and device paradigms? It is largely accepted to categorize reading into four basic types: skimming, scanning, extensive reading, and intensive reading. Skimming is to look for the gist of a text; scanning is to hunt specific information; extensive reading is to read for entertainment; and intensive reading is to read with one's full attention. In the age of electronic media, the subtle changes in reading behaviors inevitably make the first two types of reading more popular, while intensive reading is somewhat on the wane. In other words, electronic reading, with the help of various devices, has greatly improved the efficiency of fast reading, but it is difficult to focus on the same text for a long time; rather, people are accustomed to retrieving information quickly by means of skimming and scanning. In a nutshell, browsing has replaced reading. This trend has been corroborated by many empirical studies. For example, a recent study on scholarly citation reveals the downside of academic reading—readers more often than not merely read the first three pages of a document, with little patience or need to read through the whole text. The statistical results of this study were striking: 46% of the citations were limited to the first page of the document; 23%, the second page; and 77%, the first three pages.[29] This finding clearly shows that the situation has changed profoundly, even for professional readers, who no longer have the patience or time to delve into a single document in its entirety. This study on citation is no less than a statistical validation of Hayles' idea of "hyper attention". Naturally, when reading more and more tilts toward skimming and scanning, when reading is limited to the first few pages, the style and habitus of immersive reading we once had are increasingly marginalized.

From "Wolf is coming" to "Dance with wolves"

In fact, during the long history of human reading, the crisis of reading was not rare. From the oral tradition through handwritten books to printed books, reading has undergone sea changes. Some optimistic scholars specializing in book history and reading history believe that electronic reading is no more than a brief interlude in the long history of reading and that there is no need to worry about it. Many of the problems, crises, and aporias we encounter in the digital age will be solved with the development of socio-culture and the advancement of technology. The pessimists, however, have a bleak vision—the "subversion" of human reading brought about by digital electronic media simply echoes the fable story of "Wolf is coming". In fact, the debate over the ominous rise of e-reading has been going on for at least 20 years. If the e-reading is a dangerous wolf, there is little hope to reject electronic media culture from the standpoint of print culture. What matters here is not to drive away the "wolf", but how to "dance with wolves".

Let's return to the national reading report cited in the beginning of this section. The percentage of adult population exposed to digital reading in China was 58.1% in 2014, and such a drastic increase is worth further consideration. On the one hand, it shows that one's exposure to textual media is no longer limited to print books, and electronically mediated reading has become the staple of national reading, and exceeded the rate of paper-books reading for the first time. On the other hand, it can be expected that e-reading will be even more pervasive, as digital technology and devices become more popular and more affordable. Given the convenience of electronic resources and the economy of e-reading, the consumption of books will increase substantially, but the flip side of the coin seems to be alarming—the immersive and deep reading is declining significantly. This change can be acutely felt even on campus. Having said that, it is necessary to make some brief analysis of the generational aspects of e-reading.

From the perspective of generational studies, e-reading has the most salient impact on adolescent readers. The model of hyper attention and the features of e-reading have been deeply entrenched among adolescent readers. In terms of the generational aspects of e-reading, readers can be broadly grouped into three different age groups. Those with the closest tie with e-reading are called "digital natives", that is, young readers who have been exposed to the digital environment since their birth, especially the "post-80s", "post-90s", and "post-00s". As to the reading history of these generations, e-reading has become the most essential, and even the most dominant, way of reading. For these "digital natives", although reading print texts is also a part of their life, it is far less common and attractive than electronic reading. On the whole, among the "digital natives", the aforementioned symptoms of e-reading are most conspicuous. The second category can be called "digital immigrants"—people whose adolescence coincides with the stage of print culture, and print text became the medium of their elemental reading behavior; with the advent of digital age, they have been gradually attuned to sporadic use of e-reading. Compared with the "digital natives", "digital immigrants" usually maintain a delicate balance between paper-based reading and e-reading. In particular, because the habitus of reading paper-based texts has been deeply entrenched in their reading orientation, it may result in a sort of "mixed" reading pattern. For the second category of readers, immersive reading is mostly limited to paper-based texts, while other recreational or information-retrieving reading is done electronically. If "digital natives" are keen on e-reading and are most likely to develop e-reading habitus, and if "digital immigrants" are able to maintain a certain degree of balance between e-reading and paper reading, then a third type of readers chooses to keep a distance from or even rejects e-reading. This type can be named "digital aliens"—they are completely shaped by their reading experience of paper text, neither fond of nor attuned to electronic reading. If the first category comprises mostly young readers, and the second category mainly middle-aged people, then the third category comprises the elderly in terms of age distribution. Of course, there are exceptions—some from the first two groups might somehow have little knowledge about or scant experience of e-reading. For the third category of readers, e-reading is something distant and unattainable.

Such a distinction of course is very rough, but there is no denying that the reading habitus of those who grow up in distinct reading environments is very different. A deeper concern is that the younger generations, those who decide the future of our nation, are deeply influenced by the behavior and device paradigm of electronic reading, and are more prone to "infection" and "addiction" related to new technology, new devices, and new reading styles. Yet, they are often ignorance about the downside of electronic reading. In this regard, there are two conflicting views: one believes that the aforementioned trends of e-reading will be reinforced in the future, radically altering the habitus of immersive reading long nurtured by print culture, and consolidating the model of hyper attention and its browsing habitus; the other body of opinion is more optimistic—the problems incurred by today's electronic media and device paradigms can be solved by technology itself. Regardless of future developments, some effective counter-strategies should be conceived to bridle the current reading crisis before the technological antidotes are available to us. "Dancing with wolves" means that we must get close to "wolves" and understand "wolf nature", before we succeed in "dancing with wolves".

In my opinion, regarding "dancing with wolves", a key issue is how to vigorously cultivate and preserve the habitus of immersive reading at a time when electronic reading has ascendency. Print culture and electronic culture respectively represent two different stages in the history of human civilization. At first glance, immersive reading cultivated by print culture drastically differs from browsing-as-reading spawned by electronic culture. Immersive reading even seems a bit old-fashioned, quaint, and traditional. But from the perspective of reading history, it is worth noting that its decline is related to the current reading crises. The question we encounter today is not whether to read electronically or not, but how to retain the habitus of immersive reading among readers in general, while electronic reading is prevalent and dominant.

Immersive reading is characterized by a tolerance for monotony when reading an individual text. As mentioned earlier, the first three of what Hayles names four characteristics of hyper attention—focus shifting, preference for multiple information, and obsession with strong stimuli—can all be attributed to the fourth—low tolerance of monotony—as a root feature. To be more specific, focus shifting is a pattern of reading behavior, which is derived from a reader's innate gambit of readerly psychology; that she prefers multiple information means the pursuit of diversification and richness of information. One's obsession with stimulating information is a rebellion against reading monotony, but these gambits are due to readerly inability to tolerate the monotony of reading paper texts. That said, when we announce that electronic reading in the digital age has led to a change in reading habitus, we are actually referring to the decline in the habitus of "showing a high level of endurance in maintaining focus time". This change in reading habitus is a global issue, though it feels like more threatening in the context of contemporary China. The rampant spread of ultra-utilitarianism and instrumental rationality has rendered the whole Chinese society, culture, education, and even daily life increasingly fickle, with immersive reading turned anachronistic. As to this problem of reading ecology, what can we do to maintain the balance of reading? I think we can amend our way in the following aspects.

First and foremost, it is necessary to maintain readers' (especially young readers') affinity for paper-based texts. As mentioned earlier, paper texts contribute to the development of an immersive reading habitus, so there is no easier way to cultivate immersive reading than to encourage readers to love reading paper texts. Of course, at a time when electronic reading is pervasive, a new type of paper reading has also emerged—printing out electronic texts and then poring over them. This highly recommendable method combines the convenience and economy of electronic literature with the primordial tangibility of paper-text reading. An important feature of paper-based reading, as we know, is the singleness of mind and the intensity of concentration, which helps to develop on readers' part the tolerance for monotony and the ability of contemplation. Having said that, it is worth invoking Borgmann's suggestions for overcoming the limitations of device paradigms. It is necessary, he argues, to strengthen one's focus on "engagement with focal thing", such as doing handicrafts, listening to music, or jogging. It is through such activities of focus practice that one is freed from the domination of device paradigm. The same, I suggest, is true of paper-based text reading, which implies that we can promote some reading initiatives on campus, at home, or elsewhere. A reading campaign, such as "one hour of daily immersion in my favorite paper books", can free ourselves from the distractions of Internet surfing and roaming, making our eyes exposed to black ink and white pages, cleansing our mind for a short period, and enjoying contemplation for an hour. In a culture where electronic reading is dominant, cultivating one's rapport with and preference for paper books is, after all, a matter of keeping a delicate balance between electronic reading and paper reading, because the former is irresistible, even more so in the case of "digital natives". If we can sustain such a balanced relationship between the two, then the habitus of immersive reading will not be rendered obsolete. According to some comparative studies on international reading cultures, e-reading in English-speaking countries such as the United Kingdom, the United States, Canada, Australia, and New Zealand are more popular than other countries, and the e-reading industry and electronic resources are relatively developed. Of course, a major reason is that English is the current *lingua franca*, but there may be some other reasons that deserve scrutiny. In the case of China, due to poor copyright protection, e-books are not very popular, and electronic resources are not as abundant. It might have been a blessing for the traditional publishing industry in China. But how to introduce more hardcopy books to the everyday life of common readers (especially young readers) and foster an ethos of bibliophilia remains a tough conundrum. It can be expected that, with the development of various online libraries and databases, e-reading is more and more likely to be the top choice of the younger generation, with a continuous surge of e-reading. Thus, encouraging men to keep their affinity toward paper books is an important mission.

Second, it is necessary to carry out a comprehensive research on the status of e-reading in contemporary China and to make the general public aware of the strengths and weaknesses of e-reading in such a way as to arouse readers' self-awareness of the potential problems of e-reading. Any device paradigm is a double-edged sword, but its upside is usually conspicuous, while the downside is more imperceptible. That some foreign empirical studies and theories are invoked in my analysis is merely because no similar researches or data are available in China. Undoubtedly, there are similarities and dissimilarities between China's current e-reading and the situation abroad, and the distinction between the two deserves more of our attention. Empirical researches and data analysis can reveal the strengths and positive functions of e-reading on the one hand, and warn of its potential dangers on the other, especially for young readers, who are more vulnerable to such negativities and need to be wary of its consequences and take precautions. The teenager readers, with little affinity for paper text, are more attracted to e-reading. If they are not aware of the advantages and disadvantages of e-reading, and have no idea about the complex consequences of these dazzling new technological devices, they might indulge in the pleasure of e-reading, and become increasingly alienated from the immersive reading habitus over time. Their reading behavior and habitus, as a result, are inevitably transformed into something shallow and stereotyped. Research on e-reading must also go deeper into the correlation between e-reading and reading genres so that some positive and constructive tactics can be put forward—the e-reading status across different generations of readers, the relationships between different reading styles (recreational and scholarly reading, etc.) or between different reading topics (natural science and the humanities, etc.) when they concern e-reading. The study of these relationships can help readers figure out what effective approaches they should take to stay away from the haphazard of e-reading.

Third, with the premise of fully understanding the characteristics and functions of different types of e-reading, readers are encouraged to choose different reading media in line with one's reading purpose. E-reading, diverse as it is, can in general be divided into two categories: one is the e-reader (such as a kindle reader) and e-books, and another is other forms of terminal devices that provide online reading and its "hypertext". In comparison, e-readers constitute a relatively closed system, without linking with other resources during the reading process. Online reading is an infinite mesh system, with main texts linked to an infinite variety of secondary text at any time. Furthermore, it can also link to non-verbal video and audio content, which means that even SMS, WeChat, email, system notification, and advertisement may interrupt the reading at any time. Thus, online reading is associated with a situation similar to the hyper attention model fraught with distraction in reading, readers bestowed with the capacity of constantly switching back and forth between multiple targets. The two different device paradigms lead to different reading behaviors. Since e-readers are mostly limited to e-books and lacking in extensive outside links, reading is relatively simpler and more closed. Reading via other mobile devices or unmovable terminals mostly takes place with full access to the Internet, so it is conducive to "para-hypertext" browsing accompanied by frequent attention switching. Therefore, it is easy to form a "hypertext-like" browsing style with multiple goal transitions. Therefore, having understood the distinction of these two types of electronic reading, readers are expected to use different reading devices and according to one's purpose, and thus have different reading experiences. Generally speaking, for those who need intensive reading or poring over the text, the use of e-readers is highly recommendable. Despite the differences between e-books and print books, e-readers can guarantee a closed and simple reading, without producing distracting outside links, and are more conducive to the formation of immersive reading. For those who look for leisure and entertainment or engage in searching for resources, online browsing might be a better choice, as it can access a wide range of links and choose various reading styles, such as scanning, skimming, and roaming-reading. In a nutshell, savvy about the typology and functionality of e-reading, one can select different devices and reading styles. It is necessary to embrace the strengths of digital e-reading without yielding to their limitations. This is the strategy of "dancing with wolves" after knowing "the wolf nature".

Fourth, we should promote literary reading—especially the long works of literature—through which the habitus and patience associated with immersive reading can be further cultivated. Compared with other types of reading, literary reading is rather unique in that it is not only different from the research-oriented reading of scientific texts that relies entirely on rational deduction, but also very different from the newspaper reading, which allows for distractions. Literary reading requires the reader to maintain a status of contemplation, a status of "self-loss" as described by some philosophers (such as Schopenhauer)—forgetting oneself and being completely immersed in the world of literary works. An excellent exemplar is the famous British poet W. H. Auden, whose experience of reading detective novels shows that reading such fiction will make us "addicted", just like cigarettes and alcohol. The most salient feature of reading detective story is "the intensity of the craving—if I have any work to do, I must be careful not to get hold of a detective story for, once I begin one, I cannot work or sleep till I have finished it".[30] The heightened attention is typical of literary reading, not only in the case of detective novels, but also for all kinds of literary works. Therefore, literary reading has a stronger effect on the experiential and immersive aspects of reading. The reader conjures up a world created by words and feels the various emotions and desires in one's mundane existence, by grasping the meaning between the lines. "It usually suffices", just as Jin Shengtan remarks in his commentary on *Water Margin*, "to read a book one time, but *Water Margin* is an exception. I simply can't get tired of reading it, because the author casts one hundred and eight personalities in such a compelling way".[31] The one-hundred-and-eight lifelike characters are not only animated by the author Shi Nai'an's words, but also intractably imprinted in the mind of Jin Shengtan as a reader. It is in this sense that the "hyper attention" suggested by Hayles is obviously not suitable for literary reading. No wonder she contrasts a sophomore girl's reading of Dickens's novels with her little brother's obsession with video games. Literary reading cannot be a transient, fragmentary reading, nor can it be about the pursuit of sensational, diverse information. The aforementioned list the list "Those Books You Just Can't Finish Reading"—the great classics of the past the present-day young readers can't sit down through—is actually part of the consequences caused by the domination of hyper attention. In other words, literary reading requires readers to enter into a certain state of "immersion reading", especially when reading the great long works. Readers who love reading long novels must have developed the habitus of "immersive reading". When discussing the idea of device paradigm earlier on, I make reference to Borgmann's strategy to fend off distraction, that is, "focal things and practices", which perfectly applies to such a situation. Through literary reading, the reader can temporarily stay away from the distractions and domination of various devices, focusing on the solitary experience in the literary world.

Finally, we shall construe some tenable reading programs, which not only fit in with different reading circumstances (such as home, elementary and secondary schools, colleges and universities) but also take into consideration the psychological and cognitive patterns of different age groups. Although reading is a highly personal and solitary act, it is not contradictory to some collective activities in the form of reader groups. In terms of the growth cycle of an educated reader, university is the last critical period of culturalization for the young readers, so reading culture within a university is of utmost importance. At present, some famous universities in China have put forward their own recommended book lists for students, according to their scholarly traditions and disciplinary characteristics. But unfortunately, these book lists often remain only in words and have not yet become an executable project. A recent experiment made by Nanjing University might become the game-changer. Since 2015, Nanjing University has launched a well-designed "Classics Reading Program" for undergraduates, aiming at cultivating the habitus of immersive reading among young students and thus exploring a new path for liberal arts education. As the leader and participant of this program, I was fully involved in its design and operation. First of all, there were discussions among faculty members and students, followed by a committee to pick up 60, old and contemporary, classic books. These classics were divided into six units: 1) Literature and Art, 2) History and Civilization, 3) Philosophy and Religion, 4) Economy and Society, 5) Nature and Life, and 6) Globalization and Leadership. These six units are expected to cover many fields, ranging from the humanities through social sciences to natural sciences. Each unit is led by an editor-in-chief, and a total of 60 young teachers are invited to take charge of one classic book respectively, and preside over a virtual reading class of less than 100 students. Focusing on one classic book, each class carries out a variety of reading activities online and offline. At the same time, a cross-faculty teaching team was organized to offer a series of pedagogical activities, in the form of either introductory lectures or research-based tutorials. To encourage students to develop rapport with paper texts, a special reading section for classic titles is set up in our university library for students to check out or browse. The editor-in-chief for each unit is responsible for compiling an excerpt of 10,000 words, which is included in a two-volume collection entitled "The NJU Reader" (more than 600,000 words in total), and distributed to every NU undergraduate student for free. This program has been implemented for many years and has achieved good results. Through close contact with classic books, our young students have gradually developed and strengthened their immersive reading behaviors and habitus, and stimulated their rational and critical thinking skills. The implementation of this program has significantly changed the reading ecology of the campus, giving rise to a campus culture characterized by bibliophilia and diligent thinking. This project has to some extent rectified the shallow and fragmented reading pattern produced by the increasingly prevalent electronic reading.

 To conclude this part, I would like to reiterate one of my judgments: if the immersive reading habitus based on deep attention generally disappears, the browsing-as-reading pattern associated with hyper attention mode would dominate, and thereby reconfigure the national reading behavior and habitus—especially for the youth. As a result, our future reading would be in deep trouble. So, it is the high time we make the wake-up call and do something about it!

Notes

1 <http://www.cssn.cn/zt/zt_xkzt/zt_wxzt/2015sjdsr/sjdsrzqmyd/201504/t20150422_1596633.shtml>
2 See Zhou Xian, "Reconstructing Reading Culture", in *Academic Monthly* 5(2007); Zhao Yong, "Literary Reading in the Context of Media Culture", in *Chinese Social Science* 5 (2008); Yu Qiuyu, "The Reading Crisis in the Information Age", in *The Party Construction* 9 (2010); Mo Zerui, "Review of Reading Culture Research in China", in *Library Journal* 9 (2009); Liu Yongjie et al, "Review of Domestic Reading Culture Studies", in *Intelligence Theory and Practice* 12 (2012); Yang Zukui, "Analysis of the Dilemma of Reading Classic Literature", in *Library* 2 (2010).
3 Li Xinxiang. "A Study on the Individual Influence of Digitalized Reading Behavior", in *Journal of Communication University of Zhejiang* 6 (2014). p.28.
4 See John Tomlinson. *The Culture of Speed: The Coming of Immediacy*. London: Sage, 2007.
5 See Walter Benjamin. *The Work of Art in the Age of Mechanical Reproduction*. Hangzhou: Zhejiang Photo Press, 1993; Marshall McLuhan. *Understanding Media*. Beijing: The Commercial Press, 2000; Jean Baudrillard. *Simulacra and Simulation*. Ann Arbor: University of Michigan, 1995.
6 Albert Borgmann. *Technology and the Character of Contemporary Life*. Chicago: University of Chicago Press, 1987.
7 N. Katherine Hayles and Jessica Pressman, ed., *Comparative Textual Media: Transforming the Humanities in the Postprint Era*. Minneapolis: University of Minnesota Press, 2013, p.xiii.
8 There are different views on the periodization of the communication of human civilization. In addition to the quadratic approach used here, there is also a quintuple approach, which distinguishes electronic communication from digital communication.
9 See Walter One. *Orality and Literacy*. London: Routledge, 2002, pp.115–17.
10 Walter Benjamin. *The Work of Art in the Age of Mechanical Reproduction*. pp.4–11.
11 Meyer Shapiro, "On Some Problems in the Semiotics of Visual Art: Field and Vehicle in Image-Signs", in *Essential Texts in Art Theory: The Western Contemporary Period*. Ed. Zhou Xian. Beijing: Sanlian Bookstore, 2014. pp.138–140.
12 See Gabrielle Watling, ed. *Cultural History of Rea*ding, *Vol.1*. Westport: Greenwood, 2009. pp.287–304.
13 Steven Fischer. *A History of Reading*. London: Reaktion, 2003. p.205.
14 Steven Fischer. *A History of Reading*. p.162.
15 Walter Benjamin. "The Storyteller", in *Selected Writings of Walter Benjamin*. Beijing: China Social Science Press, 1999. p.307.
16 Harold Bloom. "How to Read and Why?" Trans. Huang Chanran. Nanjing: Yilin, 2011. p.5.
17 Mark Poster. *The Mode of Information: Poststructuralism and Social Context*. p.66.
18 See Wang Chaowen, ed. *An Introduction to Aesthetics*. Beijing: People's Publishing House, 1981. pp.270–271.
19 Quoted in Naomi Baron, *Words Onscreen: The Fate of Reading in the Digital World*. Oxford: Oxford University Press, 2015. p.23
20 Pierre Bourdieu and Loic Wacquant. *An Invitation to Reflexive Sociology*. Cambridge: Polity. 1992. p.127.
21 See Roland Barthes, "The Death of the Author", in *Selected Essays of Roland Barthes*. Trans. Huai Yu. Tianjin: Baihua Literary Publishing House, 1995. pp.300–308; Also see Roland Barthes, "From Work to Text", in *Foreign Aesthetics, Vol. 20*. Nanjing: Jiangsu Education Press, 2012. pp.337–343.
22 Quoted in George P. Landow, *Hypertext 3.0: Critical Theory and New Media in an Era of Globalization*. Baltimore: The John's Hopkins University Press, 2006, pp.2–3.
23 According to Espen J. Aarseth, "A nonlinear text is a work that does not present its scriptons in one fixed sequence, whether temporal or spatial. Instead, through cybernetic agency (the user[s], the text, or both), an arbitrary sequence emerges". Espen J. Aarseth.

"Nonlinearity and Literary Theory", in *Hyper/Text/Theory*. Ed. George P. Landow. Baltimore: JHUP, 1994. p.61.
24　N. Katherine Hayles. "Hyper and Deep Attention: The Generational Divide in Cognitive Mode", in *Profession* 1 (2007). pp.187–188.
25　Naomi S. Baron. "Redefining Reading: the Impact of Digital Communication Media", in *PMLA* 128.1 (2013). pp.197–198.
26　Naomi S. Baron. "Redefining Reading: the Impact of Digital Communication Media". pp.195–196.
27　Amy Kraft. "Books vs. e-Books: The Science Behind the Best Way to Read". *CBS News* December 14, 2015. <http://www.cbsnews.com/news/kindle-nook-e-reader-books-the-best-way-to-read/>
28　Naomi S. Baron, "Redefining Reading: The Impact of Digital Communication Media". p.195.
29　<http://citationproject.net/Research-questions.html>
30　W. H. Auden. "The Guilty Vicarage", in *Detective Fiction*. Ed. Robin W. Winks. New Haven: Yale University Press, 1980. p.15.
31　Jin Shengtan. "Reading the Fifth Talented Calligraphy", in *Aesthetic Literature of China Through the Ages: Qing Dynasty*. Ed. Ye Lang. Beijing: Higher Education Publishing House, 2003. p.112.

11 The construction of critical rationality in a technology-oriented society

China today has entered into a technologically oriented society, and this society and its culture raise many challenging questions for us. In this section, I will discuss one of the more complex and controversial questions, namely, how technology and its device paradigm affect the construction of subjectivity in a technology-oriented society.

Subjectivity in a technology-oriented society

Today, we find ourselves living in a rapidly changing society, a major cause being technology and its devices, such as computers, cell phones, the Internet, software programs, and interfaces. More and more technological inventions are becoming an integral part of our daily life and profoundly changing the way we live. Society as a whole is caught up in a swirl of new technological revolutions and is divided into two camps: the youth subculture obsessed with new technologies and devices, and the middle-aged and elderly subculture that is constantly being rendered obsolete. Knowledge, income, skills, cultural orientation, and even age are complicit in re-stratifying the society dominated by technology. The younger generations, as "digital natives", were exposed since their birth to a variety of digital devices that have become indispensable to their daily lives; the middle-aged and older, or the so-called "digital immigrants", are either reluctantly drawn into this intractable trend or virtually ostracized from the digital world because they are unwilling to get involved. As for the elderly, they have basically been abandoned by the digital world and have become "digital outsiders". The late German writer Günter Grass, who passed away a few years ago, had explicitly expressed his nonchalance to the Internet, computers, cell phones, and Facebook in an interview, asserting that virtual online experience cannot replace in-person experience. Glass insisted on writing his manuscript by hand, using an old-fashioned typewriter, rejecting both computers and cell phones. He once admitted,

> If I want information, I make the effort and do research. I look things up in books, in the library. I know it's all a bit slower – and modern tools can speed things up. But literature for example… You can't speed it up when you work with it. If you do, you do so at the expense of quality.[1]

Glass may seem like a dinosaur in the age of new technology, but perhaps it is only because he was detached from the technological tide and thus was able to offer some alternative but alerting observations and experiences. After all, more and more youths—increasingly younger ones—are enthusiastically embracing the fancy life and culture that new technology has brought about. The "phubber" and the "finger culture" have vividly defined the ordinary life dominated by technology in this era. The "digital natives" are constructing or have constructed their "digital habitus", which in turn reinforces the domination of device paradigm in everyday lives.

In this light, today we are undoubtedly facing an unprecedented technology-oriented society, also known as a tech-dependent society. This society is characterized by the fact that the newly invented devices, instruments, norms, and lines of thinking have fully and deeply invaded all sectors of our life world (at a quantitative level) and have become indispensable tools for social governance and citizens' daily life (at a qualitative level). The trends of social development are increasingly marked by its technological orientation (historically speaking), a fact that changes the relationship among men and between man and technology, and influences the interplay of man's mastery over technology and technology's domination of man (in terms of relationality). New developments in technology have reshaped our life world in ways that are too profound to be measurable.

One of the most important achievements of Western modernity is the Enlightenment, which ultimately helped create the reflective subjectivity and established the critical rationality of the subject. Descartes formulated the far-reaching proposition, "I think, therefore I am". Kant defined the essence of the Enlightenment as "Sapere aude! Have the courage to use your own reason!"[2] Later on, a more specific vocabulary was invented to refer to such a subjectivity and its culture—"critical intellectuals" and "critical culture of discourse", etc. However, the development of science and technology over the past two hundred years, from the Enlightenment to the present, has profoundly changed society, culture, and everyday life, leading to a series of profound subjective crises and triggering critical thinking on the part of many philosophers and thinkers. All of these led to a unique problem field—philosophy of technology and critical theory of technology, where many influential theories emerged. Heidegger points out that the essence of technology is a kind of *enframing*, in which man becomes the *Bestand*, and thus no longer meets himself (i.e., his essence). The result is the emergence of "*das Man*" in modern society.[3] Benjamin claims that the "age of mechanical reproduction" implies the "great collapse of tradition", and that art and mass movements were closely entangled in this age.[4] Adorno's reflection on fascism leads him to explore at great length the conditions for the development of the authoritarian personality in modern society.[5] Riesman finds that contemporary society is distancing itself from the "self-orientation" and increasingly turning to "other-orientation".[6] Marcuse uses a very evocative term, the "one-dimensional man", to capture and critique the new subject that has emerged from contemporary technology-oriented society.[7] McLuhan's prophecy is even more provocative: where tools extend human capabilities, those aspects of the human being will inevitably become "numb".[8] In London, for example, there was a debate over whether cabs should be equipped with GPS. The experiment yet found that drivers equipped with GPS had a dramatic loss of spatial memory for London. This example perfectly illustrates the potential impact of technology and its concomitant device paradigm on people.

The explosion of technology after the 1980s has further raised concerns among thinkers about the status of human subjectivity, and as a result has given rise to many new theories. Yet, there seems to be an implicit voice questioning the Enlightenment subjectivity, from Deleuze and Guattari's famous analysis of subjectification in human-computer systems, to Haraway's theory of cyborg, and to Stiegler's theory of the subject's individualization in the relationship between technology and time, etc. Today's social conditions are increasingly influenced by technology to such an extent that the relationship between man and technology has been reversed. As some philosophers of technology have said, if in the past man was a technological individual wielding a tool, today man is no longer such a technological individual. He either serves the machine or is a cog in the machine. The relationship between man and technology has fundamentally changed. It has been predicted that there are six types of possibilities for the change in the complex man-tech relationship in the future.

(1) Augmenting humans with technology; (2) Machines replacing humans; (3) Humans and machines working alongside each other; (4) Machines better understanding humans and the environment; (5) humans better understanding machines; (6) Machines and humans becoming smarter.[9]

Judging from the six possible changes in the future men-tech relationship, the connection between the two will become increasingly complex. As Stiegler predicts,

> Novel technical apparatuses of all sorts are to be seen: machines for circulation, communication, for sight, speech, entertainment, calculation, work, 'thought'; soon machines for feeling and for doubling oneself ('tele-presence' or tele-aesthesis, virtual reality), and for destruction. These include living machines—'chimera' and other biological artifacts currently translate not so much an organization of the inorganic as a re-organization of the organic.[10]

The situation in China since its reform and opening-up also confirms the remarkable trend toward a technology-oriented society, although unlike Western societies, China has its distinctive problems in terms of history and culture. The May Fourth Movement and New Culture Movement set in motion the modern Chinese version of the Enlightenment, with the influx of science and new thoughts, which dramatically transformed Chinese society and culture. However, the outbreak of the Sino-Japan War necessitated replacing the language of Enlightenment with that of salvation, and the modern Chinese Enlightenment was aborted and abandoned halfway. The year of 1978 saw the reform and opening-up of China and the relaunch of the ideological liberation movement and the introduction of the so-called "New Enlightenment", which established the critical subjective rationality of social practice as of the 1980s. However, this process was soon interrupted by the rapid social and cultural changes. Today, technology has gained more and more ascendancy, and consumer culture is becoming the mainstream, especially when technological devices are perfectly aligned with consumer behaviors. The construction of the critical subjective rationality has become a tough issue. The "New Enlightenment" is barely discussed, and the issue of the critical subjective rationality is seldom discussed even in intellectual circles. In addition, since the Opium War, China has always been obsessed with reviving the nation by virtue of science and technology, so the positive side of technology has been given more attention, its negative side rarely heeded. There is no doubt that the rise of technology has transformed Chinese society and culture, greatly enhancing its national power and improving people's livelihoods. And China's rise would have been inconceivable had it not been for technological progress. Unfortunately, people are usually intoxicated by the illusion of technological progress and are not sufficiently aware of its potential risks and negative effects. The impact of technological devices and their paradigms on subjectivity, the consumerist ideology caused by new technological devices, or the "device addiction" and "device dependence" symptomatic of the adolescents and youths have not been thoroughly studied. It is often the case that the bright side of technology is infinitely exaggerated, while the downside of technology is overshadowed and expelled from our sight by the euphoria generated by its advantages.

Over the last 40 years, China has undergone a series of major social reforms. Many of the social transformations that took centuries in the West have been hurried through in China in a matter of decades. China's social changes have been extraordinarily profound, and technology has undoubtedly played a remarkable role in this. From a crude and lopsided modernity at the beginning of the reform to a comprehensive modernity that emphasizes a scientific outlook on development and harmonious society, it is obvious that technological progress has been accompanied by widespread misreading and misuse. Many of the problems that China faces today—from food safety to ecological environment—are imputed to the way we approach and wield technology. Technological fetishism, apparently, must be blamed. That said, I argue that the infertility of philosophy of technology and critical theory in China today should be held accountable for providing a dangerously lenient environment for one's misunderstanding and misuse of technology.

In this chapter, I don't intend to explore the many issues of philosophy of technology and critical theory in general, but rather to focus on the question of how the device paradigm of new technologies affects the construction of subjectivity and its critical rationality in a highly technologically oriented society. Implicit in this is the intractably complicated relationship between the device paradigm and instrumental rationality. In contemporary China, the extensive and irresistible encroachment of instrumental rationality into everyday life has had a great impact on the construction of critical rationality of the subject. One observable fact is that in some sectors of Chinese society today, reflective criticality has run out of steam, while conformism and instrumental rationality are gradually gaining momentum. This raises a burning question for us: What is the relationship between the device paradigm, instrumental rationality, and the construction of subjectivity?

Device paradigm, instrumental rationality, and subjectivity

In discussing the rational behavior of modern man, Max Weber points out a tendency of rationality division and conflict, and is particularly concerned about the conflict between value rationality and purposive rationality. Starting from sociological presuppositions about the rationality of human behavior, Weber distinguishes four types of human behavior, among which value rationality and purposive rationality are the two he pays most attention to. The so-called "value rationality" refers to conscious belief in the unconditional and intrinsic value, unrelated to its outcome; the so-called "purposive rationality" refers to the realization of one's rational purpose through external objects or other means.[11] The criterion of value-rational behavior lies in the priority of value, and the premise of purposively rational judgment of behavior is the realization of purpose. The trend of modern social development is the decline of value rationality on the one hand, and the prevalence of purposive rationality on the other. As Charles Taylor puts it succinctly, instrumental (purposive) reason refers to "the kind of rationality we draw on when we calculate the most economical application of means to a given end. Maximum efficiency, the best costoutput ration, is its measure of success".[12] In particular, Weber emphasizes that these two kinds of rationality are essentially opposed to each other, because from the standpoint of value rationality, instrumental rationality is problematic; likewise, viewed from instrumental rationality, value rationality is questionable. Weber's conclusion is based on the social conditions of the late 19th and early 20th centuries. Since then, instrumental rationality has become almost the universal behavior pattern and thinking habitus for the contemporary people. However, can we venture to say that the increasingly pronounced orientation toward instrumental rationality is related to the dominance of the technological device paradigm? I think the answer is self-evident.

Let's start with Borgmann's idea of "device paradigm". Borgmann, a philosopher of technology, argues that the newly invented devices are shaping the contemporary life and are increasingly becoming a paradigm for human behavior and thinking. In his view, technology provides convenient services to people by means of devices. From the traditional way a family chop wood to make a fire, to the modern heating devices one can purchase and consume, technological advances have changed lifestyles and ideas, bringing handy and efficient services to us. The principle of instrumental rationality, that is, the minimum input for maximum return, has become the basic logic for the technology development and trendy devices. In particular, Borgmann points out that the emergence of new technological devices dissolves the inherent relationality among objects and cancels human participation, while the devices themselves are hidden in the background so that no one is aware of them. He points out that the device paradigm is characterized by two facts: the variability of means and the constancy of purpose (e.g., the purpose of heating is constant, but there are infinitely new heating devices hitting the market); and the invisibility of means and the visibility of purpose, as the purpose of a device is always obvious when it brings facilities to people, while the device itself recedes into the background. More importantly, the devices tend to be more and more "man-like" or "user-friendly". The more convenient it is to use, the greater the gap between the user and the device's complex mechanism, which is often beyond the awareness of the user.[13] The popularity of iPhones is an example—the more handy or user-friendly it is, the more unlikely for the user to figure out its technical sophistication.

If we expand the connotation of instrumental rationality—take it as a style of thinking and behavior—it is certainly related to the prevalence of herd mentality in technology-oriented societies. On the surface, the new technologies in our times have given rise to a dazzling constellation of devices, but what lies behind is often a paradigm of identity that implicitly coerces individuals into conforming to the homogeneous patterns of thinking and behavior. These newly invented devices have a largely standardized paradigm, which implicitly or explicitly turns their users into the disciples of technical thinking or instrumental rationality. According to Borgmann, the device paradigm refers to the way people deal with devices in technologically oriented societies. I want to further point out that device paradigm actually has both "hardware" and "software" dimensions—"hardware" functions in a much more palpable way, while the workings of "software" is invisible. By "software", it means the way of thinking and behavior stipulated by the device. Device paradigm is characterized by its systemization and standardization. Paradigm signifies unity (or identity thinking) and norm (which is mandatory), as developed by some select experts (standards determined by the elite). So, paradigm is a hierarchical and complex system (divided into different levels). Once the standard is established, it will reject any deviations, abnormalities, and heresies; one's mastery of standard means one's being attuned to norms.[14] More importantly, the so-called "standards" or "norms" refer not only to the visible game rules, but also to those out of sight.

History has repeatedly proved that the standard of device paradigm, with its emphasis on normativity, can easily form a symbiotic and complicit relationship with various kinds of power, reduced to a tool for authority to implement established ideologies or a means for surveillance society—the case of Snowden is a salient example. There are a variety of mobile terminals, such as laptops, cell phones, and netbooks, which yet share the same operating systems. Diverse as websites, homepages, databases, and information platforms appear to be, their contents are often homogeneous, with similar operating systems and interfaces. Therefore, the device paradigm implies not only a specific material setup, but more importantly a certain way of identical thinking, emotion, and behavior. No matter where you live in the world, or what your personal preferences are, the standardized playbooks are like "invisible hands" manipulating the device users. Behind the same playbook lurk similar frameworks of values and aesthetics. Here, I want to call attention to the digital generation gap. The younger generation in China today can be called "Device-Paradigm Generation", "digital natives", or "media generation". They have been long exposed to the all-embracing digital environments since their birth, surrounded by all kinds of technical devices. On the one hand, they are keen on the use of various devices, which are easy to use and addictive for them. As a result, this demographic group is deeply entwined with device paradigms. On the other hand, they are largely unaware of the true face of the highly digital device paradigm and its culture, because they are hooked by such devices. They often fall short of reflection and criticism, which makes them more vulnerable to the impact of device paradigm and teases out a highly digital mode of thinking, behavior, and emotion. The "Device-Paradigm Generation" is unfamiliar with, and has little interest in, traditional non-digital ways of intellectual life and cognition, creating what Stiegler calls a "short circuit" with the past. Therefore, it is particularly necessary to promote critical thinking on device paradigm among the youth, and to emphasize conscious resistance to the disciplinary power of device paradigm. Resistance to the technical politics is of course an important issue, especially when it becomes very difficult to resist technical domination by means of technology, because the pervasive technical obstacles and gaps have excluded the vast majority of users from rule-making.

If standardization usually tilts toward the technical form, then information is a matter of content. Information that conforms to normative standards, or information that is deliberately concocted to fit the technical paradigm, can be disseminated and accepted in an efficient manner. This tendency in turn reinforces the paradigms of technical devices. But the question is still whether the information would unwittingly result in conformity, in terms of thinking, emotions, values, and cultural orientations? For example, the mass production of WeChat and SMS messages is passed around among an astronomical number of users every day. However, it is easy to find that these messages are highly homogeneous (such as social news, festive greetings, pictures, memes, or emojis). It is absolutely possible that one's long-term exposure to such highly homogenized information will make him or her conform to others' thinking, feeling, and behavior. And it is also conceivable that people will lose their ability to reflect on and criticize the world independently. The convenience and utility provided by technology help to create a huge amount of homogeneous, fragmented information that can be disseminated in real time, and at the same time provide a channel—network, terminal, or various interfaces—for massive participation in the transmission of information and appeals. This has opened up a new space of virtual engagement, with the emergence of a plethora of social media and discourse circles. There are two problems that beget attention. Firstly, the highly fragmented information leads to the disintegration of an interpretative regime that features totality and complexity, and the flattening of information methods. This has contributed to the formation of what Hayles calls "hyper attention", a cognitive pattern of "media generation", which starkly contrasts "deep attention" of previous generations. In comparison, "deep attention" helps cultivate rational critical thinking and reflective subjectivity, while "hyper attention" might dissolve the construction of this subjectivity. The development of fragmented cognitive habitus inevitably leads to the degeneration of human cognition, in particular the grasp of totality. If men are indulged in fragmented, dissociated, and deceptive information flows, the totality, as theorized in Marx's historical materialism, will become increasingly inaccessible. The second problem is the "spiral of silence", which is widespread in social media. The more people who participate in social media, the more obvious the spiral of silence is—so is the "herding mentality" in social media.

In China today, this "spiral of silence" is even more pronounced. Some so-called "Big V" act as opinion leaders on social media, manipulating the emotion of netizens. Whenever a newsworthy incident occurs, it always attracts a large number of netizens within a short period of time, inciting highly emotional reactions among the mass and forming a tendentious public opinion. Dissenting opinions and independent thinking are quickly silenced by trolling. Yet, such passions and commotions online are often short-lived, and once the controversy dies down, people will soon forget about it and become nonchalant, unable to translate their affect into continuous discussions and inquiries. This kind of "intermittent hysteria" unique to Chinese social media not only exacerbates the "spiral of silence", but also leads to irrational public participation and weakens the cultivation of critical rationality of the citizenry. According to official statistics, as of December 2014, Chinese Internet users are mainly in the 0–39 age group, with a combined proportion of 78.1%. Among them, the highest percentage is found in the 20–29 age group, accounting for 31.5%. The proportion of Internet users with secondary education is the largest—36.8% graduates from junior high school, and 30.6% has received education at senior high schools or vocational schools. Students account for the largest demographical group of Internet users—23.8%.[15] According to the statistics, the bulk of Internet users is the group with (post)secondary education, but such hysterically emotional reactions displayed by social media users suggest that there is still a long way to go for this group to develop a mature and independent critical rationality. While material and technical modernization is important for China's modernization, what is more important, I believe, is the modernization of men. In other words, what the project of Chinese modernization needs at present is a critically rational citizenry, without which a comprehensive modernization of China is completely unthinkable.

Given China's integration into the historical process of globalization, the prevalence of the technical device paradigm also raises certain geopolitical issues. Those countries of technological prowess will forcefully market their culture when exporting technology. For example, the globalization of American culture has created dominant American values or ideology, and it is difficult to imagine that American culture would have such an impact, had it not been for its dominance of high technology. The introduction of a new technology and its cultural implants has become the two sides of the same coin. Whenever a new technology and its devices are introduced to a society, behind its appealing and visible materiality of technical devices lie the implicitly complex ideology or values, which have taken advantage of the situation and sneaked in. The paradigmatic cultures and ideologies that are hidden in the background are influencing us when we embrace certain technological standards and related devices. This is a subject of cross-cultural research that should be taken seriously. In an era when the world is increasingly moving toward a technology-oriented society, technological dominance and cultural hegemony are increasingly intertwined, which is a fact that compromises the diversity of cultural ecologies around the globe.

To go beyond the device paradigm?

As we have seen, the device paradigm of technology has enormous impact on the construction of subjectivity. Of course, rather than discussing its positive aspects, we focus on the negative ones of device paradigm. Then, the next question that needs to be addressed is how to resist the negative effects. Historically, contemporary thinkers who are perspicacious about the crisis of subjectivity have proposed different solutions.

Heidegger, in his "The Question Concerning Technology", borrows from Hölderlin's poem: "But where danger is, grows / The saving power also". He believes that the contemplation of technology has to take place in another sphere, that is, art. "Because the essence of technology is nothing technological", Heidegger writes, "essential reflection upon technology and decisive confrontation with it must happen in a realm that is, on the one hand, akin to the essence of technology and, on the other, fundamentally different from it".[16] This is an interesting statement, as he has pointed out that the origin of art is the self-manifestation of truth, that is, the demasking and revelation of truth. But can art rectify the domination of technology? Is this too idealistic a utopian vision? The Frankfurt School has a similar line of thinking. Both Adorno and Marcuse passionately proclaim that the new sensibility of art paves the path to the emancipation of the subject. This romantic or aesthetic modernity can be traced back to many preceding thinkers, such as Max Weber. Weber finds that the modernization that emerged firstly in Protestant countries was the product of the separation of the religious from the secular. Therefore, modernity is manifested in the differentiation of the political, economic, technological, and aesthetic spheres. He also comes to the more radical conclusion that aesthetics is the only possible way to redeem people from stereotyped cognitive and practical rationality. He writes:

> The development of intellectualism and the rationalization of life change this situation. For under these conditions, art becomes a cosmos of more and more consciously grasped independent values which exist in their own right. Art takes over the function of a this-worldly salvation, no matter how this may be interpreted. It provides a salvation from the routines of everyday life, and especially from the increasing pressures of theoretical and practical rationalism.[17]

To use art as an antidote to device paradigm may work for the time being, but its effects are limited. Many more strategies have been proposed. While analyzing the technical "device paradigm", Borgmann also proposes a counter-strategy called "focal things and practices". Borgmann's tactic is based on the premise that the technical device paradigm has caused a rupture between the moderns and the traditional way of life and that a striking disadvantage of such a rupture is that the massive deployment of various devices has led to distractions and indifference to life, and thus to an "evil (or bad)" life. In order to restore a "good" life, he proposes to change this situation by using the "focal practices", which means to concentrate one's attention on the making, creation, and experience of something, to feel the emotional pleasure and creativity involved in it, to realize one's self existence and its meaning, and to rectify the distractions and interferences incurred by the device paradigm. The "focal things and practices" include many activities, such as music, gardening, long-distance running, horse training, handicrafts, and violin making, among others. In his view, such focal practices can bring about a "focal reality" that "have engaged mind and body and centered our lives. Commanding presence, continuity with the world, and centering power are signs of focal things".[18] In fact, Borgmann's strategy is to free the subject from the distracting technological culture and to focus on the kernel of being through some contemplative activities. This reminds me of an important philosophical term "contemplation". To maintain one's independent reflective subjectivity means to keep a certain kind of "contemplative" thinking, just like yoga or Zen meditation, which allows one to reverse the habitus of hyper attention aligned with the device paradigm, and to restore deep attention. As a strategy of resistance, it is resonant with the theory of play in philosophy and aesthetics. Schiller once said that one becomes human only when one plays. Other contemporary thinkers, such as Huizinga, Lefebvre, Guy Debord, and de Certeau, have similar preference for aesthetic playfulness, believing that play can effectively resist instrumental rationality and thus manifest value rationality. However, this theory is clearly tinted with escapism, as does Heidegger's thoughts. An ultimate solution to the dominance of technical device paradigm is still nowhere to be found.

Stiegler proposes that we resist the impoverishment of the mind caused by technology with a strategy named "de-proletarianization"—that is to say, "the recovery of knowledge of all kinds", by drawing "lines of flight". For example, he makes the point that we should not passively accept cultural affairs, but take a "participatory" or "practical" approach to them—enjoying music while reading scores, or appreciating paintings while copying them. Cultural activities of this kind will transform the status of passive consumption and the impoverishment of knowledge into a more active and creative pattern of behavior. Stiegler also has an important finding: while technology has led to the "proletarianization" of knowledge, technological progress is accompanied by the "de-professionalization of instruments". He writes,

> In our epoch, and contrary to what occurred at the beginning of the 20th century, we are experiencing the de-professionalisation of instruments, their migration toward non-professionals, the re-instrumentation of the public, and the re-arming of amateurs – the ears of whom pass anew through the eyes, which pass anew through the hands. The mechanical re-organisation of perception taking place with the digital leads to the reconstitution of forms of knowledge held by audiences and publics. There thus comes to be formed a new avant-garde: one that constitutes new publics.[19]

This is a very optimistic vision, but I still doubt that the threshold of high technology would be lowered in a technology-oriented society. I find myself more in favor of Borgmann's prophecy that the more "humanized" or "user-friendly" a technical device is, the greater the gap between its user and the sophisticated construction of device. As numerous new devices are invented, it is expected that more and more users would be reduced to the slaves of their devices. We shall ask such a question: Will the accruement of devices speed up the proletarianization of device user's knowledge, thoughts, and emotion? The plain fact is that the mass is always at the bottom of "ignorance" in the modern technological system, while the technicians who control the metadata or configuration of the device are the real controllers. When they are "complicit" with mega-corporations or governments, the technical device becomes a means of social control. The collaboration between technocracy and power is inevitable in a technologically oriented society.

In my opinion, the critical theories of Heidegger and others is about resisting technology *from without*, while Stiegler's is *from within*. This is a very important strategic difference, but the question of how to find ways to subvert the domination of instrumental rationality by technical means is not answered. There is no doubt that it is a good idea to cure the malaise of technology with the panacea of technology, but the solution is not, as he argues, the lowering of technological threshold. What we need to pay attention to is, on the one hand, to take full note of the limitations and flaws of each nascent technological innovation and limit its disadvantages to a minimum; on the other hand, to design some technological means that can effectively battle and rectify these limitations and drawbacks. I fully agree with Stiegler's notion that all remedies for human malaise can in turn be toxic and even threaten human existence. So, every technological revolution brings about social disorders, which then necessitate readjustment of normativity. In this process of readjustment, we are in need of some thinkers to put forward the blueprints of reforms through critical reflection. It is for this reason that the philosophy of technology and the critical theory of technology are much needed in China today. A further question then is who will develop and promote techno-critical theory? Today we have too many technologists, but as Foucault remarks, there are few intellectuals. Edward Said also argues that true intellectuals are "amateurs"—it is through this amateurism that they resist the pressures of the professional world. In a field of knowledge production that has become increasingly bureaucratic and institutionalized, it seems to be a tough task to break free from the shackles of professionalization and to reflect on the paradigm of technical devices. How to reflect on and critique the professional from the standpoint of the non-professional? How to retain the strengths of technology and, at the same time, shake off its weaknesses? This has become a conundrum we must face in reality.

In a society where technological domination is increasingly strong, and in a culture where instrumental rationality is pervasive, it is perhaps even more important to reconstruct and uphold the value rationality as proposed by Weber. For there is nothing more effective than value rationality to detoxicate purposive rationality. According to Weber's definition, value rationality is something ethical, aesthetic, or religious, based on "conscious belief in the unconditional and intrinsic value, unrelated to its outcome". Today, if value rationality becomes sapless in some domains, people may indulge in the instrumental rationality associated with the technical device paradigm. We must understand that a society and culture that lack the guidance of value rationality may be in some serious danger and crisis. Therefore, when using all kinds of technical devices, we shall at the bottom of our heart adhere to "conscious belief in the unconditional and intrinsic value". In an increasingly technologically oriented society, it is an urgent and difficult task to build up the critical rationality of the subject.

Notes

1 Günter Grass. "Facebook is 'Crap'", in *The Local* September 5, 2013. <http://www.thelocal.de/20130905/51767>
2 Immanuel Kant. "Answering the Question: What is Enlightenment?" in *An Anthology of the Critique of Historical Reason*. Beijing: The Commercial Press, 1990.
3 Martin Heidegger. "The Question Concerning Technology", in *Selected Works of Heidegger: Vol. 2*. Ed. Sun Zhouxing. Shanghai: Shanghai Sanlian Bookstore, 1996. pp.924–954.

4. Walter Benjamin. *The Work of Art in the Age of Mechanical Reproduction*. p. 87.
5. Theodor W. Adorno et al. *The Authoritarian Personality*. New York: Harper & Row, 1950.
6. David Riesman et al. *The Lonely Crowd*. Trans. Wang Kun. Nanjing: Nanjing University Press, 2003. pp.18–23.
7. Herbert Marcuse. *One-Dimensional Man: Studies in the Ideology of Advanced Industrial Society*. Trans. Liu Ji. Shanghai: Shanghai Translation Press, 2006. pp.129–152.
8. Marshall McLuhan. *Understanding Media*. p.80.
9. Nur Bermmen. "Six Ways the Relationship Humans Have with Technology is Changing", in *Memeburn* August 6, 2013. <https://memeburn.com/2013/08/6-ways-the-relationship-humans-have-with-technology-is-changing>
10. Bernard Sitegler. *Technics and Time, 1: The Fault of Epimetheus*. Trans. Richard Beardsworth and George Collins. Stanford, CA: Stanford UP, 1998. p.85.
11. Weber writes, "Whoever acts in a purposively rational manner orients their action to the purpose, means, and associated consequences of an act, and so rationally weighs the relation of means to ends, that of the ends to the associated consequences, and that of the various possible ends to each other; hence, action that is neither affective (especially not emotional) nor traditional. The decision between competing and conflicting aims and consequences can in this way be oriented value-rationally; in this case, only the means are selected by purposively rational criteria. Alternatively, the individual can deal with competing and conflicting aims without resorting to value rationality, taking 'dictates' and 'demands' simply as given subjective feelings of need arranged on a scale that is consciously balanced according to their urgency, orienting action so that they will, as far as is possible, be satisfied in this sequence (the principle of 'marginal utility'). Hence, there are many ways in which the value rational orientation of action can relate to purposive rationality. From the perspective of purposive rationality, however, value rationality must always be irrational, the more so when action is governed by absolute values. For the more that action elevates such absolute values, the less it reflects on the consequence of such action, and the more unconditional do considerations of inner disposition, beauty, the absolute good, and absolute duty become". See Max Weber, *Economy and Society*. Ed & Trans. Keith Tribe. Cambridge MA: Harvard UP, 2019. pp.102–103.
12. Charles Taylor. *The Malaise of Modernity*. Toronto: House of Anansi, 1991. p.5.
13. Albert Borgmann. *Technology and the Character of Contemporary Life*. Chicago: University of Chicago Press, 1987. p.47.
14. Stiegler writes, "The concretization of technical objects, their unification, limits the number of their types: the concrete and convergent technical object is standardized. This tendency to standardization, to the production of mote and more integrated types, makes industrialization possible, and not the converse: it is because there is one or another tendency in the process of technical evolution in general that industry can appear, and not because industry appears that there is standardization". See Bernard Sitegler, *Technics and Time, 1: The Fault of Epimetheus*. p.72.
15. See "The 35th CNNIC Report: Analysis of the Scale and Structure of Chinese Internet Users". February 3, 2015. <http://www.askci.com/news/chanye/2015/02/03/151359b9x0_all.html>
16. Martin Heidegger. "The Question Concerning Technology". p.954.
17. H. H. Gerth and C. W. Mills, eds. *From Max Weber: Essays in Sociology*. New York: Oxford University Press, 1946. p. 342.
18. Albert Borgmann. *Crossing the Postmodern Divide*. Chicago: University of Chicago Press, 1992. pp.119–120.
19. Bernard Stiegler, "The Age of De-Proletarianisation: Art and Teaching Art in Post-Consumerist Culture", in *Essential Texts in Art Theory: The Western Contemporary Period*. Ed. Zhou Xian. Beijing: Sanlian Bookstore, 2014. pp.364–365.

12 The aestheticization of everyday life in the "post-revolutionary time"

What is "the aestheticization of everyday life"?

China has witnessed epoch-making changes in the past 40 years, progressing from an impoverished country to the world's second-biggest economy, and gradually entering a consumer society. Actually, since the second half of the 1990s, the aestheticization of everyday life has been a hot topic of the Chinese academia of aesthetics. The heated discussions on the topic reflect the profound transformation of Chinese culture and society, and demonstrate the keen perception of the academia and its theoretical response to the latter.

As we know, the conception of "aestheticization of everyday life" is not a Chinese invention, but originated from British cultural sociology. In the 1980s, the conception first appeared among some sociologists and cultural researchers centering around *Theory, Culture, Society,* and then developed into a keyword used to describe Western consumer society and postmodern culture. In light of the illustration in a dictionary, it refers to:

> Aestheticization of Everyday Life. The claim that the division between art and everyday life is being eroded. There are two senses: (1) artists are taking the objects of everyday life and making them into art objects; (2) people are making their everyday lives into aesthetic projects by aiming at a coherent style in their clothes, appearance and household furnishings. This may reach the point where people see themselves and their surroundings as art objects.[1]

In this sense, "the aestheticization of everyday life" refers to, first of all, the transformation of banal objects into works of art, which is definitely an important trend of modern art. It made its debut in the ready-made art of the French artist Marcel Duchamp at the beginning of the last century. One obvious trend of modernist art is its cultural orientation toward elitism, purism, and aestheticism, separating art from life in its pursuit of purity. However, Duchamp's sensational art, like a thunderbolt, wakens people to the fact that art is more than delicately carved novelty; art can find its way into our daily life, into everyday appliances. In the postmodernist pop art, this kind of challenge is anything but scarce, among which Andy Warhol, an American artist, enjoys his fame for his artwork of soup cans, beer bottles, news photographs, and package boxes. Anything can be made into art. His bold challenge led to the birth of the theory of artworld in contemporary Western aesthetics. However, in my view, as far as the aestheticization of everyday life is concerned, this challenge is far less important than the above-mentioned second aspect, that is, our changing everyday life into an aesthetic project.

Aestheticization has always been a prospective target with utopian overtones in the history of aesthetics, which, especially since the modern times, has developed the trend of either hunting for inspirations in the remote ancient Greek era or hoping for a beautiful future yet to arrive. It seems impossible to associate aestheticization with trivial and insipid daily routine in serious Aesthetics. One of Max Weber's famous assumptions about modernity is that aesthetics is endowed with the secular power of salvation to rescue people from the "Iron Cage" of everyday life under modernity. As Max Weber argues,

> The development of intellectualism and the rationalization of life change this situation. For under these conditions, art becomes a cosmos of more and more consciously grasped independent values, which exist in their own right. Art takes over the function of this-worldly salvation, no matter how this may be interpreted. It provides salvation from the routine of everyday life, and especially from the pressures of theoretical and practical rationalism.[2]

In Weber's argument, the aesthetic is differing from everyday life. Does it mean that his assumption ceases to be effective if everyday life is aestheticized today? Or is it possible to say that everyday life is no longer characterized with the depressive nature of iron cage?

Consumer culture in the "post-revolutionary era"

What is at stake is the implications of "aestheticization of everyday life" in those discussions. Does it imply the realization of aesthetic utopia or the aestheticization of everydayness of social life itself today?

In his *Consumer Culture and Postmodernism* (1991), Mike Featherstone elaborates the conception and points out that the aestheticization of everyday life involves two keywords: consumer culture and postmodernism. In his view, the conception can be understood as follows: first, modernist art strives to "efface the boundary between art and everyday life". On the one hand, it calls into question the traditional definition of works of art by replacing them with ready-made objects of daily life; on the other hand, it emphasizes the notion of the omnipresence of art. Second, it transforms everyday life into art. This dual focus on a life of aesthetic consumption and the need to form life into an aesthetically pleasing whole on the part of artistic and intellectual counterculture should be related to the development of mass consumption in general and the pursuit of new tastes and sensations and the construction of distinctive lifestyles, which has become central to consumer culture. The third aspect is "the rapid flow of signs and images which saturate the fabric of everyday life in contemporary society".[3] From Mike Featherstone's perspective, the trend of the aestheticization of everyday life has appeared in China with its progress toward a consumer society and culture.

In his descriptions of the aestheticization of everyday life, Mike Featherstone points out that a wide range of images, from urban planning to department stores and shopping malls, from architecture to advertisements, from commodity packing to personal clothing, have all been endowed with beauty and provided with aesthetic values. "It is this double capacity of the commodity to be exchange value and ersatz use-value, to be the same and different, which allows it to take up an aestheticized image, whatever may be the one currently dreamt up".[4] Clearly, the consumer society and its culture constitute an important context for the aestheticization of everyday life. To be specific, the aestheticization of everyday life brought about by commodity and service has been quite distinct from the aestheticization with utopian connotations in the aesthetic sense. Commodity + image = beauty. This equation has distilled the essence of the aestheticization of everyday life in the contemporary world. The French philosopher Guy Debord, who disclosed this social feature with the notion of "the society of the spectacle", went so far as to hold the view that

> the first phase of the domination of the economy over social life brought into the definition of all human realization the obvious degradation of being into having. The present phase of total occupation of social life by the accumulated results of the economy leads to a generalized sliding of having into appearing, from which all actual 'having' must draw its immediate prestige and its ultimate function.[5]

He noted in particular that the production, circulation, and consumption of commodities in capitalist society have partly changed into those of spectacles. "The world at once present and absent which the spectacle makes visible is the world of the commodity dominating all that is lived".[6] In other words, a world made visible by "spectacles" must be one dominated by commodities. In this world, what people consume is not so much the commodities themselves as their image or symbolic values, which are more important than their use values. World-renowned brands such as Coca-Cola, Hollywood movies, McDonald's, Nike, BMW, and Chanel have larger image values than their use values. Consequently, aestheticization leads to imperceptible aesthetic fetishism in daily life as commodity and service gradually assume the attraction of spectacles in accordance with the principle of attention.

Recently, one book that focuses on this aspect of aestheticization has gained popularity in the West. This book is titled *Substance of Style: How the Rise of Aesthetic Value is Remaking Commerce, Culture & Conscious-ness* (2003). Virginia Postrel, the author, stresses the urgency of contemporary aesthetics with firm conviction in the narrowness of the definition of beauty in traditional aesthetics, which cannot cater to the needs of contemporary society. The notion of aesthetics she wants to focus on bears the denotation of the object's appearance appeal and the subject's pleasure. She declares that aesthetics has grown so important that it has become part of the job for engineers, designers, real estate developers, and business managers instead of aestheticians alone. "Aesthetic creativity is as vital, and as indicative of economic and social progress, as technological innovation".[7] In spite of the absence of a clear definition for the aestheticization of everyday life, the whole book involves profound explications of and associations with this notion. From product design to environmental improvement, from daily appliances to image decoration, aesthetics in the Hegelian sense has been totally secularized into everyday life appearances. Therefore, bidding farewell to abstract philosophical exploration to enter real-life practice is one of the important implications of the aestheticization of everyday life.

It is an undeniable fact that China has become a consumer society. A careful examination of the prevalence of this notion will find its connection with the flourishing of cultural studies in China and its close relations with the growth of consumer society in China. Currently, the much-debated phenomenon of the aestheticization of everyday life in the West seems to exist in different degrees in China. If every era has its own topic (or subject), one of the post-revolutionary eras is the aestheticization of everyday life.

Since the middle of the 19th century, China has undergone too many sufferings. The radical reforms to build China into a strong country in order to expel foreign invaders have been welcomed as the most appealing social development strategy. In post-revolutionary China, Communist radicalism and idealism determined people's understanding of "aesthetics" and totally reformed their mind and body in some "unaesthetic" way. Besides, "revolutionary aesthetics" often evolved into a powerful collusion between knowledge and power, leading to the appearance of one kind of deformed "cruel aesthetics", which propounded the notion that "the more radical and revolutionary something is, the more aesthetic it becomes". Consequently, everyday life, fraught with violence, subversion, and destruction, was politicalized to the extent that all the older ways of life were completely changed as everyday life itself must be lived like making a revolution. This situation reached its climax during the Cultural Revolution with the disappearance of all aesthetic appreciation in its real sense. Revolutionary excitement replaced aesthetic pleasure, the impetuous desire to destroy took the place of aesthetic contemplation, and a unique revolutionary lifestyle characterized by thrift and poverty became the order of the day.

The advent of the post-revolutionary era suggests the arrival of a new way of life. Opening-up and reform have reshaped the Chinese people's daily life. "Allowing some people to get rich first" is more of a way of life than an economic or political policy. The call to build a well-off society is not so much a quantitative index of annual per capita income as an outline for a new lifestyle. Social progress manifests itself as a constantly changing process, such as the improvement of social productive forces and peopled living standards; on the other hand, it also brings about sudden changes in peopled psychological experience and mindset. Now that the people's long suppressed desire for material comfort during the revolutionary years has erupted, but it can never be held back like the evils from the opened Pandora's Box.

The lifestyle in the well-off society for the urban middle class has nothing to do with poverty and thrift. Chinese people nowadays are enjoying various conveniences through new technology in daily life, from television to the Internet, from mobile phones to home theatres. On the other hand, in the new consumer society, some old-fashioned entertainment and ideas in the past in accordance with Chinese hedonist traditions are now on the market again. These traditional forces, more deeply rooted than revolutions, will come to the spotlight in one way or another if conditions permit. Thus, revolutionary radicalism is replaced by material consumerism and revolutionary idealism by secular hedonism. Whether in regard to the reality of social development or to people's psychological needs, "the aestheticization of everyday life" has to be brought to the agenda. It goes without saying that it is the representation of the typical lifestyle in this "post-revolutionary era".

"Experience" and "taste": what is aestheticized?

The aestheticization of everyday life in the post-revolutionary era has always been connected with two keywords—experience and taste.

One feature of contemporary consumer society and its culture is the tendency toward a pleasant "experience" of consumption. The concept of "experience" is closely linked with aesthetics. Directly engaged with the senses, it is a process of obtaining pleasure via the senses. Thus, experience belongs to the subjective category as it involves the subject's feelings toward the external physical world. In a consumer society, however, as consumer goods transform into "spectacles" and design becomes part of everyday life, aestheticized experience has turned into a requirement of lifestyles, objects, and surroundings. Material life has changed into people's sensual pleasure of consumer goods and lifestyles accordingly. For this reason, the aestheticization of everyday life is, in essence, the pleasure of gaining perceptual experience by means of consumption. The spiritual orientation of aesthetic experience is gradually changing into the pleasure and gratification of the senses and manifests itself as fastidiousness of the senses towards consumer goods (commodities or surroundings), from the taste of drinks or food, the sight of images, clothing, environment, and HDTV, to the touch of the material and texture of banal objects. Experience has penetrated into every aspect of life and has become a key index for happiness and gratification of aestheticization.

Compared with "experience" as an internal process, "taste" literally refers to one kind of sensual response. They are two sides of a coin. In aesthetics, "taste" in English is generally translated into "*quwei*" in Chinese, which originally means taste or certain experience of food and comes to bear the meaning of certain capability, preference, and judgment in art or aesthetic appreciation due to the efforts of such modern philosophers as Kant. Nowadays, this notion has penetrated into daily life and has become a symbol of certain aesthetic capability in clothing, art, diet, and family life. The dichotomy between good and bad tastes embodies the distinction between superior and inferior ability in aesthetic appreciation. The life of "experience" regards "taste" as the standard and pursues a lifestyle of good taste.

Noticeably, "taste" has become a cover for commodity fetishism in consumer societies. A close study of advertisements shows that more and more commodities try to associate themselves with "taste" (or "good taste"). A life of good taste has become the best representation of aestheticization. The desire to consume inspired by "taste" is something more than owning goods or enjoying service; it is showing off the symbolic values of the goods or services as well. In the qualitative descriptions of goods and services, such flaunty words are used frequently as "noble", "elite", "white-collar", "petit bourgeois", and "aristocrat". Some vague words like "royal pattern" and "French flavor" symbolize life of the upper-class or exotic beauty. When it comes to family life and entertainment, "artistic temperament" or "poetic and picturesque beauty" is more appealing. All these lay emphasis on the cultural implications of goods and services, which shows that "taste" and "experience" are the core of the aestheticization of everyday life.

But the problem is how to develop the "taste" and how to have the experience.

First of all, is the "taste" overly advertised and emphasized by the mass media of consumer society commonly shared by all (human beings)? Is it innate or acquired? For this, Karl Marx proposes two different views. He believes that the nature of human beings determines that "objects are shaped according to the law of beauty". On the other hand, he stresses that even the most beautiful scenery will not attract the attention of people living in complete destitution. The first point of view tells us the fact that "love of beauty is common to all men", while the second focuses on other social conditions of beauty appreciation. It can thus be deduced that "taste" is by no means a tendency or capability that all men are born with or commonly share.

Pierre Bourdieu, a French sociologist, gave a profound historical critique of taste. He holds the view that taste is a product of society, culture, and education. He once wrote that

> [C]onsumption is, in this case, a stage in a process of communication, that is, an act of deciphering, decoding, which presupposes practical or explicit mastery of a cipher or code. In a sense, one can say that the capacity to see is a function of the knowledge, or concepts, that is, the words, that are available to name visible things, and which are, as it were, programmes for perception.[8]

His words merit deep thought. His first point is that consumption is not a natural but a decoding activity. In other words, the choice of what to consume is a cognitive process, the same way as reading is, which requires familiarity with a certain amount of words and relevant background knowledge. Second, he points out that certain "ability of judgment", or ability of choice of taste, is a prerequisite for consumption. It has something to do with cognition, which means that the good ability of choice of taste belongs to the cognitive category.

According to this point of view, we may ask: Whose tastes are those "elegant" tastes widely advertised by advertisements, the media and consumer culture in the process of the aestheticization of everyday life in China? Or, to whom does the aestheticization of everyday life belong?

Middle classes as aestheticized subjects

Here comes an inner paradox of aestheticization: as far as aesthetic pursuit is concerned, integrity of the humanity is the ultimate goal; in other words, aestheticization shared by all men is aestheticization in its real sense. In a highly stratified society, aestheticization of this kind is nowhere to find. Low-income families and people who live on minimum assurance cannot afford "elegant" taste. They have no cultural capital and no cultivation of judgment of taste, not to mention economical capital. The "aestheticization" promoted by the Chinese mass media and all sorts of marketing strategies represent only middle-class tastes and lifestyle. Although the definition of the "middle class" is still controversial, it is without doubt an important social class, or, to use other appellations, "the elite class", "the professionals", "the white collars", "the intelligentsia", etc.

Let us first turn to the situation in the West. According to the observations of Featherstone who has made an in-depth study of the aestheticization of everyday life, one of the important motives or agents is the various new cultural roles assumed by groups of people, such as "the new petites", "the new intellectuals", "the new cultural intermediaries"(from marketing personnel to advertising agents, from television producers to other professionals). Interestingly, the so-called yuppies are "selfish perfect consumers", a bunch of "narcissistic, calculating hedonists" and could be classified as "the new middle class".[9] They have formed a new kind of unique sensibility for consumer society, which is actually endless pursuit of various experiences offered by a new lifestyle.

> It can be argued that the sector of the new middle class, the new cultural intermediaries and the helping professions will have the necessary dispositions and sensibilities that would make them more open to emotional exploration, aesthetic experience, and the aestheticization of everyday life.[10]

To adapt these observations to the context of contemporary Chinese culture, we will find a similar agent in the process of the aestheticization of everyday life who may not necessarily be the same kind as the middle class in the developed societies in the West. Instead, they are the localized middle class, a special social group that grows out of a "well-off" society. They enjoy relatively higher income, better education, and more cultural capital and thus ask more from the "experience" and "taste" of everyday life. Although no analysis of social classes is attempted here, it is necessary to point out the agent of the aestheticization of everyday life in the sociological sense.

I believe that the aestheticization of everyday life per se is not an undifferentiated process of universalization but a battle field of fights between culture and ideology. The dominating social force of this field is the middle class. The promotion of the aestheticization of everyday life is the reflection of the actual situation and the cultural interest of a certain social group. But what is thought-provoking is that the aestheticization demands of the middle class often show a common social and cultural tendency. Or, to be more specific, the mass media and the cultural industry usually generalize this aestheticization with social stratification implications as a common culture shared by all people of all social classes. In this way, the specific cultural taste of certain social classes is transformed into the common demands of the entire society, thus masking the reality of differentiation in social stratification, cultural capital, and even social justice.

That is to say, the aestheticization of everyday life is, as a matter of fact, one kind of ideology of contemporary consumer society with the function of universalization.

The consumer society has a contradictory trend: social stratification leads to social separation and consumers form different consumption preferences and orientations according to their different cultural capital (as the idiom goes, "to each his own"; on the other hand, the aestheticization of everyday life, as the cultural dominant, has the trend of dedifferentiation and, masking or suppressing different consumption *taste*, promotes certain fake common taste, thus leading to the false impression that "love of beauty is common to all men". As Terry Eagleton suggests, ideology, as a means of power struggle in expressive activities of culture, would inevitably cause the dominating process of certain expressive activity, because different social classes occupy different social positions and the privileged ones will extract leadership from other classes. More importantly,

> ideology is commonly felt to be both *naturalizing* and *universalising*. By a set of complex discursive devices, they project what are in fact partisan, controversial, historically specific values as true in all times and all places, and so as natural, inevitable and unchangeable.[11]

From this perspective, the topic of the aestheticization of everyday life as one kind of ideology in a consumer society is the consumption orientation and lifestyle of the middle class that steals into the mind of common people, thus becoming the way of life and fashion for more people to pursue. Different social classes, in pursuing the aestheticization in this sense, are assimilating the consumption taste of the middle class without objection while assuming they were shaping their own lifestyle. It's reasonable to say that certain invisible shift has taken place in the aestheticization of everyday life in China today.

Some further questions

The aestheticization of everyday life in "the post-revolutionary era" is obviously a very complicated cultural phenomenon with no possibility of being evaluated in a simple way.

There is no way back to the bygone revolutionary era; neither is it possible to give positive or negative appraisal to "the aestheticization of everyday life" by employing the values of that era. We have to adopt a new idea or a new perspective. The bourgeoning of the middle class in China is a growing tendency to be welcomed. The universalization of their aesthetic taste has positive influences and is an inevitable demand of everyday life in the process of social development. But not all problems can be solved by affirming their positive sides. Some stickier issues need further study.

First of all, is "the aestheticization of everyday life" consistent with the aesthetic ideals pursued by numerous sages in history? Does the gratification people find in material things signify the fact that we are losing some more important things in aesthetics? The trend of commodity fetishism brought along by "the aestheticization of everyday life" runs counter to the non-utilitarian nature of the aesthetic spirit. In other words, "the aestheticization of everyday life" as we see it today may not be a healthy trend that might lead to an ideal state of aesthetic appreciation. In the process of social development in China, fetishism, in its endless pursuit of luxury, has given rise to a number of disconcerting trends that have outpaced the development of society and gone beyond what the ecological environment would and could allow, thereby creating a variety of potential crises unparalleled before.

Next, does "the aestheticization of everyday life" still maintain the qualities of equality, justice, and freedom indispensable to the aesthetic spirit? Based on the above argument, does "the aestheticization of everyday life" reflect a new power relation in the context of sharp conflicts between the rich and the poor in a highly stratified society? Are some more important things covered by the flashy appearances of this aestheticization, such as social injustice and the plights of the underprivileged? We should delve deeper into the social implications of this aestheticization and care for those social groups deprived of the opportunities of experiencing the same aestheticization in a generous show of humanity essential to the nature of the aesthetic spirit.

Finally, another important theoretical problem needs consideration. From the perspective of traditional philosophical aesthetics, the underlying judgment of everyday life in the context of modernity is that it always sees a repression of instrumental rationality and therefore becomes more and more rigid and tasteless, so much so that it is almost like an "iron cage" (in Weber's words). The lifestyle of the middle class often becomes the object of satire for writers, artists, and aestheticians. Aesthetics, therefore, often appears as a means of counteracting the restrictions of daily life. Weber's aesthetic "salvation", Martin Heidegger's favored "poetic dwelling", and Foucault's "the aesthetics of existence" all involve relentless attacks upon modern everyday life. On the basis of the three aspects of Featherstone's definition of the trend of the aestheticization of everyday life mentioned above, does it seem to say that modern daily life has been transformed by aesthetics to be less repressive and restrictive? In other words, has the dilemma of modernity been tided over in the process of the aestheticization of everyday life?

Notes

1. Arthur Danto famously asserts that, based on his reflections on Warhol's "Brillo Box", to see something as art requires something the eye cannot descry—an atmosphere of artistic theory, a knowledge of the history of art: an artworld. See Arthur C. Danto, "The Artworld", in *Aesthetics: The Big Questions*. Ed. Carolyn Korsmeyer. Cambridge: Blackwell, 1998. p. 40.
2. H. H. Gerth and C.W. Mills, eds. *From Max Weber: Essays in Sociology*. New York: Oxford UP, 1946. p.342.
3. Mike Featherstone. *Consumer Culture and Postmodernism*. London: Sage, 1991. pp.66–67.
4. Mike Featherstone. *Consumer Culture and Postmodernism*. pp.76–77.
5. Guy Debord. *Society of the Spectacle*. Canberra: Hobgoblin, 2002. p.9.
6. Guy Debord. *Society of the Spectacle*. p.12.

7 Virginia Postrel. *Substance of Style: How the Rise of Aesthetic Value is Remaking Commerce, Culture & Consciousness*. New York: Harper Collins, 2003. p.16.
8 Pierre Bourdieu. *Distinction: A Social Critique of the Judgment of Taste*. Cambridge: Harvard University Press, 1984. p.2
9 Mike Featherstone. *Consumer Culture and Postmodernism*. p.44.
10 Mike Featherstone. *Consumer Culture and Postmodernism*. p.45.
11 Terry Eagleton. "Ideology", in *The Eagleton Reader*. Ed. Stephen Regan. Oxford: Blackwell, 1998. p.236

PART IV

Visual Culture and Social Transformation

13 Contemporary Chinese society and visual culture

Over the past two decades, Chinese society has undergone tremendous changes, followed by the rise of local visual culture. The rise of visual culture has dramatically altered the form of contemporary Chinese culture, reshaped the way it is produced, distributed, and consumed, and even influenced cultural behavior and human perceptions. It is reasonable to argue that social transformation has given birth to contemporary Chinese visual culture and that visual culture in turn has shored up social transformation and cultural change. In this sense, the emergence of contemporary Chinese visual culture is both an inevitable product of social transformation and, in turn, a driving force behind this transformation. Based on this judgment, it is necessary to situate the study of contemporary Chinese visual culture in the context of social transformation, which is an effective approach to grasp the problems and experiences of visual culture in the case of China.

Visual culture and visual construction

"Visual culture" is an academic buzzword since the 1980s. There are many different interpretations and definitions of this term, which can be summarized as follows. One view is that visual culture is a nascent cultural form which centers on visuals as the dominant, and is very different from the once dominant language-based (or discourse-based) print culture. Visual culture ushers in, as Heidegger names it, the "age of the world image", an age characterized by "the world conceived and grasped as picture".[1] Furthermore, the society is increasingly becoming, to use Guy Debord's famous phrase, "the society of the spectacle".[2] From the perspective of cultural history, the primitive culture of mankind was a visual one, when language and writing were not fully developed and vision was dominant in human life. Later, language and writing came into being, followed by the ancient codex culture and the modern print culture. Since then, the visual became less important, and language and writing became the dominant medium for knowledge, thought, and ideology. At the beginning of the last century, the emergence of cinema sparked heated debates among many thinkers and cultural historians, who stubbornly believed in the return of a new visual culture, especially a mechanically reproduced visual culture (such as cinema) that can completely undo the previous traditions.[3] A distinguishing feature of visual culture is that it differs from traditional and modern cultures in that the dominant is neither textual nor verbal. Rather, it highly or thoroughly visualizes all aspects of society and culture. "The study of visual culture takes as one of its basic premises the idea that images from different social realms are interconnected, with art, advertising, science, news media, and entertainment interrelated and cross-influential".[4] I think there are three conditions for the emergence of visual culture. First, its rise is closely related to the advancement of visual technology. It is due to the deployment of new technologies that more and more new visual devices have invaded our daily lives and become the most convenient method for men and women to gaze at and grasp the world. In this regard, today's visual culture is very different from the dominance of visuality in primitive cultures. Contemporary visual culture is a highly technological culture. Without the diverse technologies of visual production, storage, dissemination, and presentation, contemporary visual culture would cease to exist. Second, the emergence of visual culture is accompanied by consumer society and its consumer culture. To a certain extent, it can be said that visual culture is a kind of consumer culture obsessed with pleasure—film and television, advertising, photography, online video, smartphone selfie, etc. People are not only manufacturing and disseminating images, but also, more importantly, consuming images everywhere. Nowadays, the consumer society has taken over the dominant position from the production society. Typically, on the one hand, given the all-embracing domination of consumer goods, the act of consumption has become the main means of the subject's identity; on the other hand, the consumer goods, as an infinitely inflating but empty signifier, constantly stimulate consumers' desire and expectation of consumption.[5] During this profound historical transformation, the visual becomes one of the most important and effective consumption. Visual consumption inevitably leads to the emergence of the visual spectacle, when the capital's encroachment turns the image into a commodity. As Debord points out in his analysis of the society of the spectacle: "The spectacle is the capital accumulated to the point that it becomes images".[6] The spectacle is capital, which means that the visual has been highly capitalized in the consumer society. This is certainly true of the current development of China's cultural industry, where visual consumption has become the core of the cultural industry—the so-called "attention economy" or "eyeball economy" is a case in point. Third, visual culture is the comprehensive visualization of mass media. As far as the trend of cultural development is concerned, the convergence of visual technology and consumer society is best evidenced by the mass media, and when the two began to be effectively integrated in the mass media, an unprecedented form of culture—visual culture—was born.

The process of social transformation in contemporary China is highlighted in three aspects: technological progress, consumer orientation, and mass media. Visualization and its visuality have become a crucial issue in our analysis of contemporary Chinese culture. At the beginning of the reform and opening-up, visual culture was still in its embryonic stage—the visual technology, mass media, and consumer culture have barely sprouted. The typical forms and characteristics of visual culture were not salient. By the 1990s, Chinese economy had made great strides, and so had science and technology in China. With the surge of national consumption, and owing to the rise of mass media culture, visual culture distinguished itself as a unique cultural form. It is an important phase of development for contemporary Chinese visual culture. Since entering the 21st century, visual culture has developed more rapidly, and more and more new devices of visual technology have been invented. The maturity of consumer society, the growth of consumer culture, and the rapid expansion of mass media contribute to China's further integration into globalization. Such a developing Chinese culture is deeply implicated in the dialogue and interaction with Western cultural industries. This period can be regarded as the prime time of the development of contemporary Chinese visual culture, be it the avant-garde art, popular culture, grassroots media, or urban spectacles, all of which are innovative in terms of visual imagery or spectacle. The interaction between local and globalized visual elements has made contemporary Chinese visual culture no longer a closed local spectacle, but an important part of the global visual culture.

The rise of visual culture has strongly propelled the development of visual culture studies, which is an interdisciplinary study that spans many fields of knowledge and problem fields—its interdisciplinarity is widely recognized in the academia. As far as the development of this field of knowledge is concerned, it is indebted to many disciplines, such as philosophy, aesthetics, sociology, anthropology, psychology, cognitive science, cultural studies, art history, film studies, media studies, architectural history, and design studies. Among the many issues under scrutiny in the visual culture studies, I will focus on the visual construction in contemporary China, delve into the interaction between contemporary Chinese visual culture and social transformation, and then reveal the role contemporary Chinese visual culture plays in constructing subjectivity for the public.

What is the constructive function of visual culture? How does visual culture construct our subject's identity? How does it construct our perception and understanding of social change?

According to some scholars, the so-called visual culture is the "image history" of various representational forms.[7] This view is especially illuminating for the current study. It is reasonable to argue that the study of contemporary Chinese visual culture needs to focus on the evolution of the representation of visual images, which is often closely related to social transformation. Furthermore, visual culture can be seen essentially as a visual signifying practice that unfolds within the representational system of visual signs. Within visual culture, there are hidden institutions, behaviors, ideologies, and values that are not immediately visible. It is through these visual symbolic signifying practices that the existing social structures and social relations are reproduced on the one hand; on the other hand, that existing social structures and social relations are questioned and critiqued. On the other hand, it can be a way of questioning and critiquing existing social structures and social relations. W. J. T. Mitchell tackles this issue very well. He argues that the study of visual culture should focus on "the cultural construction of visual experience in everyday life as well as in media, representation and visual arts. It is a project that requires conversations among art historians, film scholars, optical technologists and theorists, phenomenologists, psychoanalysts, and anthropologists. Visual culture is, in short, an 'interdiscipline', a site of convergence and conversation across disciplinary lines".[8] In other words, any individual subject living in the real world produces his or her own visual experiences in various ways, and these experiences will eventually be translated into some kind of "cultural construction". Be is Lu Xun's notion of "national character", or the sociological phrase "imagined community", or moderate / extreme nationalism; it is safe to say that all are inseparable from the "cultural construction of visual experience". We might ask a further question: specifically, what does "cultural construction of visual experience" refer to? Later on, Mitchell further develops his ideas into a dialectical dichotomy. He writes,

> The dialectical concept of visual culture cannot stop at defining the object of study as a certain definition of the social construction of the visual field, but must emphasize the need to explore another form of this proposition, that is, the visual construction of the social field. This is not only to say that because we are social animals, we see the way we act; it is also to show that because we are animals that see, our social planning takes the form of putting it into practice.[9]

In his statement, Mitchell explicitly mentions "the social construction of the visual field" and "the visual construction of the social field", both of which are closely related to visual culture—one takes place in the social domain and the other in the visual sphere. In fact, the two are intertwined, as the social field cannot be sustained without the visual, and vice versa. Thus, it is reasonable to say that visual culture has a certain function of dialectical construction and that the visualization of society and the socialization of vision are a dialectical process from division to unity. Therefore, the so-called "social construction of the visual field" and "visual construction of the social field" emphasize the social visual practice at the core.

How, then, is it possible for visual culture to accomplish the two kinds of dialectically related construction? The implicit premise is a sort of philosophical constructivist epistemology. The basic stance of constructivism is that the discursive practice composed of words is the primary means of knowledge and values. For example, scientific knowledge depends on the paradigm of knowledge accepted by the community of scientists, and our knowledge of the world depends on the way we interpret it.[10] The recognition about society, to give another example, depends on the corresponding social discourse, which constitutes an important means for the subject to construct social reality.[11] The most influential branch of theories is the "French Theory", represented in particular by Foucault's theory of discourse. According to Foucault, the basic unit of knowledge is discourse as speech acts in reality, and the "formation of discourse" is synonymous with the operation of knowledge, truth, and power. Therefore, discourse is not a tool for the cognitive subject, but rather the key factor that shapes the subject's cognitive activities. The tenet of this theory is encapsulated into a succinct paragraph by Stuart Hall:

> Discourse is the way in which knowledge about a particular topic of practice is referred to or constructed: a set (or configuration) of ideas, images, and practices that provide the way, the form of knowledge, in which people talk about particular topics, social activities, and institutional levels in society, and relate particular topics, social activities, and institutional levels to guide people. As is well known, these discursive structures specify what is and is not appropriate for what we say about particular topics and levels of social activity, and what we practice in relation to particular topics and levels of social activity; what knowledge is useful, relevant, and "real" in a given context; what types of persons or "subjects" that specifically characterize them. The concept of "discursive" has become a broad term used to refer to any pathway by which meaning, representation, and culture are constituted.[12]

Discourse theory refers primarily to the discursive practices constituted by language, highlighting the importance of language as a vehicle for human thought. However, these tenets also hold true, if applied to visual culture. That is to say, the visual as a discursive form is often more immediate and expressive than abstract language, and is more likely to influence the thoughts, feelings, and behaviors of the cognitive subject. We can make the case by citing a classic experiment by McLuhan. He arranged four groups of students to be exposed to the same lecture, but in different ways: reading it as a transcript, listening to the lecturer on spot, from a radio or from TV screen. By comparison, the research shows that those who watch TV best understand the lecture; radio listening is the second most effective channel; listening to the lecture in person is only better than transcript reading.[13] This classic experiment clearly proves that television as a visual medium is exceptionally effective, when compared with other reception methods. Vision plays an indisputable and decisive role in human understanding and perception of the world.

Generally speaking, language and rationality are closely related, in ancient Greek philosophy, language is reason, or, *logos*. After Socrates, there was a tendency throughout Western philosophy to emphasize language and reason and to deflate image and sensibility. Especially after the Enlightenment, human perception of image was seen as a cognitive act unreliable and perceptually biased. This also reveals the specificity of pictorial perception, bringing to the fore the strongly constructive function of vision for the subject's thinking, values, and ideology. Recently, the comparative studies on textual reading and film viewing have also confirmed the discrepancy between language and image in terms of subjective construction.[14] Of course, with the progress being made in psychology and cognitive science researches, more and more findings tend to conclude that image perception actually functions in a way similar to verbal reasoning. For example, some psychologists introduce the idea of "visual thinking", confirming that visual activities and language-based reasoning are functionally similar.[15] Even so, we are inclined to believe that the perceptual intuitiveness and emotional expressiveness of vision make visual cognition different from verbal cognition in many ways. And it is these differences that have led to the rise of visual culture as a favored field for contemporary technical devices, as an enormous industry and market for consumer culture, and as a popular channel of communication for mass media.

Therefore, the constructive function of visual discourse, as a basic form of human culture, appears to be more effective in many cases, when it comes to subjective construction. This justifies my emphasis on the two constructive functions of visual culture, especially in contemporary China, where visual technology, consumer culture, and mass media are highly developed.

From image to representation

Visual culture is a highly visualized culture. According to Raymond Williams, in each era, there are some key concepts that reflect social and cultural changes and emerge in clusters, and they form a family of interrelated keywords. These keywords on the one hand reflect the social and cultural transformation of a time, and on the other hand reflect the response from the community of ideas and intellectuals.[16] If visual culture has become the cultural "dominant" of contemporary culture,[17] then it is necessary to probe into the keyword families specific to contemporary visual culture. These keywords constitute an intellectual framework that reveals the morphology of visual culture and reflects the intellectual thoughts and interpretations in this era. Based on the status quo of contemporary Chinese visual culture and related researches, we will underscore three keywords: image, representation, and visuality.

When Heidegger refers to "the world conceived and grasped as picture", his classic statement lays bare not only the unique way of perception in visual culture, but also the medium of visual culture—image. Image is a common word with extremely complex connotations, which has been understood and interpreted differently in both Chinese and Western cultures in different periods. As a keyword of visual culture, image is a highly productive concept, related to a big family of some diverse concepts, such as representation, expression, symbol, visuality, visual institution, visual media, and visual technology. However, we believe that the core concept of visual culture is "image", and the study of visual culture must start from the image, just as literary studies must be based on the text.

The basic element of visual culture, image is found in a broad spectrum of visual culture, ranging from two-dimensional flat images (such as print advertisement) to three-dimensional images of spatial depth (such as architecture and urban landscapes), from still pictures (such as cartoon comics or paintings) to motion images (such as movies, TV, videos, video games). The concept of image may seem oddly quaint, but compared with "sign" or "language", it drives home the visuality of the research object in visual culture more accurately. Of course, in the sense of visual culture today, we need to further define or specify the concept of image, clarify its meaning, and use it correctly. On top of it, we must examine the medium-specific morphology of image and its composition. On the one hand, image is the carrier of visual culture, and the whole visual culture is built on the foundation of images; on the other hand, image is an ontological term, inundated with multi-layered visual cultural significances.

In different cultural contexts, there are different terms for "image". In classical Chinese philosophy, it is called "*xiang*"—Laozi's discussion on the relationship between Tao and Xiang, the proposition of "setting up a *xiang* in order to exhaust the meaning" in *I Ching*, Zhuangzi's character named "Xiang Wang", and the relationship between "speech", "*xiang*" (image), and "meaning" have been repeatedly discussed in Chinese aesthetics and art theory, and brought about a lot of controversies and different interpretations. In the West, the concept of image is also defined in many ways. For example, in Western languages, image and icon are conceptually different. It is generally believed that visual culture scholars prefer to use image rather than icon, because the former is more closely tied up with vision, while the latter refers to both visual and non-visual images. Some scholars point out that the contemporary usage of "image" is mainly found in three fields: one is in the cognitive sense, such as art teaching, psychology, and cognitive science; the second is in the field of art theory and art history, where various theories bestow the concept with complex connotations; and the third is visual culture studies, where image is regarded as a major feature of contemporary life and culture.[18]

Image, as the basic unit of visual culture, is both a vehicle for visual objectification and a tool for theoretical analysis. In terms of the image itself, there are many aspects to be analyzed, from its elements to structural functions, from its historical evolution to its typology. At the level of visual culture, the basic task of image analysis is to figure out how images produce meanings and what kind of impact these meanings might have on the public. This is why there are some interesting statements about the image's multiple functions and influences. For example, W. J. T. Mitchell writes a book entitled "What Do Pictures What", and Marie José Mondzain has a more provocative book title—"Can Images Kill?" To ask "what do pictures want" clearly illustrates the social and cultural functions of images themselves; the agency of pictures can have a variety of complex effects on real life. The question "can images kill" poses a more definitive question about the relationship between images and violence. Mondzain's question cancels the value-neutrality of the image itself and tethers it with social issues.

There are different approaches to the typology of image,[19] and I will adopt the triadic structure of picture, video, and spectacle. By picture, I mean all two-dimensional, flat, still images. There are many subtypes of picture—paintings, posters, print advertisements, graphic design, cartoon books, photography, calligraphy, and so on. The media forms of picture are highly diverse, from manufactured printed images and unproducible hand-made paintings, to digital photography and graphic books. The composition of picture has two characteristics. One is its two-dimensional flatness; that is to say, all pictures are composed in two dimensions, that is, length and width.[20] The other characteristic is its stillness. No matter what objects are presented—from clouds and rivers to animals and humans—an image must be still, even when it represents movement or action. Although in art history there have been a lot of attempts, theoretical and practical, to capture motion on a still surface, a picture can only suggest motion, rather than presenting it for real.[21]

The characteristics of two-dimensionality and stillness both define the way pictures exist and reveal how they are produced and received. Pictures are the staple of image output in contemporary visual culture, especially in the fields of painting, printing, advertising, and photography. Pictures constitute a vast field for the production, circulation, and consumption of images, and become the most accessible and commonplace goods for visual consumption.

Unlike the stillness of pictures, a salient feature of video is their dynamics. By video, we refer not only to film, television, and other types of dynamic images, but also to web videos based on digitalization and video technology. In comparison, there are many differences between picture and video, the most important one being, of course, the dynamic presentation of images. Unlike pictures, which exist solely in space, videos dwell in both space and time. In other words, video is temporalized by means of film projectors, or through the constantly changing images on the television screen, or through the motion pictures on the interface of computers, cell phones, iPads, or other electronic devices. The most telling example of this transformation is a digital camera, which can alternate between taking pictures and recording video. While the former function is to produce flat still pictures, the latter is to realize the spatial-temporalization of images. The invention of film more than a hundred years ago had made people rejoice in the advent of visual culture. Film as motion pictures does have a unique visual effect and appeal, but the function of videos goes beyond that. When film proceeds from silent films from sound films, the video was no longer a mere presentation of pictures; rather, it was accompanied by a variety of sound effects. Paintings do not speak, and photographs do not have sound; they rely on the power of picture itself to attract the viewer. Video, on the other hand, has more diverse technical styles and comprehensive sensory effects, coupled with fast and slow motion, freeze frames, close-ups, black-white and color pictures, etc. The development of virtual digital technology, in particular, makes video the most charming visual objects. The sci-fi blockbuster "The Wandering Earth" brings the visual effect of video to an unparalleled level, and elevates the viewer's expectations. In contrast to pictures, video represents the trend of contemporary consumer society and information technology. Visual culture should not only study visual images, but also examine sound culture. Visual-auditory integration has been realized in videos.

Pictures and videos are different, but both belong to the family of flat images. If an image goes beyond flatness and enters into three-dimensional space, then a third type of image comes into view: the spectacle. The so-called "spectacle" includes all three-dimensional images that exist in three-dimensional space, from sculpture and horticulture to architecture and cityscapes, and even natural landscapes. The various types of images with three-dimensional depth mark the way a spectacle exists, which is the same as picture in that both are still. However, the two are different in that picture is flat and spectacle is three-dimensional; it differs from video in that a spectacle is generally frozen in place, while a video changes every second. For the study of visual culture, the spectacle can be as small as interior design or sculpture, or as large as cityscape and landscape. Another important difference that distinguishes the spectacle from the first two is that both pictures and videos are images that the viewer appreciates from a distance, even when they are photographs and paintings. However, in the case of the spectacle, the viewer can enter its interior space, looking at it from all perspectives. While the first two types of image are, as Alois Riegl says, "visual", the spectacle is "tactile" in that it can be approached more closely. Another important difference between the spectacle and the picture and video is that the spectacle can exist in an infinitely extended space and in dialogue with other spectacles around it. Paintings, interfaces, and books exist on their own and are viewed independently, with the frame functioning to isolate the image from its environment. The spectacle is different. Be it a sculpture, a building, a city, or a landscape, it forms a "syntactic relationship" with the surroundings. Besides, the spectacle is placed in a larger contextual framework, serving as the foreground. Thus, the analysis of the spectacle is not limited to the spectacle itself, but needs to be extended to a broader syntactic relationship or contextual assessment.

Each of the three types of images has its own strengths and limitations, and in contemporary Chinese visual culture, no one can escape from their pervasive influence. If in traditional society and culture, images were a scarce resource that people could hardly access, contemporary visual culture has produced abundant or even excessive images. So, it is no longer the case that men turn to images, but the other way around. As Paul Klee puts it, it is an indisputable fact that it is not *I* who look at the painting, but the painting which looks at *me*.[22] As mentioned earlier, in McLuhan's classic experiment, the reason why TV is more absorbing than radio, speech, and text is that video, compared with picture and spectacle, can integrate the visual and the auditory and thus is more attractive. The first reason is that the dynamic audio-visual media can resort to all senses and function more vividly than mere pictures and spectacles do. Second, dynamic videos can represent complex and changing events and characters, and therefore are more visually effective. Third, videos can be highly virtualized, with the help of new media and new visual technologies, and can therefore make possible diverse presentations of scenes and events, expanding the space of visual imagination. Fourth, due to the emergence of more and more new visual technologies, motion pictures can not only be used in one-way dissemination, such as movies and TV programs, but also be developed into different ways of interaction between the interface and the subject (audience). Finally, in terms of the scope and immediacy of dissemination, various online videos have become the winning media because of its convenience, as well as the speed and width of their dissemination. Thus, its influence is the most prominent. From pure entertainment films and videos, to social news videos, online videos have different target audience and functions, but have become the most visually appealing and economically valuable images circulating in the current visual culture.

The study of images in visual culture will be based on the thematic analysis of image typology—content, meaning, value, or ideology of images. The thematic classification of images is important in that by doing so, one can glimpse the complex and deep content of visual culture. In fact, the classification itself is a reflection of the structure of visual culture in a specific period, and the specific classification reflects not only the changing perspective of visual culture research, but also the evolution of images in visual culture of a certain period. For example, that the subject of avant-garde art has changed from the images of great heroes to that of everyday life reflects the profound transformation of visual experience resulting from China's social transformation since the reform and opening-up. For example, in popular culture (especially TV series), the image of characters is no longer "productive idols" who advance ground-breaking ideas and concepts, but "consumer idols" who sport their flamboyant lifestyles. It reveals the change in Chinese visual experience as Chinese society departs from idealistic culture and embraces consumer culture. Another example is urban landscapes (spectacles), which also take some noticeable thematic forms in the process of urbanization. On the one hand, in some mega-cities (e.g., Beijing and Shanghai), the international style has become the dominant of its urban landscape. On the other hand, in some smaller and medium-sized cities (such as Hangzhou, Suzhou), there is an obvious tension between traditional local characteristics and international popular styles, which gives rise to the prevalence of hybrid styles. In my opinion, there are two aspects that need to be noted in the study of image thematics in contemporary Chinese visual culture. One is a critical and reflective stance on contemporary visual culture—being critical is a very important quality for cultural studies, without which it cannot be called cultural studies. Visual culture studies can easily slip into some kind of phenomenological description, or even a value-neutral analysis. In fact, what contemporary visual culture studies usually fall short of is a sharply honed critical and reflective edge. The ordinariness and banality of various mechanisms, modes, and images in visual culture often dull people's thinking and analysis of them. We need to discover some unique critical perspectives that distance themselves from the object of study so as to better reflect on it. The thematic analysis of image typology is a feasible research path, which helps us reflectively and critically probe into the interiority of visual culture, focusing on different themes and genres, and thus revealing the changing social culture and the concomitant transformation of subjectivity and ideology. Second, the thematic analysis of image typology focuses on content and analytical contextualization, which provides us with a possible path to explore contemporary visual culture associated with Chinese experience. Although in contemporary Chinese visual culture there is a lot of cat-copying of and borrowing from the West, some local TV programs with high ratings are basically Chinese versions of hot Western TV shows. However, an interesting question is what changes have been made to these Chinese versions, what local elements have been added to these seemingly copied programs, and what kind of China-specific interpretation and visual experiences are revealed. Needless to say, of course, there are purely local visual phenomena in these TV shows. Thus, the proposed thematic analysis of image typology needs to highlight the locality and Chinese characteristics of contemporary visual culture.

Visual culture is a highly visualized culture, as a result of which "the world is conceived and grasped as picture" (Heidegger's words). Whether the culture is highly visualized or grasped as an image, the core concept of visual culture—image (picture, video, spectacle, etc.)—is actually the same. Image is the basic unit of visual culture studies, but image is never an isolated, static object, which is always caught in the cycle of production-dissemination-reception and derives rich and diverse meanings from it. If turning our attention to the process of image circulation, we will touch on another core concept of visual culture—representation. The meaning of "representation" is rather complex. In the light of lexical construction, it means *re-present* in English. According to the Oxford English Dictionary, it means "a description or depiction of someone or something in a particular way", such as a photograph or a documentary. Representation actually points to a relationship between the real world and its symbolic embodiment—to *re*-present the real in the world of experience (such as men, objects, or events) via language, symbols, or signs. It is a kind of "signifying practice" in a particular context, an examination of the way visual meaning is produced and received.

As to the studies of representation, there are many different methods and approaches. A noticeable theory of late is Stuart Hall's definition of representation from the perspective of cultural studies. According to Hall, representation actually consists of three elements: things, concepts, and signs, which in pairs constitute two different systems of relations. The first system is of correspondence between things and concepts, where a given thing, whether it is a natural object or a social phenomenon or a person, always corresponds to a particular concept. For example, a horse or a tree always corresponds to a specific concept, and the two will not be confused; a horse is a horse as much as a tree is a tree. The second system is of correspondence between concepts and signs, because a concept is intrinsic and needs to be presented through external signs—abstract language ("horse" or "tree"), or pictures (such as the horse painted by Han Gan or the tree painted by Guo Xi), or videos (footages of horses or trees). To put it bluntly, representation is the complex relationship between the two systems linked by the three elements.[23] Through the dualistic relationship among the three elements and the two systems, it is easy to see that the transition from the real horse or tree to the symbolized horse and tree is not a mirror-like reflection (re-presentation). First, there is a transformation from the objective things to the subjective concepts; second, it is a process of transformation from subjective concepts to objective signs. These two processes also indicate the cycle from the signifier to the signified and then the signifier. During the cyclical process, one can find different ways, methods, perspectives, and techniques of representation. The ancient Chinese painter Han Gan and the modern French painter Courbet are very different when painting a horse. Therefore, the same referent has a very different representation under the pens of different artists. I think that the most crucial aspect of representation lies in the variation and differences created in this process. Here, it is useful to invoke Gombrich's "schema theory". In his analysis of artistic style, Gombrich observes that the same landscape can be represented rather differently in the eyes, minds, and hands of different artists. In particular, he analyzes two paintings of Derwentwater in England, one of which is drawn by an unknown English painter of the Romantic period, and the other by the Chinese painter Jiang Yi. His question is why the same landscape conjures up stylistically different representations? Because each artist is deeply influenced by his or her own artistic tradition and has developed his or her own unique visual schema, which works like a "sieve"—let certain things pass through while block other things. No wonder a particular artist's painting inevitably embodies a unique personal style. His conclusion is rather intriguing: "Painting is an activity and the artist will therefore tend to see what he paints rather than paint what he sees".[24]

Based on Gombrich's conclusion, it can be inferred that whether it is painting, photography, film, TV series, or animation, advertising, video, museums, etc., there are different possibilities and variations in between—from the human or object in the real world, to subjective concepts, to the objectified languages, signs, symbols, or images. Therefore, the representation of images in visual culture is by no means a mirror-like reproduction, but a volatile and changeable innovation and reconstruction. At this point, I need to call attention to two important issues. First, there is no such thing as identity between the person or object in the real world and the symbolic representation; rather, there are distances and differences between them, which bring infinite possibilities for image production and allow for the implant of different ideologies and values. Second, this process is subject to what a semiotics scholar calls encoding—the production and reception of meaning, the encoding of image production, and the decoding of image perception. During the process of encoding, there arise distances and differences. Not only do the production and reception fields of visual culture consist of tension, but the two fields are linked by a relationship with tension.

Next, we will dwell upon the issue of image representation from the perspective of encoding and decoding. As mentioned earlier, image is a fluid sign in visual culture, produced by various actors in a specific context, then entering a certain communication field, and finally reaching a specific recipient in a specific context. The signifying practice of image producers is actually a process similar to "encoding" in informatics, while one's appreciation of these images is equivalent to "decoding". Returning to the definition of representation, encoding is a complex process of converting a person or object from the real world into a sign, and the very person or object will take on a completely different symbolic form. Therefore, encoding inevitably involves many cultural and political issues—how to reflect major historical events, how to represent social changes, how to capture daily life and its imagination, how to arrange and design various characters, etc. There are quite a lot of differences, when it comes to mainstream culture, elite culture, and popular culture. It can be said that coding is a complex ideological embedment procedure, where the culture, history, politics, and values to which the coder belongs are covertly implanted in images. In the case of contemporary Chinese visual culture, there are complex interactions between the encoding of various visual cultural images and a society that is undergoing great changes. In fact, in the diverse forms of image production, we can glimpse different representations of the changing China today—some representations are positive, some critical and negative, and others nostalgically vigilant and anxious about changes. These different ways of coding constitute a sophisticated semantic field of images, revealing the complexity and diversity of social changes and people's reactions to them in contemporary China.

If there is difference in encoding, then the same is true of decoding. When image products of visual culture enter the field of reception, reception groups of different times, places, and cultures will inevitably bring about differences and diversity. In his analysis of viewers' reception of TV, Stuart Hall points out the complex correlation between encoding and decoding. On the one hand, encoding establishes certain boundaries and parameters, and decoding occurs within the framework of these boundaries and parameters, without which decoding cannot happen. On the other hand, due to the information asymmetry between encoders and decoders, this inevitably leads to the inconsistency between decoding and encoding, resulting in the differences between the production and reception of the meaning of images. For example, in the encoding and decoding of TV, there are three decoding styles that differ in terms of their distance from encoding. The first type of decoding, as pointed out by Hall, is "dominant-hegemonic" decoding, in which TV viewers basically understand the content of TV programs in accord with the intention of the coder; the second type is "negotiated" decoding, in which TV viewers partially accept the coding intention and have their distinctive take on it—understanding is the result of negotiation. The third type is "antagonistic" decoding, in which the receiver completely subverts the intention of the coder and forms his or her own counter-interpretation.[25] In fact, the three different decoding methods outlined by Hall are only a basic classification of the ever-changing decoding process, and the real situation is far more complex and diverse. In both cases, they are all about the production of meaning, and the study of representation is an inquiry into how meaning is constructed:

> Meaning is thus not stable. A red poppy does not mean anything, meaning is what we attribute to it. It is us that give it a name, and give it a value (cultural, financial, historical, even organizational in the case of the Royal British Legion). Meaning is dependent on culture, geography, language, heritage, education, and it is through processes of representation that it is inscribed; through the "words we use ... the stories we tell ... the images ... we produce, [and] the emotions we associate" (Hall 1997: 3).[26]

To investigate the relationship between image and representation is to examine in depth the relationship between real people or objects and concepts or signs. At the micro level, this relation is embodied in the process of encoding and decoding of images; and at the macro level, it involves the process of production, dissemination, and consumption of signifying practices. There are many rules and axioms for encoding and decoding images in visual culture—some are obvious, while others are implicit. Exploring the rules of encoding/decoding entails an in-depth analysis of visual culture representations. In particular, there are many tacit principles of representation— How is visual narrative sequentially or causally arranged? Which is at the center and which at the periphery? What is highlighted and what obscured? What is celebrated and what is frowned upon? It is these tenets that embody the value orientation of visual culture and its constructive function for the subject. They have an intractable relationship with the transformation of contemporary Chinese society.

From representation to visuality

The extension from image to representation is a passage from the basic units of visual culture to the production of meaning in the signifying practice. This extension necessarily involves visual experience, how and what people see. Once we consider the question of how and what to see, the third core concept of visual culture, visuality, logically surfaces. The question of visuality is not necessarily raised in semiotic studies in general, or in cultural studies in its broad sense. This is not the case with visual culture studies, which, as a special field, is to a considerable extent centered on visuality, thus forming a special interdisciplinary knowledge system.

Since the emergence of visual culture studies, the concept of visuality has been constantly discussed and redefined, especially due to the influence of poststructuralism and cultural studies, and has been endowed with new meanings. It, together with concepts such as "visual regime", "subjectivity", "interactive subjectivity", "ways of seeing", or "gaze", forms a complex family of keywords. In my opinion, visuality is, after all, closely tangled up with the two kinds of construct of visual culture I discussed earlier, and it highlights the social nature of the visual.

There have been many theories and ideas about vision. For example, Hegel holds that among all human senses, vision and hearing are the only "free" and "cognitive" senses, because they can perceive things from a distance. Psychologists describe this feature as "distant senses", which means that vision and hearing can grasp objects from a certain distance away, while other senses (taste, touch, and smell) must be close to the object to obtain perception. Following Hegel's line of thought, it can be inferred that vision is more "free" and "cognitive" than hearing, because the former is more diverse and complex than the latter, which is conditioned by the purity of sound and the rhythm of sound vibration. Therefore, it is not an exaggeration to say that vision is the most important perceptual channel for the subject to grasp the objective world. However, how does a person perceive the world through his or her vision? What are the visible and invisible rules of visual cognition?

Visual culture researchers emphasize that vision, as a human sense, is highly socialized and does not function by itself. In fact, this point is fully illustrated by a large number of expressions about vision in our ordinary language, such as "wise eyes", "fiery eyes", "discerning eyes", "mouse eyes", "cold eyes", "wide-opened eyes", "kind eyes", and "crystal and scintillating eyes". When we talk about a person's cultural identity, we are actually saying that a person belongs to a certain culture, ranging from the cultural identity of a nation-state to the identity of a small ethnic group and gender class. These identities are to a large extent constructed by the visual. And vision itself is a constructed cultural faculty, for there is no such thing as a "naive vision" or "natural sight". According to Gombrich's theory on visual schema, a painter tends to see what he wants to paint rather than what he sees, and the same is true of ordinary people. John Berger has proposed a very influential concept called "ways of seeing"—anyone sees the world and the self in a certain way, and these ways are not innate, but are constructed within a societally specific context. So, he has a very classic conclusion:

> We only see what we want to see. Wanting to see is an act of choice, the result of which is that what is seen is brought within the reach of our eyes". He further argues, "The way we see things is affected by what we know or what we believe.[27]

Berger's words illuminate the profundity of the idea of visuality—human vision is a product of social, historical, and cultural construction. Since the reform and opening-up, Chinese society has undergone profound changes, which are not only at the material level, but are reflected in the evolution of "ways of seeing". It is through the bewilderingly rich image production of visual culture, and through a variety of representational practices, that different ways of viewing social change have been constructed. We can even describe each decade since 1970s as a cycle, which corresponds to a distinct "ways of seeing". From the "Post-50s" Generation to the "Post-00s" Generation, after every ten years, a unique way of viewing for a generation would pop up—these demographical groups are very different in terms of how and what they see. Therefore, the core concept of visuality is not only about vision itself, but also about the construction of individual subjectivity and interactive subjectivity in a specific historical stage. In this sense, visuality is, to put it bluntly, a certain kind of constructed subjectivity and interactive subjectivity.[28]

If visuality is seen as a certain inevitable "way of seeing" acquired by the subject, then a further question is how this way is formed and operates? By asking this question, we have expanded visual culture thinking from image analysis into a broader socio-visual field. Now, visuality turns to more complex cultural and political aspects of ways of seeing and its social institutions and paradigms. As far as the definition of visuality is concerned, I find the classic definition proposed by Foster in the 1980s especially enlightening:

> Why vision and visuality, why these terms? Although vision suggests sight as a physical operation, and visuality sight as a social fact, the two are not opposed as nature to culture: vision is social and historical too, and visuality involves the body and the psyche. Yet neither are they identical: here, the difference between the terms signals a difference within the visual-between the mechanism of sight and its historical techniques, between the datum of vision and its discursive determinations-a difference, many differences, among how we see, how we are able, allowed, or made to see, and how we see this seeing or the unseen therein. With its own rhetoric and representations, each scopic regime seeks to close out these differences: to make of its many social visualities one essential vision, or to order them in a natural hierarchy of sight. It is important, then, to slip these superimpositions out of focus, to disturb the given array of visual facts (it may be the only way to see them at all).[29]

One of the central ideas that Foster emphasizes here is that visuality is ultimately about how people see or are seen in a particular "visual regime" and that the study of visuality is about how this seeing itself is shaped, by exposing how the "visual regime" masks the complexity and volatility of looking and produces some sort of ordered visual structure. This view is actually indebted to Marx's ideological theory of the "dominant ideology of the ruling class", a theory that features acute socio-cultural criticality. According to Marx, every age has its own dominant ruling ideology. This ruling ideology operates through a complex web of discursive practice, a hidden principle being to "give a universal form to one's ideas, portraying them as the only reasonable and universally meaningful ideas".[30] That said, there is always a "ruling ideology" of visual culture in a society, which inevitably imposes an order upon visual images and signifying practices, distinguishing between what kind of seeing is sensible and legitimate, and what is unsensible and illegitimate. Such a distinction thus demarcates two different visual boundaries—what can be accepted, and what should be rejected. In the case of Chinese visual culture, which is obviously more complex, we need to further examine several types of visualities and take their tense relations into consideration.

In terms of the visual culture produced by the social changes in China since the reform and opening-up, I believe that there are three different kinds of visual subcultures, each of which has created its unique visuality. The first is the mainstream culture and its dominant visuality—such a visuality is more often than not characterized by the advocacy of established cultural regime and tinted with its orthodox doctrines. The visuality of mainstream culture tends to emphasize the political correctness and to strengthen moral and ethical guidance, and the result is a visual representation paradigm that stimulates positive values and aims at the social benefits of a whole culture. This has created a unique "way of seeing" with distinctive Chinese characteristics, which is strengthened and sustained by means of institutional management and resource allocation. The visuality of mainstream culture is a "way of seeing" enforced from the top down, the purpose of which is to ensure its dominant position in the field of China's contemporary visual culture. The visuality of mainstream culture establishes complex rules and paradigms of viewing—some are explicit rules, written in the form of documents and management protocols, and some are tacit norms, which are red lines no one shall cross. The mainstream visual culture stipulates how and what one can see—images and representations that conform to its visuality norms are strongly promoted and massively reproduced, while those that defy the rules are removed from sight, marking the existence of stern visual taboos. Of course, there is a wide "gray area" between the approved and the disapproved, so it is no rare to witness some visual practices that waltz near the red lines and "exploit the loopholes".

The second type of visual subculture can be loosely categorized as entertainment-oriented popular culture, which differs from the highly institutionalized mainstream culture and is market-oriented and highly industrialized. The visuality shaped by this subculture features the pursuit of pleasure and entertainment. If the mainstream culture has existed long before and after the reform and opening-up, only with some changes made to its form, the entertainment-oriented popular culture is a product of the reform and opening-up and the market economy, a product of the convergence of economy and culture. Entertainment-oriented popular culture has a lot to do with the progress of visual technology and the development of consumer society, with the decline of the pre-reform culture championing idealism and frugality, and with the national strategy of developing cultural industries and cultural soft power. Unlike the top-down administration of mainstream culture, entertainment-oriented popular culture is bottom-up and has a large base of audience and consumer market. As the essential orientation of this visuality, entertaining pleasure requires that the image production and representation must conform to the "pleasure principle"—such production must create the pleasure associated with mass entertainment, and must enthrall the audience. If the visuality of mainstream culture seeks for propaganda and edification, the entertainment-oriented popular culture is oriented to the pursuit of ratings and the production of visual pleasure. Actually, entertainment is a rather sophisticated business. On the one hand, entertainment is not only tinted with carnivalization but also akin to hysteria; when the thirst for entertainment goes too far, it is at the risk of reducing everything to game and slapstick. On the other hand, the competitive exploitation of visual cultural resources by the visual nature of entertainment-oriented popular culture leads to the tendency to use visual resources in any way possible, so it often crosses some political On the other hand, the visual nature of entertainment-oriented popular culture has led to the exploitation of visual resources, which are inflated exceedingly to the point of crossing the bottom lines of politics, ethics, or culture. Once some obvious or even hidden bottom line is touched, the production of such entertainment images is immediately halted, as is often the case in China's current popular culture. It is worth noting that, within this overall entertainment culture, with the popularization and enhancement of the Internet and mobile terminal technologies, a grassroots media culture with both entertainment and social functions has burst onto the scene, which constructs a hybrid visuality between entertainment, information, and politics, and also creates a significant tension between entertainment, information, and politics.

The third visual subculture is the elite culture, which comes from the cultural elite and the intellectuals. It also produces a particular visuality or "way of seeing". Over the forty years since the reform and opening-up, this culture has undergone a remarkable change from prosperity to decline, from center to periphery. In the early years of the reform, this culture functioned as an important agency for social change in China, creating a series of visual images and creative representational paradigms that rectified and critiqued the wrongdoing of the Cultural Revolution. With the deepening of the reform, China witnesses the infiltration of economic laws in the cultural sphere, with the increasing stratification of intellectual, artistic, educational, and cultural domains. Also, the change of socio-political realities in China gradually deprives the elite culture of its autonomy, criticality, and elitism—it was either assimilated by mainstream culture or co-opted by popular culture, becoming less and less influential. Despite the decline of Chinese elite culture and the drastic changes that followed, this culture still remains indispensable to the integrity of contemporary Chinese culture. The visuality it helps construct is functionally irreplaceable, especially in terms of visual innovation and self-reflexive critique of visual experience.

Finally, let's return to Foster's definition of visuality—visuality is "how we see, how we are able, allowed, or made to see, and how we see this seeing or the unseen therein". In fact, each type of visuality has its own visual norms of how to see and what to see, with different orientations and different visual experiences, and with even more different ideas, values, and ideologies as implied by them. For the current reality of Chinese visual culture, the three kinds of visuality are in a very complex web of interaction, forming a dynamic structure of negotiation. The visuality of mainstream culture is a dominant visuality, playing a self-evident role of cultural hegemony, and making a restrictive impact on the other two sorts of visuality. The visuality embodied in entertainment-oriented popular culture claims a large market and audience, and has become the most influential visuality at present. On the one hand, it forms an interactive and cooperative tie with mainstream culture, and on the other hand, it often draws on resources and methods related to elite culture and transforms them into visual resources with commercial value. The visuality of elite culture is under unprecedented pressure from both mainstream culture and popular culture while adhering to its autonomy and innovation. If we consider contemporary Chinese visual culture as a field, then the three kinds of visuality in this field are intricately entangled and interact with one another, leading up to a situation where multiple actors coexist with reconciliation and tension. It is precisely because of the status of multiple tensions that we have confidence in and expectation of Chinese contemporary visual culture.

Notes

1 Martin Heidegger. "The Age of the World Image", in *Selected Works of Heidegger*. Ed. by Sun Zhouxing. Shanghai: Shanghai Sanlian Bookstore, 1996. p.899.
2 See Guy Debord. *The Society of the Spectacle*. London: Black and Red, 1977.
3 Béla Balázs. *Film Aesthetics*. Beijing: China Film Press, 1979. pp.28–29; Walter Benjamin. *The Art of Work in the Age of Mechanical Reproduction*. p.4.
4 Marita Sturken and Lisa Cartwright. *Practices of Looking: An Introduction to Visual Culture*. Oxford: Oxford University Press, 2001. p.7.
5 See Jean Baudrillard. *The Consumer Society*. Trans. Liu Chengfu. Nanjing: Nanjing University Press, 2008.
6 Guy Debord. *The Society of the Spectacle*. p.33.
7 Norman Bryson, et al., *Visual Culture: Images and Representations*. Hanover: Wesleyan University Press, 1994. p.xvi.
8 W. J. T. Mitchell. "Interdisciplinarity and Visual Culture", in *Art Bulletin* 77.4 (Dec. 1995). p.540.
9 W. J. T. Mitchell. *What do Pictures Want?* Chicago: University of Chicago Press, 2005. p.345.
10 See Thomas Kuhn. *The Structure of Scientific Revolutions*.
11 See Peter L. Berger and Thomas Luckman. *The Social Construction of Reality*. p.173.
12 Stuart Hall, ed. Representation: Cultural Representations and Signifying Practices. London: Sage, 1997. p.6.
13 See Marshall McLuhan, "Sight, Sound and the Fury", in *Radical Aesthetic Frontiers*. Ed. Zhou Xian. Beijing: Renmin University Press, 2003. p.340.
14 In comparing three different modes of interaction—orality, print, and electronic culture—Mark Poster points out that textual reading is closely related to the cultivation of autonomous rational subjectivity. He writes, "Speech constitutes subjects as members of a community by solidifying the ties between individuals. Print constitutes subjects as rational, autonomous egos, as stable interpreters of culture who, in isolation, make logical connections from linear symbols. Media language replaces the community of speakers and undermines the referentiality of discourse necessary for the rational ego. Media language – contextless, monologic, self-referential – invites the recipient to play with the process of self-constitution, continuously to remake the self in 'conversation' with differing modes of discourse. Since no one who knows the recipient is speaking to them and since there is no clearly determinate referential world outside the broadcast to provide a standard against which to evaluate the flow of meanings, the subject has no

defined identity as a pole of a conversation". See Mark Poster, *The Mode of Information Poststructuralism and Social Context.* Cambridge: Polity, 1990. p.46.
15 See Rudolf Arnheim. *Visual Thinking.* Berkeley: University of California Press, 1969.
16 Raymond Williams. *Keywords: A Vocabulary of Culture and Society.* Trans. Liu Jianji. Beijing: Sanlian Bookstore, 2005. p.4.
17 The concept of "the dominant" was coined by Roman Jacobson, and it means the major or decisive factors that govern the overall structure. According to Jacobson, different periods of literature have different dominant factors. For example, Renaissance literature was characterized by realistic mimesis, so "the dominant" was visual verisimilitude; Romantic literature champions emotional expression, musicality being "the dominant"; modern and contemporary literature focuses on language and its experimentation, so language becomes "the dominant". See Roman Jakobson, "The Dominant", in *Language in Literature.* Cambridge: Harvard University Press, 1987. pp.41–46.
18 James Elkins and Majia Naef. *What is an Image?* University Park, PA: University of Pennsylvania Press, 2011. pp.1–2.
19 Mitchell charts five types of images: 1) the graphic (i.e., pictures, statues, designs); 2) the optical (i.e., mirrors, projections); 3) the perceptual (i.e., sense data, "species", appearances); 4) the mental (i.e., dreams, memories, ideas, fantasmata); and 5) the verbal (i.e., metaphors, descriptions). See W. J. T. Mitchell, *Iconology: Image, Text, Ideology.* Chicago: University of Chicago Press, 1987. pp.9–10.
20 Since Manet and Cézanne, Western modernist painting abandoned the perspectivism characteristic of the Renaissance art, and returned to the two-dimensional flatness, bringing to the fore the flatness of painting as a two-dimensional art and revealing the essence of painting as a flat image.
21 Lessing in "Laocoon" famously discusses how painting can represent movement through stillness. The essence of visual art is to choose the most suggestive moment, turning beauty into charm. Modernist painting, on the contrary, has also made many explorations in this respect—from the Impressionists (such as Degas and Manet), who represented horse racing, to Duchamp's Cubist work "Nude Descending a Staircase", which represents the continuous movement of a figure's descending a staircase.
22 Zhou Xian. *The Turn of Visual Culture.* Beijing: Peking University Press, 2008. pp.58–60.
23 See Stuart Hall, ed., *Representation: Cultural Representations and Sign Signifying Practices.* p.19.
24 Ernst Gombrich. *Art and Illusion: A Study in the Psychology of Pictorial.* Trans. Yang Siliang and Xu Yiwei. Hangzhou: Zhejiang Photo Press, 1987. p.101.
25 See Stuart Hall. "Encoding/Decoding", in Cultural Studies: A Reader. Ed. Luo Gang and Liu Xiangyu. Beijing: China Social Science Press, 2000. pp.356–358.
26 Jenny Kidd. *Representation.* London: Routledge, 2016. p.5.
27 John Berger. *Ways of Seeing.* New York: Penguin, 19728.
28 Sunil Manghani, Arthur Piper and Jon Simons, eds., *Image: A Reader.* London: Sage, 2006. p.227.
29 Hal Foster, ed. *Vision and Visuality.* Seattle: Bay Press, 1988. p.ix.
30 Karl Marx and Fredrich Engels. "Feuerbach", in *Selected Works of Marx and Engels*, Vol. 1. Beijing: People's Publishing House, 1972. p.53.

14 From text reading to picture reading

Visual "hegemony" in the time of "picture reading"

In 2004, Lin Bai's *A War of One's Own* was published as "A New Illustrated Reader", which caused some repercussions among readers. According to the author,

> This is the eighth edition…it's designed by the poet Ye Kuang-zheng. He told me on the phone that he designed every page. The upper layer of cover is stamped with silver, and the cover painting is by Li Jin…Ye said that Li Jin's painting is dedicated to *A War of One's Own*, while Lin wrote *A War of One's Own* especially for Li Jin. I did not believe it at first, when I finished the reading, I found that there was really some truth in this statement.[1]

In fact, this format of illustrated text was nothing new in history—the classical novel with "illustrated fine-lined portraits" is a case in point. But what is the difference between this new edition labeled "A New Illustrated Reader", and the classical novel with "illustrated fine-lined portraits"? What is new about the "new illustrated reader"? This reminds us of a buzzword, the "Time of Picture Reading".

This "New Illustrated Reader" has 238 pages, with 212 illustrations (with some repetitions). In the words of the project planner Ye Kuang-zheng, "almost every page has been designed". With so many pictures embedded in the text, the number of images alone distinguishes itself from the traditional illustrated novel. Historically, in the case of traditional Chinese graphic books (including the novels with illustrated fine-lined portraits), illustrations were always subordinate to the text. The illustrations are merely to assist the explication of key passages or texts. The overwhelming proportion of text shows the pattern of traditional Chinese illustrated books—the text carries more weight than pictures. Today's popular picture books, however, tilt toward a balance between pictures and words. Such a change is not only reflected in the ratio of pictures and words; more importantly, it reflects a change in the mindset of the publishing industry. The question we should ask is why, after seven editions of "A War of One's Own", the eighth edition featuring new illustrations was released. Obviously, the text of the latest edition remains the same, but more than 200 new pictures painted by the artist Li Jin were added. It is these images that attract readers to the new edition. If this judgment is valid, then it can be inferred that the real "selling point" in the time of picture reading is no longer the original written text, but the picture of novel, exquisite, and visual appeal. In these new editions of illustrated books, pictures seem to occupy a dominant position, and the text is reduced to a minor role. The proliferation of images is found not only in books, but also in magazines, newspapers, guide books, and even in teaching materials. It seems to signal a profound change in the traditional culture dominated by the text. If any reading material lacks images, it will lose its luster and allure, falling short of visual impact on readers. This is the new law of the time of picture reading, in which images form a unique "eyeball economy". It may be inferred that contemporary reading style has undergone some kind of transformation—readers are now more attuned to the immediacy of pictures, rather than textual interpretation.

From the aesthetic point of view, words and images are different in that images are immediate and concrete, while words are abstract and associative. Reading a text can evoke rich associations and polysemy in the mind of the reader. Words have a unique signifying function in explicating the connotations of phenomena and the depth of ideas. The result of pictorialization is to render meaning in a sensual and visual way, which undoubtedly adds new gusto and pleasure to reading. The abstract word and the visual image can illuminate each other, which undoubtedly makes reading playful—the back-and-forth transition from text to image transforms reading comprehension into visual directness. As Lin Bai puts it, "The beauty is that whether one looks at the pictures before reading the text, or read the text before looking at the pictures, he or she will always find the interesting correspondence between the two".[2] Lin Bai's statement speaks to the "intertextuality", as well as the "interesting correspondence" between words and images, but this line of argument implies a looming "crisis", because between the two lies a certain tension. On the one hand, the image can produce effective interpretation of the text, and on the other hand, there is much misinterpretation and distortion. In the first case, the illustrated books help to "popularize" the books themselves, thus broadening the readership. However, in the second case, the tension between pictures and words may affect the reader's understanding of the text—for instance, some authors turn the literary classics into "comic books". Originally, these classics are mostly known for their profundity, and the ancient classical Chinese is not only their unique medium of expression, but also a necessary condition and path for readers to understand these classic books. However, in the time of picture reading, such books have been widely "popularized" and transformed into "picture books"—the unique language used in these books is reduced to "flat" or even "vulgar" expressions. For example, Cai Zhi-zhong's cartoon series illustrates the esoteric thoughts of the Chinese classics into a form of cartoons, which may help readers understand these ancient classics, but maybe at the risk of caricaturing and oversimplifying the profound thoughts of ancient thinkers. If readers' understanding of ancient wisdom and thought is limited to such caricatures and paraphrasing, and if what remains in their memory are no more than flat caricatures, will this lead to the distortion and obliteration of these ancient classics? When some purely linguistic works of art, such as Tang poems and Song lyrics, are transformed into cartoons, the unique charm of words and the rich associations they evoke, as a result, are rigidly fixed in the frames of some specific images. If so, can the reader still experience the poetic quality of language in the literary works?

The prevalence of "picture reading" may unwittingly change people's reading habitus, a potential result being the reader's preference of pictures over the text. I think that the most worrying implications of the era of picture reading is the "hegemony" of images over words, a hegemony that will marginalize the status of words. In the era of picture reading, the word may be reduced to the subordinate of the image, while the image obtains the status of "the dominant" of culture. Also, the public is more inclined to embrace the pleasure of picture reading, showing less interest and enthusiasm for textual reading. In particular, when too many illustrations are added to the text, the original narrative pattern and logic of the text are disrupted. As the inner logic of the text is unhinged, the reader's attention will be shifted from the text to the images themselves. What's worse, the reader's contemplative and meditative approach to the text is derailed and sabotaged.

In a nutshell, there is a smokeless "war" between images and words in the era of picture reading. This "war" is now extending to more and more cultural fields.

The continuous "colonization" of literary works by film and television is another facet of this "war". Due to the unprecedented expansion of the image industry, more and more non-image cultural resources have been exploited pictorially in the era of "picture reading". Many classical and modern literary masterpieces have been adapted to the screen of film and television, or turned into comics and serial picture books. There is nothing wrong with this. However, a deluge of images and films are produced to promote the reputation and popularity of literary masterpieces, while only a few readers pay attention to the literary texts themselves, because watching movies and TV is easier and more pleasurable than reading novels. Especially among youth readers, the preference for "reading pictures" seems to have replaced the pleasure of textual reading. That readers' enthusiasm has shifted from textual books to graphic ones suggests a subtle change in what readers' eyes are attuned to. In the face of the unprecedentedly developed and market-oriented film and television industry, literature has to change its own "ecology"—there are more and more writers who earn their livelihood by writing for films and TV series, who strive to produce "literary works" that can be shown on, or even customized for, the screen. The result is that, on the one hand, the visuality stipulated by the film and TV industry is imposed on the text, forcing literature to abide by their typical visual requirements; on the other hand, writers who write exclusively for the screen gradually lose their independence and autonomy, living a "parasitic" life attached to film and television. What's more, the great lure of blockbuster films and TV drama works has also changed the way a writer rises to fame, stimulating him or her to enlarge cultural capital by some paraliterary means. Some famous directors commission writers to write for the screen and provide them with a paraliterary route to "fame". What is more interesting is that literary works will also gain a larger market and readership with the success of film and television adaptations—the "win-win" strategy is exemplary in the case of *The Wandering Earth*. However, it is still too early to assess the consequences: Is it beneficial to the development of literature itself, opening up new space for literature? Or, is it possible to render literature more marginalized, reducing it to the "running dog" of the hegemonic film and television?

Not only is there "hegemony" of images over words in the relationship between film and literature, but the visual media also pose a great threat to the written media, such as TV's dominance over newspapers. Bourdieu notes the challenge of television to traditional textual media, such as newspapers. He points out that television has gradually gained ascendancy in the newsroom in terms of economic and symbolic power, so the newspaper industry is facing a new crisis, and many newspapers have gone out of business as a result of the rise of television.[3] In particular, he analyzes the competition between television and newspapers, which is, to put it bluntly, a tension between images and words. This relationship is particularly evident in the print journalists' worship of television and their disillusionment with the written words, as television's influence far exceeds that of newspapers. The charm, power, and appeal of television are, after all, derived from the image. In other words, the advantage of images over words is an indisputable fact in contemporary culture.

At this point, I would like to ask the following questions: Does the advent of the "era of picture reading" mean that the culture of words-as-the-dominant has been replaced by the culture of images-as-the-dominant? Is it possible to say that today images are more magical and attractive than words? Is there indeed a hegemony of images over words today? Roland Barthes' remark provides a positive answer to these questions:

> This is an important historical reversal, the image no longer illustrates the words; it is now the words which, structurally, are parasitic on the image. The reversal is at a cost; in the traditional modes of illustration the image functioned as an episodic return to denotation from a principle message (the text) which was experienced as connoted since, precisely, it needed an illustration; ... Formerly, the image illustrated the text (made it clearer); today, the text loads the image, burdening it with a culture, a moral, an imagination. Formerly, there was reduction from text to the image; today, there is amplification from the one to the other.[4]

The phenomenon addressed by Barthes is a significant trend in contemporary visual culture, where the traditional master-slave relationship between words and images, or texts and pictures, is now reversed. And it is no longer the text or the words that dominate the image, but the opposite is true—the image has gained an unprecedented "hegemony". The result is that the "hegemony" of the image not only threatens the text or the words, but also makes it a parasitic and marginalized medium.

Image fetishism

The "age of picture reading" is marked by the establishment of the hegemony of images, which indicates a profound transformation from a language-as-the-dominant culture to an image-as-the-dominant culture. So, how do we make of this historical transformation?

Scott Lash offers an approach of semiotic political economics. He argues that the prominence of visuality in contemporary society can be analyzed from the perspective of "regime of signification", which consists of two aspects. The first is the "cultural economy", which includes the relations of production, reception conditions, and consumption structures of specific cultural products. The second is the mode of meaning, which points to the complex relationship between the signifier, the signified, and the referent of cultural signs as stipulated in semiotics.[5] Lash's theory is illuminating for our inquiry into the "age of picture reading".

From the perspective of "cultural economy", the hegemony of images in the era of picture reading is reflected in the fact that the production, circulation, and consumption of symbols in contemporary culture are all defined by an image-centered mode. Guy Debord describes it as the advent of the society of the spectacle. He writes:

> [T]he spectacle is both the result and the goal of the dominant mode of production. It is not a mere decoration added to the real world. It is the very heart of this real society's unreality. In all its particular manifestations — news, propaganda, advertising, entertainment — the spectacle represents the dominant model of life. It is the omnipresent affirmation of the choices that have already been made in the sphere of production and in the consumption implied by that production. In both form and content the spectacle serves as a total justification of the conditions and goals of the existing system. The spectacle also represents the constant presence of this justification since it monopolizes the majority of the time spent outside the production process.[6]

That is to say, spectacle becomes not only a central element in the structure of production, but also a dominant factor in human activities beyond production. In the first case, the production of commodities is accompanied by the production of images of various forms—from product design, to brand label, to advertising planning. The result is that the marketing of commodities depends to a considerable extent on image-based planning, dissemination, and publicity, which are not totally related to the quality of products. Therefore, the product is the image. It is easy to understand why images have become an important intangible production resource in the era of picture reading. Also, we can figure out why commodity fetishism has evolved into a new image fetishism, and more and more commercial competition has been transformed into the competition for image resources. Now, let's elaborate on the productiveness of images themselves.

Production in contemporary society is to a considerable extent structured on the basis of images, which are productive elements with great potential. By the word "productive", I mean that not only are images produced as objects, but images themselves can bring about the conditions and resources indispensable for this production itself. When it comes to the relationship between production and consumption, as Marx points out, production is direct consumption and consumption is direct production—each is its antithesis, but at the same time, there is a mediating movement between the two. This is because, on the one hand, in consumption the product becomes a real product, and consumption creates new needs for production; on the other hand, production provides the materials and objects for consumption. It determines the means of consumption and creates the need for products.[7] In this light, the productiveness of the image creates new means and needs for consumption, providing the possibility of visualizing new materials and objects for consumption. Thus, the image itself is not just a dispensable element, but one of the most important factors of production. The image is both an object to be produced and at the same time an object that produces the need and desire for more production. Images not only make commodities real, but also create real demands and more desires for them. For Debord, the spectacle has become the "totality of social reality" and the ultimate goal of social production is the symbol of the spectacle. Because the law of the "society of the spectacle" is that what is visible is good, and what is good must be visible. This is what the popular phrase "attention economy" means, and images (the spectacle) are the basic means of producing consumers' "attention". So Debord concludes that "[a]s indispensable embellishment of currently produced objects, as general articulation of the system's rationales, and as advanced economic sector that directly creates an ever-increasing mass of image-objects, the spectacle is the leading production of present-day society".[8] From this point of view, the traditionally language-based print culture inevitably led to a new pattern in which images and words coexisted in an evenly matched manner. All the aforementioned trends of "picture reading" came into being, and the hegemony or dominance of images was thus logically established. In addition, the electronic media itself technically ensured the efficiency and convenience of image production and dissemination, while consumer culture shaped an ideology of euphoria, and the structure of entertainment and consumption became image-centered.

Furthermore, to interpret the characteristics of the "hegemony" of images in the era of picture reading, one needs to pay special attention to the cultural and political implications of such a "hegemony", which can be summarized as the new tendency of "image fetishism". Marx's analysis of classical capitalism points out that the commodity production of capitalism mystifies commodities somehow, and the material relations of commodity exchange obscure the social relations between producers. The realization of the exchange value of commodities leads to the misconception that the commodity itself has some kind of magic power, thus leading to one's worship of the commodity. If there is a shift from commodities to images in contemporary social development, it is reasonable to assume that the traditional "commodity fetishism" has morphed into a new "image fetishism" in the era of picture reading.

Fetishism was a religious practice prevalent in primitive societies. Conceptually, fetishism is the worship of material, inanimate objects as something with universal magical powers and as something that can bring good luck to people. In contemporary cultural studies, the concept of fetishism is widely used in different fields. In Marx's political economics, fetishism is both ideological and deceptively false. In Freud's psychoanalysis, this concept is usually interpreted as sexual fetishism, which refers to a certain misplacement caused by scarcity and the surrogate gratification it entails. Broadly speaking, fetishism has the following two characteristics:

first, the tendency of fetishism is always to mystify material, inanimate things, giving such things transcendent magical power; second, fetishism always entails a certain religious worship, which constitutes the veneration of the above-mentioned magical things. From commodity fetishism to image fetishism, I believe these characteristics not only remain but become more and more prominent.

As images become popular in the era of picture reading, they are inevitably "enchanted". Governed by the new law of "attention economy", images seem to have all kinds of magical functions—they determine the market share of certain goods, influence people's perception and acceptance of a brand, and even allow some to shape or confirm their individual identity, as well as national, class, racial, and gender identities. It can create the world of virtual reality, provide a sensual, pleasure-seeking lifestyle unique to this era, and so on and so forth. Most importantly, when commodities are transformed into images, commodity fetishism is accordingly transformed into image fetishism, and many of the magical powers that people wrongly ascribe to commodities are logically transferred to images; the worship of magical commodities naturally shifts to that of images. The popularity of illustrated books in the era of picture reading is precisely because the "selling point" is anchored on the image, and the new strategy of book marketing is dedicated to catching consumers' attention. Speaking of commercial competition, different brands of products are largely similar in terms of quality, but the publicity of their images makes the remarkable difference. The magic of commodity images is its productiveness. From the consumers' vantage point, owning a brand-name product is ultimately no more than an illusion sustained by the product's images, a symbolic or semiotic value realized in its images (trademark, advertisement, celebrity lifestyle, fashion, social status, etc.). In this sense, the symbolic value of the image is perhaps more important than the use value of the product itself.

Obviously, image fetishism exaggerates the function of images and "enchants" it. The "hegemony" of images is, after all, a manifestation of this tendency toward fetishism. The magic of images is due to the fact that images as the culturally "dominant" are suitable for the hedonistic ideology of consumer society. The phrase "commodity as image" itself indicates the nature of images as something to consume, and that the image as a consumer object provides not only the use value of a material commodity, but also a more semiotic or symbolic value.

From the "linguistic turn" to the "pictorial turn"

Theoretically speaking, the advent of the "era of picture reading" can be described as another "turn"—our present-day culture is bidding farewell to the "linguistic turn", and entering a new period defined by "the image turn". According to the American philosopher Richard Rorty, while ancient and medieval philosophy was concerned with human ideas, contemporary philosophy centers on the issues of language. He writes: "philosophical problems are problems which may be solved (or dissolved) either by reforming language, or by understanding more about the language we presently use".[9] In this statement, Rorty emphasizes the important fact that many of the problems discussed in philosophy have no transcendental basis.

As Wittgenstein asserts, "all philosophy is critique of language".[10] This shift is the so-called "linguistic turn". Some even argue that the "linguistic turn" began in as early as the 18th century during the Enlightenment.

The "linguistic turn" marks the trend to discard the traditional epistemological model of subject-object dichotomy, to forcefully subvert the simple correspondence between mind and reality, and to question the traditional notion of language as natural, neutral, transparent, and instrumental, thus highlighting the important argument that human recognition and knowledge are shaped through language. In other words, the core issue of the "linguistic turn" is that language and meaning are productive, constructed, and creative. Our knowledge, perceptions, and ideas—and even the real world—are closely related to linguistic construction. Sociologists Peter L. Berger and Thomas Luckmann write,

> This reality-generating potency of conversation is already given in the fact of linguistic objectification. We have seen how language objectifies the world, transforming the *panta rhei* of experience into a cohesive order. In the establishment of this order language realizes a world, in the double sense of apprehending and producing it. Conversation is the actualizing of this realizing efficacy of language in the face-to-face situations of individual existence. In conversation the objectifications of language become objects of individual consciousness. Thus the fundamental reality-maintaining fact is the continuing use of the same language to objectify unfolding biographical experience.[11]

This means that our experience of the real world is nothing more than a function of socially determined language. Under the "linguistic turn", which highlights the important role of language in social life, various ideas closely related to linguistics and semiotics have proliferated, and some linguistic concepts (such as language, discourse, text, meaning, signifying, narrative, vocabulary, grammar, syntax) are widely applied to other fields. Linguistic models and methods became the universal models and methods of research in the humanities and social sciences in the 20th century.

With the "postmodern turn" since the 1960s, the "pictorial turn" surfaced quickly. In 1994, two European and American scholars simultaneously proposed the "pictorial turn" or the "iconic turn", which was later renamed the "visual turn".[12] W. J. T. Mitchell, who was the first to propose this turn, even argues that the "linguistic turn" already has the embryo of the "pictorial turn". In other words, the "linguistic turn" actually anticipates the advent of the "visual turn". He writes:

> I want to call this shift "the pictorial turn." In Anglo-American philosophy, variations on this turn can be traced early on to Charles Peirce's semiotics and later in Nelson Goodman's "language of art", both of which explore the conventions and codes that underlie nonlinguistic symbol systems and (more importantly) do not begin with the assumption that language is a paradigmatic for meaning. In Europe, one might identify it with phenomenology's

inquiry into imagination and visual experience; or with Derrida's "grammatology," which de-centers the "phonocentric" model of language by shifting attention to the visible, material traces of writing; or with the Frankfurt School's investigations of modernity, mass culture, and visual media; or with Michel Foucault's insistence on a history and theory of power/knowledge that exposes the rift between the discursive and the "visible," the seeable and the sayable, as the crucial fault-line in "scopic regimes" of modernity.[13]

Mitchell's argument points to a tradition in Western culture that has traditionally regarded speech acts as the highest form of mental activity, a rational activity; visual images and visual perception, on the contrary, are a secondary form of interpretation of ideas, inferior and unreliable. Therefore, the "pictorial turn" is actually a challenge to the "linguistic turn", a challenge that profoundly unsettles the hegemony of language (especially speech).

Back to the question of the era of picture reading. If the proposition that the advent of the era of picture reading means that language-as-the-dominant culture has given way to image-as-the-dominant culture is valid, the shift from "linguistic turn" to "pictorial turn" therefore is a logically clearer elucidation of this shift. In my opinion, the "pictorial turn" contains at least two levels of meaning.

First, it marks the fact that contemporary culture is increasingly structured and centered on images. Many sectors of contemporary society and culture are subject to visualization—film, television, photography, advertising, fashion, beauty treatment, fitness, cartoons, video games, the Internet, theme parks, urban planning, etc. A myriad of new visual forms and technologies have burst onto the scene and widely influenced contemporary people's understanding and interpretation of the world they dwell in. Here, I would like to point out one finding during the "linguistic turn", a finding that is still important for one's inquiry into the "pictorial turn". It is that if language is an important channel for constructing our social reality, then, in the same sense, it can be argued that images in contemporary culture are equally important for constructing our social reality. In comparison, images have shaped our perception of the real world more effectively and powerfully than words. The explosive proliferation of images or videos in contemporary visual culture inevitably has an increasingly profound impact on present-day subjectivity, ideologies, and perception. During the First Gulf War, computer simulations and satellite television broadcasts of the battles greatly changed the audience's perception of the nature of the war, of its progress, of humanitarian disasters, and of the world. Television coverage of terrorist attacks can shape public opinion and public reaction to a considerable extent. Video games provide not only superficial visual pleasure, but also complex ideologies. Today, in the era of picture reading, it would be difficult to make sense of the events that take place in the world had it not for the visual images supplied by the mass media. That is why the French sociologist Baudrillard makes a radical statement that the Gulf War was simply a "television event". The viewers around the world learned about the war from television (especially from the Western television media). The role of images is clear when one looks at the crucial impact of advertisements on our daily lives and ideologies. As early as the 1930s, Heidegger predicted the arrival of the "age of the world picture":

> Understood in an essential way, "world picture" does not mean "picture of the world" but rather, the world grasped as picture... The world picture does not change from an earlier medieval to a modern one; rather, that the world becomes picture at all is what distinguishes the essence of modernity.[14]

Second, the shift from the "linguistic turn" to the "pictorial turn" not only marks a remarkable cultural change, but also brings about a serious challenge to the language-centered mode of thinking and research methodology. We have seen that in the 20th century, under the influence of the "linguistic turn", all fields of the humanities and social sciences adopted the linguistic model as a research method, and even the study of images was constrained by the hegemony of linguistics. Words, sentences, grammar, syntax, metaphors, and other linguistic concepts were widely deployed in other fields, ranging from art history to film studies. This is precisely what vexed Mitchell. Therefore, it is obvious that visual culture studies are in need of new methods and concepts appropriate to the visual and the pictorial. Mitchell writes,

> It is the realization that *spectatorship* (the look, the gaze, the glance, the practices of observation, surveillance, and visual pleasure) may be as deep a problem as various forms of *reading* (decipherment, decoding, interpretation, etc.) and that visual experience of 'visual literary' might not be fully explicable on the model of textuality.[15]

This means that linguistic thinking or methodologies are not suitable for the study of the visual experience, and that viewing images have many features that are different from reading texts, and that they need to be parsed according to the paradigm of a new visual culture that cannot simply be explicated by applying linguistic models. In this sense, the rise of visual culture is not only the emergence of a new cultural form, but also demands a new paradigm of thinking. As to the first aspect, language-as-the-dominant culture gives way to image-as-the-dominant culture, and this transformation is closely related to the development and changes of contemporary society. As to the second aspect, a unique thinking paradigm suitable for visual culture emerges, which also leads to a shift in the research paradigm from the "linguistic model" to the "visual model". It has also led to a paradigm shift from a "linguistic model" to a "visual model". As Mirzoeff remarks,

> The emergence of visual culture develops what WJ.T. Mitchell has called 'picture theory,' the sense that some aspects of Western philosophy and science have come to adopt a pictorial, rather than textual, view of the world. If this is so, it marks a significant challenge to the notion of the world as a written text that dominated so much intellectual discussion in the wake of linguistics-based movements such as structuralism and poststructuralism.[16]

At this point, we can draw two tentative conclusions: first, in terms of contemporary social production, circulation, and consumption, images themselves have gained a supreme "hegemonic" status, forming a dominance over language; second, in terms of the development of images, their internal structure has also undergone profound changes. The contemporary visual symbols in the era of picture reading are no longer the traditional paradigm based on similarity, but increasingly tend to refer to the new structure of self-referential simulacrum. Lash compares the "culture of discourse" and the "culture of images", shedding light on the cultural significance of the "pictorial turn":

> In this context the discursive (l) gives priority to words over images; (2) valuates the formal qualities of cultural objects; (3) promulgates a rationalist view of culture; (4) attributes crucial importance to the meanings of cultural texts; (5) is a sensibility of the ego rather than of the id; (6) operates through a distancing of the spectator from the cultural object. The "figural" in contradistinction: (l) is a visual rather than a literary sensibility; (2) devalues formalisms and juxtaposes signifiers taken from the banalities of everyday life; (3) contests rationalist and/or "didactic" views of culture; (4) asks not what a cultural text "means", but what it "does"; (5) in Freudian terms, advocates the extension of the primary process into the cultural realm; (6) operates through the spectator's immersion, the relatively unmediated investment of his/her desire in the cultural object.[17]

This comparison underscores several important differences. The first is the medial difference: discursive culture is centered on language, endowing language or text with supreme finitude; in pictorial culture, images overwhelm language and become the dominant factor. Second, discursive culture is a rationalist culture, which focuses on form and champions rationalist values. Borrowing a term from psychoanalysis, this culture is based on the principle of rationality, which Freud called the "principle of reality". In contrast to discursive culture, pictorial culture tends to be more sensual, abandoning reason and embracing pleasure, excluding formalist principles and equating symbols with everyday ready-mades. Such a culture inevitably leads to what a psychoanalyst calls "id", replacing the "reality principle" that defines discursive culture with the "pleasure principle". Finally, because of these two differences, discursive culture is necessarily a "contemplative" culture, in which the actor of cultural activities maintains a certain aesthetic distance from the object, while pictorial culture, on the contrary, excludes the "halo" of the object and turns to the "shock"—as a result, the distance between the subject and the object disappears.[18] As some scholars observe, in the contemporary visual culture, sensual, pleasurable, immediate, and distance-free experiences are the dominant forms. The most typical morphological difference is found between reading a book and watching a movie. Reading is a typical form of "contemplation", which allows the reader to repeatedly experience the deep meaning of the work, to chant and pause for meditation, thus keeping the aesthetic subject at a certain distance from the object. Watching a movie is rather different, as the audience is completely immersed in the ambience created by the cinema, the distance between the subject and the object gone. The transient, immediate pleasure makes the subject forget its own existence, and the subject's desire enters directly into the object's context.

At this point, we have interpreted the new cultural politics of the "picture-reading age" from a new perspective, which marks not only a new ideology but also a change in the communicative subjectivity. On this point, Mark Poster makes a compelling point in comparing television and words as two modes of communication:

> The language/practice of TV absorbs the functions of culture to a greater degree than face-to-face conversations or print and its discursive effect is to constitute subjects differently from speech or print. Speech constitutes subjects as members of a community by solidifying the ties between individuals. Print constitutes subjects as rational, autonomous egos, as stable interpreters of culture who, in isolation, make logical connections from linear symbols. Media language replaces the community of speakers and undermines the referentiality of discourse necessary for the rational ego. Media language – contextless, monologic, selfreferential – invites the recipient to play with the process of selfconstitution, continuously to remake the self in "conversation" with differing modes of discourse. Since no one who knows the recipient is speaking to them and since there is no clearly determinate referential world outside the broadcast to provide a standard against which to evaluate the flow of meanings, the subject has no defined identity as a pole of a conversation.[19]

Although Poster's comparison seems to be a bit mechanical and absolute, it also speaks to the differences between the two cultures. We have reason to believe that the advent of the "age of picture reading" has intractably changed our culture, the pattern of literature, and our cultural values. The important thing is not only to see this change, but also to understand the root of this change, and then to address this change with ease.

Notes

1. Lin Bai. *A Man's War.* Beijing: October Literature and Art Publishing House, 2004. p.1.
2. Lin Bai. *A Man's War.* p.1.
3. Pierre Bourdieu. *On Television.* Trans. Xu Jun. Shenyang: Liaoning Education Press, 2000. p. 48, pp.57–58.
4. Roland Barthes. "The Photographic Message", in *A Barthes Reader.* Ed. Susan Sontag. New York: Hill and Wang, 1982. pp.204–205.
5. See Scott Lash. *Sociology of Postmodernism.* London: Routledge, 1990.
6. Guy Debord, *The Society of the Spectacle.* p.7.
7. Karl Marx. "A Contribution to the Critique of Political Economy", in *Selected Works of Marx and Engels*, Vol. 2. Beijing: People's Publishing House, 1972. pp.93–96.
8. Guy Debord, *The Society of the Spectacle.* p.8.
9. Richard Rorty. *The Linguistic Turn.* Chicago: The University of Chicago Press, 1967. p.3.
10. Ludwig Wittgenstein. *Tractatus Logico Philosophicus.* Trans. He Shaojia. Beijing: The Commercial Press, 1985. p.38.
11. Peter L. Berger and Thomas Luckmann. *The Social Construction of Reality.* London: Penguin, 1967. p.173.

12 See Martin Jay. *Downcast Eyes: The Denigration of Vision in Twentieth-Century French Thought*. Berkeley: University Press of California, 1994; also see Nicholas Mirzoeff. *An Introduction to Visual Culture*. London: Routledge, 1999.
13 W. J. T. Mitchell. *Picture Theory*. Chicago: University of Chicago Press, 1994. pp.11–12.
14 Martin Heidegger. "The Age of the World Picture", in *Off the Beaten Track*. Eds. and trans. Julian Young and Kenneth Haynes. Cambridge: Cambridge UP, 2002. pp.67–68.
15 W. J. T. Mitchell. *Picture Theory*. Chicago: University of Chicago Press, 1994. p.16.
16 Nicholas Mirzoeff. *An Introduction to Visual Culture*. pp.5–6.
17 Scott Lash. *Sociology of Postmodernism*. p.175.
18 Walter Benjamin. *The Work of Art in the Age of Mechanical Reproduction*.
19 Mark Poster. *The Mode of Information*. pp.65–66.

15 Spectacle cinema and visual culture

In 2003, Zhang Yimou, a trailblazer of the "Fifth Generation" of Chinese film directors, released a new film called *Hero*. Some reviewers thought that *Hero* did not have a complete plot, falling short of a profound theme, and failing to create authentic characters. Zhang Yimou has his own opinion:

> After two years, when speaking of a movie in your memory, you will definitely forget its storyline. But what you will always remember is the scene that lasts a few seconds...... But I think, after a few years, whenever *Hero* is mentioned, you will remember those colors — for example, you will remember, against the cloud of yellow leaves, there are two women in red flying around. On the surface of the mirror-like lake, there are two men communicating with martial arts, who swoop on the water like birds, like dragonflies. Images like these will definitely impress the audience. So that's what I feel proud of.[1]

Zhang's words speak to a certain truth about the development of contemporary film—in an era of visual culture, spectacle films are replacing narrative films as the dominant form.

Narrative cinema and spectacle cinema

Aesthetically, film as a visual art has both linguistic and visual dimensions (this was the case even before the emergence of sound films). As a kind of text, film is deeply tied up with linguistics not only because of its dialogues and scripts, but also due to the discursive feature of a film's narrative structure. From a historical perspective, film is akin to theater, which is to a considerable extent more discursive. For exa, the dramatic structure itself is linear (e.g., Aristotelian closed dramatic structure), the storiness and plot elements displayed by narrative all add up to the linguistic quality of drama. In my opinion, traditional cinema was imbued with large dramatic component and therefore carried more discursive features. Some of Hitchcock's thriller films, for example, have a strong dramatic and plot-driven character, and their dialogues also assume a central role. Many black-and-white films of the 1930s and 1940s in China, for example, also have such narrative elements—they are more like visual reproductions of literary works. Therefore, literariness is used to be the core of cinema, which was embodied in script, dialogues, voice-over, plot structure, film narrativity, and so on. Accordingly, it is reasonable to assume that the "ideal type" of such films is the so-called "narrative films", which take narrative as the mode of discourse.

The very concept of narrative cinema reveals the centrality of narrative in film, which is structured in tandem with the requirements of narrative. Therefore, how a film presents its plot, shapes its characters, and writes its dialogues becomes the basics of narrative cinema. Narrative is originally a literary concept, and in the literary sense, the purpose of narrative aims to narrate events. It takes two forms: the first is a simple narrative that models on chronicle; the second is a narrative that follows a plot arrangement, which embodies certain artistic laws and morphology. The gist of literary narrative lies in the artistic emplotment, which makes the ordinary occurrences engaging—this explains the charm of narrative, the art of storytelling. According to the structuralist Gérard Genette, the concepts of story / narrative / narrating are different: "The 'story' consists of the events, in temporal and causal order, before they are put in words. The 'narrative' is the written words, which Genette also calls 'narrative discourse.' 'Narrating' involves the relations between the speaker/writer (the narrative 'voice') and the audience/reader".[2]

If we transpose the idea of literary narrative to film, then film is also a narrative art. The narrativity of film is presented most notably as montage, or, more precisely, as narrative montage. The basic principle of montage combination is some kind of narrative or logical (causal) or temporal sequence, which reflects certain rational rules, intended to combine different footages or images into a law-abiding whole, thus conveying specific meanings and producing a dramatic effect. The temporal or logical structure of film governs its narrative montage—the former refers to the sequence, while the latter is about the cause-and-effect relationship, both of which constitute the tenets of narrative montage. Hitchcock's films, be it *Rebecca* or *Rear Window*, are masterpieces of narrative cinema. In these works, montage serves the function of narrativity, and the unfolding of the plot is logical and temporal. As a result, a rational structure unique to narrative film itself is established. From the perspective of the discourse/image dichotomy, narrative film is closer to the model of discourse, and therefore tends to be more in line with rational structure and principles. Its integrity, structuredness, and orderliness do not come from the images themselves, but from the narrative logic or causality behind them. It is in this sense that narrative films are more inclined to foster characters, explore profound themes, and construct complex plots. These are precisely what Zhang Yimou's *Hero* lacks, and perhaps what he deliberately avoids.

With the development of film, spectacle film has gradually replaced narrative film as a dominant paradigm. British film theorist Laura Mulvey was the first to point out the phenomenon of "spectacle" in cinema. Drawing on psychoanalysis, she believes that the spectacle is related to the sexual difference, which "controls images, erotic ways of seeing" in cinema.[3] Of course, the concept of spectacle in cinema originates from the French philosopher Guy Debord's analysis of the "society of the spectacle". According to Debord, the production, circulation, and consumption of commodities in contemporary society have become the production, circulation, and consumption of the spectacle. Thus, the spectacle-as-commodity phenomenon is omnipresent, and the spectacle holds up to view a world that is simultaneously present and absent, "a world of the commodity dominating all living experience".[4] Obviously, Debord explains the spectacle in terms of the society—in contemporary society, traditional modes and laws of production have been invalid, and what matters now is the production, flow, and consumption of spectacle. In fact, according to Debord's line of thinking, the whole film industry is inevitably reduced to the product of the society of the spectacle. Unlike Debord, Mulvey's analysis is conducted from a uniquely feminist perspective, addressing the following questions: What kind of relationship between seeing and being seen does the visual pleasure provided by film originate from? Is there an inequality between the different sexes involved? She argues that the stylistic magic of Hollywood cinema derives from the "skilled and satisfying manipulation of visual pleasure" and that her work is "to make way for a total negation of the ease and plentitude of the narrative fiction film".[5]

Mulvey believes that the visual pleasures of cinema consist of scopophilia (voyeurism) and narcissism—in the first case, looking itself is a source of pleasure, but in the second case, self-construction is through the pleasure of being looked at. She particularly emphasizes the importance of visual pleasure, so that providing visual pleasure by satisfying scopophilia and narcissism becomes the primary task of cinema. Mulvey raises two important issues. First, women, as objects of desire for male viewers, are placed in an unequal position of being passively looked at and shown, while men are the active seer. Second, in order to maximize the provision of the object (i.e., female body) to be seen by viewers of scopophilia (voyeurism) and narcissism, cinema (and also other forms of media) necessarily chooses to be hinged on visual pleasure. It is thus inevitable to expel or suppress those narrative requirements that contradict or negate visual pleasure. That is why Mulvey says,

> [I]n the musical song-and-dance numbers break the flow of the diegesis... The presence of woman is an indispensable element of the spectacle in normal narrative film, yet her visual presence tends to work against the development of a story line, to freeze the flow of action in moments of erotic contemplation.[6]

This observation touches on the "cultural turn" of contemporary cinema from narrative cinema to spectacle cinema.

After Mulvey, spectacle cinema is developed into mainstream cinema. Some have found that narrativity and structure are less and less important in contemporary cinema, and that narrative integrity, complex linear structure, and plot arrangement have become far less important than spectacle scenes.[7] Others have found that contemporary mainstream films are increasingly emphasizing the representation and expression of the body, especially in erotic films, where the "unrestrained repetition of sex scenes" has replaced narrative. There is also a clear "suppression of voice" in such films, echoing the new idea that voice is increasingly "a support for a certain visible presence of the body".⁸ This tendency, as Lash remarks, was

> reinforced in the mid and late 1980s in which the blockbusters box office hits have been, for example, the Indiana Jones films and Ghostbusters and the Stallone and Schwarzenegger films which have catered especially to an audience in their early teens, and use plot as an excuse for a succession of spectacular events.⁹

What's more, this shift not only appears in commercial films, but also gradually finds its way in avant-garde films and art films. In other words, the spectacle as a new film form has taken over almost all cinematic styles or genres, becoming "the dominant" of contemporary cinema. Lash firmly maintains,

> My point in this context is that in films of recent years 'spectacle' — especially if we expand the definition of spectacle to include also images marked by the aggressive instinct — does not any longer become subordinated to narrative. That is, there has been a shift from realist to postmodernist cinema, in which spectacle comes heavily to dominate narrative.[10]

Rush's analysis differs from the general film theories in that he places more emphasis on the social institutions of signification. In his view, as far as the history of cinema is concerned, there are four types of cinema that have been involving continuously: the first is the realist narrative cinema, which is what we call the traditional narrative cinema. It has two main characteristics—spatial perspectivism as discovered during the Renaissance; the linear narrative structure of the 19th century realist novel, with a closely connected "head", "body", and "tail". The second genre is the modernist film or "discursive" film. In Lash theory of "mode of signification", image is opposed to discourse, which he sees as rational, formalistic, and language-centered; image is pleasurable, anti-rationalistic, and image-centered.[11] Based on this categorization, Lash argues that modernist films, or those of the avant-garde, tend to be discursive in nature, dedicated more to questioning film narratives or representations themselves and expanding the possibilities of cinematic representation. Such films are quite different from the later spectacle films. The third genre is the mainstream postmodern cinema. These films are entirely "pictorial" or "spectacular". Its main characteristic is the overriding of image over discourse, or the domination of spectacle and the suppression of narrative. This kind of film elevates the visual pleasure of images to a dominant position, and all filmic elements must cater to this requirement. The fourth genre, which Lash has categorized as 'transgressive' postmodernist cinema, is similar to postmodern cinema in that it is figural and privileges spectacle. But what distinguishes this type of film from postmodern cinema is that it problematizes reality itself.[12]

Speaking of the shift from narrative cinema to spectacle cinema, what is worthy of closer investigation?

First of all, let's analyze montage, the most important structural and signifying device of film. As mentioned before, narrative montage is structured according to certain narrative principles or relationships, and its main purpose is to create a certain plot and meaning through the grouping of disparate images. However, in a film of spectacle, the rational principle of montage assemblage has given way to the pleasure principle, that is, the visual pleasure of spectacle. As a result, the complete narrative linear structure is subverted by the spectacles. In other words, the primary task of the spectacle film is to present visually attractive and pleasurable images through the assemblage of images. The montage of spectacle is entirely different from that of narrative in that it is no longer tethered to the meaningful relationship of narrative, but in direct service of the production of visual pleasure. This implies an important change; that is, the grouping of images relies on the superficial and immediate visual pleasure, rather than the in-depth semantic relationship of narrative, which inevitably results in the deconstruction of narrative owing to the spectacle. For the sake of the spectacular effect, montage can disregard narrative requirements, and even interrupt the continuity and structure of narrative so as to highlight the visuality of the spectacle. In this cinematic form, the rules of traditional narrative cinema are transformed into the principle of spectacular visual structure, where the spectacle rules the narrative and changes it. With a little analysis of a spectacle film like *Titanic* or *Hero*, it is not difficult to prove this point. Of course, this does not mean that narrative no longer exists in spectacle films—the core of the problem is that narrative no longer has its autonomy and dominance; rather, it has become subordinate to the spectacle. In this sense, the film of spectacle entails the conquest of the spectacular effects and principles over the narrative principles inherent in montage.

Second, the second characteristic of spectacle films is that the importance of discursive elements in cinema has diminished. Discursiveness is a broad concept here, meaning a filmic genre that relies on narrative and literariness. Based on Lash's dichotomy between discourse (linguistic signs) and image (visual symbols), it is reasonable to assume that narrative cinema tends to be discourse-centered, focusing on the narrative and storytelling, and on the dialogue of the characters and the drama of the plot. Therefore, literariness (including scripts, etc.), emplotment, storiness, and characterization are the basic requirements of discursiveness. From the perspective of traditional narrative cinema, a successful film depends first and foremost on a good literary script, and on storyline and characterization. Discursiveness stands out as the dominant of narrative films. Spectacle films yet follow a different path, taking image as the dominant, highlighting the figural nature of the film itself, downplaying or even weakening the discursive aspects, strengthening the impact of visual effects, and even forming what some film critics call the "tyranny" of image over sound. This tendency is particularly evident in the so-called action films and shoot-'em-ups. These films tend to focus on spectacular action, relegating dialogue and narration to the less important position—that is to say, the linguistic elements are reduced to serve the plastic and visual functions of image. Zhang Yimou's *Hero* is a salient case in point.

Third, another characteristic of the spectacle film lies in the "spectacle" itself. We can invoke Bakhtin's idea of "carnivalesque" to illustrate this point. The spectacle helps the film truly realize its own pure ontology of visual arts—the film no longer yields to other non-visual requirements, but conforms to the tenets of its own visual spectacle.

The spectacle as the dominant in cinema

The so-called "spectacle", in my opinion, is videos and pictures with strong visual appeal, or fantastical videos and pictures created by various high-tech filmic methods.

Specifically, the spectacle of contemporary cinema can be divided into four main types: the first is the spectacle of action, that is, a myriad of thrilling action scenes. From cowboy fights in westerns, to gun battles and stunts in crime films, to exotic action designs in sci-fi films, the list can go on forever. Lately, Chinese *kung fu* has been widely used as a new and visually appealing action spectacle, and has taken root in mainstream Hollywood films. This is evidenced by the rise of Hong Kong *kung fu* star Jackie Chan in mainstream Hollywood cinema. Ang Lee's *Crouching Tiger, Hidden Dragon*, and Zhang Yimou's *Hero* are also known for their action-centered spectacles. The action spectacle is of course centered on the visual effects of the action itself, so in many mainstream films, the hyperbolic and sensational action far exceeds the needs of plot-making and characterization. Action itself has become the main goal in its own right.

The second kind of spectacle can be boiled down to body spectacle, which is related to action spectacle, but not exactly the same. Body spectacle is, simply put, the marshaling of various filmic devices to show and represent the body. Action spectacle not only involves bodily kinesis, but is associated with various kinds of machinery and props, such as horses, firearms, automobiles, airplanes, and motorboats. In contrast, body spectacle is limited to the human body itself. Showing the body has different implications in the film of spectacle, in the sense of gender, the female body as a passive object to be seen, according to feminist critics, is a type of body spectacle. In such a spectacle, women become the object of male gaze. Thus, to satisfy the male audience's scopophilia and narcissism becomes a fundamental demand for the reproduction of female body. Mulvey aptly remarks:

> Thus the woman as icon, displayed for the gaze and enjoyment of men, the active controllers of the look, always threatens to evoke the anxiety it originally signified.... Going far beyond highlighting a woman's to-be-looked-at-ness, cinema builds the way she is to be looked at into the spectacle itself. Playing on the tension between film as controlling the dimension of time (editing, narrative) and film as controlling the dimension of space (changes in distance, editing), cinematic codes create a gaze, a world, and an object, thereby producing an illusion cut to the measure of desire.[13]

On the other hand, masculinity is also an element of body spectacle, and many films take pains to show the muscular physique, gritty character, and power of the male body—the films starring Stallone and Schwarzenegger might be exemplary in this regard. Perhaps we can ask rhetorically: Is it the acting skill of Stallone and Schwarzenegger or their stunningly masculine body that make them qualified for the spectacle film? Put it another way: Had it not been for their body desired by spectacle movie audience, could they have garnered such reputation?

The third can be called the speed spectacle. It also has something to do with the action spectacle. In order to create more visually sensational scenes, a unique type of spectacle film that flaunts high speed has been developed. The narrative mode of traditional narrative films can no longer meet the visual demands of contemporary audiences, and "speedy viewing" and "viewing the speed" constitute the typical forms of speed spectacle. In this regard, *Live and Let Die*, *The Fast and the Furious*, and the "James Bond" series can be regarded as exemplary works. Highlighting speed as a spectacle in the film has particularly complex reasons. First of all, contemporary life has long been free from the traditional static form. As some philosophers put it, the most prominent phenomenon of contemporary culture is the so-called "dynamics". Therefore, the accelerated rhythm of life has also been accompanied by men's demand for speed in visual forms. Second, advances in communication technology make fast viewing possible. Paul Virilio finds that reading books, a traditionally slow method of communication or reception, no longer has an advantage over modern image communication technologies. He argues that in an era of satellite television, the simultaneous transmission of images (live broadcasting) is far more convenient and attractive than the text. Therefore, the hegemony of television is the triumph of speed, the triumph of real time over deferred time.[14] I think the same is true of movies. The advancement of film technology has made it possible for images to be presented at a high speed, which makes it possible for viewers to see in films those speedy spectacles that otherwise cannot be seen in everyday life. Films such as *Live and Let Die* are the product of speed spectacle and exemplify how a film makes use of speed to create special visual effects. Speed here contains two layers of meaning—one is the speed or rhythm of shots pieced together, and the other is the speed of the movement of objects or human body within the frame. Speed spectacle is thus the combination of these two kinds of speed. From the perspective of film reception, when the audience is accustomed to a certain visual paradigm provided by the speed spectacle, the thirst for speed naturally arises on the part of viewers. Therefore, in contemporary mainstream films, the slow, verbose, and lengthy narrative is obviously no longer able to cater to the audience's visual desires—"speedy viewing" and "viewing the speed" become the staple of the speed spectacle.

The fourth type can be called the scene spectacle, which refers to the spectacular and rare scenes of various milieus and environments. Natural wonders belong to such a category—they are some inaccessible landscapes that are visually attractive and distinctive, such as icebergs, snow-capped peaks, canyons, waterfalls, deserts, and oceans. *Hero* focuses on the natural landscape with distinctive spectacular characteristics—from Jiuzhai Valley to the Northwest desert boxwoods. The function of spectacle is, as Sontag remarks in her analysis of photography,

> Photographic seeing meant an aptitude for discovering beauty in what everybody sees but neglects as too ordinary. Photographers were supposed to do more than just see the world as it is, including its already acclaimed marvels;

they were to create interest, by new visual decisions… The urge to take photographs is in principle an indiscriminate one, for the practice of photography is now identified with the idea that everything in the world could be made interesting through the camera.[15]

Virtual spectacles are another example, usually found in sci-fi films—virtual spectacles created by high technology are either set in the future, such as *The Wandering Earth* or *A.I.: Artificial Intelligence*, or set in outer space, such as *Star Wars*, or even in the underwater world. The third subtype is the human landscape, such as famous historic sites or world-famous cities. Such human landscapes abound especially in some Chinese and foreign historical films and constitute a unique visual element. Scene spectacles are an integral part of spectacle films, and they not only contribute to the spectacle-ness of such films, but also become an important resource for the filmic visual pleasure. It is noteworthy that in narrative films, due to the need for narrative clues and rhythm, the scene is often subordinated to the narrative function—the scene, so to speak, does not have independent value. In spectacle films, in contrast, in order to maximize the visual impact of the spectacle, the scene often receives excessive attention. These scenes are sometimes so digressive that they deviate from the main storyline or character relationships, and acquire a relatively independent visual value. The spectacle itself is an independent part of the film, which has to strengthen or even abuse its spectacular elements for the sake of visual effects. One example is the grand scene of Qin Palace in *Hero*.

A case study of the spectacles in *Hero*

Hero is a worthy sample of spectacle films. First, there is a clear tension between narrative and spectacle in *Hero*. On the surface, the film bears the hallmark of a narrative film, as the film is centered around a conversation between the assassin Nameless and Qin Shi Huang. Except for the voice-over and subtitles as latent narrative elements, the film basically unfolds during a question-and-answer session between Qin Shi Huang and Nameless. As the most important character, Nameless actually assumes the dual role of narrator and protagonist. On the one hand, he narrates the story under Qin Shi Huang's imposing questioning, and on the other hand, he intervenes in the complications of character relationships and multiple alternative plots. To be more specific, there are nine narrative sections in *Hero*, seven of which unfold in the form of a dialogue between the King of Qin and Nameless; another two passages are narrated either by Nameless or by Chan Jian. Two elements emerge here: one is functional (i.e., the King of Qin asks Nameless), which mainly runs through the whole film and invokes different spatial-temporal scenes; the other is Nameless' (and Chan Jian's) reply, which is an account of various possibilities of this attempted assassination. Obviously, the first structural or functional element is of secondary importance in the film—it is mainly to demonstrate the fighting scenes of four assassins. If the dialogue between the King of Qin and Nameless is in the "present tense", then the narrative of Nameless and Chan Jian belongs to the "past perfect tense"—the alternation of the two tenses constitutes the basic structure of the film. Such a structure is very similar to that of the detective films based on Agatha Christie's novels. However, if we further compare the two, it is easy to find that despite the structural similarities, they have very different focuses. In the detective films adapted from Christie's works, the interrogation conducted by the detective Poirot is analogous to that by the King of Qin, while Poirot's own speculation or the suspects' narration is equivalent to Nameless'. For example, in *Murder on the Orient Express*, the storyline is also divided into several segments, but they are tied together by a narrative logic. Therefore, the logicalness of Poirot's reasoning becomes the narrative logic of the entire film. In contrast, *Hero* is neatly divided by spectacles and presents a loose structure that lacks logical coherence—it is especially the case when the King of Qin questions Nameless, because there is no such thing as logical or even structural integrity or consistency between these interrogation scenes and Nameless' storytelling. In *Hero*, the tension between narrative and spectacle is presented as spectacle's dominance over narrative. Narrative is at best a secondary functional element in this film. In this sense, the fragmentary and flashback structure of *Hero* provides more freedom for time-space shifts and scene making on the one hand, and creates favorable conditions for the spectacle effect on the other.

This brings us to the second aspect of *Hero* as a spectacle film: the superimposition of scenic spectacles. To some extent, one of the most outstanding features of *Hero* as a spectacle film is the spectacular scenes. Its humanistic and natural landscapes are the finest ones among Chinese films. Unlike the virtual scenes in sci-fi films, *Hero* is distinguished by the richness of visual effects of natural scenes. When explaining the characteristics of the film, Zhang Yimou always said that the scenes should be "unique and pleasing to the eye". So, the film producer chose the most representative natural landscapes in China: the first is Dunhuang in the west, representing the desert and the Yardang Landform; the second is also in the northwest, that is, the Inner Mongolia poplar woods; the third is Jiuzhaigou Valley in the southwest, featuring mountains and lakes; and the fourth is a passing shot of Guilin in Guangxi, the short Guangxi Guilin. The first two types of landscape have a rough, gritty, massive sublimity, while the last two belong to the beautiful and the pleasant. The two distinctive styles of landscape constitute the very unique natural wonders in *Hero*. It is worth noting that although the attempted assassination of Qin Shi Huang did happen in history, *Hero* is never limited to the topography of Kingdom Zhao (now Shanxi and Hebei) when it comes to the choice of setting; rather, the priority is the visual effects evoked by the landscape itself. That is why the film was shot in Jiuzhaigou Valley in Sichuan, poplar woods in Inner Mongolia, and even Guilin in Guangxi. The selection of scenery sites shows the centrality of visual spectacle in the film, which has little to do with the historical time and space. Rather, to be more precise, the visual effect of the scenes is more important than the authenticity of historical space related to the story. In addition, the artificial landscape of the film is also quite spectacular. In general, there are two types of man-made landscapes in the film: one is the Qin Palace, an architecture rich in national characteristics and imperial grandeur. Both the open square and the grand palace give the film a special visual impact. The second type is the Library and the Book Depository of Kingdom Zhao—in particular the Book Depository, which is arranged with great care. There is a circular totem field in the middle, around which lie massive bamboo slips like a city wall—this is a special humanistic landscape with Chinese cultural characteristics. The fictionality and formal beauty of these landscapes transcend historical authenticity itself. Some of the scenes in *Hero*—the walk of Nameless to meet the King of Qin sitting in front of the palace hall, for example—is particularly breath-taking and majestic; the march of the troops in procession through the expansive desert is also full of sublimity and tension. A special point to emphasize is that, in addition to the natural colors of these landscapes themselves, the film highlights them with striking hues. The scenes in Qin Palace are mainly depicted in black and brown, while the scenes in the poplar woods are in yellow, the interior of the Book Depository in blue, the Yardang landform in brownish-yellow, the Jiuzhaigou and Guilin in green, and so on and so forth. The combination of the color schemes with filmic themes tends to highlight the spectacular visual effect of the scenes. Furthermore, even the colors of the costumes in such environments are carefully designed so as to highlight the color contrast or visual harmony. For example, the red clothes of Feixue and Ruyue in the yellow poplar forest form a strong visual contrast; in the Book Depository, Chan Jian and Feixue are in a sword battle decorated by the art of calligraphy, both dressed in green to accommodate the ambient greenish tone; Chan Jian tries to stab the King, fighting in the black Qin Palace hall, which is intentionally decorated with ornate bright green drapery. Zhang Yimou believes that the color scheme of *Hero* will greatly impress the audience, and the cinematographer Christopher Doyle also said, "Color is really important and very bright, and has a strong visual impact. Different colors will bring about different color associations".[16] Doyle's remark unveils the true meaning of the film's visual spectacle.

The third aspect of *Hero*'s spectacle is the martial arts scenes, which Zhang Yimou believes are the most challenging, and most remarkable, part of the film. Altogether, there are seven martial arts scenes that deserve further scrutiny:

Scene 1: Nameless and the Qin soldiers, fighting with Chang Kong in the rain in the Chess Hall. (Duration: 7 minutes)

Scene 2: Fei Xue battling Ru Yue under a sky imbued with yellow leaves in a boxwood forest. (Duration: 4 and 1/2 minutes)

Scene 3: Fei Xue and Nameless fighting in the Qin camp in a desert. (Duration: 4 minutes)

Scene 4: Chan Jian and Nameless fighting above water in Jiuzhaigou. (Duration: 4 minutes)

Scene 5: Chan Jian and Fei Xue, Nameless and Ru Yue, fighting in the Book Depository. (Duration: 4 minutes)

Scene 6: Chan Jian and Fei Xue, fighting their way to the Palace; Chan Jian fighting the King in the Palace. (Duration: 4 minutes)

Scene 7: Chan Jian and Feixue, fighting in a mileu of Yardang Landform. (Duration: 3 minutes)

The running time of *Hero* is 1 hour and 32 minutes, one third of which, according to my statistics above, is dedicated to martial arts scenes, let alone some sporadic fight scenes. If these martial arts scenes are removed, *Hero* will no longer be in possession of its *heroism*, and its visual appeal and spectacle will be greatly weakened. Therefore, Zhang Yimou reiterates that the most attractive and challenging aspect of the film is the representation of Chinese *kung fu*. And the action director Cheng Xiaodong says even more bluntly: "We want every shot, every idea to be innovative, to be unseen, to be novel. Action must also be very interesting".[17] No wonder there are so many creative martial arts scenes capturing your attention like never before, making our eyes wide open. Regardless of the elements of martial arts, the gritty Yardang landscape, the picturesque valley, the Qin Palace, and the Book Depository of historical and cultural characteristics are appealing in their own right. Also, action modeling in the film is extremely varied—in particular some martial arts scenes that supposedly take place in mind, which not only extends the boundary of human imagination but transcends the limits of the human body and the laws of nature. For example, in Scene 4, Chan Jian and Nameless fight above the lake. The two men sometimes plummet to the surface of the water, with a sharp sword making ripples, or sometimes beat the water to support their flying body, or sometimes chase each other by skimming the vast expanse of the lake, like birdmen. The two men can rotate vertically, or play out a whirlwind on the water, evoking the legendary totem of a soaring dragon or a leaping tiger. The cinematography of *Hero* is unique: on the one hand, there is the unfolding of subjective shots that capture the two men's mind; on the other hand, it is laced with objective shots to demonstrate a full range of martial arts. Not only are there overhead high-angle shots, but also the film features some upward low-angle shots from underwater, highlighting the visual charm of Chinese *kung fu* from different perspectives. What's more interesting is the visual details, such as the water droplets transformed into deadly weapons during the battle—the two men have to use their swords to fend off the bullet-like droplets. In short, the quality of *Hero* as a spectacle film is salient. If we interpret *Hero* through the lens of the spectacle, then it can be said that the film has elevated the level of spectacle films in contemporary Chinese cinema. The film's impressive box office revenues are sufficient to show that, in the context of socio-cultural transformation in contemporary China, and against the backdrop of the visual cultural turn, the spectacle film has its legitimacy and *raison d'etre*. At the same time, the success of this film also suggests that, first, there is a prospect for Chinese films to take the route of the spectacle paradigm; second, Chinese and even global audiences recognize and relish such kind of oriental spectacle films.

From narrative to spectacle: The significance of cultural transformation

From narrative films to spectacle films, there are several aspects of change that are worth reflecting on.

First, the rise and popularization of spectacle films indicate that there is a shift from a discourse-centered paradigm to an image-centered paradigm in cinema itself. There is no doubt that cinema is essentially a visual art, an art of image montage and assemblage. But in the course of development, there are actually two different types cinema, namely, traditional discourse-as-the-dominant one and contemporary image-as-the-dominant one. In terms of the visual-culture turn, there is a shift from a discourse (language)-dominated cultural form to an image (video)-dominated cultural form in terms of the overall cultural styles. In the case of cinema alone, there is a similar shift—to be more precise, this shift within cinema is a manifestation of the change of overall cultural styles. If we compare the works of the "fifth generation directors" (such as Zhang Yimou) with those of previous generations (such as Xie Jin), we can easily find a clear difference: the former focus more on visual spectacle, while the latter are better at narrating stories and forging characters. I think this difference is derived from the diversified conception of cinema. In other words, spectacle films are more suitable for the visual requirements of contemporary visual culture and consumer society.

Second, as a result of the shift mentioned above, another question naturally arises. The evolution from the discourse-dominant narrative cinema to the picture-dominant spectacle cinema is again presented as a transformation from the mode of temporal depth to that of spatial flatness. It is worthwhile to invoke Jameson's theory here. In his view, modernist art is characterized with a sense of history or time, the representation of which can be described as the depth mode, while the overall composition of postmodernist art tends to be spatially flat. Jameson remarks, "In short, objects fall into the world and become decoration again; visual depth and systems of interpretation fade away, and something peculiar happens to historical time".[18] Clearly, narrativity itself is embedded in an art of time, a way of reflecting on past realities or inner journeys through time. It is therefore reasonable to assume that in narrative-driven cinema, temporal relations are constantly transformed into logical associations of narrative elements and processes. The sense of history or the past and its depth of interpretation often becomes the dominant paradigm of narrative cinema. In contrast, the increasing emphasis on the pleasure-seeking of the spectacle itself has led to the repression of narrative, often making the visual elements more prominent than the narrative. Therefore, the narrative inevitably gives way to the spectacle. Such a situation demonstrates the fractured and fragmented nature of time (narrative) in the spectacle films themselves. In this regard, *Hero* can be considered an exemplar.

Third, the shift from narrative cinema to spectacle cinema has another important meaning, which is the shift from rational culture to jouissance culture. When discussing the emergence of mechanical reproduction culture represented by cinema, Walter Benjamin distinguishes between aura and shock. When contemplating traditional art, one can perceive the "aura", while the art of mechanical reproduction merely offers a brief, intense experience, like a bullet penetrating one's chest. Such a distinction can also be applied to the art of mechanical reproduction—cinema—itself. In a comparative sense, narrative cinema is closer to the art of "aura", while spectacle cinema is of the type of shock. Narrative cinema entails, to a certain extent, the viewer's active participation and interpretation, and the viewer is expected to follow the narrative threads to grasp the meaning of plot, characters, and themes. Therefore, there is interaction between the film and the audience from a distance, the reception process being closer to aesthetic contemplation. Spectacle films emphasize the direct visual impact and jouissance created by images. And the narrative is dismembered into fragments, sacrificing its totality. The visually stunning images therefore impress the audience visually—the visual, as Benjamin puts it, is transformed into the tactile. Further, if combining this theory of Benjamin with Freud's psychoanalysis, we can better grasp, in terms of the psychology of the subject, the cultural characteristics of pleasure aroused by spectacle films. That is to say, the spectacle cinema is more inclined to the viewer's ego and its principle of visual pleasure. Thus, we have reasons to believe that such a cinema is the product of the jouissance culture that defines contemporary consumer society.

Notes

1. *Hero* (DVD) is published and distributed by Guangzhou Audio and Video Publishing House.
2. See Wallace Martin. *Recent Theories of Narrative*. Ithaca: Cornell University Press, 1986. p.108.
3. Laura Mulvey. "Visual Pleasure and Narrative Cinema," in *Film Theory and Criticism: Introductory Readings*. Eds. Leo Braudy and Marshall Cohen. New York: Oxford UP, 1999. p.833
4. Guy Debord. *The Society of the Spectacle*. p.12.
5. Laura Mulvey, "Visual Pleasure and Narrative Cinema". p.835.
6. Laura Mulvey, "Visual Pleasure and Narrative Cinema". p.837.
7. See P. Coates, *The Story of the Lost Reflection*. London: Verso, 1985.
8. See S. Heath, *Questions of Cinema*. London: Macmillan, 1981. pp.185–190.
9. Scott Lash, *Sociology of Postmodernism*. pp.175–191.
10. Scott Lash, *Sociology of Postmodernism*. p.188.
11. Scott Lash, *Sociology of Postmodernism*. p.175.
12. Scott Lash, *Sociology of Postmodernism*. p.191.
13. Laura Mulvey. "Visual Pleasure and Narrative Cinema". p.840–843.
14. James der Derian, ed., *The Virilio Reader*. Oxford: Blackwell, 1998. p.16.
15. Susan Sontag. *On Photography*. New York: Rosetta Books, 2005. p.68–86.
16. See *Hero* (DVD), published and distributed by Guangzhou Audio and Video Publishing House.
17. See *Hero* (DVD), published and distributed by Guangzhou Audio and Video Publishing House.
18. Anders Stephanson. "Regarding Postmodernism: A Conversation with Fredric Jameson". *Universal Abandon? The Politics of Postmodernism*. Ed. Andrew Ross. Minneapolis, MN: The University of Minnesota Press, 1989. p.4.

16 Wang Guangyi's *The Great Criticism* and pop iconography

The strategies of *The Great Criticism* and its different interpretations

Hampered by social closure and cultural isolation since 1949, Chinese contemporary art tends to imitate, borrow, and convert different artistic languages, styles, and themes from Western modernism. When most Chinese artists were preoccupied with cat-copying Western art, Wang Guangyi took the world by surprise with his *The Great Criticism* series. The seemingly simple pop images captured the Western imagination, and in turn boosted "the domestic sales of exported commodities", namely, the phenomenal promotion of Wang's status and influence as an artist in China through earning symbolic capital in the Western art circle.

This shortcut for Chinese artists to acquire symbolic capital is noteworthy whose spirit is well encapsulated in a Chinese idiom that "the fragrance of blooming flowers can only be appreciated by outsiders beyond the garden walls". What Wang and like-minded artists usually do is to adopt the style and vocabulary of Western art with an eye on the Western criteria of aesthetic evaluation. After obtaining recognition and reputation in the west, the artist usually returns to the domestic art circle and transforms the foreign symbolic capital, including exhibitions, professional critiques, social reception, and auction performance, into his personal art resources back home. The most successful contemporary Chinese artists, the so-called "F4" or Flower Four (Zhang Xiaogang, Yue Minjun, Wang Guangyi, and Fang Lijun), all followed the same route. Successful examples of similar kind can also be found in other art fields such as literature, architecture, music, and drama. This strategy to a great extent has altered the contemporary terrain of Chinese arts since the New Culture Movement in the early 20th century. Chinese artists are no longer passive imitators; instead, they are now able to ride the tide of international arts. Wang Guangyi apparently discovered, utilized, and benefited from this shortcut. Of course, I am not meant to give a normative value judgment here, but merely a descriptive statement. That is to say, whether or not this strategy implies postcolonial subtleties across different cultures is not to be discussed here.

In this light, an intriguing question arises: Why does the Western artworld take a shine to Wang Guangyi and give his *The Great Criticism* series so much attention and recognition? Are there any differences between the work's acceptance in China and in the west? I select two representative views among western scholars which reveal similar judgments and different focuses. In general, they outline the mainstream opinion on *The Great Criticism* series. The first opinion comes from the Italian critics with whom Wang has a close connection. Demetrio Paparoni said,

> In the early 1990s, Wang Guangyi was already well-known in the west for his The Great Criticism series which combines the worker-peasant-soldier (WPS) images from propaganda posters of the Mao era with logos of western commercial brands. Such a juxtaposition expresses the artist's desire to picture two kinds of preaching that serve to hone people's mind: socialist nations are dedicated to maintaining the political propaganda of the press, and western capitalist nations try to create a satisfactory design of products. Wang Guangyi particularly chose the western commercial logos in order to indicate the consumerist fetishism in this society.[1]

Another opinion is raised by the U.S. scholar Mary Bittner Wiseman, who specifically commented on the value and significance of *The Great Criticism* in her review of the characteristics of Chinese contemporary art:

> Political themes from the Cultural Revolution joined Pop Art in a series of oil paintings by Wang Guangyi, one of which, Great Castigation: Coca-Cola [1993], combines the image of three workers lined up side by side with the soft drink logo. Only the heads and raised left arms of the second and third workers can be seen. The first clutches a red book and all the three hold one large fountain pen whose nib lies just above the second C in the white letter 'Coca-Cola' and whose length appears to be the pole of a red flag. If the first C is communism, then the second, the one threatened by the pen's nib, is "capitalism"...The conjunction of the two reduces the revolutionary workers and the logo of China's most popular company to kitsch, trivializing the ideologies of Maoism and Western economies. To reduce Maoism to kitsch is to subvert its authority over the people's beliefs and values. *Great Castigation: Coca-Cola* is nothing more than an exemplification of materialism, historical and consumer, where "nothing can escape being material.[2]

For Paparoni, the purpose of *The Great Criticism* is to criticize the two kinds of propaganda that are seemingly different but in effect similar. One is the Chinese socialist preaching, and the other is the advocacy of Western materialism and commercial culture; they both are a method of "brainwashing" designed to instigate some concept or mode of behavior. Wiseman also found a subversion of authority in Wang's *The Great Criticism* for she interpreted the two capital Cs in Coca-Cola respectively as "communism" and "capitalism". Although the huge brush is pointed toward the second C(capitalist), she stressed on the work's criticism of the authority in Maoist political pedagogy (as in the first C), which, by reverting to kitsch, vulgarizes Maoism and Western economy.

The distinct iconological feature of *The Great Criticism* is the juxtaposition of socialist propaganda from the Cultural Revolution and famous Western commercial brands. The brainwashing function identified by Paparoni and Wiseman's interpretation of the subversive import represents the prevailing views on the series in the west. Based on this understanding, Wang Guangyi has been favorably reviewed by many Western critics and thus accumulated considerable volumes of symbolic capital, which not only established his status in the west, but also catapulted him to the apex of Chinese contemporary art.

Nevertheless, it must be noted that the interpretations of the same series in China is completely different from those in the west. The discrepancies and differences uncover some key issues regarding how to take grasp of Wang's *The Great Criticism*. Here, we may quote Chinese critic Gao Minglu who says:

> Even though Wang Guangyi and some other artists' political pop acquired popularity abroad, but not at home, the social mentality reflected in their political pop, the aesthetic character and even the commercial value are in tune with the "Mao fever". Most political pop painters share an ambivalent attitude towards the Cultural Revolution. This ambivalence combines love and hate, and they even admire the power of Mao's discourse and its aesthetic features...More than that, Mao's power to control and create media is worshipped as well...If the political pop of the early 1990s was ironically intent upon deconstructing something, it is the utopian illusion of Mao's myth of Cultural Revolution as well as self-mockery and repudiation of the painters' own humanistic sentiments in the mid-1980s. However, this does not indicate a complete opposition to Mao's aesthetic values or the way in which Mao's political discourse went popular, nor does it express an ironic twist on some kind of illusory myth as believed by some western critics. Instead, these artists still worship power. This is because in a society with a pyramid-shaped power hierarchy, any social group that resides within the structure and is subject to its shaping force, yearns for the rulership at the top of the pyramid. And avant-garde art makes no exception. It is just in these terms that Maoist revolutionary popular art, the 1985 Art Movement, and political pop are all embedded in the same historical totality and proceed from the same origin of utopian logic...They know it at heart that despite being the opposite and opponent of the power, they also crave for it. And as the descendants of the utopia, they collude with what has already become they own tradition. The love-and-hate mentality of varying degrees can be found with the new generation of artists since the 1985 Movement.[3]

In the domestic cultural and historical context, Chinese critics made a conclusion that is totally different from the Western critics. Gao saw the ambiguous relationship between Wang's works and the authority, especially the "love and hate" relationship, that potential complicity between avant-garde artists and the authority. Gao's judgment that "Maoist revolutionary popular art, the 1985 Art Movement, and political pop are all embedded in the same historical totality and proceed from the same origin of utopian logic", evidently different from the views of the Western counterparts, deserves further contemplation. Suspending the existing conclusions and current mode of thinking, we are capable of arriving at some new ideas or conclusions by delving into *The Great Criticism* series more critically. In what follows I will try to give a reinterpretation of the series in close connection with the artist's career development from an integrated perspective of psychoanalysis and iconographic rhetoric.

The social context and individual experience of The Great Criticism

I would like to first review Wang's life experience since his early years. In 1957, Wang Guangyi was born into a poor worker's family in Harbin[4]. From 1966 to 1968, when the Cultural Revolution was in full swing, Wang was at the Freudian "latency stage". 1978 saw China ushered into the new era of opening-up, and in 1980, he was admitted into the Department of Oil Painting of China Academy of Art in Hangzhou where he completed his BA degree program in 1984. At a stage of "identity crisis" as termed by Erik H. Erikson, Wang was embarking on his "North Pole" series. In 1985, he left Harbin for Zhuhai in Guangdong province, and perhaps since Guangdong was the earliest pilot area of China's opening-up policy, the movement prompted a sharp change in his artistic style. Wang soon completed a "Post-Classic Series" followed by "Red Reason" and "Black Reason" series. It is noteworthy that in both series, he creatively painted Mao's images upon a gridded background, the practice of which, according to himself, was first started at the end of 1986[5]. It can be argued that there would be no *The Great Criticism* series without the Mao Zedong series, because from a psychoanalytical perspective, there lies a hidden subtext of collective memory—the Cultural Revolution that has left an indelible mark on Wang Guangyi's adolescence. Although the revolution had long ended, the memory of it has stayed in Wang's unconscious.

As indicated by Wang's interviews, *The Great Criticism* was created by chance, but in fact it was not. He left Zhuhai for Wuhan under immense pressure since his work "Mao Zedong" was published on *Time* magazine. Later, he met his close friend Zhang Peili in Hangzhou, and their conversation sparked the original inspiration for *The Great Criticism* series. Wang Guangyi said:

> I went to Hangzhou, and at Lao Zhang's place he found me a book about mastheads during the Cultural Revolution. Later Liao Wen also looked for these materials in Beijing. Because I hadn't read that for a long time, I felt excited when Lao Zhang handed me the book, so I started this after I came back. At first, I did not think of doing stuff like Coca-Cola; I just wanted to enlarge the picture in the beginning, so I can decide after one piece was finished. The size was one meter by one meter, and done through gridding because there was no way to get it done but to paint exactly the same. Still, I thought it was a problem as it subtly suggests some kind of cultural mode. At that time, I just had some foreign cigarettes and cokes, and cokes were still a luxury back then, those in bigger cans. I placed the coke beside the canvas when I painted, and coincidentally found that this was good. I could not make out where to put it, but I felt "that's it!" when the painting was

finished. "Coca-Cola" brought me good fortune because the Italian magazine *Flash Art* unexpectedly published this piece of work on the front cover of a 1991 issue.[6]

Wang's words call for special attention here. First, Wang Guangyi's excitement at the sight of the Cultural Revolution mastheads means that these images used to be very familiar to him but had faded out over the time. We can presume that Wang was already learning how to paint during the Cultural Revolution when such images were ubiquitous and became the raw materials of his iconographic memories. This is like bumping into an old friend who you haven't seen in years. I think personal pictorial memories by shaping the latent psychological impetus for the works of similar type to appear in Chinese contemporary art are vital to the creation of *The Great Criticism*. Second, Wang initially applied the gridding method to achieve a vivid imitation of the original images of the Cultural Revolution. The artist's intention invites reflection. It stands to good reason that given his professional training at China Academy of Art, he is fully capable of reproducing a copy of the original image. For one thing, he had used gridding to paint the "Mao Zedong" series, and for another, enlargement upon gridding, though necessary for the duplication of a portrait which entails precision of details and proportion, is actually superfluous for copying a coarsely crafted masthead by unprofessional people in the revolution. I think it more or less reflects Wang's complicated attitude toward images of the Cultural Revolution when he found that "there is no way to get it done but to paint exactly the same" and intuitively discerned "a problem as it subtly suggests some kind of cultural mode". Based on the understanding of the "cultural mode", he thought it would be a failure if the duplicate was not exactly the same. Why didn't Wang use the gridding method to paint the numerous "The Great Criticism"? My guess is, once the gridding method had incorporated those images into his visual-conceptual experience and formed what he called "the cultural mode" (in Gombrich's terms, a "schemata", to be explained later), he was able to reach an "accustomed and proficient" stage, just like an experienced potter who can draw various patterns on a greenware at will. Therefore, even though Wang Guangyi has created many pieces of *The Great Criticism* from 1990s to 2007, he never mentions again the gridding method. The schemata of *The Great Criticism* have completely established itself as the signature of the "Wang style", and an iconological model of the political pop in Chinese contemporary art. Third, the appearance of Coca-Cola in the painting is said to be sheer accidental due to its physical closeness to the canvas and "chance" of being put into the painting. But in my opinion, there is an inevitability underlying the seeming contingency. There is certainly a purpose to serve for the artist to paint the typical images of WPSs who hold red flags, pens, "the Red Books", and dominated Cultural Revolution mastheads. Likewise, the presence of the coke can in the painting is by no means without a purpose. In the late 1980s, China's economy and society had obviously progressed, and the trade-oriented economy made it possible for foreign products from common soft drinks to expensive luxuries to enter the daily life of Chinese people. So much so that foreign brands have melted into the background of the daily life of artists like Wang Guangyi and adding the logo of Coca-Cola into the painting is simply beyond a "convenient" move dictated by chance. When Wang was working on the first piece of *The Great Criticism*, he had to find some current counterparts for the quotidian mastheads in the revolution. A picture that shows only a duplicated masthead of the Cultural Revolution with no connection to the present day would probably lose much of its attraction to the contemporary audience. Some contemporary clues would be necessary to form a comparative graphic structure. The logo of Coca-Cola therefore became a sensible choice under the circumstances as Wang happened to find a can of coke near at hand, and this is the inevitability underlying the contingency.

Another question that interests me is why did Wang Guangyi feel excited when he saw the Cultural Revolution mastheads? Why did he immediately decide to put the image into the painting, and what drove him to make such a decision? Sometimes, the decision made by an artist can be emotional and hasty, but what prompted Wang Guangyi to the decision to image the Cultural Revolution and Coca-Cola seems even more intriguing. In order to clarify this question, I would like to start with Gombrich's theory of schemata. Wang Guangyi is also familiar with the theory for he attended China Academy Art when the art historian and his theories had found many followers there. When comparing the differences in the graphic maneuver of the paintings of Derwentwater by Chinese artist Jiang Yi and an anonymous British artist, Gombrich made a philosophical comment:

> We see how the relatively rigid vocabulary of the Chinese tradition acts as a selective screen which admits only the features for which schemata exist. The artist will be attracted by motifs which can be rendered in his idiom. As he scans the landscape, the sights which can be matched successfully with the schemata he has learned to handle will leap forward as centers of attention. The style, like the medium, creates a mental set which makes the artist look for certain aspects in the scene around him that he can render. Painting is an activity, and the artist will therefore tend to see what he paints rather than to paint what he sees.[7]

According to this theory, Wang's excitement about the mastheads is what Gombrich called "matching", a correspondence between what he sees and what he is looking for, or he sees what he is going to paint. This is a process of "sieving", that is, "a selective screen which admits only the features for which schemata exist", and in this way "the sights which can be matched successfully with the schemata he has learned to handle will leap forward as centers of attention". Then, what are the schemata in Wang's visual experience? No doubt, the four-year undergraduate training has shaped many professional schemata, especially an iconographic model of oil painting. But I especially want to point out that in Wang's individual psychological development, he has experienced the Freudian latency stage (from five to adolescence), and subsequently the Eriksonian stage of "identity crisis" (12 to 19), largely coinciding with the ten-year time span of the Cultural Revolution. On the one hand, he felt small due to his family's poverty, but his worker's family background also left him and his family unscathed in the Cultural Revolution. His memories of the revolution therefore were very different from those of the persecuted artists. At the same time, Wang had a burning passion for art and studied extremely hard; he was not only familiar with the popular Cultural Revolution mastheads; he actually drew some of them himself. In the post–Cultural Revolution era when the reform and opening-up were launched, Wang tried to seek out new iconographies from past cultural memories, and always looked for "matching" images from the existing schemata, among which there are mastheads of the Cultural Revolution. On the one hand, they evoked the old memories of the Cultural Revolution, and offered a possibility for Wang to get over his "identity crisis". Therefore, the mastheads of the Cultural Revolution awakened his complex visual experience and filled him with heightened excitement.

Simply put, "identity crisis" is the crisis of not knowing "who I am", a common question in the art circle, particularly striking with young artists who have not yet established their distinctive artistic style. For every artist, the question of "who am I?" is more often rephrased as "what is my style?" The second question, symptomatic of the identity crisis, constantly baffles and even torments the artist. Wang has expressed on different occasions that *The Great Criticism* brought him good fortune and established his status in the domestic and international art circles. Such acknowledgment undoubtedly confirms the resolution of his identity crisis. From *Mao Zedong* to *The Great Criticism: Coca-Cola*, it marks an important transitional period for Wang who, freed from previous identity crisis, just began to establish his identity as a political pop artist in the art circles home and abroad with *The Great Criticism* being his stylistic symbol.

Both the 1990s and the ten-year Cultural Revolution (1966–1977) have seen earth-shaking changes in China. Fraught with traumatic memories, these mastheads certainly invite different responses from different people. The artists who suffered in the Cultural Revolution would voluntarily stave off or even reject these images linked to their miserable memories. However, born into a worker's family, Wang Guangyi did not suffer for his family background, so these images were not repulsive to him. Furthermore, dislocated from the historical context in which they were created, their political significance and cultural violence have been much subdued. And yet, they do revive the artist's visual memories of the past; in Wang's words, "the Cultural Revolution to me is not what it is to the general public (in a politico-economic sense) … For an average man, he may care more about the facts and outcomes of a historical event; but for an artist, he cares more about the visual complexity within a visual pattern that can be brought by a historical event. … When I put together 'The Great Criticism' and 'Coca-Cola', its spirit points to the relationship between fetishism and utopia".[8] I think the first half of Wang's words is credible; he explicitly expressed that the visual complexity within the visual pattern of the Cultural Revolution has an influence on him. However, the second half is not as convincing since it is difficult for him to self-consciously criticize "utopia" and "fetishism" when he started to create *The Great Criticism: Coca-Cola*. Just as he confessed, he had discussions with some critics after this work was completed, and these discussions to a great extent encouraged him.[9] Perhaps the so-called "double criticism" of utopia and fetishism was inspired by the interpretation of critics. Wang Guangyi himself admires a saying of Derrida: "Writing precedes thinking", from which he has developed his own motto: "working precedes thinking".[10]

Oxymoron in T*he Great Criticism: Coca-Cola*

In the early 1990s, Wang Guangyi's visionary mind captured the complicated meanings of mastheads of the Cultural Revolution, and more creatively, he made a connection between the mastheads and the logo of Coca-Cola, and set the basic iconological pattern for his *The Great Criticism* series, which brought him immediate fame. As for the mastheads of the Cultural Revolution, they have sunken into oblivion in the new era of China's reform and opening-up policy, and their reappearance evokes different reactions in different viewers. But in the increasingly stratified and commercialized west, these political and utopian revolutionary images, like the portrait of Che Guevara, have been invested with some new visual magic. The reason why Wang Guangyi chose these rebellious WPS images, I think, is that they seemed strikingly Chinese, simple, and historical. More importantly, these images were born with a kind of pop art characteristics, very much in keeping with the iconology of pop art. It is easy to presume that if Wang Guangyi followed Warhol's paradigms of Coca-Cola bottles or Mao Zedong, he would never have achieved his current success. His sagacity lies in his full awareness about the necessity to apply Warhol's techniques to genuine Chinese images for the invention of a new kind of Chinese pop art. The combination of the utopian revolutionary images and the most popular Western commercial symbols gives birth to the Chinese contemporary pop art distinctively different from Warhol's American pop.

Among Wang's *The Great Criticism* series, the most famous is *The Great Criticism: Coca-Cola,* the cover piece on the Italian magazine *Flash Art*. In order to analyze *The Great Criticism*, I would like to draw two lines here. First, the following discussion is focused on those juxtaposed foreign commercial logos; as for other series, such as those about WTO, *Time* magazine, artists, museums, are not considered in this discussion. Second, I will narrow down the scope of these works to the Coca-Cola series for they are the most representative ones. Roughly estimated, Wang Guangyi painted no less than 22 pieces of *The Great Criticism: Coca-Cola* from the 1990s to 2007.[11] The time span is long, and the images, colors, and compositions vary from one to another, but one symbol remains constant, that is, the logo of Coca-Cola (see figures below).

There are several iconographic aspects about Wang's *The Great Criticism: Coca-Cola* series. First, the center of the painting is occupied by a number of people (ranging from two to dozens) who form a group portrait. But the grouping method, ambience, relative surroundings, and manners of these people in each painting are very different. Second, the characters' actions are highly exaggerated and dramatized, like a stage performance. In other words, the scenarios do not come from real situations in everyday life, but deliberately posed for enhanced impact and attraction. Apparently, there are two concerns underlying such rendition, namely, the origin from the necessary visual features of the Cultural Revolution propaganda, and the iconological requirement of pop art to be succinct and impressive. Third, the images obviously carry the style of a poster, which is also the most common styling approach in pop art. *The Great Criticism: Coca-Cola* can be put on exhibition in museums, and decorate domestic space too (see figure 10). It seems very proper to apply Hamilton's classic conclusion about the secret of pop art to *The Great Criticism: Coca-Cola*: "[p]opular, transient, expendable, low cost, mass produced, young, witty, sexy, gimmicky, glamorous, big business".[12] For instance, there are no neutral colors or transitional colors, only the contrastive matches between red, yellow, black, and blue, highly suggestive of the features of advertisements and posters. However, these features fall short of the full manifestation of pop art style, and the streamlined typeface of Coca-Cola either foregrounded or figured in the background becomes the linchpin. This involves the fourth aspect, the logo of a product. One major characteristic of the Western pop art is the direct incorporation of daily commodities or advertisements. Artists from Hamilton to Warhol all did the same. Using commercial logos in paintings is nothing new. But in my opinion, the most innovative aspect of *The Great Criticism* series is the juxtaposition of the well-known Western commercial logos and stereotypical WPS images, which brings in a special tension. As I have mentioned before, mere duplication or appropriation of the Cultural Revolution mastheads is not innovative, and can hardly draw attention from the art circles home and abroad. It is exactly through the introduction of Western commercial logos into the artwork that a unique strategy of visual rhetoric falls in line. This involves a complicated phenomenon in contemporary Chinese society and culture: the relationship between the culture of the utopian revolution and the ecstasy of consumerism.

Myriads of discussion have been done about the pairing of these two entirely different or even antithetic subjects. Some believe that both result from seemingly opposed yet essential the same "brainwashing" phenomenon, which represent the two dominant ideologies of the contemporary society. Some find this juxtaposition "a criticism against the Western commercial culture prevailing in China".[13] Some consider these works highly parodical and game-like, which inadvertently reduces their critical thrust to the minimum and infinitely raises their humorous effects.[14] Still others see Wang's efforts to integrate two entirely different artistic forms. I would like to approach *The Great Criticism* from a new perspective, that of the visual rhetoric.

A fundamental visual rhetorical strategy that runs through *The Great Criticism* series is oxymoron. In order to explain this strategy, I will borrow the idea of rhetoric from historiography. Nearly all analyses of *The Great Criticism* have mentioned the binary opposition in the combination of images, that is, the combination of highly political and revolutionary images of the Cultural Revolution at home and the typical commercial brands of the Western capitalist society. In terms of the principles of pictorial composition, Wang adopts juxtaposition, which is very common in Western pop art. Though juxtaposition in artworks is commonplace in the west, as we can see in Hamilton and Warhol, Wang Guangyi's way of doing juxtaposition differs from the Western style with two obvious features. The first is the sharp opposition between the revolutionary images of *The Great Criticism* and the consumerist commercial logos which originally belong to two entirely different ideologies and discursive systems. When they are framed in one piece, an oxymoronic effect comes into being. Oxymoron, according to OED, is "a figure of speech that yokes together two seemingly contradictory elements. Oxymoron is, thus, a form of condensed paradox". In terms of rhetoric, oxymoron reveals the distinction of the composition of the image while juxtaposition, as mentioned by many art critics, is just a neutral explanation, which is unable to clarify the true characteristics of the visual rhetoric of *The Great Criticism*.

In general, the key of oxymoron is the syntactic combination of two antonyms, and this is a common rhetorical phenomenon in language. For example, Shakespeare used this figure of speech many times in *Romeo and Juliet*. Romeo says, "O heavy lightness! Serious vanity! Mis-shapen chaos of well-seeming forms! Feather of lead, bright smoke, cold fire, sick health! Still-waking sleep".[15] Nearly every phrase is a combination of antithetic words, which seems illogical for they form a paradoxical semantic structure. Another example is the oxymoronic description of a "black sun" in Sholokhov's *And Quiet Flows the Don*. The basic structure of oxymoron is the combination of two semantically antithetical words, which builds up a special structure of semantic tension, like Romeo's "heavy lightness" or "cold fire". Oxymoron originates from the deeply rooted mindset of binary opposition because polarized concepts like true and false, good and evil, and beautiful and ugly provide the most convenient pattern of thought. Wang Guangyi has talked on several occasions that he was deeply influenced by such thought pattern. As he admitted,

> people who grew up in a socialist country like China tend to see the world in binary opposition. I don't want to make a judgment about the existence of such a mindset. But I would like to remind the audience of a vision and mindset which represents another value system and is on the verge of oblivion.[16]

According to Foucault, the mindset of binary opposition is essentially a form of power because there will always be the dominator and the dominated, implying some kind of "will-to-knowledge" or "will-to-truth" and hence manifesting a power relation, for instance, the denial of falsehood by truth, goodness's dominance over evil, beauty's transcendence beyond ugliness. These are all realized through this discursive strategy.[17] In fact, art is one of the important ways to implement these discursive strategies. The history of art is replete with various models of binary opposition, and the juxtaposition of images is not a simple comparison between two different objects, but the recognition and reinforcement of a certain power relation. Ever since modernism, especially in the era of postmodernism, art has often been mobilized to deconstruct the long-trenched discourse of binary opposition. This is true of avant-garde art, and also true of pop art as it erodes upon the barrier and opposition between fine art and mass culture or commercial culture. One interpretation of *The Great Criticism: Coca-Cola* is that Wang bridged the gap between the revolutionary discourse and the commercial discourse, thus establishing a new form of discourse. I doubt this interpretation. Can we make an assumption that *The*

Great Criticism: Coca-Cola implies a simultaneous confirmation and negation of the utopian revolutionary images of the Cultural Revolution and the logo of Coca-Cola? Or is it possible that he has a negative attitude toward them both?

I think Wang is more likely to have adopted the "double mindset" of oxymoron. The so-called "double mindset" means absorbing two opposed ideas in a unified thought mechanism without taking an affirmative or critical stance. Wang is probably one of those artists who work with the "double mindset" for he has expressed it many times that he did not intentionally stick to one concept or stance when he was creating *The Great Criticism* series, and that he intended to be more "neutral". He said,

> I think the reason why people remember *The Great Criticism*--even if they don't like it, they remember it anyway--is that I have no 'stance'... a neutrality shapes it. Everyone thought I was 'attacking' something as if I had a specific stance, but in fact people came to see that I did nothing, or maybe it's just all sorts of contingent factors that gave meaning to my *The Great Criticism*.[18]

In order to clarify this paradoxical phenomenon, let us break down the oxymoron in *The Great Criticism: Coca-Cola*. For an oxymoron, there is not only one standard structure, but multiple with varying degrees of opposition. At least we can categorize three types of oxymoronic structures that are different in their degree of opposition: 1) complete opposition and contradiction, in which A and B are in sharp opposition, causing an intense situation of mutual denial, that is, A is a clear negation of B and vice versa, like "the black sun" et cetera; 2) relative opposition and contradiction, in which A and B are in mild conflict and no obvious mutual negation can be found. This gives rise to a relatively stable tension, such as "dim dawn"; 3) a peaceful structure of differences, in which A and B are not in obvious opposition or contradiction; they are just different, but this difference is not negative and mutually exclusive, as in the neutral concept of "juxtaposition".

Most reviews on *The Great Criticism* series are concerned about the first type of conflict, that is, the complete opposition and contradiction. Through my interpretation of many of Wang Guangyi's works, I think the aforementioned three types are all present in the series, and the first type is arguably not as common as the second or the third. Therefore, *The Great Criticism: Coca-Cola* also has three degrees of oxymoronic structures. Figure 1 is the work that first brought Wang Guangyi fame, and it has a complete contradictory structure in which the WPSs wave the red flag high and hold the pen tight with the pen tilting to the logo of Coca-Cola, and this reflects the sharp opposition of two different discourses. But upon closer examination of his other works, you will find pictorial structures with entirely different tensions. For instance, in Figure 2, the WPS adopts the composition of USSR propaganda pictures. The three WPS characters uphold the hammer, the sickle, and the Red Book, which stand for workers, peasants, and the Cultural Revolution respectively. But the treatment of the relationship between the group portrait and the logo is very different from Figure 1. The three characters in Figure 2 are beaming, in sharp contrast to the serious and dramatized visages in Figure 1. The hammer, the sickle, and the Red Book, which are held high by the three characters, are on the same level with the logo, as if the characters are also holding up Coca-Cola. Figures 8 and 9 utilize the stage photo of the "model opera" during the Cultural Revolution. Figure 8 uses the stage photo of ballet *The Red Detachment of Women*. Two female soldiers dance trippingly, their movements are smooth and joyful, and the logo of Coca-Cola is just like a piece of the stage backdrop, outlining the merriment of the female soldiers, as if their happiness comes from drinking Coca-Cola. The painting shows no sign of "great criticism". Figure 9 borrows a stage photo of *Taking Tiger Mountain by Strategy* for the same effect. If Figure 1 is the complete opposition and contradiction, then Figure 2 is the relative opposition and contradiction, and Figures 8 and 9 clearly show a peaceful structure of differences. Considering the fact that *The Great Criticism: Coca-Cola* series are created over nearly two decades from the 1990s to 2007 and Wang's explicit expression of his "neutral stance" or "lack of stance", the relationship between the artist's intention and the themes in his works cannot be reduced to a double negation of two ideologies as some critics suggest.

The image-text intertextuality of T*he Great Criticism: Coca-Cola*

There is yet another iconological feature of *The Great Criticism* series that is worth analysis: the images of different characters from the mastheads of the Cultural Revolution plus the textual logos of Western commercial brands. When joining the two different cultural symbols, Wang Guangyi did not choose the images of the Western products, but consistently used the textual logo. Why so? This is an intriguing question.

The practice of "textual picture" is widespread in Western pop art. For instance, Robert Indiana's *LOVE* (1968) is a simple combination of two letters on top and two down below. Another example is Warhol's *Close Cover Before Striking* (Pepsi-Cola, 1962), which illustrates the bottle cap of Pepsi-Cola with a sentence at the center, "say 'Pepsi Please'". Another common combination of pictures and words is the textual narrative of cartoons or comics like Roy Lichtenstein's *M-Maybe* (A Girl's Picture, 1965). Wang Guangyi handles the images and words in a way different from the image-text blending in the Western pop art in that he only uses the textual logos of commodities instead of their actual images. Warhol's Coca-Cola series, such as *Green Coca-Cola Bottles* (1967), which consists of three Coca-Cola bottles in the middle and the textual logo at the bottom, exemplify such cross-reference and mutual explanation of the image and the text. But only a few works of *The Great Criticism* series use the actual images of Western commodities, and they were all created in the early 1990s. For instance, *The Great Criticism: Tang* (1990) features three cups containing different volumes of Tang juice, and *The Great Criticism: Marlboro* (1990) presents a facsimile of a Marlboro pack at the center. From then on, the images of commodities hardly appear in Wang's paintings; only textual logos are featured. What does this suggest? A reasonable speculation is that Wang believes the images of real products affect the simplicity of the painting and do not contribute to the pure opposition of the graphic and textual symbols, while simple contrastive patterns are often found with pop art.

Next, the theory of intertextuality in deconstruction would be employed to analyze this phenomenon.

Intertextuality originally refers to the literary phenomenon in which one text constantly mentions, alludes, or refers to another, thus setting up a complex dialogic relationship between the texts. The situation is somewhat different for *The Great Criticism: Coca-Cola* because first, this is a graphic text, not a linguistic work; second, it has both images and texts, constituting the intertextuality between words and images, and this is what I am concerned about.

According to the Western art theory, images and words belong to two completely different domains. Lessing's *Laocoon* specifically discusses the differences between painting and poetry. However, the development of art often ignores boundaries and artists love to break down conventional artistic categories and bring together what has previously been separated apart. This is all too common in art since modernism, and postmodernism sees its growing popularity in hybridity. As American critic Leslie Fiedler's slogan "Cross the Border, Close the Gap" goes, it is possible to mix anything together.

In *The Great Criticism: Coca-Cola* series, "the great criticism" consists of two sides; the images from the mastheads of the Cultural Revolution and the text of Coca-Cola as two elements of the oxymoron, each represents two entirely different cultures and ideologies. From the perspective of intertextuality, we have reasons to take the images of the WPSs in the foreground as the center of the painting, and the logo of Coca-Cola as the background. Viewed in this way, these two elements form a "quotation": the textual logo of Coca-Cola in the back is like a quotation made by the main body of the painting, the images of the WPSs. The image quotes the text as its background, and brings in an oxymoronic effect. According to the linguist Stefan Morawski, there are three types of quotations in an intertextual relationship: the authoritative quotation, the erudite quotation, and the ornamental quotation. If we take the logo of Coca-Cola as a quotation of the visual text, it is topologically similar to the third type, the ornamental quotation. Morawski pointed out that the authoritative quotation is the "leading actor" in a text, while the other part of the text takes a supporting role. The Scriptures or quotes of a great leader fall into the type just as the saying goes, "I annotate the canons". The erudite quotation aims to convince people. The quote and its context act upon each other, such as the quotation in scientific studies. The ornamental quotation, emerging as the opposite of the authoritative quotation, is not independent, but furnishes an explanatory account for the main text, in a spirit as of "[t]he canons annotate me".[19] However, in *The Great Criticism: Coca-Cola*, the text as a quotation is not entirely cast in a supporting role. In a sense, it is a textual logo quoted by the main image and also a self-referential object of reference. Based on this understanding, we can add the fourth type of quotation, that is, the contrastive type. Coca-Cola as a quotation of the painting is in a contrastive relationship with the group portrait of the characters. In fact, the logo "Coca-Cola" has no special meaning whatsoever; it is just a symbol of a brand. However, when put in the frame of *The Great Criticism:*

Coca-Cola, this quotation is invested with delicate subtlety and complexity, whose referential function makes it both the background and the foreground, the ornament and the subject.

Primarily, the image-text intertextuality calls forth a tensile structure of Chinese and Western cultures. The contrast of local images and Western texts reveals the complicated connections between China and the west. Ever since the Opium War, China had been on deeply troubling terms with the west. The Western powers forced into China with their warships and cannons. From the invasion of the Eight-Nation Alliance and their reckless burning and looting of the Old Summer Palace, the establishment of concessions in Shanghai and other coastal cities, and down to the Korean War, the west had been regarded as a hostile force against China. On the other hand, since the late Qing dynasty, China had begun to learn from the west and tried to catch up with its Western counterparts in areas ranging from modern education, science and technology, social institution, ideology and culture, and of course to literature and art. The craze for learning from the west can be best encapsulated in Wei Yuan's remark of "[b]eat the foreigners by learning from their advantages". The love-and-hate mentality has essentially shaped Chinese people's conflicted opinions of the west. Such is the historical context of *The Great Criticism: Coca-Cola*, hidden in the contrast between the image and the text.

Second, this series pit the home-grown revolutionary tradition against the Western commercial culture. In terms of themes and mode of expression, they are two totally different ideological symbols. *The Great Criticism* stands for an idealistic culture, an ascetic culture of privation, which is similar to Puritanism. However, Coca-Cola stands for the culture of materialism, which advocates the pleasure of consumption. A mere glance at the slogans of Coca-Cola over the years will reveal its consumerist culture and pursuit after pleasure and comforts: "Enjoy Thirst" (1923), "Makes Good Things Taste Better" (1956), "We've Got a Taste for You" (1985), and "Open Happiness" (2009). Two entirely different ideologies, contrast with, refer to, negate, or coexist with each other, which in fact demonstrates the profound transformations that contemporary China has been going through.

Lastly, the image-text intertextuality also suggests of the contrastive relationship between history and current development. The Cultural Revolution that *The Great Criticism* represents has already been stored away in people's memories. However, even if the era is long gone, popular trends like "Red (revolutionary) Songs", "Mao Fever", and "Revival of the Culture of the Educated Youth" clearly show that the past culture still claims an intangible and potential sway over Chinese society today. On the other hand, Coca-Cola, a symbol of the American consumerist culture, has already blended into the everyday life of Chinese people as cola drinking is a common practice among Chinese youths. *The Great Criticism: Coca-Cola* bridges the historical and the contemporary. But to Chinese viewers of different generations, they will have different responses. For those who have experienced the Cultural Revolution, the visual experience of *The Great Criticism* refreshes their memory as if it were only yesterday, and they must have some secret apprehension for the extensive infiltration of the Western commercial culture. Those who were born in the 1980s and 1990s after the opening-up tend to have much weaker response to the strong contrast. The images of WPSs or the model opera of the Cultural Revolution, feeling so much like a parody, are strange to them. On the contrary, they are too familiar with Coca-Cola to actually pay attention to it. The historical distance in the painting compounded by the cultural gap between different generations in Chinese society necessitates highly complicated reception of the artworks.

As a trendsetter of Chinese contemporary art, Wang Guangyi has initiated and led the development of pop art in China. Shaping the iconology of Chinese pop art, *The Great Criticism* series has been hailed as a classic model in the history of Chinese contemporary art. From the intentions of the artist, to *The Great Criticism* series, and to the different comprehensions and interpretations of Chinese and Western critics, we can see the complexity of Chinese contemporary art. Wang Guangyi himself embodies the idea of complexity because on the one hand, he stresses upon the role of artists as the critic of society and culture, and on the other hand, he professes to have a "neutral stance" or "no stance". He believes that artist cannot make out their own intentions when they create their own works, but he also cares most about "the politics of art" and its deconstructive function. All the above underscores the necessity of a reconsideration of every aspect of Chinese society and culture, which has conditioned Wang's paintings. Any simple and biased explanation may fail to wholly grasp the complexity of *The Great Criticism* series. Therefore, it is necessary for us to focus on the "field" where various forces converged and entwined from the Cultural Revolution to the era of opening-up, and examine the "field" where Wang Guangyi's personality and psyche came to be fully developed, and finally to the "field" where *The Great Criticism* series were produced. The complex relationships between the three fields hence demand a correlation analysis of various forces instead of fixing upon any of them while missing the rest.

Notes

1 Demetrio Paparoni. "Wang Guangyi and the Empty Complexity", in *The Art and Thoughts of Wang Guangyi: A Collection of Critiques and Interviews*. Ed. Wang Junyi. Beijing: China Youth Publishing Group: 2015. p.143.
2 Mary Bittner Wiseman. "Subversive Strategies in Chinese Avant-Garde Art", *Journal of Aesthetics and Art Criticism* 5.1 (2007). pp.112–13.
3 Gao Minglu. "Kitsch, Power, Complicity, Political Pop", in *Lion Art* (1995). Qtd. in Wang Nanming, "The Battle between Gao Minglu and Li Xianting", *Art Observation* 6 (2006). p.100.
4 In a talk with a friend, Wang mentioned his family background, "My family was very poor in my childhood. My father was a simple and honest road builder, and my mother was a kind-hearted and introvert housewife. My father's paltry wages were the only income for a family of seven or eight people. My family background and plain appearance made me feel below others in society". See Yan Shanchun, "Wang Guangyi in the Tide of Contemporary Art", in *The Art and Thoughts of Wang Guangyi: A Collection of Critiques and Interviews*. Ed. Wang Junyi. Beijing: China Youth Publishing Group, 2015. p.35.
5 Li Xianting. "The Artistic Experience of Wang Guangyi", in *The Art and Thoughts of Wang Guangyi: A Collection of Critiques and Interviews*. Ed. Wang Junyi. Beijing: China Youth Publishing Group, 2015. p.237.

6 Ibid, pp.239–240.
7 E. H. Gombrich. *Art and Illusion*. Hangzhou: Zhejiang Photography Press, 1987. p.101.
8 Huang Zhuan. "The Classical World in Contemporary Art: On Wang Guangyi", in *The Art and Thoughts of Wang Guangyi: A Collection of Critiques and Interviews*. p.178.
9 Li Xianting. "The Artistic Experience of Wang Guangyi", in *The Art and Thoughts of Wang Guangyi: A Collection of Critiques and Interviews*. Ed. Wang Junyi. Beijing: China Youth Publishing Group, 2015, p.240.
10 Lv Peng, "A History of Criticism: Wang Guangyi's Artistic Experience", in *The Art and Thoughts of Wang Guangyi: A Collection of Critiques and Interviews*. p.91.
11 According to the author of "The Portfolio of Wang Guangyi, 1984–2014", in *The Art and Thoughts of Wang Guangyi: A Collection of Critiques and Interviews*, from 1991–2007, there are 22 paintings themed *The Great Criticism: Coca-Cola* collected in this book.
12 Tilman Osterwold. *Pop Art*. London: Taschen, 2003. p.71.
13 Li Xianting's remark, qtd. in Lv Peng, "A History of Criticism--Wang Guangyi's Artistic Experience". p.93.
14 Lv Peng, "A History of Criticism: Wang Guangyi's Artistic Experience", p.91.
15 William Shakespeare. *Romeo and Juliet*, in *The Complete Works of Shakespeare, Volume 4*. Nanjing: Yilin Press, 2006. p.20.
16 Meriwether. "About the Socialist Visual Experience: An Interview with Wang Guangyi", in Wang Junyi eds. *The Art and Thoughts of Wang Guangyi: A Collection of Critiques and Interviews*. p.232.
17 See Michel Foucault. "Discourse on Language", in *Critical Theory Since 1965*. Eds. H. Adams and L. Searle. Tallahassee: Florida State of University Press, 1986.
18 Huang Zhuan. "Visual Politics: Another Wang Guangyi", in *The Art and Thoughts of Wang Guangyi: A Collection of Critiques and Interviews*. p.100.
19 Stefan Morawski. "The Basic Functions of Quotation", in *Sign, Language, Culture*. Ed. A. J. Greimas. The Hague: Mouton. pp.690–705.

17 Spatial practices in the space of haze city

Haze city as a problematic

On a winter day in 2015, I traveled from Beijing to Nanjing on a high-speed train. The haze in Beijing had haunted me for several days, and I looked forward to the long ride back to Nanjing so that I could finally break away from the besiegement of haze. However, while the train was racing on the rail, it struck me that the haze had kept me company like a shadow all the way. When we arrived in Jinan, the smog was even heavier than that in Beijing; after passing Xuzhou, we were navigating through the dense haze, and when we finally reached Nanjing, the haze seemed to have weakened, but the city was cloudy and foggy. This trip was a shocking experience that opens my eyes to the dire situation of environmental pollution in China. It forced me to recognize that most of the economically developed areas in China from north to south are almost entirely enveloped in the gloomy haze. The severity of air pollution and the size of its scope are unprecedented in Chinese history. Although this travel experience seems a bit incidental, the shock makes me feel that the production of space in many large cities in China has entered a new form: living under the haze has become the daily experience of contemporary Chinese urban life. Haze has completely changed our city image, spatial experience, and lifestyle.

China has experienced rapid development, thanks to 40 years of reform and opening policy, and is now the world's second largest economy. Industrialization and urbanization have boosted each other, the rural population has undergone urban migration, city territory has rapidly expanded, per capita income has significantly increased, and the housing situation has experienced substantial improvement. Nevertheless, in this rapid urbanization process, the problem of environmental degradation has become increasingly exacerbated. Since May 2013, the National Air Quality Monitoring Network has expanded its operation from 113 major cities to more than 338 prefecture-level cities and above, and the country has established a total of 1,436 air quality monitoring sites, watching over six kinds of major pollutants, including PM 2.5 particulate. Take the Beijing-Tianjin-Hebei region for instance. The region encompasses 13 large- and medium-sized cities, including Beijing, Tianjin, Shijiazhuang, and Xingtai, with an area of 183,400 square km and a population of about 85 million. Located in the Bohai economic belt and nurturing industries of energy, metallurgy, equipment manufacturing, and electronics, it is one of the most economically developed regions in China. However, according to recent years' air quality data, Shijiazhuang has the lowest annual air quality: only 52% of good air quality, which means that there is air pollution in the city for about half of the year. The second lowest is Beijing with the rate of 69% and air pollution for about one third of the year.[1] These data demonstrate clearly that China now faces a severe environmental problem of air pollution.

Smog is a man-made environmental problem of air pollution, which affects human beings' perception, cognition, and conception of space. According to Lefebvre, the space in which human beings exist is in fact a kind of spatialization.[2] And spatialization includes three interrelated dimensions: the physical, the mental, and the social:

> It is a question of discovering or developing a unity of theory between fields which are given as being separate... Which fields?... First, the physical, nature, the cosmos, —then the mental (which is composed of logic and formal abstraction)—finally the social. In other words, this search concerns logico-epistemological space—the space of social practices—that in which sensible phenomena are situated in, not excluding the imaginary, projects and projections, utopias.[3]

Inspired by Lefebvre's conception, I divide the spatialization of haze city into three dimensions: the physical, the experiential, and the social. Physical spatialization refers to the physical composition and change of urban space that take place due to the haze; experiential spatialization is slightly different from Lefebvre's formal abstraction, referring especially to the subject's perception and experience of physical spatialization. If physical spatialization is a kind of production of space, then the subject's experience is a kind of production of space as well. Finally, social spatialization carries a wide range of connotations, and I would concentrate on one aspect of Lefebvre's triad, namely, spatial practice.

I do not attempt to comprehensively discuss China's environmental problems here, but rather focus on spatial practices in the space of haze city. In the triadic production of space by Lefebvre, "spatial practice, which embraces production and reproduction, and the particular locations and spatial sets characteristic of each social formation".[4] Furthermore, he points out that spatial practice consists in a projection onto a (spatial) field of all aspects, elements, and moments of social practice.[5] Based on Lefebvre's theory of spatial practice, I would develop a new triad focusing on the case of haze city and emphasize three dimensions of people in the space of haze city, such as experience, behavior, and discourse. Just like Lefebvre's "spatial triad" (representational space, representation of space, and spatial practice), I propose another triad of spatial practice in which there are three closely related aspects. In my view, spatial practice involves residential or tourist-risk experiences, stress behaviors, and resistance discourse in the case of haze city.

Here, I would further discuss an issue about the new triad. That is the dynamic interrelationships of three dimensions of the new triad. As I mentioned above, the triad of spatial practice in haze city consists of three factors: experience, behavior, and discourse. The experience of the triad is a process of directly perceiving haze space and becomes a source of knowledge or cognition of the environment. Therefore, the experience of residents or tourists in a haze city is quite different from that of those living in a clean city. More important, haze experience always influences and even alters people's behavior. Facing a risk environment, the risk experience inevitably leads to various stress behaviors. In psychology, it is agreed that stress behavior is a kind of defense response generated by unfavorable circumstances or experiences. Needless to say, haze space in city as a risk circumstance causes people's strain or tension and even a variety of stress behaviors. If we define the stress behaviors in terms of the transaction between people and the environment, then we should pay attention to various discourses of meaning production arising from this situation. Generally speaking, such discourses on the haze space strongly demonstrate a growing discontent which produces a kind of "counter-speech" against environmental pollution.[6]

It is reasonable to say that the space of haze city in China is a form of special spatialization concerning a kind of social practice. Such social practice is just so-called "spatial practice" defined by Lefebvre. In the case of haze space, I want to narrow "spatial practice" to the new triad, including risk experience, stress behavior, and resistance discourse. In the following sections, I will focus on the process of spatial practice in haze city from risk experience through stress behavior to resistance discourse.

The logic of visualization of in the space of haze city

As I have said above, the first of the triad of spatial practice in the haze city is the experience through human vision. Although visualization is not the critical point of reflection in Lefebvre's theory of production of space, he still offers numerous links between spatialization, visualization, and spatial practice. He argues, "A further important aspect of spaces of this kind is their increasingly pronounced visual character. They are made with the visible in mind: the visibility of people and things, of spaces and of whatever is visualized by them".[7] He discusses in particular the logic of the visualization of space:

> It may be said of this space that it presupposes and implies a logic of visualization. Whenever a "logic" governs an operational sequence, a strategy, whether conscious or unconscious, is necessarily involved. So, if there is a "logic of visualization" here, we need to understand how it is formed and how applied.[8]

To illustrate his ideas, Lefebvre analyzes representation of space developed by Tuscan painters, architects, and theorists and focuses on perspective on which social practice bases. He reminds us that the vanishing line, the vanishing point, and the meeting of parallel lines at infinity were the determinants of a representation, at once intellectual and visual. This representation, which had been in the making for centuries, now became enshrined in architectural and urbanistic practice as the code of linear perspective.[9] He also employs modern architecture as his illustration. He points out that the arrogant verticality of skyscrapers introduces a phallocratic element into the visual realm; the purpose of this display of the need to impress is to convey an impression of authority to each spectator. Therefore, verticality and great height are spatial expressions of potentially violent power.[10]

Adopting Lefebvre's logic of visualization, I would like to further develop it and explore visual experience in the space of haze city. It should be kept in mind here that vision is the most important of human senses because vision is a cognitive organ as Hegel puts it. Heidegger suggests, we have entered an age of world picture by which he means to view the world as a picture, rather than a picture of the world. There is a good reason to combine vision and experience in spatial practice. That is to say that local people or tourists in a haze area always have directly visual experiences of smog surroundings. Visualization is the most prominent feature of haze as a weather phenomenon. The spatialization of haze city manifests itself more conspicuously through its visualization. Human perception, cognition, and experience of space depend on the visuality of space, and visibility is one of the most fundamental conditions of spatial practice. To put it another way, the experience of space is primarily a kind of visual experience of space, without which the construction of subjectivity by space would cease to exist. I will consider further how important visual experience is to constructing people's recognition of haze space. I suggest that visual perception and its experience form the visual construction of space in a specific space leading their cognition and attitude toward space, which results in a corresponding visual ideology. This process constitutes the subject's production of visuality in space. According to Foster, visuality involves ways of seeing, which involves how we see, how we are able, allowed, or made to see, and how we see this seeing or the unseen therein.[11]

In the following section, what I will examine is how the low visuality of smog space form a particular visual experience and how people response to their personal situations. In China's existing scientific research, the haze refers to the horizontal visibility of air drops below 10 km due to the conglomeration of solid and liquid particles (especially PM 2.5).[12] By this definition, an intuitive experience of haze refers to low visibility and the compromise of normal visual perception of space. In simple terms, the transparency and visibility of urban space disappear. For example, in a period from October 8 to December 7 in 2011, for more than 40% of the time, the atmospheric visibility of Beijing's urban area was below 5 km.[13] According to Weather China, on December 20, 2016, the visibility in some parts of Beijing was below 50 m and that in the Capital International Airport, it was 300 m. As a consequence, 169 flights had to be cancelled and multiple expressways closed.[14]

The phenomenon of haze is not something new in our daily experience. A common phenomenon is heavy fog. Nevertheless, heavy fog is only temporary, mostly at dawn or early in the morning, dispersing gradually as the sun rises. The haze, however, is quite different. It would last usually for a week or 10 days, until the arrival of the weather conditions (such as wind or rain) that drive it away. In other words, haze is an enduring meteorological condition. This has fundamentally changed the original experience and cognition of urban space by local residents and tourists, resulting in a brand-new visual experience of a hazy urban space.

Due to the reduction in visibility, the consequence in terms of spatial cognition is the variation of urban visual form. Just imagine. As the air visibility drops below 50 m, many of the city spectacles that should have been in sight in under normal conditions just vanish before our very eyes. The Palace Museum, the Great Wall, the new CCTV Tower, or the Bird's Nest Stadium, when enveloped by dense haze, presents completely different visual effect, which results in a unique visual experience.

In his discussion of urban landscape, Moser poses an interesting idea of sensual fatigue due to information overload.

> I, however, believe that the intrusion of haze has completely changed the spatial visual form of the city (such as Beijing), and its consequences are less visual fatigue than visual deficiency because many spectacles under the haze simply disappear before our very eyes. As a result, daily experiences and memories of the once familiar city become estranged and peculiar under the haze. This leads to a visual construction of space specific to the haze city and a particular visual experience of haze that results from it. The visual experience of space toward haze has not only changed the city residents and tourists' impressions on the city but it also caused concerns about future environmental development and a sense of crisis about self-survival.[15]

In analyzing Western representation of space, Lefebvre indicated the logic of visualization resulted in linear perspective. However, in facing haze space and its visual experience, we have to change Lefebvre's logic of perspective visualization to a new one, namely, the logic of spatial disorientation and "compressed flat space".

The primary feature of the spatial form of haze city is the disappearance of transparency and the sense of distance. The composition of the urban space that was once clear and transparent has now become a huge container filled with turbid gas, in which everything is blurred. The landmark structures or streets of the city can no longer be seen; the horizon in the distance vanishes; and the skyline that was originally the symbol of people's memory of the city's visual image is also obstructed. Haze has substantially changed people's visual perception, blocking their lines of sight, which results in the following visual experiences. First, the sense of distance disappears. Generally speaking, people rely on distance to grasp the real world. Distance as a measure of the structural relation between objects is an important indicator in terms of establishing objects' interrelation. Haze causes visibility to disappear so that humans can see objects only close to them, but not far away. The visual experience of finding orientation in the city based on distance thus becomes ineffective. A resident who has long lived in a particular city can still use his daily experience and memory to compensate for his confusion about orientation when distance disappears. However, when first-time tourists visit a city in the haze, they completely lose their sense of direction and their ability to establish an overall visual grasp of the urban space. As a result, their memory of the urban space is next to nothing.

Second, the disappearance of the sense of distance means that the city turns from three-dimensional composition to two-dimensional composition. It may be possible to interpret the phenomenon of haze with the theory of perspective in the history of art. The so-called "perspective" is a representational method to create the illusion of three-dimensional depth on a two-dimensional plane. However, since perspective depends largely on people's daily visual experience, and since the ratio between length, width, and depth is an important visual experience in people's daily experience, people's grasp of reality depends on the experience of perspective. For example, objects or human figures are always bigger in the near and smaller in the far, and the close views are clear, but the distant views are vague. From this point of view, perspective is not only a kind of magic that creates three-dimensional depth on a two-dimensional plane but also a basic function for people to visually grasp their everyday life world. The problem is when everything is obscured in the haze and the only things in view are what one sees in the front, perspective disappears from the visual experience of haze.

This situation is quite similar to the paradigm shift in the history of Western art. The Renaissance artists discovered perspective so that two-dimensional paintings could vividly reproduce the sense of spatial depth of the real world, thus changing the direction of the development of Western painting. When it comes to Impressionism in the 19th century, especially Manet's work, painting has increasingly turned to flatness and back to the spatial composition of the two-dimensional plane, which is particularly evident in the American abstract expressionist painting. The deep perspective disappears from the scene of painting.[16] The haze's reconstruction of urban space is quite similar to this shift in that, due to the haze, people's visual perception of the city turns from three-dimensional depth into a plane in much shorter distance. Haze has caused people's sight to be blocked, with the consequence that the city's visuality of depth has been greatly compressed into a plane in short range. The obstruction and compression of sight have modified people's perception of urban space, resulting in a unique visual experience. In the dense haze, a particular position or neighborhood is no longer a reference for the visual cognition at present, but only a marker on the map. Third, the haze has led to the disappearance of edge. Distance and perspective reveal the characteristics of spatial visual cognition in terms of the spatial relation of distance, but the disappearance of distance and perspective is in fact closely related to another important visual phenomenon—the disappearance of the edge. The edge refers to "[a] line which marks the limits of an area; a dividing line", signifying the division and demarcation of different areas. In terms of human's spatial vision, edge has a very important function. It demarcates the subject's location and moving distance and also marks the spatial relation between districts and neighborhoods of different sizes. When haze fills the urban space, these edges of spatial district that can be visually grasped simply disappear, and people's visual ability to determine the edge between districts thus disappears along with it. The haze destroys the determinacy of all objects' contours and visual forms and the edges of various districts or neighborhoods, causing the edges of spatial division to be blurred.

Kevin Lynch once said that people rely on five elements to identify a city's image: paths, edges, districts, nodes, and landmarks.[17] When haze is severe enough to submerge these identifications of the urban image, the city will lose its determinate function of constructing visual impressions. Submerged in haze, the city is no longer in its old normal state but demonstrates an estranged visual form. This is detrimental to a city, especially to cities like Beijing, which possesses a long history and a venerable image. The unique visual experience caused by the low visibility of the haze city not only changes the original visual image of the city but also changes people's cognition of urban space. All the wonderful expressions of the particular cultural memories and literary rhetoric concerned with the city completely vanish due to this visual experience, which fundamentally changes people's view of the city, causing its original image to be subverted.

The haze blurs visual references and time periods. Under normal conditions, the city often presents two different kinds of looks: that of the daytime and that of the night. Some cities show completely different looks and styles in the day and at night. When the haze hits, especially in severe haze conditions, the normal sunshine is so obstructed, the sky so dark, and the paths and neighborhoods so indistinct, in that the lighting system has to be turned on in the daytime. Thus, haze produces a period that is neither day nor night. It blurs the rhythm of day and night, resulting in a conflict between people's visual impression and their biological clock time. This may be the temporalizing of the spatial form specific to haze; its function is to confuse the time rhythm of day and night, as well as people's visual cognition.

It can thus be said that, due to its low visibility, the spatial vision of the haze constructs a different visual form, which contains various crises and inevitably causes people to experience cognitive disorientation and emotional anxieties.

The patterns of stress behavior in the haze city

The second factor of the new triad I have suggested above is stress behavior responding to haze circumstances. I would like to make some observations on the several patterns of such stress behavior and probe the relationship between people's behavior and their poor surroundings.

In haze-prone areas, such as the Beijing-Tianjin-Hebei region, the meteorological changes of space have caused many social issues, including changes in the behavioral tendencies of people living in the haze city. This is a social issue that deserves close attention. The visual construction of the space of haze city contains a series of complex consequences behind the vision, which spawns a series of new behavioral tendencies and patterns. This is one of the connotations of the so-called "spatial construction of vision".

Haze is a risk space that directly signifies air pollution and creates human health problems. Many studies have revealed the impact of PM 2.5 on human health. One study finds that for every 10 $\mu g/m^3$ increase in PM 2.5 concentration, the rate of acute mortality, respiratory disease, and cardiovascular mortality would increase respectively by 0.40%, 1.43%, and 0.53%.[18] According to a research conducted by Peking University School of Public Health, "An Assessment on the Health Hazards and the Economic Loss of PM 2.5", it is estimated that 2,349 deaths were caused by PM 2.5 in Beijing in 2010, accounting for 1.9% of the total death number that year, and the economic loss amounts to nearly 1.86 billion yuan; 2,980 deaths were caused by PM 2.5 in Shanghai, accounting for 1.6% of the total death number that year, and the economic loss amounts to nearly 2.37 billion Yuan.[19] While obstructing people's sight, haze has also brought greater dangers to the surface. That is why the visual construction of haze space is also changing people's behavioral patterns.

In Beijing, urban residents pay a high degree of attention to haze. According to one survey, 96% of the respondents have clearly felt the decrease in spatial visibility caused by haze; 85% of the respondents have felt that the air has peculiar smell in haze weather; 96% of the respondents agree or fully agree that the haze problem of Beijing is critical, with 77.32% of them fully agreeing.[20] When urban residents have such high awareness toward the haze, how does their visual cognition affect their behavioral tendency? One observable change is that residents of haze city start taking an increasing amount of "isolation" measures, to isolate themselves in indoor environment that is temporarily insulated from the haze air, or to simply flee the city when it is under haze attack.

One major feature of modern life is the timetable. For working-age residents living in a metropolis, time can be divided into three major parts: work hours, family time, and social time. To switch from one part to another needs the corresponding traffic time, such as going to work, picking up children, or visiting relatives and friends. In all three situations, a certain amount of outdoor time is required. Under severe haze conditions, one significant tendency of people's behavior is to minimize the time spent on outdoor activities and to stay indoors as much as possible, to reduce the time and frequency of being exposed directly to the haze environment, so as to reduce the possibility of breathing in smog.

The motivation behind this behavioral tendency to reduce outdoor activities comes from two factors. The first is the emergency response measures issued by the government. During periods of severe haze that reaches the level of air orange or red alarm, local governments have taken a series of measures to reduce daily activities and restrict traffic. For example, from December 19 to 21 in 2016, when haze hits the level of a red alert, the Beijing Municipal Department of Education issued emergency response measures, ordering primary schools, kindergartens, the Children's Palace, and extracurricular educational institutions to suspend class, and secondary schools (including junior high, senior high, and secondary vocational schools) to implement a flexible suspension of class. The Beijing Municipal Commission of Transportation mandates that during periods of heavy air pollution that reaches the level of a red alert, motor vehicles that meet the standard have to follow the odd-and-even license plate number rule.[21] It is necessary for the government to issue a timely public notice. The release of emergency measures serves to persuade people to stay indoors as much as possible, while compulsorily ordering primary and secondary schools to suspend class, which substantially reduces people's outdoor activities and strengthens their alertness and self-protection in the face of the extreme haze weather.

In the face of the severe haze, in addition to those official orders and emergency response measures that appear in the newspapers, individual isolation measures are more widespread. Individuals reduce their public and outdoor activities, close doors and windows, and stay in office or at home. As a personal stress response to the risky environment, reducing the time and frequency of going out will inevitably lead to a certain degree of spatial isolation tendency. Although indoor space is not entirely effective in warding off haze, it is preferable to direct exposure to the turbid haze air. To keep the indoor space clean, a variety of haze PM 2.5 testing equipment and air purification equipment become popular as a necessary installation for families to deal with haze. Due to urban residents' concerns about the health problems caused by haze, and due to the decrease in their public outdoor activities and the increase in their isolation tendency, the city's function has also changed. Lefebvre points out that the city has three most fundamental functions. The first is the informative function: the city provides various perceptions; the second is the symbolic function: the architectures, monumental buildings, or urban infrastructures constitute a social and cultural whole with symbolic signs; the third is the recreational function: the city provides the public with a variety of activities and games.[22] The city functions as the source of information changes due to the haze: public interaction and information exchange turn to indoor communication on the Internet; the symbolic function completely changes due to the low visibility, and the city image under normal conditions in the past now hides away; and outdoor recreational activities are significantly reduced and turned to indoor spaces, with many large-scale public recreational activities canceled or postponed.

It is obvious that haze has led human behaviors toward isolation, but to reduce outdoor activities and to stay indoors will also cause a series of other complex problems. From local governments' orders to restrict outdoor activities to individuals' internalized self-isolation, human beings, by reducing their everyday social and public activities, may also experience some new psychological disorders or emotional problems. Being isolated indoors may lead to mild depression. These complex emotional disorders may in turn lead to the increase in conflicts in workplace or at home, causing people to lose balance in behaviors and in mental status.

Parallel to the behavioral tendency of self-isolation is the tendency to flee the city in severe haze conditions, which is a new development that emerges in the recent periods of frequent haze attack in the Beijing-Tianjin-Hebei region. People usually escape in two ways: one is to have a short-term travel when the haze hits, breathing in fresh air in other places, enjoying the sun, beach, and beautiful sceneries. People jokingly call this kind of escape "the escape-from-haze trip" or "the lung-washing trip". Unfortunately, this kind of short-term travel is only a measure of expediency. People return to their resident city when the haze passes and the air turns clean. Another more radical act is to relocate the whole family in other cities where there is either little to no haze, which is an effective strategy to break away from the harm of haze once and for all. However, both "the lung-washing trip" and the family relocation process require corresponding material conditions and economic means. Therefore, the escape from the haze city has become a behavioral tendency with social stratification implications. Only the middle class and above are likely to afford the choice of fleeing the haze city, while for the lower classes, this kind of escape is nearly out of the question. Here are two examples. The movie star Zhang Ziyi microblogs the following words on November 26, 2016:

> Severe haze again in Beijing. The adults can wear breathing masks, but no child is willing to wear masks. They feel suffocated and breathless. They

resist instinctively...What can I do? Poor children! Indoors, I choose countless air purification equipment; outdoors, I have no other option but to take her straight to the airport.[23]

She took her child on a plane to the United States, and soon the microblog attracted heated discussions and criticisms. Many Internet users exclaimed: "Only when you have money can you afford to do whatever you want". These heated discussions manifested the problem of social inequality: not everyone can afford the choice to escape the haze city. Another example relates to the effect of public opinion, that is, how to prevent the escape of certain distinguished persons from producing the "domino effect". In recent years, many professionals have no other choice but to leave the Beijing-Tianjin-Hebei region and move to Hainan, Guangzhou, Shenzhen, and even some cities in the southwest such as Yunnan and Guizhou. In the spring of 2016, a well-known scholar of communication studies at an established university in Beijing publicly announced his decision to leave Beijing for Guangzhou. This news was immediately interpreted as "going south to escape the haze" and was discussed so heatedly on the Internet that it turned into a "media event" in no time. It is said that the protagonist of the incident received enormous pressure and severe criticism from the authority, which quickly deleted the relevant information online, to prevent the incident from getting negative publicity.

The haze-prone areas not only bring about local residents' desire to flee but also cause a lot of problems for the tourists who come to visit. Take Beijing again for example. The image of "Beijing with a fresh autumn" depicted in textbooks of primary and secondary schools in the past no longer exists because of the frequent attack of haze. Haze arrives with autumn, and in winter, the haze frequently visits, completely changing the look of the city. For tourists, the haze city is a dangerous place to visit. According to statistics, due to haze, in 2013, the total number of domestic tourists to Beijing decreased by 8.9% and that of the foreign tourists by 27.5%. Some foreign media have classified Beijing as one of the global travel destinations to be avoided in tourism.[24] Leaving aside the rapid decline in the number of tourists, those who visit during the haze time not only feel concerned about their health but also experience disappointment and frustration in not seeing anything at all, thus feeling tedious about their travel and sightseeing. Studies have shown that haze reduces the scenic spots' appeal to the tourists, damages the quality of the photos taken, results in a decline in the overall quality of the trip, and causes the traffic to be neither safe nor smooth, all of which increase the difficulties and risks of traveling.[25]

For a very long time, since Beijing is the capital and the imperial city in history, Beijing citizens have developed a feeling of identification with the city and a sense of superiority. However, during the SARS epidemic in 2004, Beijing was among the severely afflicted regions. As a result, Beijing's image and the self-esteem of Beijingers suffered an unprecedented blow. Late, as haze heavily affects Beijing, Beijing as the capital again suffers a serious blow. Living in Beijing was once the dream of many outsiders of Beijing, but now because of the serious haze, this dream becomes questionable not only in the eyes of the outsiders but also for Beijing citizens themselves. One study points out that every city has its own urbanity and its residents have a feeling of identification with their city. "Urbanity constitutes one of the sources of that feeling of belonging to a community personified by a place, in other words, an identity that is closely linked to the territory and its characteristics / distinctiveness, and becomes a major identity component".[26] As Beijing becomes more and more unfit to live in due to haze, the cultural factors that take pride in Beijing's special political status and history form a sharp conflict with people's self-protection of health. The haze has created a sense of frustration for the Beijingers. They have to endure the harsh environment of haze. In contrast, some peripheral cities that do not have the political, cultural, and historical importance exclusive to the capital are now much sought after due to their clean water and blue sky. It is thus obvious that, due to haze, Chinese people's approval and evaluation of cities have now undergone a subtle change.

The resistance discourse in the space of haze city

The last factor in the new triad of spatial practice in the space of haze city is a variety of discourses growing out of people's emotional expressions. Although there are a lot of different discourses, the most distinctive futures of them are toward a resistant expression. China has very strict regulations and censorship system on the press. People's resistance discourses have to use multiple tactics in order to keep away from official censorship. In my view, the most effective tactics is to produce humorous expressions in the popular discourse by which a resistant humor culture against haze space has developed in China.

In discussing city image, Lynch points out that the analysis of city contains three components: identity, structure, and meaning. Identity refers to distinctiveness; structure refers to the spatial relation between observer and object; and meaning is another form of relationship, which is more complex and changeful.[27] Lefebvre poses a triple dialectic in the analysis of urban space, one of which is the so-called representational spaces. According to him, representational spaces embody complex symbolisms and are linked to the clandestine side of social life and to art.[28] If we combine Lynch's views with Lefebvre's views, we would find that the meaning of city image is embodied not only in the physical urban spectacles but also in the signifying practices of people who live in the city using various symbols. I believe that in the study of urban space, this embodiment of symbolism is as important as various physical spatial practices. This is an indispensable dimension of understanding the spatial practice of urban space. As a serious problem of China's contemporary urban environment, haze not only reconstructs urban spatial practices, forms a special visual form of space and people's corresponding behavioral pattern, but also spawns a unique spatial culture—"the folk humor culture of haze". This kind of culture is characterized by its comic style, which profoundly reflects the mentality of the lower- class people in a civil society under the authoritarian cultural governance. It resists ideological control in a variety of witty and humorous ways and evades the authority's strict monitoring of the media, embodying certain characteristics of the resistance culture. The folk humor of haze shares some similarities with what Bakhtin describes as the carnival of the Middle Ages: "Thus carnival is the people's second life, organized on the basis or laughter. It is a festive life".[29] It forms a folk culture in opposition to the official culture. In a similar way, people in China suffering from the consequences of haze have formed a "folk culture of humor", which employs humorous discourses and carnivalesque actions to engage in pungent criticism of the official discourse on the haze issue. The folk humor culture directly addresses harmful effects of haze, but in a more subtle and oblique way, thus carrying with it complex political and cultural meanings. As a subculture, it simultaneously reflects the helplessness and anxiety of people at the bottom of society about the environmental degradation in severe environmental conditions of haze, while it also serves as a way for them to release their anger and anxiety in a manner that produces therapeutic effects and restores mental balance in the face of risk situations.

One form of the folk humor culture is the realistic and symbolic use of the mask in the extreme haze conditions. For ordinary people, the simplest way to fend off haze is to wear a mask when going out. Masks become a necessity for people's life when the haze hits. It is reported that for only 2 days—January 11 and 12 in 2013—China's largest online shopping platform Taobao and T-mall received 23,000 mask orders nationwide for a total of nearly 500,000 masks. A variety of jokes and performance art about masks emerge one after another. Masks turn from a simple tool to defend against air pollution into a warning sign of environmental degradation.

For example, some people use the technique of collage to make the Chairman Mao portrait on the Tiananmen Rostrum wear a mask, launching an acute criticism against the increasingly serious air pollution recently. This picture is widely circulated around the Internet, resetting the sharp contrast between history and reality. In Mao's time, even though the level of China's socioeconomic development was still very low, China's environment was indeed pleasant, the air was clear and fresh, and haze did not exist. Now, times have changed. Even our wise and great leader would not be able to foresee that the earth-shaking changes occurring later in China would lead to such rapid deterioration of the living environment. He, if still alive, could not resist the invasion of haze either and would have to wear a mask to prevent inhaling toxic air. This highly symbolic picture of the contrast between history and reality evokes people's memories of the pleasant environment of Mao's time and satisfies their nostalgic mentality, while, with the picture of the great leader wearing a mask, people are able to express their strong dissatisfaction with the present state of the environment, thus containing a kind of ironic humor and covert criticism. The protesting image of the great leader, compared with that of the general public, is clearly more influential and authoritative.

As masks gain popularity, their manifestation as a symbol goes far beyond the scope of its practicality. People or animal, living or nonliving, as long as they exist in the urban space of haze, can wear a mask to issue a protest. The statue of the former president of Peking University on campus was made to wear a mask. On Wangfujing Street, the sculptures that depict marketplace life also wear tight masks. Young people, while shooting wedding photographs in public places, wear gas masks as an exaggerated gesture. The newly weds are immersed not so much in the joy of being married as in their worries about haze, and these worries are directed not only at their own generation but also at the health of the next generation.

Another interesting visual image is a person who not only wears a mask himself on a walk but also gives his dog a mask. This performance art expresses people's concerns about the fate of animals in a haze environment. Haze is caused by human beings, but it also exerts negative effects on other species. If people can consciously protect against the haze, what can animals do? Has haze also deprived animals of their right to life? There have already been numerous studies on the impact of haze on human beings, and there is no denying its relevance. Who knows the harm of the environmental degradation caused by haze has on animals? Perhaps the owner gives her dog a mask only out of her affections for her pet, but the interpretation of such a picture undoubtedly puts forward more complex issues. Therefore, masks as a cultural symbol of the haze period carries extremely complicated political, social, and cultural meanings. They motivate people to rethink the relationship between human beings and their environment. Haze blocks people's sight, while people have to wear masks to block their contact with the haze air. Haze not only gives rise to significant increase in rich visual images but also produces various forms of literary expressions about haze. Apart from many literary works about today's urban life that touch the issue of haze, numerous self-deprecating and ironic WeChat jokes reflect people's deep anxiety about the haze. Through the use of humor, these jokes alleviate this anxiety and the emotional disorders that come with it. Take a representative joke spread around group chats of WeChat as an example:

> Haze is a macro-control measure that has eight positive effects on China: 1) The social security and retirement issues that the government is worried about is smoothly solved; 2) The high housing prices in Beijing and Shanghai is suppressed; 3) The problem of overpopulation is resolved; 4) The problem of unproportioned aging demographic structure will be gradually solved; 5) The medical and health industry is expected to replace real estate in short time as the pillar industry of China's economy; 6) The air purification equipment and other related industries rise fast; 7) The indoor lifestyle drives the development of the Internet; 8) A natural military protection zone is formed, and the hostile forces dare not covet it.

This joke first affirms the positive function of haze, which lays down an ironic tone: fog is not only not a serious problem but also a new opportunity to solve many of China's thorny issues. The first four issues are related to the livelihood of the people, such as social security, housing prices, and aging; the next three issues are related to industrialization, such as the medical and air purifier industries and Internet development; the last one touches on the issue of national security. Haze has many benefits, so its rationality and legitimacy are ironically confirmed. This joke seems to describe the necessity of haze on the surface, but deep down implies profound questioning. Haze cannot solve the difficulties of livelihood, industry, and security, and it may also lead these problems to further deterioration. The writer cleverly describes the negative effects of haze as positive, as the cure for China's current problems, enabling people to cry and laugh at the same time while reading it. The joke hits two birds with one stone. While pointing out that China now faces serious problems, it also releases deep concerns about the haze crisis in an ironic and humorous way. Thus, it ironically produces what psychoanalysis describes as the "catharsis" effect.

Although such humorous expressions have some of the characteristics of Bakhtin's alleged carnivalesque humor speech of the marketplace, it still has its own distinct features. In analyzing the humor of carnivalesque marketplace speech, Bakhtin points out that the marketplace speech incorporates many things that are excluded and forbidden by the official culture, thus forming a new language in the carnival atmosphere.[30] However, I want to point out that the language used in China's current folk humor of haze is not banned or excluded by the official culture. Its language and expressions are precisely those praised and normalized by the official culture. One feature worth analyzing is its unique rhetoric. It manipulates the correct expressions of official norms to convey implied meanings completely different from the expressions themselves so that an incisive ironic effect could be achieved. The reason why this kind of irony is popular is, on the one hand, the reality of China's current speech control, and, on the other hand, its evolution into a unique Chinese-style irony that turns official speech into its opposite meanings.

Haze is a serious challenge that China's development of urban space now faces. It is a man-made phenomenon of environmental deterioration that reconstructs a city's spatial form to a considerable extent and gives birth to new experience, behavior, and discourse. In the spatial vision of haze city, the low visibility causes the city to turn from a transparent deep space into a turbid flattened space. People's blocked sight leads to further defamiliarization of space. The spatial experience of haze intensifies people's visual perception of the potential danger of haze; so, it inevitably triggers a behavioral tendency to reduce outdoor public space activities. Self-isolation or escape from the haze city also becomes realistic choices for people, which exacerbate social inequality of urban spatial rights. From visual experience and behavioral tendency of isolation, the folk humor of haze uses irony as its leading verbal and visual rhetoric. The ironic folk humor expresses people's worries and resentment against the environmental deterioration, while it reveals people's helplessness about the status quo of air pollution. Since it is difficult to form a grassroots environmental movement in contemporary China, the folk humor culture of haze carries a certain psychological function of self-treatment. In contemporary China, the tension between the recognition of the environmental deterioration and the expectations of environmental improvement is apparent. Since haze is a phenomenon caused by air pollution due to a variety of complex reasons, ordinary people are unable to figure out the cause of the haze, let alone controlling it. Therefore, their recognition of the current environment is associated with their worries about future uncertainties. In light of the tendency of China's socioeconomic development, the management of haze would not improve substantially in the short term. But there have appeared optimistic signs. Xi Jinping, China's president, has declared in his state address: "Gold Mountain or silver mountain are not as good as clear rivers and green mountains". Since he took office, the

Chinese government has taken considerable measures to curb environment deterioration and control industrial pollutions and achieved some visible effects. In 2016, Chen Jining, the Minister of the Ministry of Environmental Protection, asserted that China's atmospheric environment management has improved, especially in the Eastern and central regions. The situation of heavily polluted areas such as the Beijing-Tianjin-Hebei region has also shown signs of improvement. Nevertheless, the haze space of Chinese cities will for a considerable period of time continue to exist as a complex visual experience, a behavioral pattern, and a resistance discourse. In environmental psychology, people have developed a certain kind of "resilience" toward the crisis environment or the traumatic situation. Adger, Brown, and Waters define resilience as "the capacity of a system to absorb disturbances and reorganize while undergoing change so as to still retain essentially the same function, structure, identity and feedbacks".[31] Under China's specific political, cultural, and social conditions, it remains to be seen in which way people's "resilience" will develop. Will it disappear altogether due to the further degradation of the environment or because of environmental improvement? We can only wait and see.

Notes

1 See Ma Xiaoqian et al. "The Spatial and Temporal Variation of Haze and its Relevance in the Beijing-Tianjin-Hebei Region", *Regional Research and Development* 35.2 (2016). pp.134–138.
2 See Rob Shields. *Lefebvre, Love and Struggle*. London: Routledge, 1999.
3 Henri Lefebvre. *La Production de L'espace*. L'Homme et la societe. 1974. p.19.
4 Henri Lefebvre. *The Production of Space*. Oxford: Blackwell, 1991. p.33.
5 Henri Lefebvre. *The Production of Space*. p.8.
6 Judith Butler. *Excitable Speech*. New York: Routledge, 1997. p.15.
7 Henri Lefebvre. *The Production of Space*. pp.75–76.
8 Henri Lefebvre. *The Production of Space*. p.98.
9 Henri Lefebvre. *The Production of Space*. p.41.
10 Henri Lefebvre. *The Production of Space*. p.98.
11 Hal Foster, ed. *Vision and Visuality*. Seattle: Bay Press, 1988. p.ix.
12 See Yu Xingna et al. "Optical properties of Aerosol during Haze Fog Episodes in Beijing", *Environmental Science* 33 (2012). pp.1057–1062.
13 See Ma Zhiqiang et al. "Comparison of Influence of Fog and Smog on Visibility in Beijing", *Research of Environmental Science* 25 (2012). pp.134–138.
14 The visibility in some parts of Beijing was below 50 meters, and 169 flights had to be cancelled, with 6th Ring Road closed. See "Weather China", *Ifeng News* December 20, 2016. <http://news.ifeng.com/a/20161220/50444083_0.shtml>
15 Gabriel Moser. "Cities", in *The Oxford Handbook of Environmental and Conservation Psychology*. Ed. S. D. Clayton. Oxford: Oxford UP, 2012. p.205.
16 See Clement Greenberg. "Modernist Painting", in *The Collected Essays and Criticism: Modernism and Vengeance, 1957–1969*. Ed. J. O'Brian. Chicago: University of Chicago Press, 1960.
17 Kevin Lynch. *The Image of the City*. Cambridge: MIT Press, 1960. pp.46–47.
18 Xie Peng and Liu Xiaoyun. "Exposure Response Functions for Health Effects of Ambient Particulate Matter Pollution in China", *China Environmental Science* 29 (2009). pp.1034–1040.
19 See Pan Xiaochuan, et al. *Dangerous Breathing: Health Hazard and the Economic Loss Assessment of PM 2.5*. Beijing: China Environmental Science Press, 2012.

20 Peng Jian et al. "Smog's Impacts on Tourism Willingness and Decision-Making of Beijing Residents", in *World Regional Studies* 25.6 (2016). pp.128–137.
21 See "Beijing Sounds Red Alert for Haze", in *Sina News* December 17, 2016. <http://news.sina.com.cn/c/2016-12-17/doc-ifxytkcf7897975.shtml>
22 Henri Lefebvre. *Du rural à l'urbain*. Paris: Anthropos, 1970.
23 See "Money Means Freedom! Zhang Ziyi Takes Her Daughter to the Airport to Flee Beijing Because of Severe Haze", in *Sohu Entertainment* November 27, 2016. <http://yule.sohu.com/20161127/n474240879.shtml>
24 See Peng Jian et al. "Smog's Impacts on Tourism Willingness and Decision-Making of Beijing Residents".
25 Cheng Jining. "Haze Management is in the Second Stage", in *Sohu News* March 11, 2016. <http://news.sohu.com/20160311/n440087124.shtml>
26 Gabriel Moser. "Cities", in *The Oxford Handbook of Environmental and Conservation Psychology*. p.212.
27 Kevin Lynch. *The Image of the City*. pp.8–9.
28 Henri Lefebvre. *The Production of Space*. p.33.
29 Mikhail Bakhtin. "Folk Humor and Carnival Laughter", in *The Bakhtin Reader*. Ed. P. Morris. London: Arnold, 1994. p.198.
30 Mikhail Bakhtin. "Folk Humor and Carnival Laughter". p.204.
31 W. Neil Adger, et al. "Resilience", in *The Oxford Handbook of Climate Change and Society*. Eds. J. S. Dryzek, R. B. Norgaard and D. Schlosberg. New York: Oxford University Press, 2011. p.698.

Index

Note: Page numbers followed by 'n' refer to notes.

Aarseth, Espen J. 159n23
Abrams, M. H. 50
accommodation 93, 96n19, 130–131, 136n11
administration-oriented cultural institutions 112
Adorno, Theodor W. 36–38, 41, 162, 169; *Dialectics of Enlightenment* 43
aesthetic culture 11; autonomy in 37; backdrop of 5; changes in 23; classical mode of 27; in contemporary China 13; dissociation of 26; effort of 12; field of 5; highly productive for 4; producers and consumers of 24; production and consumption of 15, 18; significance of 14
aestheticization 174, 175, 179, 181; of everyday life (*see* aestheticization of everyday life); happiness and gratification of 177; inner paradox of 178; representation of 177
aestheticization of everyday life 173–174, 180–181; consumer culture in "post-revolutionary era" 174–177; "experience" and "taste" of consumption 177–178; middle classes as aestheticized subjects 178–180
aesthetics 8, 11, 30, 37, 176, 177, 180, 181, 187; autonomy of 38; Chinese academia of 173; creativity 176; culture (*see* aesthetic culture); domain of 48; history of 174; isolationism 34; and knowledge 51; notion of 175; radical conclusion 169; studies 145; values and 166

Against Communication 35
Against Interpretation 35
age: of cultural tragedy 32; of electronic media 151; of picture reading 207, 215
agrarian laborers 33
alien culture 91, 94, 102
amateurism 171
American art 62
American consumerist culture 243
American culture 61, 168
American intellectual elites 61
ancient codex culture 185
Anderson, Benedict R. 80–82, 103, 106, 120
And Quiet Flows the Don (Sholokhov) 239
Ang Lee 222
"antagonistic" decoding 197
anthropological thinking 6
anthropology 2, 3, 187
anti-China Sinologists 68, 69
anti-culture 36
anti-traditionalism 54, 107
"aphasia" of Chinese literary theory 49, 54, 83
archeology 2, 139
aristocratic culture 27, 28, 39, 41
Artaud, Antonin 88
Art Movement, 1985 232
assimilation 131, 135n11
attention economy 186, 209, 210
Auden, W. H. 157
"aura" 228
authenticity 8, 56–57, 59, 67, 101, 105–107, 116, 140, 225–226
autonomy 7–12, 14, 26, 33, 36–38, 41, 61–62, 100, 105, 114, 201–202, 206, 221

avant-garde art 16, 17, 35, 41, 42, 187, 194, 232, 239
avant-gardism 42

Bakhtin, Mikhail 28, 29, 120, 257, 259
Bao Zheng 82
barometer 4
Baron, Naomi 150
Barthes, Roland 93, 147–148, 207
Baudrillard, Jean 139, 212
Bauman, Zygmunt 48, 79, 99, 101, 124
Beckett, Samuel 87, 88
Beijing Municipal Department of Education 253
Bell, Daniel 33, 40
Benjamin, Walter 3, 124, 125, 139, 142, 143, 162, 228, 229
Berger, John 198–199
Berger, Peter L. 79, 211
"bipolar" feature of public psychology 118
Bloom, Harold: *How to Read and Why* 144
Book Depository 226–227
Borgmann, Albert 136n12, 139–140, 165, 169, 170
boundary effect 79
Bourdieu, Pierre 5, 8–12, 16–18, 146, 147, 178, 207
Brecht, Bertolt 2
British Educational Association 127
British Library 127
browsing-as-reading pattern 158

Cai Zhi-zhong 205
Cao Shunqing 49, 51
capitalism 16, 32, 36, 37, 40, 42, 43, 66, 125, 209, 231
capitalist "super-democracy" 35
Cartesian: "cogito" 75, 76, 78, 98; notion of subjectivity 75, 80; "reflective subject" 129, 162; subjectivity 76, 78
"catharsis" effect 117, 259
CCTV *see* China Central Television Station (CCTV)
Central Committee of the CPC 113
centralized administrative system 11
Che Guevara 237
Cheng Xiaodong 227
Chen Jining 260
Chiang Yee 68
China 1, 2, 25, 27; academia of aesthetics 62, 64, 173; aesthetic culture 4, 5, 13, 15, 17; atmospheric environment management 260; backwardness. 51; civilization 55, 63–65, 67, 68, 142; communication culture 121; contemporary art 230–234, 244; contemporary reading culture 137; contemporary urban environment 256; contemporary visual culture 202; critics 232; cultural and economic differences 23; cultural awareness 61; cultural changes in 6; cultural communities 49; cultural context 66; cultural differentiation in 14; cultural industry 113; cultural institutions 113; cultural studies 33; culture 1, 23, 32, 47, 53, 63, 66; diasporic literature 73; economic reform 112; economy and society 11, 137, 186–187, 234; environmental pollution in 246; environmental problems 247; "Four Great Inventions" 142; GDP 111; invention 173; knowledge 67; literary history 82; literature and art in 12; media and cultural industry 117; media culture 111; modernization 168; monolithic information flow in 126; opening-up policy 233; political democratization in 120; rapid development in 62; reform and opening-up policy 74, 237; science and technology in 187; social and cultural modernization 32; social changes in 164, 200; social cultures 111, 112; social transformation 194; socioeconomic development 257, 259; theory issues 258; tradition 68, 82, 104, 235; traditional publishing industry in 155; transformation into modernization 54; urban culture and country culture 23; younger generation in 166
China Academy of Art 233–235
China Central Television Station (CCTV) 113, 114, 250
China economy: and culture 10; soaring development of 111
China Internet Network Information Center (CNNIC) 118, 119
Chinese Enlightenment 163
Chinese media culture 111–118, 121, 122; administration and market in 114;

decision-makers of 112; topography of 114
Chinese society 185; analysis of 7; and culture 1; democratization of 126; historical development of 6; integration and totality of 9
Chinese Theories of Literature (Liu) 50
Christie, Agatha 225
citizenship 131, 132, 134
civilization 23–26, 32, 35, 40, 55, 63–65, 67–69, 89, 141–143, 154
Civil Rights movements 62
classical Chinese culture 27, 29, 30, 32, 39, 41
classical Chinese literary theory 115
classical tradition of Chinese poetry 57
classic Freudian psychoanalysis 75
"Classics Reading Program" 158
"clickbait" 128
Close Cover Before Striking (Warhol) 241
CNNIC *see* China Internet Network Information Center (CNNIC)
codex culture 141–143, 185
coding-decoding process 87
coding, in interactivity 87–88
"*cogito*" 75, 76, 98
cognitive construction 146
cognitive modes 127–129, 149
cognitive psychology 82, 145
collective reading habitus 146
colonial discourse 101
colonialism 69, 71, 89
commemorative ceremonies 106, 107
commodity fetishism 38, 180, 208–210
communication mode 121
communication theory 18
communist radicalism 176
comparative textual media (CTM) 140, 143
complex mechanism 166
The Condition of Postmodernity: An Enquiry into the Origins of Cultural Change (Harvey) 123
conformity 18, 35, 40, 73, 167
Confucian Chinese culture 31, 104
Confucianism 30
Connerton, Paul 106
conservatism 5, 13, 35, 49
conservative fundamentalism 107
constitutive otherness 79
consumer culture 39–40, 112, 126, 164, 174, 178, 186, 187, 190, 194, 209; growth of 187; in "post-revolutionary era" 174–177

Consumer Culture and Postmodernism (Featherstone) 174
consumer idols 194
consumerism 5, 117, 177, 238
consumer society 3, 118, 179–180
consumption 3, 12, 14–18, 24, 27, 33, 37–39, 114, 117, 118, 125, 137, 153, 170, 174, 175, 177, 178, 180, 186, 187, 192, 208, 209, 214, 219, 243
contemplation 79, 145, 155, 157, 169, 170, 176, 214, 219, 229, 232
"contemplative" culture 214
"contemplative" thinking 170
contemporary Chinese aesthetic culture 12–14, 47, 58, 78, 185, 201; context of 179; mass culture in 43; real vista of 23
contemporary Chinese literary theory 49–51
contemporary Chinese media culture 115, 122; broader vista of 118; dualistic system in 112; duality of 117
contemporary Chinese visual culture 185, 187, 190, 193, 194, 196, 202
contemporary consumer society 177, 179, 192, 229
contemporary culture 106, 190, 207, 208, 212, 223
contemporary image-as-the-dominant one cinema 228
contemporary media culture 118
contemporary micro culture 126
contemporary Omnimedia 138
contemporary thinkers 168, 170
contemporary visual culture 186, 190, 192–194, 200, 202, 207, 212, 214, 228
contemporary visual symbols 214
contemporary Western aesthetics 174
contextualization 76, 92, 125, 130, 134, 194
conventional forms of entertainment discourse 118
cosmopolitan identity 102
counter-culture 36
creativity 15, 38, 39, 169, 176
critical cultural sociology 4–6, 14, 15
critical theory 6, 16, 43, 63, 162, 164, 171
Croce, Benedetto 81
cross-cultural commonalities 70
cross-cultural communication 75, 86, 88, 90
cross-cultural psychology 69
cross-cultural research 69, 86, 168
cross-cultural studies 86–88, 90, 91–92, 95

cross-cultural text, interpretive strategy about 93–95
Crouching Tiger (film) 222
crucial factor 9, 139
CTM *see* comparative textual media (CTM)
cultural analysis 2, 3, 18
cultural commodities 38
cultural community 47–49, 52–56
cultural conservatism 5
cultural contexts 66, 73, 81, 87, 91, 92, 191
cultural contradictions 17
The Cultural Contradictions of Capitalism (Bell) 40
cultural conventions 27
cultural correctness 88–90
cultural differentiation 12–14, 26, 30
cultural disparities 23
cultural diversity 97, 100, 135
cultural economy 4, 208
cultural elitism 5
cultural forms 24, 26, 30, 47, 82, 98, 123, 134, 146, 185, 187, 213, 228
cultural fundamentalism 59, 83, 102
cultural harmony 30
cultural hegemony 27, 28, 67
"cultural history" approach of CTM 141
cultural identity 49, 53, 54–59, 61, 80, 82–84, 97, 98, 101–105, 107, 198
cultural imperialism 6, 90
cultural industrialization in Western countries 112
cultural industry 12–13, 16, 35, 43, 113–114, 117, 179, 186
Cultural Industry Revitalization Plan 113
cultural institutions 111–114
cultural interpretation 4, 17, 92, 93, 95
cultural legitimacy 47, 48, 54, 56, 57, 59
cultural legitimation 48
cultural miniaturization 135
cultural modernity 8, 23, 32–33, 35
cultural modes 13, 24, 26, 233, 234
cultural morphology 28
cultural nihilism 51, 83
cultural paradigms 4
cultural praxis 52, 55
cultural production 3, 14–18, 27, 86
cultural production-reception mode 14–18
Cultural Revolution, the 10–11, 66, 176, 201, 231–238, 240–244
cultural shock 1
cultural sociology 2–6, 15–18, 173
cultural studies 2–4, 82; China 33; critical theory and 43; flourishing of 176; perspective of 195; poststructuralism and 198; psychoanalysis to 74–77; quality for 194; unicity of 71; Western scholars of 39
cultural subjectivity 62, 131
cultural supremacism 68, 90
cultural topography 112
cultural transformation 6–14
"cultural turn" of contemporary cinema 219
culturati 40, 43
culture: aesthetic culture (*see* aesthetic culture); alien culture 91, 94, 102; American consumerist culture 243; American culture 61, 168; ancient codex culture 185; anti-culture 36; aristocratic culture 27, 28, 39, 41; Chinese economy and 10; Chinese media culture (*see* Chinese media culture); Chinese society and 1; classical Chinese culture 29; codex culture 141–143, 185; Confucian Chinese culture 31, 104; consumer culture (*see* consumer culture); "contemplative" culture 214; contemporary Chinese media culture (*see* contemporary Chinese media culture); contemporary Chinese visual culture 185, 187, 190, 193, 194, 196, 202; contemporary culture 106, 190, 207, 208, 212, 223; contemporary micro culture 126; contemporary visual culture 186, 190, 192–194, 200, 202, 207, 212, 214, 228; counter-culture 36; and cultural sociology 2–6; discursive culture 214; dominant culture 12, 13, 16, 38, 41, 77, 99, 114, 207, 212, 213; electronic media culture 105, 154; elegant culture 35; elite culture 13, 27, 196, 201, 202; entertainment-oriented popular culture 201, 202; e-reading culture 150–153, 155–156; European culture 89; feudal culture 29; folk culture 27, 29, 41, 257; global culture 102; Greek culture 31; harmonious culture 31; image-as-the-dominant culture 213; language-as-the-dominant culture 213; market-based institutional reform of media culture 113; mass culture 5, 12, 13, 16, 35–43,

212, 239; media culture 111–118, 121–122, 129, 130, 152; micro culture (*see* micro culture); modern culture 32, 33, 35, 37, 41, 185–186; modern print culture 141, 185; modern Western culture 42; oral-auditory character of oral culture 141; patrician culture 27, 28, 30, 41; politicization of 58; popular culture 13, 35, 39, 41, 187, 194, 196, 200–202; primitive culture 24, 25; print culture (*see* print culture); of reproduction 3; "ruling ideology" of visual culture 200; social culture 6, 26, 40, 111, 112, 194; socio-culture 73, 139, 152; sociology culture 2, 3; spiritual culture 38; strong supremacism of native culture 69; structural-functional perspective of media culture 114; topography of Chinese media culture 111, 114; traditional Chinese culture 23, 51; traditional culture 52, 59, 102, 185–186; visual culture 128, 138, 147, 185–202, 207, 212–214, 217, 228; visual subculture 200, 201; vulgar culture 35; weak supremacism of native culture 69; Western carnival-style culture 29; Western commercial culture 238, 243; Western cultures 9, 28, 29, 32–33, 37, 39, 42, 52, 53, 58, 71, 88, 190, 212, 243; Western media culture 116; youth subculture 161
cyber-violence 118, 122
cyclical process 195

Davis, Fred 56, 57
Debord, Guy 175, 185, 186, 208, 209, 218–219
decision-makers of Chinese media culture 112
decoding 178; diversity of 93; encoding and 196–197; of image perception 196; in interactivity 87–88; model 102
deconstruction 93, 130, 221, 242
de-contextualization 92
dedifferentiation 180
deep attention 127–128, 149–151, 158, 167, 170
deep reading 145–146, 151, 153

defamiliarization 28, 38, 259
dehumanization 41
democracy 14, 58
democratization 5, 40, 104, 120, 126
descriptive definition 63
de-traditionalization 54
device paradigm 132, 134, 136n12, 139–140, 147, 152–157, 161–171
"Device-Paradigm Generation" 166, 167
Dialectics of Enlightenment (Adorno) 43
diaspora 74
Dickens, Charles 127, 149, 157
différance 79, 93
differentiation 7–9, 11–15, 25, 26, 30, 32, 33, 35, 37, 40, 56, 67, 99, 103, 114, 115, 169, 179
digital: aliens 153; habitus 162; immigrants 153, 161; natives 153, 155, 161–162, 166; outsiders 161
digital age 138, 139, 152–154; "hypertext" and "hyper attention" in 146–150
digitalization 147, 192
discourse 2, 6, 8, 10, 18, 38, 47, 49, 50, 52, 54, 56, 57, 64, 67, 76, 79, 80, 82, 84, 89, 94, 101, 111, 114–118, 122, 124, 138, 144, 162, 167, 185, 188–190, 202n14, 211, 214, 215, 218, 220, 221, 227, 228, 232, 239, 240, 247, 248, 256, 260
discourse-centered paradigm 227
discourse-dominant narrative cinema 228
discursive culture 214
discursiveness 221
discursive turn 79, 80
distinctive knowledge paradigm 86
division of media discourse 114–117
dominant culture 12, 13, 16, 38, 41, 77, 99, 114, 203n17, 207, 210, 212, 213
"dominant-hegemonic" decoding 197
"double criticism" of utopia and fetishism 237
"double mindset" of oxymoron 240
"doxxing" 121
Doyle, Christopher 226
dualistic system, in contemporary Chinese media culture 111, 112, 117, 121
Duchamp, Marcel 173
Durkheim, Émile 7
dynamic audio-visual media 193
dynamics 6, 27, 29, 92, 192, 223

Eagleton, Terry 180
"earls of Ho" 97, 98

economic reforms 11
eidetic intuition 91
Eight-Nation Alliance 243
electronic media culture 105, 152, 154
electronic reading 158
elegant culture 35
Eliot, T.S. 39
elite culture 13, 27, 196, 201, 202
encoding 196, 197
Engels, Fredrick 17, 95, 96n23
Enlightenment, the 8, 16, 124, 129, 162–164, 189, 211
entertainment 14, 40, 41, 84, 111, 112, 114–120, 122, 126, 135, 152, 156, 163, 177, 178, 186, 193, 200, 201, 208, 209
entertainment discourse 115; conventional forms of 118; market-oriented mechanism of 116
entertainment-oriented popular culture 201, 202
environmental psychology 260
"era of picture reading" 210
e-reading culture 150–153, 155–156
Erikson, Erik H. 74, 75, 233
Eriksonian stage of "identity crisis" 235
essentialism 74, 76, 78, 79, 83
Euro-centric reference framework 66
Eurocentrism 6, 74
European culture 89
European societies 143
European tradition 62
everyday life 2, 81, 100, 155, 162, 164, 169, 187, 194, 214, 223, 237, 243, 251; aestheticization of (see aestheticization of everyday life)
"experience" of consumption 177–178
extensive reading 152
eyeball economy 186

face-to-face communication 133, 141
face-to-face cross-cultural communication 86
fascism 162
fast reading 137–158
Featherstone, Mike 99, 105, 174–175, 179, 181; *Consumer Culture and Postmodernism* 174
Feixue, Chan 226
fetishism 36, 38, 164, 175, 177, 180, 181, 207–210, 231, 236, 237
feudal culture 29
Fiedler, Leslie 242

Fifth Plenary Session of the Fifteenth Central Committee of the Party 113
First Opium War of 1840 47
Fisher, Steven 93, 143
Flash Art, Italian magazine 234, 237
'fluid' modernity 101
focal practices 169
focal reality 169
folk culture 27, 29, 41, 257
folk literature 28
formalism 106, 214
"formation of discourse" 188
"42nd Statistical Report on the Development of the Internet in China" 118
Foster, Hal 199, 201, 249
Foucault, Michel 52, 67, 76, 78–80, 93, 171, 181, 188, 212, 239
fragmentation 78, 106, 124–125, 128
fragmicronization 124, 126–135
Frankfurt School 16, 36, 41, 43, 169, 212
"French Theory" 188
Freudian latency stage 235
Freud, Sigmund 74, 80, 209, 214, 229
Friedman, Jonathan 101; *Cultural Identity and Global Process* 99
friend-*versus*-foe logic 12, 14
fundamentalism 59, 83, 102, 107
fusion of horizons 70, 71, 90–94

Gadamer, Hans-Georg 70–71, 91, 93
gadget-lover 132
Gan, Han 195
Gao Minglu 232
Geertz, Clifford 4, 17; *The Interpretation of Cultures* (Geertz) 3
genealogy 1, 74
generalization process 99
Genette, Gérard 218
Giddens, Anthony 18, 54, 59, 100
global culture 102
globalization 16, 56, 61, 62, 73, 75, 77, 84, 97, 100, 104–107, 187; of American culture 168; and identity crisis 98–103
glocalization 100
Gombrich, Ernst H. 67, 68, 93, 196, 198; "schema theory" 195; theory of schemata 235
Goodman, Nelson 211
grand narrative 77, 124, 130, 131
Grass, Günter 161
grassroots media 111, 118–122, 187, 201

Great Castigation: Coca-Cola 231
The Great Criticism: image-text
    intertextuality of 241–244;
    oxymoron in 237–241; social
    context and individual experience
    of 233–237; strategies of 230–233
The Great Criticism: Coca-Cola 236–240,
    242–243
The Great Criticism: Marlboro 241
The Great Criticism: Tang 241
Greco-Roman classicalism 62
Greek culture 31
Greenberg, Clement 39, 42
Green Coca-Cola Bottles 241
Gresham's Law 39, 40
Gu, Ming Dong 64, 65
Guo Moruo 50
Guowei, Wang 92, 96n17

Habermas, Jürgen 7–8, 12, 18, 33, 71, 90,
    117; communicative rationality 70;
    *The Structural Transformation of
    the Public Sphere* 14
habitus 146, 150–152
Hall, Stuart 67, 76–81, 83, 87, 88, 93, 102,
    189, 195–197
Haraway, theory of cyborg 163
hard-core theory 86
harmonious culture 31
Harvey, David 100–102, 123
Hauser, Arnold 25, 27, 41
Hay, Denys 89
Hayles, N. Katherine 127, 131, 149, 151,
    152, 167
haze city 246–247; resistance discourse in
    256–260; space of 248–252; stress
    behavior in 252–256
hedonism 5, 40, 41, 177
hedonistic ideology of consumer
    society 210
Hegel, Georg Wilhelm Friedrich 31, 32, 37,
    198, 249
Hegelian sense 176
hegemony 38, 41, 58, 67, 73, 75, 76, 89,
    204–213, 223
Heidegger, Martin 32, 90, 169, 170, 181,
    185, 190, 213, 249
"herding mentality" in social media 167
hermeneutics 70, 86, 94
Hero (film) 217, 218, 221, 222, 224–228
heterogeneity 56, 65, 73, 98, 125
heterogeneous cultural factors 99, 101
heteronomy 37

Hidden Dragon (film) 222
high-level integrity 24
Hirsch, Eric D. 94, 96n22
Hitchcock 217, 218
Ho 97, 98
Hobsbawm, Eric 78, 80, 81, 83, 84, 106
Hölderlin, Friedrich 169
homesickness 56, 83, 105
homogenization 98, 99
Howe, Irving 38
How to Read and Why (Bloom) 144
human civilization 24, 25, 141, 142, 154,
    159n8
human-computer systems 163
humanities, cross-cultural studies of 86–87
Hu Shih 50
Husserl 91
hybridity 23, 56, 101–102, 106, 116, 242
hyper attention model 127–129, 131, 146–
    154, 156–158, 167, 170
hypertext 146–151, 156
hysteria 117, 118, 168, 201

Ibsen, Henrik: *A Doll's House* 88
iconic turn 211
iconography 230–244
iconological model 234
idealism 176
ideal types 5, 6, 24, 42
identification 74–77, 79, 82–84, 85n24, 93,
    94, 98, 99, 251, 255, 256
identity 36, 40, 49–51, 53–59, 61, 166, 187,
    196, 198, 256, 260; construction
    54–57; crisis 54, 74, 97–104, 107,
    233, 235–236; in locality 103–107;
    as phenomenon/problem 73–74;
    politics 58; from psychoanalysis to
    cultural studies 74–77; signifying
    practice in literature 81–84;
    theories 77–81, 93
ideology 9, 12, 17, 27, 36, 41, 58, 63, 64,
    66, 67, 75, 76, 79, 89, 90, 123,
    132, 147, 164, 168, 179, 180, 185,
    189, 193, 194, 199, 209, 210, 215,
    243, 249
image 66, 75, 99, 100, 149, 175, 176, 186,
    189–197, 199, 200, 205–210, 212,
    220, 221, 223, 228, 234, 235, 239,
    241–243, 246, 250–252, 254–258;
    fetishism 207–210; typology
    193, 194
image-as-the-dominant culture 213
image-centered mode 208

image-centered paradigm 227
image-text intertextuality, of *The Great Criticism* 241–244
imaginative art 145
imagined communities 80–82, 103, 106–107, 120, 188
immersive reading 141–147, 151–158
imperialism 6, 67, 69, 71, 89, 90
Indiana, Robert: *LOVE* 241
industrialization 33, 40, 246
infotainment 116, 126
instrumental rationality 138, 147, 154, 164–168, 170–171, 181
integration 7, 9, 10, 13, 14, 75, 94, 99, 168, 187, 192
intensive reading 152
intentional misinterpretation 66, 67
interactive context 90–93
interactivity 87–88
inter-contextual position 87
intercultural studies 69–72, 87
inter-interpretations 94
inter-lingual position 87
intermittent hysteria 168
interpretation 1, 3, 4, 17, 18, 35, 49, 64–67, 70, 71, 84, 86, 87–95, 102, 125, 130, 132, 148, 150, 151, 185, 190, 191, 194, 197, 205, 212, 213, 228, 232, 237, 239, 240, 244, 258
interpretive communities 86, 93–95
interpretive strategy 93–95
intersubjectivity 18, 70, 71, 87–90, 94
intertextuality 87, 93, 205, 242, 243
invented traditions 80–81, 83–84, 106
Iser, Wolfgang 86

Jackie Chan 222
Jacobson, Roman 203n17
Jameson, Fredric 36, 103, 104, 228
Jaspers, Karl 25
Jian, Chan 226
Jiang Yi 195, 235
Jose Ortega y Gasset 35, 41; *The Revolt of the Masses* 34

Kantian transcendental subject 78
Kant, Immanuel 92–93, 162, 177
key opinion leader (KOL) 128
kitsch 38, 39, 42, 66, 231
Klee, Paul 193
knowledge system of Orientalism 89
KOL *see* key opinion leader (KOL)
Korean War 243

Kristeva, Julia 93
Kroeber, Alfred L. 2
Kuhn, Thomas 47–48, 124

Lacan, Jacques 75, 80
language 2–4, 10, 11, 15, 28, 36, 37, 49, 50, 53, 56, 67, 75, 77, 79, 80–82, 87, 93, 103, 104, 106, 123, 141, 144, 145, 150, 163, 185, 189–191, 195–198, 202n14, 203n17, 205, 206, 210–215, 230, 239, 259
language-as-the-dominant culture 213
Laocoon (Lessing) 242
Larrain, Jorge 98
Lash, Scott 4, 25, 26, 208, 214, 220
Lash theory of "mode of signification" 220
late modernity 77–78
law of "attention economy" 210
Lefebvre, Henri 254, 256; logic of visualization 249–250; theory of production of space 248; theory of spatial practice 247
legislatorial process of cultural legitimation 48
legislators 47–48
legitimation 24; debate 48–54; and legislators 47–48; re-legitimation and identity construction 54–57
Lentricchia, Frank 69
Lessing, Gotthold Ephraim: *Laocoon* 242
Liao Wen 233
Li Bai 82
Lichtenstein, Roy: *M-Maybe* 241
Li Jin 204
Lin Bai 205; *A War of One's Own* 204
linguistic model 211, 213
linguistic studies 80
linguistic turn 79, 210–215
Lin, Yu-sheng 53–54
"liquidation" effect 101
liquid modernity 101
literary critics 51, 73
literary discourse 84
Literary Machines (Nelson) 148
literary reading 144, 157
little narratives 129, 130
Liu, James J. Y.: *Chinese Theories of Literature* 50
Liu Yandong 113
local discourse 101
localization 77, 84, 98–100, 103
logos 189, 231, 237–239, 241
LOVE (Indiana) 241

Löwenthal, Leo 35, 41
Luckmann, Thomas 79, 211
Lu Xun 23, 82, 188
Lynch, Kevin 251, 256
Lyotard, Jean-François 124, 129–130

MacDonald, Dwight 39
"Major Social Events and the Influence of Network Media" 119
Mao era 231
Maoism 66, 231
Mao Zedong 233, 234, 237
Marcuse, Herbert 34, 36, 169
marginal literature 28
market-based institutional reform of media culture 113
Marxism 6, 16
Marx, Karl 7, 12, 15–17, 24, 32, 100, 125, 135n7, 167, 178, 199, 208, 209
mass culture 5, 12, 13, 16, 35–43, 212, 239
massive urbanization process 35
May Fourth Movement, the 1, 9, 53, 57, 78, 88, 163
McLuhan, Marshall 31n3, 123, 132, 139, 162, 189, 193
mechanical solidarity 7
media 14, 15, 35, 39, 40, 76, 81, 87, 102–105, 111, 124, 125, 127, 129, 137, 139–141, 145, 146, 148, 149, 151, 152, 154, 167; audience 117–118; culture 111–118, 121–122, 129, 130, 152; discourse 114–117; framework 140; generation 127, 167; institutions 112–114; language 202n14, 215
Mercer, Kobena 98
meta narratives 8
Meyerhold, Vsevolod 88
Meyrowitz, Joshua 103, 105
micro cognitive paradigms 134
Micro Cultural fragments 134
micro culture 127–129, 131–135; cultural symptoms of 123–126; objective consequence of 129; subjectivity of 129
micro device paradigms 134
"Micro Era" 123, 131
micro information 126, 130, 131, 133
micro narrative 125–126, 129–135
micronization 123, 124
micro politics 6, 125, 127, 129–135
micro reading 128
micro subject 125–129, 131–134

middle classes, as aestheticized subjects 178–180
Mills, C. Wright 5
mind-boggling theories 147
Ming Dong Gu 63, 69
Mirzoeff, Nicholas 213
misinterpreted knowledge, Sinologism as 66–69
Mitchell, W. J. T. 187, 188, 191, 211–213
M-Maybe (Lichtenstein) 241
mnemonic devices 106
mode: of information 125, 135n7; of production 16, 17, 125, 135n7, 208; of signification 4, 220
modern: art 31, 33–36, 41, 173; Chinese poetry 49, 50, 52–53, 57; culture 32, 33, 35, 37, 41, 185–186; print culture 141, 185; social development 165; societies 7–9, 11, 12, 23, 34–35, 40, 124, 142, 162; tradition of Renaissance 62; Western culture 42
modernism 33, 35, 36, 38–39, 42, 230, 235, 239, 242
modernity 7, 8, 23, 31n2, 32, 33, 35, 56, 59, 76–79, 81, 100, 101, 107, 124, 130, 162, 164, 169, 174, 181, 212, 213
modernization 7–8, 23, 32, 35, 51, 54, 56, 61, 99–100, 104, 131, 135, 139, 168–169
modesty and harmony (*zhonghe*) 30
Mondzain, Marie José 191
Mongolian and Tibetan ethnic groups 82
Morawski, Stefan 242
morphology 24, 28, 29, 190, 218
Moya, Paula M. L. 74
multiculturalism 58–59
Mulvey, Laura 218–219, 222
Munch, Edvard 88
Murder on the Orient Express (film) 225

naïve poems 32
narcissism 38, 41, 219, 222
narrative cinema 217–222, 228
National Air Quality Monitoring Network 246
nationalism 53, 54, 77, 81, 105, 118, 188
nation-state's cultural ethnicity and identity 61
naturalism 76, 78
natural sciences 10, 11, 67, 86, 156, 158
negotiated code 88
"negotiated" decoding 197

Nelson, Theodore H.: *Literary Machines* 148
neologism 6, 99, 116, 124
New Culture Movement 88, 163, 230
New Democratic Revolution (1919–1949) 112
New Enlightenment 163, 164
New Poetry 49–52, 55–57
new visual paradigm 141
Nietzsche, Friedrich 53, 147
Nisbet, Robert 57
Noelle-Neumann, Elisabeth 133
"non-linear textuality" 148
normative system of cultural conventions 27
North American Indians 62
nostalgia 31, 56, 57, 99, 105
notion of aesthetics 37, 175

Offe, Claus 9
online reading 150, 156
ontological security 54–57
Opium Wars 1, 164, 243
oppositional code 88
oral-auditory character of oral culture 141
oral-auditory paradigm 141
organic solidarity 7
Orientalism 58, 59, 62, 88–90, 93, 94
orthodox literature 28
otherizing 58
oxymoron 237–241

Pandora's Box 176
pantheism 24
Paparoni, Demetrio 231
paper-based printed texts 143
paper-based text reading 147, 148, 153, 155
paper reading 153, 155, 157
paradigm 3, 4, 12, 15, 16, 47–49, 64, 86, 130, 132, 134, 139–141, 145–148, 152, 154–156, 161, 162–171, 188, 199–201, 211, 213, 214, 218, 223, 227, 228, 237, 251
paradigmatic cultures and ideologies 168
"paradigmatic revolution" of Sinology 71
"para-hypertext" browsing 156
"para-literary" forms 82
parallelogram 95, 96n23
Parsons, Talcott 7, 12
particularism 99
patrician culture 27, 28, 30, 41
Peirce, Charles 211
performativity 106

perspective 6, 15, 36, 42, 69–71, 74, 79, 82, 114, 115, 117, 120, 125, 129, 138, 139, 142, 143, 145, 153, 154, 172n11, 175, 180, 181, 185, 193–196, 208, 215, 218, 219, 221, 223, 227, 233, 238, 242, 248–251
perspectivism 142, 203n20, 220
phenomenological reduction 91
philosophical constructivist epistemology 188
physical spatialization 247
Piaget, Jean 92, 93, 96n19; genetic epistemology 130, 135n11
pictorial turn 210–215
picture 5, 99, 119, 128, 144, 149, 167, 185, 190–195, 204–210, 212, 213, 222, 231, 233, 235, 240, 241, 249, 257, 258
picture-dominant spectacle cinema 228
picture reading 128, 204–210, 212–215
Pinter, Harold 88
pleasure principle 201, 214
pluralism 103
Poggioli, Renato 42
political correctness 70, 90, 200
political discourse 10, 111, 114–118, 122, 232
politicization of culture 58
pop art 173, 237–239, 241, 242, 244
popular culture 13, 35, 39, 41, 187, 194, 196, 200–202
post-Cartesian metaphysics 76
postcolonialism 61, 74
Poster, Mark 135n7, 144, 202n14, 215
post-Fordist production mode 77
postmodernism 3, 4, 61, 79, 124, 174, 239, 242
postmodernist pop art 173
postmodernity 23, 130
postmodern turn 211
Postrel, Virginia: *Substance of Style: How the Rise of Aesthetic Value is Remaking Commerce, Culture & Conscious-ness* 175
"post-revolutionary" age of consumerism 117
post-revolutionary China 176
post-revolutionary era (age, or time) 174–177, 180
post-secondary diploma-holders 119
post-structuralism 93
Pound, Ezra 42
pre–Micro Culture era 125

prescriptive definition 63
primitive culture 24, 25
primordial cultural mode 24
"principle of reality" 214
principle of spectacular visual structure 221
print culture 143, 154; and immersive reading 141–146
private media *see* grassroots media
pro-China scholars 68
production 3, 4, 8, 14–18, 24, 27, 33, 36, 61–63, 65, 66, 71, 77–80, 86, 87, 94, 100, 112, 114–118, 120, 121, 124–126, 138, 142, 148, 167, 171, 172n14, 175, 186, 192, 194, 196, 197, 199–201, 208, 209, 214, 218, 219, 221, 246–249
"production-reception" mode 17
productive idols 194
productiveness 208–210
productive prejudice 91
product of modernity 81
"proletarianization" of knowledge 170
propaganda 10, 112–114, 116, 117, 119, 121, 201, 208, 231, 238, 240
psychoanalysis 74–78, 209, 214, 218, 229, 233, 259
pure intersubjectivity 70, 90
purity 7, 33, 56, 59, 107, 145, 173, 198
purposive rationality 165, 171, 172n11
pyramid-shaped power hierarchy 232

Qin Shi Huang 224, 225
quasi-obligatory repetition 80, 81
Qu Yuan 82

radical anti-traditionalism 54, 107
radicalism 13, 49, 52, 176–177
rationalism 8, 169, 174
rationality 8, 70, 118, 129, 134, 138, 144, 145, 147, 154, 162–171, 172n11, 181, 189, 214, 258
rationalization 99, 169, 174
rational principle of montage assemblage 221
"reading on the prowl" 149
real art 26
realist narrative cinema 220
Rebecca or *Rear Window* (film) 218
The Red Detachment of Women 241
Redfield, Robert 3
reform and opening-up 1, 7, 9–14, 74, 88, 104, 112, 137, 138, 163, 186, 194, 199–201, 236, 237

re-legitimation 53–58, 61
Renaissance literature 8, 33, 62, 107, 129, 143, 203n17, 220, 251
representation 31, 33, 77, 81, 84, 93, 97, 105, 177, 187, 189–202, 219, 220, 227, 228, 247, 248, 250
representational spaces 247, 256
research method of the humanities 86
resistance discourse, space of haze city 256–260
retraditionalization 54–59
The Revolt of the Masses (Jose Ortega y Gasset) 34
revolutionary aesthetics 176
revolutionary idealism 177
revolutionary radicalism 177
Riegl, Alois 193
Riesman, David 35, 40, 162
Robertson, Roland 102; *Globalization: Social Theory and Global Culture* 99
Rogers, Carl Ransom 40
romantic art 31
"Root Seeking Literature" 104
Rorty, Richard 210
"ruling ideology" of visual culture 200

Said, Edward 58, 62, 88–90, 171
scanning 149, 152, 157
scene spectacles 223, 224
schema theory (Gombrich) 195
Schiller, Friedrich 24, 32, 170
Schubart, Wilhelm 31
secular hedonism 177
seismic shifts 1
self-legitimization 8
self-media *see* grassroots media
self-referential theory on subjectivity 79
semantic production 17, 18
sentimental poems 32
sexual fetishism 209
Shakespeare, William 39
Shapiro, Meyer 142
Shengtan, Jin: *Water Margin* 157
Shklovsky, Viktor 28
Sholokhov, Mikhail: *And Quiet Flows the Don* 239
sign 3, 8, 38, 144, 190, 196, 241, 257
significance of cultural transformation 227–229
signifying practice 76, 77, 79, 81–84, 187, 195–197, 200, 256
Simmel, Georg 32, 35–37

simulacrum 214
simulation 212
Sino-Japan War 163
Sinologism 61–65; intercultural studies 69–72; as misinterpreted knowledge 66–69
"Sinologist mood" 64
Sinologization of politics 68
Sinology 64, 65, 68, 71
skimming functions 151, 152
Smith, Anthony D. 56, 104
smog 247
social animal 73, 188
"social construction of the visual field" 188
social culture 6, 26, 40, 111, 112, 194
social differentiation 13, 26, 35
social evolution 6–14
social hierarchy 26
"social inheritance" of community 2
socialist egalitarianism 7
socialist market-oriented economy 112
social stratification 179, 180, 254
social transformation in contemporary China 186
societal sectors 7
"the society of the spectacle" (Debord) 185
socio-cultural context 73, 81, 107
socio-cultural sectors 111
socio-cultural transformation in contemporary China 227
socio-culture 73, 139, 152
sociological imagination 5, 6
sociology culture 2, 3
soft power 112, 113, 200
soft theory 86
software "addiction" 132
solidarity 7, 76
'solid' modernity 101
Sorokin, Pitirim 26
spatial axis 99
"spatial construction of vision" 252
spatial fluidity 102
spatial practices, space of haze city 246–248; logic of visualization 248–252; patterns of stress behavior 252–256; resistance discourse 256–260
spatial turn 259
spectacle 123, 175, 177, 186, 187, 191–193, 208, 209, 250, 256; of culture 3; as dominant in cinema 222–224; in *Hero* 224–227; significance of cultural transformation 227–229

spectacle-as-commodity 219
spectacle cinema 228–229; narrative cinema and 217–222
speed spectacle 223
Spengler, Oswald 32, 35
spiral of silence 127, 133, 134, 167, 168
spiritual culture 38
standardization 35, 38, 39, 166, 167, 172n14
standard of device paradigm 166
Star Wars (film) 224
stereotypical modes of traditional political propaganda 117
Stiegler, Bernard 163, 167, 170, 171, 172n14
stress behavior, in haze city 252–256
strong supremacism of native culture 69
structural functionalism 7
structural-functional perspective of media culture 114
The Structural Transformation of the Public Sphere (Habermas) 14
stylish alienation 34
subculture 3, 15, 26–28, 37–39, 41, 123, 128, 161, 200, 201, 257
subjectivity 1, 38, 57, 62, 74–80, 123, 124, 127–129, 131, 132, 134, 139, 144, 145, 165–168, 170, 187, 194, 198, 199, 212, 215, 249; in technology-oriented society 161–164
Substance of Style: How the Rise of Aesthetic Value is Remaking Commerce, Culture & Consciousness (Postrel) 175
super-ego 74
symbolic capital 230, 232
symmetrical intersubjectivity 18
systemic cognition 134
systemic reforms 10–11
systemization 166

Tao Yuanming 82
taste 8, 15, 17, 27, 28, 38–40, 48, 73, 115, 138, 146, 174, 177–180, 198
Taylor, Charles 165
tech-dependent society 162
technological domination 171
technological innovation 176
technological inventions 161
technology 10, 15, 33, 62, 119, 120, 125, 127, 132, 139, 140, 143, 147, 152–154, 161–170, 176, 186, 187, 190, 192, 200, 223, 224, 243

technology-oriented society 168, 170; subjectivity in 161–164
temporal axis 99
tensions in media institutions 112–114
text 4, 50, 86–88, 90–95, 128, 142–145, 147, 148, 150–156, 190, 193, 204–207, 211, 213, 214, 217, 223, 241–243
text reading 128, 145, 155
textuality 147, 148, 213
"textual" medium of oral culture 141
The Great Criticism: image-text intertextuality of 241–244; oxymoron in 237–241; social context and individual experience of 233–237; strategies of 230–233
Third Culture 102
Third Space 102
"Tianya," community management committee 120
time-space compression 77, 100–102, 106
Titanic (film) 221
Tomlinson, John 98, 103
Tönnies, Ferdinand 124
topography of Chinese media culture 111, 114
totality 9, 13, 24, 36, 71, 76–78, 95, 124–126, 130, 134, 135, 167, 209, 229, 232
totemism 24, 25
tradition 3, 8, 15, 16, 41, 50–59, 62, 68, 73, 76–78, 80, 81, 83, 84, 88, 99, 101, 105–107, 121, 152, 162, 195, 212, 232, 235, 243; authority 47, 53; Chinese aesthetics 27; Chinese culture 23, 51; Chinese graphic books 204; Chinese poetry 50; cinema 217; culture 52, 59, 102, 185–186; deep-attention model 149; discourse-as-the-dominant one cinema 228; narrative cinema 220, 221; philosophical aesthetics 181; social mobilization 133; societies 8, 23, 35, 101; storytellers 141; symbolic resources 104
transformation 1, 2, 7, 11–15, 18, 23, 24, 32, 33, 52, 54, 57–59, 61, 73, 77, 79, 84, 94, 103, 111–114, 123–125, 132, 138, 143, 148, 164, 173, 185–187, 190, 192, 194, 195, 197, 205, 207, 213, 227, 243, 244
'transgressive' postmodernist cinema 220

triad of spatial practice 247–248
true-or-false logic 11, 12
Tu Fu 82
Turner, Bryan S. 56
"12th National Reading Survey Report" 137
typical cross-cultural research of the humanities 86

unintentional misinterpretation 66, 67
universalism 99
universalization 99, 179, 180
urbanity 256
urbanization process 194, 246
urban population 40
utilitarianism 24, 25, 128

value rationality 165, 170–171, 172n11
Vasari, Giorgio 62
Virilio, Paul 223
virtual community 120
virtual digital technology 192
virtual spectacles 224
Virtuous Discussions of the White Tiger Hall 30
visual-auditory integration 192
visual construction 185–190, 249–253
visual consumption 186, 192
visual culture 128, 138, 147, 185–202, 207, 212–214, 217, 228
visual hegemony 204–207
visuality 186, 190, 197–202, 206, 208, 221, 249, 251
visualization 186, 188, 212, 248–252
visual model 213
visual regime 198, 199
visual subculture 200, 201
visual thinking 189
visual turn 211
vulgar culture 35

The Wandering Earth (film) 206, 224
Wang Guangyi 66; *The Great Criticism* (*see The Great Criticism*)
Warhol, Andy 173, 237; *Close Cover Before Striking* 241
A War of One's Own (Bai) 204
Water Margin (Shengtan) 157
"ways of seeing" 198, 199, 218, 249
weak supremacism of native culture 69
Weber, Max 7, 12, 33, 165, 169, 171, 172n11, 174, 181; concept of legitimation 47; cultural sociology

17; definition of men 3; disciple of 8; idea of legitimation 47; observation 124; religious sociology 17; sociology 16–17, 24, 47; theory 26; works of 6
Web 2.0 technologies 120
WeChat 123, 125, 127, 134, 137, 156, 167, 258
Wei Yuan 243
Wen Tian-xiang 82
Western academia 3, 33, 62
Western aestheticians 35
Western art theory 242
Western carnival-style culture 29
Western-centrism 68, 69, 71
Western civilization 32, 89
Western commercial culture 238, 243
Western commercial symbols 237
Western consumer society 173
Western countries 112
Western critics 232, 244
Western cultures 9, 28, 29, 32–33, 37, 39, 42, 52, 53, 58, 88, 190, 212, 243
Western culture supremacism 71
Western economies 66, 231
Western ideology 66, 67
"Westernization" of New Poetry 50, 52–57, 98
Westernized ideology 67
Western languages 145, 191
Western literary theory 49
Western media culture 116
Western modernism 230
Western modernity 162
Western modernization 35
Western painting techniques 142
Western pop art 238, 241
Western power/knowledge 88, 89, 243
Western scholars 3, 31n2, 39, 66
Western Sinologists 62, 64, 67
Western Sinology 64–66
Western societies 34, 163
Western supremacism 89
Western supremacy 89
Western theory 49, 50
Western thinkers 37
White Deer Plain 104
White, Hayden 83, 84
Williams, Raymond 190
Wilson, Robert N. 39, 40
Wiseman, Mary Bittner 66, 231
Wittgenstein, Ludwig 79, 211
Wolf Totem 104
worker-peasant-soldier (WPS) 231, 234, 238, 240, 242, 244

xiang 191
Xi Jinping 259

Ye Kuang-zheng 204
youth subculture 161
Yury Tynyanov 28

Zhang Peili 233
Zhang Yimou 217, 218, 221, 222, 225–227
Zhang Ziyi 254
Zhou Jiugeng 121
Zhou Ning 64, 69

For Product Safety Concerns and Information please contact our EU representative GPSR@taylorandfrancis.com
Taylor & Francis Verlag GmbH, Kaufingerstraße 24, 80331 München, Germany

www.ingramcontent.com/pod-product-compliance
Lightning Source LLC
Chambersburg PA
CBHW052133010526
44113CB00035B/2024